| READING |

Basic   Intermediate   Advanced   Expert

| LISTENING |

Basic   Intermediate   Advanced   Expert

Informative passages

HACKERS APEX LISTENING includes informative and interesting listening passages on a variety of academic topics and everyday situations in a university setting.

Useful online study materials

HACKERS APEX LISTENING provides access to quality online study materials at HackersBook.com. These include streaming audio recordings of all passages accessible through QR codes in the book.

HACKERS

APEX
LISTENING
for the
TOEFL iBT®

Advanced

HACKERS

Preface

Preface

Thank you for purchasing *HACKERS APEX LISTENING for the TOEFL iBT Advanced*. The TOEFL iBT is a highly challenging exam, so it is important to select an effective study guide. All of us at Hackers Language Research Institute are confident that this publication will be an invaluable resource as you prepare for the TOEFL iBT.

HACKERS APEX LISTENING for the TOEFL iBT is a series of comprehensive study guides for students planning to take the TOEFL iBT or for those wanting to improve their general English listening skills. This series includes four books that progress in difficulty. Students can begin at the level that matches their current abilities and then move on to the higher ones. All of the books in this series provide step-by-step question-solving strategies for every TOEFL question type. These are based on thorough research and years of instructional experience. Each book also includes informative and interesting listening passages that enable students to improve their English listening skills and familiarize them with academic topics and spoken English used in everyday university settings. Furthermore, students will receive access to quality online study materials that are designed to help them get the most out of the books in this series. Key features of *HACKERS APEX LISTENING for the TOEFL iBT* books include:

- Detailed explanations and question-solving strategies for all TOEFL Listening question types
- A large number of high-quality TOEFL Listening passages and questions
- Two full-length TOEFL Listening tests
- Dictation exercises to enhance listening comprehension ability
- Vocabulary exercises to review essential vocabulary that appeared in the passages
- An answer book with complete scripts, Korean translations, and lists of key vocabulary
- Access to streaming audio recordings of all passages through QR codes
- Access to supplementary study materials online (www.HackersBook.com)

Thank you again for choosing *HACKERS APEX LISTENING for the TOEFL iBT Advanced*, and we wish you all the best whether you are preparing to take the TOEFL iBT in the near future or simply hoping to develop your English listening skills overall.

Table of Contents

How to Use This Book

1. Understand the Question Type

Each chapter includes an Overview page that provides essential information about the featured question type and key strategies for answering it. Make sure you fully understand the strategies before moving on to the Example section, where you can apply the key strategies to short conversation and lecture passages with one question each.

2. Improve Your Skills with Listening Practice Exercises

Each chapter includes four Listening Practice exercises, which consist of two conversation and two lecture passages. These will help you become more familiar with the featured question type, as well as other question types. Each exercise is accompanied by a dictation section so that you can enhance your listening comprehension ability.

3. Take the iBT Listening Tests

Each chapter includes two iBT Listening Tests, which consist of longer conversation and lecture passages with 5 to 6 questions each that are similar to those that appear on the TOEFL iBT. Taking these tests will enable you to improve your listening comprehension skills and prepare for the TOEFL iBT.

④ Review Essential Vocabulary

At the end of each chapter is a Vocabulary Review, which includes questions on essential vocabulary from the chapter. You will be able to easily memorize the vocabulary words through various types of questions.

⑤ Evaluate Your Progress with Actual Tests

The book includes two Actual Tests, which are full-length listening tests that include passages and questions that closely match what appears on the TOEFL iBT. They provide an excellent opportunity to apply the skills you have learned and evaluate your progress.

⑥ Check the Answer Book

The Answer Book specifies the correct answer choice for all questions and provides complete scripts and Korean translations of all passages and questions. It also includes a list of key vocabulary words from each passage with definitions.

About the TOEFL iBT

What Is the TOEFL iBT?

The TOEFL (Test of English as a Foreign Language) iBT (Internet-Based test) includes Reading, Listening, Speaking, and Writing sections to comprehensively assess English ability. Although most tasks require the application of only one of these skills, some require the use of two or more. The TOEFL iBT is designed to measure a student's capacity to use and understand English at a university level and is, therefore, much more difficult than many other English proficiency tests.

TOEFL iBT Structure

Section	No. of passages and questions	Time (min.)	Score	Notable Features
Reading	• 3-4 Passages • 10 Questions/Passage	54-72	30	• Each passage is approximately 700 words long.
Listening	• 2-3 Conversations • 5 Questions/Conversation • 3-4 Lectures • 6 Questions/Lecture	41-57	30	• Speakers have various accents, including American, British, Australian, etc.
10-minute break				
Speaking	• 1 Independent Task • 3 Integrated Tasks	17	30	• Independent Tasks ask you to state your opinion about a specific topic. • Integrated Tasks ask you to provide a response based on reading and listening content.
Writing	• 1 Integrated Task • 1 Independent Task	50	30	• Integrated Tasks ask you to provide a response based on reading and listening content. • Independent Tasks ask you to write about a specific topic.

Total Time: Approximately 3 hours 30 minutes / Total Score: 120

■ TOEFL iBT Listening Section

The TOEFL iBT Listening Section largely consists of conversations and lectures. Conversations mainly take place in university settings, and lectures discuss topics from different academic fields covered in university lectures. Note-taking is allowed while listening to conversations and lectures. Therefore, the ability to listen, understand, and organize information is more important than relying on memory. The test consists of 2 to 3 Parts with either 11 or 17 questions. Each Part has 1 conversation and 1 to 2 lectures.

■ TOEFL iBT Listening Question Types

Question Type	Description
Main Purpose/Topic	Choose the answer choice that best represents the main idea of the conversation or lecture.
Detail	Choose the answer choice that corresponds to specific information or important details introduced in the conversation or lecture.
Function	Choose the answer choice that best describes the underlying function or purpose of a speaker's specific statement.
Attitude	Choose the answer choice that best represents the speaker's attitude or opinion regarding a specific matter.
Organization	Choose the answer choice that best describes the overall organization of the passage or the relationship between ideas in the passage.
Connecting Contents	Choose the answer choices that correspond to related ideas clearly stated in the passage.
Inference	Choose the answer choice that can be inferred based on relevant information in the passage.

NOTE-TAKING

Strategies for Note-taking

1. Write down the main idea using key words.

Listen carefully to the beginning of the conversation or lecture. Write down the main idea in a short sentence or phrase using key words.

2. Organize information into subtopics and categories.

Identify the subtopics and organize the information into groups or categories. Listen for signal words (First of all, Secondly, Now, Later, Then, Another, etc.) used to introduce subtopics.

3. Write down the supporting details.

Write down the supporting details for each subtopic or category. Especially for lectures, it is good to take notes according to how the lecturer gives supporting details. For example, the lecturer may give the definition of a term, compare two or more ideas, or give a list of important items.

4. Do not try to write down everything.

Make your notes brief and do not try to write down every single word. Include only essential key words. It is also helpful to use symbols and abbreviations of your own.

Note-taking Example

Script

> P: Today we are going to continue our discussion on the differences between mammals and reptiles. One of the key traits that distinguish these two types of animals is the way that they control their body temperatures. I'm sure you have all heard the expressions "hot-blooded" and "cold-blooded," right? Well, it's actually a bit more complicated than that. Basically, mammals rely on their ability to burn fats and sugars to generate heat as required. In contrast, reptiles depend on external factors, such as the sun, to warm their bodies, or cold water to cool them. OK... Let's look at these functions in a bit more detail.

Note

diffs. bet. mammals & reptiles: way they ctrl. body temp.	— *Main Topic*
1. mammals: burn fat & sugar → heat	— *Type 1*
2. reptiles: ext. factors	— *Type 2*
e.g. sun → warm	
e.g. cold water → cool	*Examples of Type 2*

Common Symbols and Abbreviations

The key to note-taking is writing down only the essential information of the conversation or lecture. Using symbols and abbreviations will allow you to make your notes brief and accurate. With symbols and abbreviations, you can write down more information in a quick and efficient way. Below are some commonly used symbols and abbreviations.

1. Symbols

Symbols can save you time and increase the amount of information you write down about a passage.

=	equals; to be	K	1,000	X	not, no
+	and; plus	&	and	/	per, each
>	more than	∴	therefore/so	/day	per day
<	less than	←	from	/h	per hour
↑	increase	@	at	/w	per week
↓	decrease	#	number (of)	∵	because

2. Abbreviations

There are several methods to make abbreviations, but make sure to keep your method consistent. Here are some ways to make abbreviations.

· Omit latter part: European → Eu
· Omit vowels: movement → mvmt
· Omit middle letters: government → govt

e.g.	for example	usu.	usually	info.	information
prob.	problem	w/	with	sum.	summary
ppl	people	cf.	compare	psych.	psychology
rsn.	reason	c.	century	Qs	questions
etc.	and so on	max.	maximum	pics	pictures
i.e.	that is; in other words	min.	minimum	w/o	without
intro.	introduction	fr.	from	vs	versus
concl.	conclusion	tech	technology	ea.	each
b.f.	before	reg	regular	btw	by the way

www.HackersBook.com

CHAPTER 01

Main Purpose/Topic

Main Purpose/Topic

Main Purpose/Topic questions ask you to determine the main idea of a conversation or lecture. Main Purpose questions focus on the purpose or reason the speaker is discussing a particular topic in the conversation or lecture. Main Topic questions ask you to identify the main subject or what the speakers are discussing overall.

Incorrect answer choices often contain exact words and phrases you hear from the passage, but they focus on minor points (examples, supporting ideas, etc.). Therefore, make sure that your answer choice paraphrases or restates the main idea of the entire passage.

■ **Question Format**

Main Purpose
- Why does the student go to see the professor?
- Why is the man speaking to the woman?

Main Topic
- What is the conversation/lecture mainly about?
- What is the main topic of the lecture?

■ **Key Strategies**

- **Step 1** — Listen carefully to the start of each passage. The main idea is usually mentioned clearly near the beginning of the passage.

- **Step 2** — Pay attention to the signal words that are commonly used to introduce the main purpose or topic of the passage. Examples for conversations include: *I'm interested in* and *I was wondering if*. Examples for lectures include: *Let's talk about* and *I want to take a look at*.

- **Step 3** — Select the answer choice that best expresses the main idea of the passage.

Example

Answer Book p. 2

A. Listen to a conversation between a student and a professor.

Note-taking

C1_ExA

Why does the student go to see the professor?

(A) To submit the first draft of his report

(B) To request an explanation for his grade

(C) To ask for more time to do an assignment

(D) To explain the reason for missing a class

Answer Book p. 2

B. Listen to part of a lecture in a geology class.

Note-taking

C1_ExB

What is the lecture mainly about?

(A) The process of forming a polar desert

(B) The reason a region is classified a desert

(C) The factors that limit rainfall in Antarctica

(D) The differences between various ecosystems

Listen again and fill in the blanks.

A.

C1_ExA_D

S: Hi, Professor Watkins. I've been sick recently, so I was wondering _____

_____ .

P: _____ , Morgan. You have to submit it tomorrow just like everyone else.

S: Couldn't you _____ ?

P: I explained on the first day that _____ .

S: I know, but I really was sick. I have a note from the doctor...

P: I assigned the paper _____ . So you've had enough time

to work on it. I suggest that you finish it tonight and _____ .

B.

C1_ExB_D

P: When you think of a desert, you probably think of a hot, dry, place _____ .

Well, surprisingly, _____ is actually cold and icy. I'm

referring to the Antarctic Polar Desert. It's an ecosystem that _____

_____ .

Now, to understand _____ , we first need to

define what a desert is. So, uh, a desert is any area of land that receives less than 25

centimeters of rain each year... Um, _____ .

And Antarctica receives just over five centimeters of rain and snow per year. As a result,

the entire continent is technically _____ .

Listening Practice 1

Listen to a conversation between a student and a university facility manager.

C1_P1

Note-taking

1 Why does the student go to see the manager?

(A) To submit an application form

(B) To find out about university clubs

(C) To ask about a practice space

(D) To get permission for an event

2 What does the manager say about the repair work in room 302?

(A) It was scheduled months before.

(B) It will be finished in the afternoon.

(C) It was requested by a professor.

(D) It usually happens twice a year.

3 According to the conversation, what might have caused a problem with a notification?

(A) The student did not reply to an e-mail.

(B) The university updated a computer program.

(C) The group got confused about a room number.

(D) The manager lost an important document.

4 What will the student probably do next?

(A) Review a list of building policies

(B) Choose a different day for practice

(C) Visit another department in the building

(D) Discuss a situation with other group members

Listen again to part of the conversation. Then answer the question.

5 What does the student imply when she says this: 🎧

(A) The group does not want to bother other people.

(B) The room needs to have some sound equipment.

(C) The group enjoys listening to music at a high volume.

(D) The room should be located somewhere quiet.

Dictation

Listen again and fill in the blanks.

W: Um, do you know where I can find the university facility manager?

M: Actually, that's me. What can I do for you?

W: Oh, great. Um, I'm a member of the dance club, and _____.
We went to our usual practice room, but it was locked.

M: I just want to check... _____?

W: Well, we reserved it several months ago for the same time every week. There's never been a problem before, so we were quite surprised _____.

M: OK... What's the room number?

W: Um, it's room 302 in the Ryder Building.

M: Just a minute... Oh, that's right. It's closed because _____.
The repair work will be finished later this afternoon... Nobody told you about this? You should have been notified that there was _____.

W: No, and I checked my e-mail just before I came here.

M: I see. Actually, the university recently _____, but there have been some issues with it. That could be why you weren't told. Hopefully, everything will be back to normal soon.

W: OK, but what can we do now? We still don't have a room to use.

M: Here's what we'll do. Let me check if there are _____. I'll try to reserve one of them for you.

W: Thank you. Um, I should tell you that _____... So you probably should not put us next to a place where people are trying to study.

M: That's fine. Could you come back in 20 minutes? I'll need some time to _____
_____.

W: OK. I'll just go to the lobby to talk with the rest of the group. I need to _____
_____.

M: Oh, in that case, please talk outside the building. There are people working and I don't want you to disturb them.

W: All right. We can meet outside.

Listening Practice 2

Listen to part of a lecture in a psychology class.

C1_P2

Note-taking

1 What is the lecture mainly about?
(A) The common habits of successful people
(B) How working together can lead to career success
(C) The personal achievements of successful people
(D) How different personality types achieve success

2 According to the professor, what is a quality of extroverts?
(A) Speaking in a loud voice
(B) Losing energy talking to others
(C) Making careful decisions
(D) Needing others' approval

3 According to the professor, why do introverts dislike talking in front of groups?
(A) They are easily exhausted by a large audience.
(B) They want to avoid receiving attention.
(C) They feel uncomfortable in big spaces.
(D) They are afraid of making a mistake.

4 What is the professor's opinion of introverts?
(A) They should be encouraged to work alone.
(B) They have many good characteristics.
(C) They should try to be more outgoing.
(D) They have fewer strengths than extroverts.

Listen again to part of the lecture. Then answer the question.

5 Why does the professor say this: 🎧
(A) To disagree with a point
(B) To criticize introverts as leaders
(C) To emphasize that an idea is true
(D) To stress the importance of research

‖ Dictation ‖

Listen again and fill in the blanks.

C1_P2_D

P: OK, so we've spent some time recently talking about the behavior of successful people. Today, we'll move on to the _____.
But first, let's be sure everyone understands what the terms mean. Um, extroversion and introversion are two opposite personality types that explain _____. Extroverts are people who gain energy from spending time with others and _____. They are usually better at acting than thinking. They are confident and more likely to take risks. _____ and making decisions quickly. Introverts, however, are the opposite of extroverts. They, uh, feel exhausted after talking to people and _____. In general, introverts are more likely to think long and hard before acting. They pay attention to small details and are generally more anxious than extroverts. They often appear more serious or shy. Oh, and _____. So introverts feel nervous about talking in front of large groups.
Anyway, that's a basic overview of extroverts and introverts. Um, I want to focus on how we, as a society, _____. People often assume that extroverts are more likely to succeed in life. And it's true that many successful people, like politicians and celebrities, are outgoing. In reality, however, _____.
In fact, many artistic and scientific geniuses, like Van Gogh, Einstein, and Darwin were introverts. They produced some of history's greatest ideas and creations. This was because they could work well alone and focus on their ideas. _____, too. This is not my opinion... It's supported by research.
For example, one study showed that _____.
They tend not to listen and lose energy while working on projects. In contrast, introverts listen well and actually gain more energy as projects progress. And another study estimates that over half of the world's CEOs are introverts.
Does that mean employers shouldn't hire extroverts? Not at all. But it does indicate that both extroverts and introverts have _____. Ideally, extroverts are at their best when they work in large groups. Their personality makes them excellent salespeople and speakers. But that doesn't mean they make the best leaders. My point is that we should think again about success. We shouldn't force introverts to be more like extroverts. Instead, _____...
And there are many!

Listening Practice 3

Listen to a conversation between a student and a university employee.

C1_P3

Note-taking

1 Why does the student go to see the university employee?
  (A) To sign up for a job-training program
  (B) To inquire about job opportunities
  (C) To submit an application for a job
  (D) To complain about some job requirements

2 According to the employee, what are department assistants expected to do?
  (A) Prepare lessons for classes
  (B) Help students with assignments
  (C) Complete tasks on a computer
  (D) Show students around a campus

3 What should the student do to become a department assistant?
  (A) Pass a computer test
  (B) Have a high grade point average
  (C) List her past experience
  (D) Submit a recommendation letter

4 What will the student most likely do next?
  (A) Call a department
  (B) Go to an interview
  (C) Complete a form
  (D) Visit another office

Listen again to part of the conversation. Then answer the question.

5 What does the student mean when she says this: 🎧
  (A) She expected lower pay.
  (B) She thinks the employee made a mistake.
  (C) She prefers to work part-time.
  (D) She does not know when she can start.

Dictation

Listen again and fill in the blanks.

C1_P3_D

M: Good afternoon. How can I help you?

W: Hi, my name's Becky Williams. I'm a third-year student here. I'm interested in _____. Do you know if there are any positions available?

M: Yes. There are some in the English and math departments. Which one are you interested in?

W: Well, I'm planning to _____. So, uh, I'm more interested in the English department.

M: OK. And have you done anything like this before?

W: No, but I think I can do the job. I'm very organized and _____.

M: Great. You'll be working and studying at the same time. So you'll need to _____. Other than that, are you good with computers? You'll _____. You'll, um, need to send and receive messages, print documents, copy files, and so on.

W: I'm sure I can do all of those tasks.

M: All right. You need to have a few requirements to qualify. The first is that _____ _____. So there are no issues there. However, you also need to have a high grade point average of 3.0 or more. _____ _____. Otherwise, you will lose the job.

W: That shouldn't be a problem. My grades are good.

M: Terrific. Now, do you have any questions before I give you the application form?

W: Yes, uh, could you tell me _____?

M: Oh, sure. You'll get $11 an hour. And you'll be paid once a month.

W: Is that right? That's excellent. _____. Could I get the form now?

M: Here you go. Make sure _____. You don't need to include all the details, though, since there will be an interview later.

W: Thanks! I'll _____. Um, when should I submit it?

M: I'll need it back by the end of the week. You'll be notified about the interview after that. Good luck!

Listening Practice 4

Listen to part of a lecture in a history class.

C1_P4

Note-taking

---

1 What is the main purpose of the lecture?

(A) To show why the UK entered World War I

(B) To describe how armies can change the results of a war

(C) To explain why the UK army had many young volunteers

(D) To discuss the advantages of conscription

2 According to the professor, why was the UK army small?

(A) It lost many soldiers in a previous war.

(B) It was the last country to join a war.

(C) It only had to defend a small country.

(D) It did not force people to join the army.

3 What does the professor say about the UK army's campaign to find volunteers?

(A) It only lasted for a couple of months.

(B) It produced better results than expected.

(C) It cost the government lots of money.

(D) It was promoted in countries overseas.

4 According to the professor, what is one reason that many young people joined the UK army?

(A) They heard stories about war from family members.

(B) They were paid more in the army than in their jobs.

(C) They had a wrong idea about war.

(D) They wanted to visit some foreign countries.

Listen again to part of the lecture. Then answer the question.

5 Why does the professor say this: 🎧

(A) To criticize the actions of young soldiers during World War I

(B) To suggest that the UK army paid attention to soldiers' ages

(C) To show how difficult it was to know a person's age during the war

(D) To emphasize how careless the UK army was about requirement

‖ Dictation ‖

C1_P4_D

Listen again and fill in the blanks.

P: World War I was mainly fought between two groups of countries: the Central Powers and Allied Powers. The countries in these groups had agreements with each other. _____, the other countries in the group had to join as well. So when Germany attacked France in 1914, the UK went to war against Germany the next day. Um, Germany, of course, was a Central Power, and the UK and France were Allied Powers. Anyway, what I want to focus on is _____ _____. How did this happen?

At the start of World War I, the UK had a small army. It had around 700,000 soldiers. In comparison, Germany had nearly two million soldiers ready to fight. One of the reasons for the UK's small army was that, for over a hundred years, _____. Um, this means no one was forced to join.

So _____ from the first day of the war... It published requests for help in newspapers and put up posters in public places. And, in towns across the country, leaders gave speeches that encouraged men to join the war. Uh, _____. In fact, the UK army found five times more people than it expected in just a few weeks. Now, even though the UK army attracted potential recruits of all ages, a large number were very young. The minimum age to join the army was 18. However, _____. You see, back then, few people had birth certificates that showed their real age. So someone could easily pretend to be older. If a young person just said he was 18, joining was easy. _____. By the time the war ended in 1918, around 250,000 soldiers under the age of 18 had joined the army. Some were as young as 12.

Young men joined the army for many reasons... Uh, some believed the army's campaign and _____. Others wanted to get away from their towns because there were no jobs for young people. Many also grew up reading stories about wars and war heroes. They wrongly thought that going to war would be like an exciting adventure. A lot of young people also _____. If they didn't join, people would think they were afraid.

Answer Book p. 8

TOEFL Listening

C1_T1

Note-taking

1 What are the speakers mainly discussing?

(A) The student's grade in a class

(B) The availability of a book for class

(C) The professor's rules for a class

(D) The subject of a class·assignment

2 Why was the student not able to participate in a discussion?

(A) He was busy with other assignments.

(B) He did not read some material.

(C) He thought that a lesson was hard.

(D) He was not interested in a topic.

3 What does the professor say about the university's policy on book orders?

(A) It is updated every year.

(B) It makes books cheaper for students.

(C) It helps the school reduce costs.

(D) It was recommended by the bookstore.

4 What is the student's opinion of a university policy?

(A) It would benefit employees at the school.

(B) It should be used at more universities.

(C) It could be explained better to students.

(D) It might make a situation difficult for students.

Listen again to part of the conversation. Then answer the question.

5 Why does the professor say this: 🎧

(A) To point out a different problem

(B) To express her confusion about a request

(C) To show that she has another solution

(D) To emphasize how long a process could take

C1_T1_D

Listen again and fill in the blanks.

S: Professor Taylor? Um, I'm George Davis. I'm one of the students in your science class. I wanted to _____.

P: Sure, George. Are you having difficulties with it? I noticed that you did not _____.

S: Actually, the discussion was interesting. However, I didn't participate because I wasn't able to do the reading assignment before class.

P: Why not? Have you been busy with other work?

S: No. Um, the issue is that _____.

P: I see. Did you check the campus bookstore?

S: Yes, I went right away after I signed up for your class, but _____ _____.

P: Right. This happens every year. The bookstore only buys a small number of books at the start of the semester. So _____.

S: But why doesn't the bookstore just order more copies?

P: It's part of a university policy. The university doesn't let the campus bookstore _____ _____. That way, they can use the money they save for other important uses, like buying office equipment.

S: But then, what are students supposed to do when they can't find a book? That policy doesn't seem fair. It makes it harder for students to find the books they need.

P: I agree. However, _____. Um, this happens in the first few weeks of the semester. These students may sell their books to other students.

S: Oh... So does that mean I can still _____?

P: Yes, but you might have to wait one or two weeks... Oh, but hold on. Actually, I have the book right here. _____ and make copies of the pages you need for the reading assignment.

S: Really? That would be very helpful!

P: Hmm... Now that I think about it... _____ who don't have the book yet. I'll ask about that at our next class on Thursday.

S: That's a great idea. I think everyone would appreciate it, Professor Taylor.

Answer Book p. 9

TOEFL Listening

C1_T2

FILM

Note-taking
_____

_____

1 What is the lecture mainly about?

    Ⓐ Why some films are in black-and-white

    Ⓑ The role of artists in Hollywood films

    Ⓒ How movies about crime are made

    Ⓓ The development of a style of film

2 According to the professor, what effect did World War I have on German filmmakers?

    Ⓐ It led them to make films about war.

    Ⓑ It made them create works about dark topics.

    Ⓒ It changed their views about Germany.

    Ⓓ It forced them to work with criminals.

3 According to the professor, why did German filmmakers paint their walls in dark and light colors?

    Ⓐ They needed to save on costs.

    Ⓑ They were inspired by American artists.

    Ⓒ They wanted to copy a European style.

    Ⓓ They had cameras of low quality.

4 What did American filmmakers contribute to film noir?

    Ⓐ The use of camera techniques

    Ⓑ Specific major character types

    Ⓒ The hero and the antihero

    Ⓓ Simple and happy endings

5 According to the professor, what happened to film noir by the 1950s?

    Ⓐ It inspired many foreign films.

    Ⓑ It continued to grow in popularity.

    Ⓒ It became darker and more complex.

    Ⓓ It started to focus on positive subjects.

Listen again to part of the lecture. Then answer the question.

6 What does the professor imply when he says this: ∩

    Ⓐ Sam Spade's character was based on Sherlock Holmes.

    Ⓑ Viewers did not usually see violence on film.

    Ⓒ Sam Spade did not have many positive qualities.

    Ⓓ The actor who played Sam Spade was not famous.

‖ Dictation ‖

Listen again and fill in the blanks.

P: Imagine a scene from a black-and-white movie... A man in a coat is walking down a city street at night. It is raining and the street is full of shadows... It's the kind of scene you might see in the typical film noir movie. Film noir is a style of film that was popular in the 1940s. Its name came from the French word for *black* because _____ _____. Let's talk about how it developed.

Film noir movies were partly inspired by German artists who painted about the negative aspects of modern life in Germany. But, uh, German filmmakers were also greatly affected by the shocking violence of World War I. This caused them to _____ _____, like crime and horror. Changes in the German film industry also influenced the appearance of film noir. In the early 1900s, _____ _____ because of the country's economic problems. So, instead of lighting scenes with expensive equipment, they painted walls in dark and light colors. Later, other Europeans copied the unusual German films. And, before World War II started, many of these European filmmakers left Europe to work in Hollywood.

In Hollywood, _____. This led to the creation of film noir. The Europeans created the appearance and feel of film noir, but _____ _____. Two of the most common character types in film noir were the antihero and the femme fatale. The antihero was a male figure who did the right thing eventually but sometimes did bad things. The femme fatale was a woman who used her beauty to trick other people. Normally, _____, such as a murder or robbery. This created dramatic tension that continued throughout the movie. And film noir stories did not always end well. _____.

Now, let's consider an example. One of the most famous film noir movies is called *The Maltese Falcon*. It was filmed in 1941. It includes Humphrey Bogart as a private detective named Sam Spade and Mary Astor as the femme fatale. Before the movie came out, people thought detectives should be like Sherlock Holmes, _____ _____. Sam Spade surprised viewers. _____ _____ toward criminals. During the movie, he even smiles at a character just before punching him in the face.

Film noir's popularity grew throughout the 1940s. Around the world, other filmmakers copied the appearance, characters, and stories about crime. However, by the 1950s, new forms of film noir developed that had darker themes and more complex characters and stories. Since then, generations of filmmakers have continued to

_____.

Vocabulary Review

Answer Book p. 11

A. Choose the correct word for each meaning.

notify outgoing continent ecosystem

1 to give someone official information: _____

2 a natural environment where plants and animals live: _____

3 one of seven large land groups that the world is divided into: _____

4 friendly and preferring to be around others: _____

B. Fill in the blanks with the appropriate words from the box.

approval budget tension exception behavior

5 Some people might not like the rules, but they must be followed without _____.

6 The students were warned about their _____ in class after getting into a fight.

7 Tim told a funny joke that broke the _____ in the room.

8 Some teens will do anything to gain the _____ of their friends.

9 We must stick to the _____ because there is not enough money.

C. Choose the closest meaning for each highlighted word.

10 I called the restaurant to reserve a table for lunch on Thursday.
(A) book　　(B) control　　(C) assert　　(D) describe

11 Some of the elements of a good story include the characters and the setting.
(A) purposes　　(B) benefits　　(C) parts　　(D) notes

12 Ms. Taylor is busy and does not want to be disturbed.
(A) replaced　　(B) alarmed　　(C) bothered　　(D) confused

13 People often assume that the members of a group all behave the same way.
(A) believe　　(B) acquire　　(C) pretend　　(D) affect

14 It is estimated that the global population will grow to 10 billion over the next 30 years.
(A) measured　　(B) valued　　(C) decided　　(D) predicted

CHAPTER 02

Detail

Detail

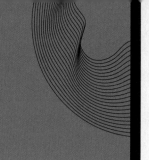

About the Question Type

Detail questions ask you to identify specific details or facts that are mentioned in a conversation or lecture.

Correct answers restate specific information explicitly mentioned in the passage. Incorrect answers contain new, contradictory, or irrelevant information. Some questions may require you to select more than one correct answer choice.

Question Format

- According to the conversation, what is ~?

- What does the professor say about ~?

- According to the professor, what are the reasons for ~? *Choose 2 answers.*

- What are the two examples the man gives of ~? *Choose 2 answers.*

Key Strategies

- **Step 1** — Identify the main topic and focus on important information supporting the main idea. For example, listen carefully for definitions, examples, reasons, results, and features.

- **Step 2** — Listen carefully for signal words that are commonly used to introduce supporting ideas. Some examples include: *For instance, To illustrate, That's because, As a result, Similarly,* and *On the other hand.*

- **Step 3** — Select the answer choice that best presents the information from the conversation or lecture. Remember, the correct answer often paraphrases information, or repeats it using different words.

Example

Answer Book p. 11

A. Listen to a conversation between a student and a professor.

C2_ExA

Note-taking

What does the professor recommend that the student do?

(A) Take several practice tests

(B) Read a textbook carefully

(C) Study with other students

(D) Ask questions during class

Answer Book p. 11

B. Listen to part of a lecture in a city planning class.

C2_ExB

Note-taking

What are two benefits of green roofs? *Choose 2 answers.*

(A) They help roofs last longer by taking in water.

(B) They save costs by requiring little maintenance.

(C) They reduce energy by keeping buildings cool.

(D) They improve city life by providing spaces for resting.

▌▌ Dictation ▌▌

Answer Book p. 11

Listen again and fill in the blanks.

C2_ExA_D

A.

S: Excuse me, Professor Gibson. Are we still going to _____?

P: Yes, of course. It will happen on October 18. I've already placed this on the schedule. Are you _____?

S: Um, a little bit. I've been reading the textbook for class, but _____ _____.

P: Well, let me give you some advice. I recommend that _____. It will help you understand the lessons in the book.

S: You mean _____ from the class?

P: Yes, exactly. That way, if you don't understand a lesson, another student can explain it to you.

C2_ExB_D

B.

P: One problem with urban environments is the lack of trees and plants. And one solution is to build green roofs. _____ because they reduce carbon dioxide in the atmosphere and provide a habitat for birds. Moreover, they can _____... Plus, green roofs keep buildings cool, which means there is less need for air conditioning.

Now, there are two types of green roofs: intensive and extensive. The main difference between them is _____. An intensive roof can have soil that's more than a meter deep. So _____. An extensive green roof has less soil. It is good for covering a wide area with grass, but it doesn't have many other uses.

Listening Practice 1

Answer Book p. 12

Listen to a conversation between a student and a university employee.

C2_P1

Note-taking

1 What is the conversation mainly about?

(A) Buying tickets for a concert

(B) Finding a room for visitors

(C) Changing a hotel reservation

(D) Inviting participants to an event

2 What does the employee say about rooms at the conference center?

(A) They can be used only for two nights.

(B) They are currently closed for repairs.

(C) They are normally reserved in advance.

(D) They must be paid for online.

3 What is a benefit of going to Sugar Falls?

(A) It is close to the university.

(B) It is going to have a special exhibition.

(C) It is a quiet place to visit.

(D) It is the city's biggest tourist attraction.

4 Why does the student ask the employee for other options?

(A) He is worried about transportation.

(B) His father does not like cultural events.

(C) His parents do not enjoy outdoor activities.

(D) He is concerned about the costs of an activity.

Listen again to part of the conversation. Then answer the question.

5 What does the student mean when he says this: 🎧

(A) He would like a cheaper option.

(B) He changed his mind about a plan.

(C) He wants to reserve one more room.

(D) He requires more assistance.

Dictation

C2_P1_D

Listen again and fill in the blanks.

W: Good morning, and welcome to the student center. How can I help you?

M: Hi, I'd like to ask about rooms. Um, my parents are coming to visit and _____ _____. They're watching me play in a music concert.

W: That's wonderful. There are some good hotels nearby.

M: Oh, actually, _____. Um, most of the hotels in the area are expensive.

W: I see... The university does have rooms at the conference center. But they're usually _____. When are your parents coming?

M: Um, the concert is on Saturday, May 7. They will be here on Friday and _____ _____.

W: All right, let me check... Oh, we actually have a couple of rooms that can be used on those nights. _____ if you'd like...

M: That's great. Um, how much is it for each night?

W: Well, a room usually costs $75 a night. But, because you're a student here, it would just be $45. That's _____.

M: I agree! Just one more thing. My parents _____. However, I've only been a student here for a couple of months, so I don't really know where to take them. Could you, uh, _____?

W: Oh, Sugar Falls is a good option... It's close and _____. A bus goes from the conference center to the falls twice a day. You can even go swimming if you like. There's more information on the city's website.

M: Actually, is there anything else? My parents don't like doing things outside or being in nature. They _____.

W: Then, what about the Metropolitan Art Gallery downtown? They have a special exhibition right now. Plus, _____. You can take a taxi or a bus to get there.

M: That sounds good. Thanks for your help!

Listening Practice 2

Listen to part of a lecture in an economics class.

C2_P2

Note-taking

---

1 What is the lecture mainly about?

(A) The changing attitudes of modern consumers

(B) The growth of an economic system

(C) The advantages of having many assets

(D) The similarities of different business environments

2 What is the professor's attitude toward the sharing economy?

(A) She worries that it is becoming too large.

(B) She thinks it will make products more expensive.

(C) She believes it has some negative effects on society.

(D) She feels it has caused a great change in the economy.

3 According to the professor, how does digital technology contribute to economic globalization?

(A) It lets companies find international partners.

(B) It lowers the cost of shipping products overseas.

(C) It makes businesses compete with each other globally.

(D) It provides access to individuals around the world.

4 Why does the professor mention jewelry making?

(A) To specify a common idea people have for starting a business

(B) To show that some people in the sharing economy are wealthy

(C) To offer an example of a business found on a digital platform

(D) To describe a kind of asset that is often underused

5 What do researchers say about the future of the sharing economy?

(A) It will make up a bigger percentage of markets.

(B) It will force many workers to leave their jobs.

(C) It will cause more business to be done online.

(D) It will grow at a slower rate than today.

Dictation

C2_P2_D

Listen again and fill in the blanks.

P: These days, the business environment is changing rapidly. And one of the outcomes of these changes has been the growth of the sharing economy. Um, the sharing economy is an economic system in which _____.
Let's discuss this in more detail…
Um, so, in the sharing economy, _____. An asset is anything that has value to someone else. It can be a physical object like a car or even a skill like designing a website. _____, they are called underused assets. The sharing economy lets people share underused assets in exchange for money.
In recent years, _____. It is truly an economic revolution. There are many reasons for this, but I'll just give a couple… The first is economic efficiency. People have learned that _____ _____. This allows sellers to make money and buyers to save money. Uh, the second reason is _____. With digital technology like apps and smartphones, people can get instant access to sellers and buyers from all over the world… In this way, _____ _____…
Now, let's look at a couple of well-known examples to help us understand the sharing economy better… One good example is eBay. eBay lets people buy and sell products directly… Uh, imagine that you have a hobby, like making jewelry… Where would you sell them? Most likely, you'd use a digital platform like eBay. By using eBay, _____ or even a personal website. You can simply join the sharing economy… Another example is Uber. Uber _____ _____… Anyone with a car can make money by offering ride services through Uber. And riders can use an app to instantly order the service. By sharing the car, _____… And the rider can save money by renting a ride instead of buying their own car.
The success of companies like eBay and Uber has attracted many companies to the sharing economy. It is _____. Um, according to a study, the sharing economy was less than 6 percent of all markets in 2013… But, by 2025, researchers expect it to be around half of all markets.

Listening Practice 3

Listen to a conversation between a student and a student activities office employee.

C2_P3

Note-taking

1 Why does the student visit the student activities office?

(A) To get information for a school event

(B) To register for a course at another university

(C) To apply for membership in a student club

(D) To reserve seats for a student performance

2 What does the employee say about the school's policy?

(A) It was changed recently.

(B) It only applies to some clubs.

(C) It limits what the school can pay for.

(D) It will be discussed at a meeting soon.

3 What will the student be required to do at the end of a trip?

(A) Provide refunds to students

(B) Submit receipts from a trip

(C) Write a letter to the school

(D) Put money into a bank account

4 What will the student probably do next?

(A) Meet with a university employee

(B) Attend an event of the drama club

(C) Discuss a plan with other club members

(D) Look at event venues around campus

Listen again to part of the conversation. Then answer the question.

5 Why does the student say this: 🎧

(A) To show it is allowed to have an event

(B) To give an example of a successful event

(C) To explain why an event was delayed

(D) To describe how an event space was used

C2_P3_D

Listen again and fill in the blanks.

W: Hi. I'm looking for the student activities office. I'm the president of the dance club and I have some questions about _____.

M: Yes... What would you like to know?

W: Um, our club will be joining a dance competition in Seattle next month. But _____. We have to pay for hotel rooms, transportation, and meals for all the members...

M: I'm sorry, but the university cannot pay for all of those things. The school's policy is to _____.

W: Oh, I understand. What I mean is, um, we would like to hold an event on campus to raise some money. I just wasn't sure _____.

M: I see. In that case, you will need the school's permission first. _____ and return it to me when you're done.

W: Thank you. But, uh, _____?

M: Certainly. Um, the most important one is to keep a record of the money you make from the event. And you need to _____. The money can only be used for club-related activities.

W: Got it. But, um, will it be OK to use the money for our trip, then?

M: That will be fine... Just make sure to _____. Now, um, what kind of event are you having?

W: Um, the drama club had a play last month... It seemed popular and the tickets were $10 each. We were thinking of doing something similar. Maybe we'll do a dance performance.

M: OK, and _____?

W: I'm not sure about the exact date yet... I'll need to talk about it with the other club members.

M: OK. Discuss it over the next couple of days. _____, though. You still need to find a place on campus for your event, and, uh, that also takes time.

Listening Practice 4

Listen to part of a lecture in an environmental science class.

C2_P4

Note-taking

_____

1 What is the lecture mainly about?

(A) The importance of fish in ecosystems

(B) A solution to the problem of overfishing

(C) The different types of harmful fishing practices

(D) A set of regulations for fishers

2 What is the professor's attitude toward fishing in international waters?

(A) He thinks it should be against the law.

(B) He considers it a problem even if it is legal.

(C) He believes it benefits only a few countries.

(D) He feels that it is not an easy issue to solve.

3 According to the professor, what is a factor that contributes to IUU fishing?

(A) The funding provided by governments

(B) The cost of maintaining fishing boats

(C) The lack of good places to fish

(D) The high price of rare types of fish

4 What does the professor say about the impact of IUU fishing? *Choose 2 answers.*

(A) It lowers the income of legal fishers.

(B) It causes conflicts between countries.

(C) It forces fish to move to warmer waters.

(D) It worsens existing environmental problems.

Listen again to part of the lecture. Then answer the question.

5 Why does the professor say this:

(A) To emphasize the seriousness of a problem

(B) To say that a problem will last a long time

(C) To correct an error in an earlier statement

(D) To remind students about the subject of a test

▌▌ Dictation ▌▌

C2_P4_D

Listen again and fill in the blanks.

P: Fish is an important part of people's diets... I mean, over a billion people eat it every day. The demand is so great that some fishers will do almost anything... Unfortunately, _____. Although there are laws and agreements that regulate fishing, there are serious problems caused by illegal, unreported, and unregulated fishing, _____. Let's review each of these problems in detail.

So, uh, the first problem is illegal fishing. Illegal fishing is _____ _____. These laws may be national, regional, or international... They may include laws about a country's rivers, lakes, and coastal waters... Then, the second problem is unreported fishing. Um, many times, fishers must report when, where, and how much fish they've caught. However, _____.

By doing so, they can have more fish to sell for money. Finally, the third problem is unregulated fishing. This refers to _____. These areas are usually in international waters.

S: Um, what's wrong with that? It's not illegal to catch fish in international waters, right?

P: That's right. And it's because nobody owns international waters. However, it's still a big concern because _____.

Now, what is a common factor with each of these problems? Well, the reason they happen is because of money. _____... Just think of the high demand for fish like tuna and salmon that we eat. And, the rarer the fish, _____. This, of course, greatly contributes to IUU fishing...

Sadly, what these illegal fishers don't realize is the impact that their activities have on the planet. I mean, _____. Um, there is an estimate that the global economic losses from IUU fishing are about $23 billion a year. This includes income losses for those who fish legally. And then there is the impact of IUU fishing on ocean ecosystems... Fish are already suffering from the effects of global warming. But IUU fishing makes this even worse. And, as I said before, _____, and it only grows higher as the world's population keeps growing...

So _____. Regulations allow fish populations to recover so that there is enough for future generations of people to eat... When IUU fishers violate these regulations, _____ but also an important food source for humans... Make no mistake... IUU fishing affects everyone.

Answer Book p. 17

TOEFL Listening

C2_T1

Note-taking

1 Why does the student go to see the professor?

 Ⓐ To discuss some important works of Shakespeare

 Ⓑ To ask about an overseas academic program

 Ⓒ To get information about a professor from England

 Ⓓ To invite the professor to watch a performance

2 What does the professor say about his course?

 Ⓐ It is offered twice a year.

 Ⓑ It is popular among students.

 Ⓒ It will definitely interest the student.

 Ⓓ It will include some challenging topics.

3 Why does the professor want his students to read about ancient Greek theater?

 Ⓐ It will be the subject of a final exam.

 Ⓑ It is going to be part of a course next year.

 Ⓒ It has many examples of famous tragedies.

 Ⓓ It inspired the writing of several plays.

4 What is mentioned as a benefit of joining the program?

 Ⓐ Finishing a requirement in less time

 Ⓑ Learning some new languages

 Ⓒ Meeting students from other colleges

 Ⓓ Studying with a famous professor

Listen again to part of the conversation. Then answer the question.

5 What does the student mean when she says this: 🎧

 Ⓐ She does not know where to stay for the summer.

 Ⓑ She has already made plans to visit another city.

 Ⓒ She wants to do more than study while abroad.

 Ⓓ She is thinking about joining a different program.

Dictation

Listen again and fill in the blanks.

C2_T1_D

S: Hi, Professor Williams. My name is Amelia. Do you have a minute? I want to ask about the study-abroad program in England.

P: Sure, no problem. Are you interested in _____?

S: Yes, I think so. I mean, I've always wanted to visit England. But, uh, it's also my first year here. So _____.

P: It shouldn't be that hard. Courses in the study-abroad program are usually _____. What is your major, by the way?

S: It's English literature, but I especially like drama. I want to write plays for the theater one day.

P: Oh, then _____. It will be all about Shakespeare and his plays. We're going to study famous tragedies, like *Othello* and *Hamlet*.

S: Really? That's perfect. I've read some of his tragedies before.

P: That's good. I will also be _____. It'll be about ancient Greek theater.

S: What does that have to do with Shakespeare?

P: Well, some of Shakespeare's plays were _____, so I think it's a good idea to understand the topic.

S: I see... Um, this all sounds great. But are we going to _____ _____? I'm not sure I want to spend the entire summer in a classroom.

P: Oh, don't worry about that. We'll definitely have other activities. For instance, _____ of Shakespeare's *Macbeth* at the Globe Theatre. We'll also visit his hometown, Stratford-upon-Avon...

S: Did you say the Globe Theatre? Isn't that the actual theater where Shakespeare's plays were performed?

P: No, but _____. I've been there several times and my students always love it.

S: That sounds exciting. _____ to joining the program?

P: Yes, actually. Completing the course will _____. And it's only four weeks long. That's much shorter than a normal college semester.

S: Wow! That is great. Can I sign up today?

C2_T2

PSYCHOLOGY

Note-taking

1 What is the main topic of the lecture?

   (A) Ways to evaluate mental health

   (B) Reasons people feel different emotions

   (C) Characteristics of a mental disorder

   (D) Behaviors that improve mental health

2 According to the professor, what can be considered a symptom of a panic attack?

   (A) Sick feelings in the stomach

   (B) Problems with walking properly

   (C) Sudden necessity to speak loudly

   (D) Difficulties with breathing

3 What is the professor's attitude toward panic disorder?

   (A) She believes it can result in serious issues.

   (B) She is worried that it is becoming more common.

   (C) She thinks researchers are close to finding a solution to it.

   (D) She feels it is caused by relationship problems.

4 How are experts trying to learn about the causes of panic disorder?

   (A) By reviewing past experiments

   (B) By studying people's brains

   (C) By talking to health professionals

   (D) By comparing different disorders

5 According to the professor, what is one way of treating patients with panic disorder?

   (A) Making them do regular exercise

   (B) Asking them to discuss their thoughts

   (C) Encouraging them to spend time with family

   (D) Helping them change their sleeping habits

Listen again to part of the lecture. Then answer the question.

6 Why does the professor say this: 🎧

   (A) To show that a topic has been well researched

   (B) To apologize for providing incorrect information

   (C) To explain how people with anxiety usually act

   (D) To emphasize that anxiety is a natural reaction

Dictation

C2_T2_D

Listen again and fill in the blanks.

P: OK, we've been talking about mental disorders. Um, these are conditions of the mind that

affect _____. So, if a person is normally happy,

a mental disorder can make them feel unusually sad, angry, or afraid... Now, there are

many kinds of mental disorders. Today, we will go over panic disorder.

First, let me be clear. Feeling anxiety is normal. In fact, _____

_____. It's a natural response to everyday situations that are stressful.

Um, let's say you did something bad and you're afraid to tell your parents about it.

This fear can cause your body to react in certain ways. Maybe your heart beats faster,

your hands start to sweat, or you feel a little dizzy. These are _____

_____.

Once in a while, however, anxiety attacks can become more serious. When this happens,

they are called panic attacks. _____.

They can also happen suddenly and for no clear reason. You could be walking

down the street or just sitting at home when you have a panic attack. Symptoms

of panic attacks can include cold skin, sweating, and chest pain. Many times,

_____, which can be extremely frightening.

Some even feel like they are about to die. Thankfully, panic attacks usually don't last

very long. Um, maybe five to ten minutes at most. But the anxiety they cause can

_____.

You see, people who have experienced even one panic attack can become very afraid of

having another one. So _____. For instance, if

they had a panic attack while driving a car, they may avoid driving ever again. Just imagine

what a severe problem this can be. A panic attack can happen almost anywhere without

warning. So, instead of living a normal life, _____

_____. As a result, they may have trouble doing things like

keeping a job.

Currently, researchers believe that _____.

These may include stress, family history, and the environment. Unfortunately, experts

are still not completely sure why it happens. They hope to find answers by studying

the human brain. _____, they can

develop better ways to treat it. Right now, people who suffer from panic disorders

have to see a mental health professional. The mental health professional will usually
_____. Then, the condition may be
treated with medicine or the patient may be encouraged to discuss his or her concerns
with a therapist.

Vocabulary Review

A. Choose the correct word for each meaning.

| urban | prefer | demand | exhibition |

1 related to a city or life in the city: _____

2 the need or desire of a market for specific products and services: _____

3 to want one option over another: _____

4 an event where objects such as art are shown to the public: _____

B. Fill in the blanks with the appropriate words from the box.

| worsened | lifespan | illegal | disorder | symptoms |

5 The city has made it _____ for drivers to park on major streets during the day.

6 You should see a doctor if you are worried that you have _____ of the disease.

7 The car's unreliable brakes _____ the public's opinion of it.

8 Poor lifestyle habits such as smoking can lead to a heart _____.

9 Mayflies only live for 24 hours, which is the shortest _____ of any animal.

C. Choose the closest meaning for each highlighted word.

10 The website lets you instantly see stock prices as they change throughout the day.
(A) rightly
(B) suddenly
(C) hurriedly
(D) immediately

11 The speaker called to confirm her attendance, so she will definitely be at the event.
(A) easily
(B) certainly
(C) finally
(D) closely

12 Business activities must be regulated for the safety of all consumers.
(A) improved
(B) controlled
(C) coordinated
(D) normalized

13 Trees can help soil absorb water and therefore reduce the risk of floods.
(A) go over
(B) push away
(C) take in
(D) let out

14 The traffic police pulled him over for violating the speed limit.
(A) disobeying
(B) opposing
(C) enforcing
(D) resisting

CHAPTER 03

Function

Function

About the Question Type

Function questions ask you to determine the true meaning or intention behind a speaker's statement. This is usually different from what the speaker states directly.

These questions require you to listen again to part of a conversation or lecture. Some examples of the possible functions of a statement include: to explain a concept, to give an opinion, and to make a comparison.

Question Format

Listen again to part of the lecture. Then answer the question.
P: *********************
Why does the professor say this: 🎧

Key Strategies

- **Step 1** — Listen carefully to the replay, and then identify the intention behind what the speaker has said within the context.

- **Step 2** — Focus on the words that the speaker emphasizes and the tone of voice that they use. They often indicate the true intention behind statements.

- **Step 3** — Select the answer choice that best represents the true meaning or intention of the speaker.

Example

C3_ExA

A. Listen to a conversation between a student and a professor.

Note-taking

Listen again to part of the conversation. Then answer the question.
What does the student mean when he says this:

(A) He would like to send the paper earlier.

(B) He will not be finished at that time.

(C) He cannot understand what the professor said.

(D) He can complete the research without any help.

B. Listen to part of a lecture in a history class.

C3_ExB

Note-taking

Listen again to part of the lecture. Then answer the question.
Why does the professor say this:

(A) To explain why a holiday is popular

(B) To agree with the choice of a date

(C) To emphasize that a celebration is important

(D) To point out the need for more holidays

‖ Dictation ‖

Answer Book p. 20

Listen again and fill in the blanks.

A.

C3_ExA_D

S: Hi, Professor Mitchell. I was hoping I could talk to you. Um, it's about the paper I'm writing for your economics class.

P: Oh, hi, Kevin. Are you having difficulties with your research?

S: Yes, I am. Um, I'm not quite sure _____. I think a lot of my ideas are important. But I'm worried that some of them might be unrelated.

P: I see. I'd be happy to _____. Send me a copy this evening and I'll take a look.

S: Did you say this evening? I have to go to football practice and I won't be home _____.

P: Don't worry. Just send me _____.

B.

C3_ExB_D

P: Since tomorrow is Juneteenth, I thought we might take some time to talk about this important holiday. So what exactly is Juneteenth? Well, it began in the 19th century _____. You see, slaves in Texas were freed on June 19, 1865. However, it wasn't until 2021 that _____ _____. I would say it's a good thing they did. Today, it's the only holiday that remembers the end of slavery.

Now, in the past, celebrations of Juneteenth usually included small family gatherings and church ceremonies. Recently, however, _____. In fact, many cities across the United States hold parades and festivals on the occasion.

Listening Practice 1

Answer Book p. 21

Listen to a conversation between a student and a student services office employee.

C3_P1

Note-taking

---

1 What is the student's problem?

(A) He has no meals for the end of the semester.

(B) His request for a refund was not approved.

(C) He purchased more meals than he needed.

(D) His meal plan cost much more than expected.

2 What does the student say he is planning to do?

(A) Try a different meal plan

(B) Buy his meals outside campus

(C) Fly out of the country over break

(D) Join a program to study abroad

3 What does the employee think about the university's refund policy?

(A) She does not understand why students dislike it.

(B) She believes that it should be explained more clearly.

(C) She thinks that it is helpful to the university.

(D) She does not feel that it is fair to students.

4 What does the employee suggest that the student do?

(A) Call the office when he has decided

(B) Wait until next semester to change his plan

(C) Make an appointment to speak with an employee

(D) Visit the office before a busy period

Listen again to part of the conversation. Then answer the question.

5 Why does the employee say this: 🎧

(A) To encourage the student to choose later

(B) To express support for the student's decision

(C) To emphasize the seriousness of a problem

(D) To suggest a way to improve a situation

‖ Dictation ‖

C3_P1_D

Listen again and fill in the blanks.

M: Excuse me. Is this the student services office?

W: Yes, it is. What can I help you with?

M: Um, I need to talk to someone about my meal plan. I bought the largest one with 225 meals. But, um, I've only used around half. What can _____?

W: Um, how many do you have left, exactly?

M: I think there are 100 left. And, um, each one is $15. So _____. I was hoping to get some money back so I can buy a plane ticket to Spain. I'm planning to spend summer break overseas.

W: Well, you have the option to _____. But then, you will only get back half of the money _____.

M: I see... That doesn't seem like a reasonable policy.

W: Well... Personally, I think you're right. Students should be able to _____ _____. But I can't do anything about it.

M: Then, I need to think of another solution. Maybe I can _____. If I sell it at a cheap price, I'm sure someone would buy it.

W: I don't think that's a good idea. _____ is against university rules. If you are caught doing that, you won't be allowed to get another meal plan next semester. You wouldn't want that to happen, would you?

M: Definitely not. I didn't know that. I'd better think about it some more. When do I have to _____?

W: Well, there are only two weeks left _____. And changes have to be made before the winter break. But it's very busy during the final week. Students sometimes have to wait for hours before they can talk to one of our staff. _____ _____, if you can.

M: OK. I'll do that. Thanks for all of your help.

W: My pleasure. Feel free to call us if you need more information.

Listening Practice 2

C3_P2

Listen to part of a lecture in a physiology class.

Note-taking

1 What is the lecture mainly about?

(A) Why people should avoid dangerous situations

(B) Changes in the human body when sleepy or hungry

(C) How the human body reacts to potential threats

(D) The difference between physical and psychological threats

2 What is the professor's attitude toward the danger faced by early humans?

(A) She thinks it was more psychological than physical.

(B) She believes it gave them limited options.

(C) She feels it caused them to migrate to new areas.

(D) She disagrees it was more dangerous than modern threats.

3 According to the professor, what is an effect of the release of chemicals by the nervous system?

(A) The heart rate decreases.

(B) The body shakes uncontrollably.

(C) Muscles loosen up.

(D) Blood pressure increases.

4 According to the professor, what can people do to reduce the effects of the body's response to stressful situations?

(A) Express what they are feeling

(B) Think of positive experiences

(C) Slow down their breathing

(D) Stretch their arms and legs

Listen again to part of the lecture. Then answer the question.

5 Why does the professor say this:

(A) To illustrate an incorrect belief about the fight-or-flight response

(B) To explain that fighting or running away is not always possible

(C) To highlight the relationship between stress and survival

(D) To point out that a reaction can happen even without a threat

Dictation

Dictation

Listening Practice 3

Listen to a conversation between a student and a professor.

C3_P3

Note-taking

---

1 Why does the student go to see the professor?

    (A) To request a new group for a project

    (B) To discuss a problem with another group

    (C) To ask if his group can choose a new topic

    (D) To learn more about a group presentation

2 What is the professor's opinion of the Midland Zoo?

    (A) It pays very well for internships.

    (B) It has several excellent researchers.

    (C) It should receive more city funding.

    (D) It performs important studies.

3 Why does the student want to learn about various subjects?

    (A) He is no longer interested in animal studies.

    (B) He must improve his grades to apply to graduate school.

    (C) He has to choose a major before he graduates.

    (D) He is not sure what to study in graduate school.

4 What will the student probably do next?

    (A) Select a new topic for a class project

    (B) Finish some homework assignments

    (C) Tell his group what he has learned at the zoo

    (D) Send an email to some of his group members

Listen again to part of the conversation. Then answer the question.

5 What does the professor mean when she says this: 🎧

    (A) The student should work hard at the internship.

    (B) The student was recommended for the internship.

    (C) The student deserves the internship.

    (D) The student is required to do an internship.

Dictation

Answer Book p. 24

C3_P3_D

Listen again and fill in the blanks.

P: Hi, Brad. Is something wrong?

S: No, Professor. I just need to talk about our animal studies course.

P: Sure. What's on your mind?

S: I want to _____. Right now, I'm in the group that is studying _____.

P: Oh... Is there a problem with your group?

S: No. But _____ at the Midland Zoo. I'm learning about how animals live in that environment. So I'd like to join another group because _____.

P: Well, congratulations on the internship. That's a great zoo. I mean, _____ _____. But also, some of the best researchers work there.

S: Yeah, I was lucky to be _____. Um, it was really competitive.

P: That's more than just luck, you know. You've always been an excellent student. But I think you should stay in your current group. They can _____. And the project could also help your work at the zoo.

S: That's true. But I'd like to learn about new things. I want to _____, but I don't know what to study yet. That's why I want to learn about various subjects before I graduate.

P: Hmm... I understand what you mean. That sounds like a good idea. Um, do you know _____?

S: Well, the topic about marine animals sounds interesting. Can I join that group?

P: But then, your current group will have one less member if you leave. That will _____.

S: Oh... I didn't think about that. Is there anything I can do to help them?

P: _____ with your original group? You can join the other group after you do that.

S: Of course. I'll go talk to them right away!

Listening Practice 4

Listen to part of a lecture in an earth science class.

C3_P4

Note-taking

1 What is the main topic of the lecture?
   (A) How geothermal energy was invented
   (B) The main advantages of geothermal energy
   (C) How people have used geothermal energy
   (D) The technology utilized in geothermal energy

2 What does the professor say about a spring?
   (A) It contains lots of small rocks.
   (B) It is water that comes from under the ground.
   (C) It becomes cooler when it meets the air.
   (D) It can cause floods during a storm.

3 What does the professor say about a town in France?
   (A) It has the oldest hot spring in the world.
   (B) It learned about hot springs from China.
   (C) It benefits from hot springs in various ways.
   (D) It only uses its hot springs in the winter.

4 What does the professor imply about new technology?
   (A) It could replace the use of generators.
   (B) It makes heat and electricity at the same time.
   (C) It has made generators cheaper to build.
   (D) It makes new generators more powerful.

Listen again to part of the lecture. Then answer the question.

5 What does the professor imply when he says this:
   (A) The town spent too much money on equipment.
   (B) The people of Larderello used the wrong method.
   (C) The generator took too long to be built.
   (D) The town's first generator produced little electricity.

∥ Dictation ∥

C3_P4_D

Listen again and fill in the blanks.

P: You know we can produce energy from sources like the sun, wind, and water, right?
But did you know that we can also _____?
Well, this is called geothermal energy. Today, we will examine some of the ways

_____.

Geothermal energy comes from deep within the earth's mantle. The mantle has
temperatures of up to 4,000 degrees Celsius, which is, um, _____.
Most of the heat in the mantle has existed for millions of years. Sometimes, the heat goes
up and gets released above the ground. Now, _____
and appears above the surface of the earth, this is called a spring. And, when a spring is
heated by geothermal energy, what does it become? Um, can anyone take a guess?

S: _____?

P: That's right. And this brings us to how geothermal energy was first used.
_____. Uh, the ancient Chinese and Romans used hot springs
for bathing. In fact, there is a hot spring in northeastern China that is among the oldest
in the world. People have been using it for about 3,000 years. Meanwhile, in France,
_____ since the 1300s. It built pipes to move
water from the spring to people's houses. This provided many important benefits. For
instance, the springs provided hot water for bathing and kept houses warm in the winter.
OK, _____. You see, hot water
produces lots of steam. And, uh, this steam can be used to _____
_____. First, the steam passes through pipes that go into a
building. Inside the building, the steam causes a large wheel to move. As the wheel moves,
it creates energy. This energy is then _____.
The first generator to produce electricity this way was built in the town of Larderello, Italy,
in 1904. At first, the generator made electricity for just five light bulbs. That's not great...
But, 10 years later, _____. Today, it provides electricity to
millions of people.
Anyway, geothermal energy is important because _____
_____. The only disadvantage is cost. It can be expensive
to find the right location and to build a powerful generator. This has improved in recent
years, though, with the introduction of new technology.

Answer Book p. 27

TOEFL Listening

C3_T1

Note-taking

1 What is the student's problem?

   Ⓐ She borrowed the wrong book from the library.

   Ⓑ She forgot to return a book to the library.

   Ⓒ She got a book with a missing section.

   Ⓓ She lost a book that was needed for a course.

2 Why does the librarian plan to contact another student?

   Ⓐ To find out the location of a library book

   Ⓑ To ask them to pay for a damaged item

   Ⓒ To update some account information

   Ⓓ To determine when a book will be returned

3 What must the student do to get the book from another library?

   Ⓐ Complete an online document

   Ⓑ Sign up at an office

   Ⓒ Send a university an e-mail

   Ⓓ Contact another librarian

4 What does the librarian suggest the student do to save time?

   Ⓐ Schedule another visit with him

   Ⓑ Acquire a book in person

   Ⓒ Contact another bookstore

   Ⓓ Request home delivery of a book

Listen again to part of the conversation. Then answer the question.

5 What does the librarian imply when he says this: 🎧

   Ⓐ The library only has one copy of every book.

   Ⓑ The student should return on another day.

   Ⓒ The book may be available at a later date.

   Ⓓ The student cannot get a copy of a book.

Dictation

Listen again and fill in the blanks.

C3_T1_D

W: Hi. Uh, could I show you something? It's about this book. _____
_____ last night.

M: A problem? What do you mean? Is it the wrong book?

W: Well, _____. If you look inside, you'll see it's
missing. I need that part of the book to write my essay.

M: Really? Let me take a look... Hmm, you're right. It looks like _____
_____.

W: Why would someone do that?

M: I'm not quite sure. They could have easily copied the pages that they needed. Anyway, I'll
check the records and _____. They will have
to pay to replace the book.

W: OK... But that doesn't help me with my problem. Like I said, I need that chapter to
complete my assignment. Does the library have _____?

M: Um, let me check... Yeah, it's not your day. And the book is no longer published, so you
probably won't find it in a bookstore. That means it's going to _____
_____.

W: I really need to get another copy of that book. There must be another way to get it. Do
you have any suggestions?

M: Well, there is one other option. Why don't you see _____?

W: All right... How exactly can I do that?

M: Well, the easiest thing to do would be to use the interlibrary loan system. If the book is
available, you can _____. You will be notified by
e-mail when the book arrives. Then, you can pick it up...

W: That actually sounds pretty simple. _____?

M: Well, it can take up to two weeks. The book has to be sent here from another location.
However, if I were you, _____. That will save you
some time.

W: OK. That would work better for me. If another library has it, I'll go there as soon as
possible.

Answer Book p. 28

TOEFL Listening

C3_T2

BIOLOGY

Note-taking

1 What is the lecture mainly about?

(A) Why some insects change their shape

(B) How scientists study the lives of insects

(C) The process of metamorphosis in an insect

(D) The physical differences between insects

2 What does the professor say about a caterpillar's cocoon?

(A) It provides food for a young caterpillar.

(B) It has a smooth and shiny appearance.

(C) It gives a caterpillar protection.

(D) It usually takes several days to form.

3 What happens to some of a caterpillar's organs as it develops?

(A) They produce lots of proteins.

(B) They release chemicals in the brain.

(C) They combine to form new parts.

(D) They change shape to fit the body.

4 According to the professor, what are imaginal discs?

(A) Cells that form body parts

(B) Places where butterflies grow

(C) Color patterns on a pupa's skin

(D) Smaller insects inside the pupa

5 Why do butterflies wait one to two hours before flying away?

(A) Their wings have to be dry.

(B) They have to gather as a group first.

(C) Their wings take time to fully open.

(D) They only fly at certain times of the day.

Listen again to part of the lecture. Then answer the question.

6 Why does the professor say this: 🎧

(A) To explain how a butterfly breathes

(B) To illustrate a step in a process

(C) To define a technical term

(D) To emphasize the strength of a cocoon

Dictation

C3_T2_D

Listen again and fill in the blanks.

P: In our last class, I mentioned that some insects go through a process called metamorphosis. During this process, insects change their physical form as they grow. A good example is caterpillars, _____

_____.

OK, so, caterpillars hatch from little eggs. When a caterpillar comes out of its egg, _____. First, it eats its own eggshell, and then it eats the leaves of plants. This allows _____. It grows so fast that its skin changes four or five times, and it becomes about a thousand times bigger than its original size.

After about two weeks of eating, chemicals in the caterpillar's brain tell it to go to the next stage of metamorphosis. At this stage, the caterpillar _____

_____. The silk is sticky and is used by the caterpillar to attach itself to a leaf or branch. Then, the caterpillar continues to produce silk until its entire body is covered in it. This silk covering is called a cocoon, and _____. The cocoon takes about one day to form.

When the cocoon is complete, the caterpillar's outer shell and other parts of its body are broken down into smaller proteins. At this point, the caterpillar is now a pupa, and _____. Of course, some parts of the caterpillar are never broken down. These include organs from inside the insect's body, like the stomach or the brain. These organs are not destroyed, but _____

_____. At the same time, the pupa has other groups of cells called imaginal discs. Imaginal discs are _____.

They are quite thin and flat, and each one holds a unique set of cells. These cells determine _____. So some imaginal discs will form a butterfly's eyes, others will form the wings, the legs, the antennae, and so on. This stage of development usually lasts from a few weeks to a month, but, for some kinds of butterflies, it can take up to two years.

_____, the pupa is now an adult butterfly. However, it is still inside the cocoon and must break through the cocoon to open its wings. The monarch butterfly, for example, does this by breathing in air. _____ and makes it grow larger. This stretches out the cocoon and causes it to break open.

_____, it must wait one to two hours for its wings to dry completely before it can fly away. When that happens, _____ _____ and is now ready to begin its adult life.

Vocabulary Review

A. Choose the correct word for each meaning.

| organ   psychological   solution   hatch |

1 a way of dealing with a problem: _____

2 to be born from an egg: _____

3 relating to the human mind and how it works: _____

4 an inner part of the body that serves an important purpose: _____

B. Fill in the blanks with the appropriate words from the box.

| officially   competitive   replace   attach   possibility |

5 Getting into a top university is highly _____, so study well.

6 You should _____ your car's tires with new ones every six years.

7 Ivy plants can _____ themselves to walls and grow 30 meters above the ground.

8 The government _____ announced its position after rumors were spread online.

9 Scientists are exploring the _____ that there is life on other planets.

C. Choose the closest meaning for each highlighted word.

10 As long as our plan is reasonable, management will likely approve it.
(A) unique   (B) honest   (C) convenient   (D) practical

11 The building collapsed because it was not built on solid ground.
(A) ancient   (B) regular   (C) firm   (D) continuous

12 You will notice several interesting features of the artwork if you look at it closely.
(A) overlook   (B) consider   (C) observe   (D) expect

13 Each year, powerful storms threaten the lives of people on the island.
(A) enrich   (B) scare   (C) approach   (D) endanger

14 Flowers release a scent that attracts bees and other insects.
(A) clear   (B) emit   (C) loosen   (D) submit

CHAPTER 04

Attitude

Attitude

About the Question Type

Attitude questions ask you to identify the speaker's attitude or opinion regarding ideas mentioned in a conversation or lecture.

These questions require you to recognize the speaker's feelings, likes and dislikes, or reasons for particular feelings. These questions sometimes require you to listen again to part of the listening passage.

Question Format

- What does the man/woman mean/imply when he/she says this:
- What is the professor's attitude toward ~?
- What is the professor's opinion of ~?

Key Strategies

- **Step 1** — Pay close attention to parts of the talk where the speaker expresses personal opinions, suggestions, or feelings.
- **Step 2** — Listen to the speaker's tone of voice and way of talking. This can make it easier to identify the speaker's attitude towards a topic.
- **Step 3** — Select the answer choice that best illustrates the speaker's attitude or opinion.

Example

Answer Book p. 29

A. Listen to a conversation between a student and a professor.

Note-taking

C4_ExA

What is the professor's attitude toward the student's situation?

(A) He is concerned that the student has made a poor choice.

(B) He is surprised that the student has already started her paper.

(C) He is confident that the student has done enough research.

(D) He is upset that the student has not listened to his suggestion.

Answer Book p. 29

B. Listen to part of a lecture in an environmental science class.

Note-taking

C4_ExB

Listen again to part of the lecture. Then answer the question.
What does the professor mean when he says this:

(A) He is worried that a symptom is more serious than expected.

(B) He hopes that the problem of red tides will be solved soon.

(C) He believes a phenomenon has become more common.

(D) He thinks a red tide is especially dangerous for some people.

Dictation

Answer Book p. 29

Listen again and fill in the blanks.

A.

C4_ExA_D

S: Hi, Professor. I'm getting ready to start my economics paper. These are _____
_____. What do you think?

P: Let's see... Uh, I'm afraid _____. The ones you've
chosen are quite old. _____ since these were published.

S: I thought they would be good because they are well-known.

P: Yes, they are very good books and articles, but _____
_____. We read a lot of recent articles in class... Do you still have
them?

S: Of course. I kept everything from your class.

P: Well, _____. That would be a good place
to start.

B.

C4_ExB_D

P: Every summer in different parts of the US, _____.
This phenomenon is called a red tide. Uh, it is _____
_____. A red algae bloom has serious consequences for sea life
as well as humans. Some species of red algae _____
_____. These can cause health issues for people on the shore.
_____ and, um, a burning feeling
in the eyes. And, if anyone with breathing problems is planning a trip to the beach during
a red tide... Well, let's just say it'd be better to make other plans.

Listening Practice 1

Answer Book p. 30

Listen to a conversation between a student and an assistant in a language lab.

Note-taking

C4_P1

1 What is the woman's problem?

(A) She wants to reserve a seat for a test.

(B) She is having an issue with some equipment.

(C) She does not know how to use a device.

(D) She cannot install a program on a computer.

2 Why can't the man get new speakers from the supply room?

(A) He needs to ask for approval first.

(B) He is unable to contact the head of a department.

(C) He does not have access to the supply room.

(D) He has to check that a computer part is available.

3 Why does the woman mention the problem with her laptop?

(A) To explain why she reserved a space at the lab

(B) To describe a common issue with computers

(C) To confirm that she already downloaded a file

(D) To emphasize the importance of computer maintenance

4 What does the man offer to do for the woman?

(A) Send a document to a department

(B) Leave a message at an office

(C) Allow her to use the seat for assistants

(D) Replace some equipment she needs

Listen again to part of the conversation. Then answer the question.

5 What does the man mean when he says this:

(A) He feels that he cannot meet a deadline.

(B) He believes an item will take too long to fix.

(C) He thinks he will need some better tools.

(D) He wishes there was something he could do.

C4_P1_D

Listen again and fill in the blanks.

W: Hi. Um... I have a problem. I'm hoping you can help me.

M: Sure. What can I do for you?

W: I'm using the computer in that seat over there... It's, uh, number 51. I reserved it so _____ for my Spanish class. The test is in 10 minutes, but _____.

M: Oh, really? Let me see if there are any other ones available... Hmm, it seems that we're full this morning. Midterms are this week, so _____.

W: I understand. But I really need to take the exam. Do you think _____ _____?

M: The, uh, service engineer is _____. He should be back in about three hours.

W: Hmm... Is there anything you can do in the meantime?

M: I'm sorry. I'd fix them myself if I knew how.

W: The exam is going to start soon. If I miss it, my grade will be affected. How about _____? We could connect them to the computer I'm using.

M: I would do that if I could. But _____. And the request needs to be approved by the head of the maintenance department.

W: But this is kind of urgent... Can't you just get the speakers first and the approval later?

M: No, I can't do that. _____ or I could lose my job. Besides, the service engineer has to check the speakers first to _____. The problem could be caused by something else.

W: I don't know what to do.

M: Hmm... Don't you have your own computer?

W: Yes, but my laptop is old. _____, either. That's why I reserved a spot here at the language lab.

M: I see. Well, I don't need speakers to do my work, so why don't you take my seat, instead? It's usually only for student assistants. However, since you have an exam now, _____.

W: Really? That's so thoughtful of you!

Listening Practice 2

Answer Book p. 32

Listen to part of a lecture in an ecology class.

C4_P2

Note-taking

---

1 What is the lecture mainly about?

  (A) Why endangered deer species need protection

  (B) How the increase in deer influences the environment

  (C) The consequences of overhunting a deer species

  (D) The effects of too many deer on human settlements

2 According to the professor, what contributes to the disappearance of some plants in the forest?

  (A) The activities of animals reduce the amount of soil.

  (B) Deer prefer to eat specific types of leaves and plants.

  (C) Many animals use leaves to build their nests.

  (D) Large numbers of deer step on the plants.

3 What is the professor's attitude toward the damage deer are doing to forests?

  (A) It will have an impact on people's food sources.

  (B) It is too late to prevent it from happening.

  (C) It can only be stopped by people.

  (D) It has negatively affected the number of deer.

4 According to the professor, what are two ways to reduce the number of deer? *Choose 2 answers.*

  (A) Hunting large numbers of deer

  (B) Removing the deer's food sources

  (C) Building fences and walls around forests

  (D) Introducing more natural predators to forests

Listen again to part of the lecture. Then answer the question.

5 Why does the professor say this: 🎧

  (A) To suggest that deer can be found in many kinds of habitats

  (B) To introduce another species that can be harmful to crops

  (C) To show that deer are not responsible for all crop damage

  (D) To suggest that deer do not only threaten agriculture

‖ Dictation ‖

Listen again and fill in the blanks.

C4_P2_D

P: Recently, we discussed endangered animals. Now, let's talk about a species that is doing well, the white-tailed deer. About 90 years ago, _____. Due to overhunting, there were only about 300,000 left in the US. But today, there are about 30 million... Obviously, _____. So now, let's consider what the effects of this population increase are on the environment.
But first, we need to understand _____. In fact, this is the key to its success. This species lives in a variety of different habitats. They can survive in grasslands, wetlands, and, of course, forests... Uh, and they also live well near humans, especially, um, _____...

S: I've heard that they do a lot of damage to crops. Doesn't that _____ _____?

P: Yes. The losses are huge. In fact, deer are responsible for more than half of all crop losses caused by wildlife. And that's only the tip of the iceberg... As I was saying, these deer can have _____... Um, they significantly influence the plants that grow there. Generally, _____ _____, which can stop plants from growing. And they only eat certain kinds of plants. So, uh, these plants begin to disappear. Why is this a problem? Well, this can _____ in the forest. And this reduces the food sources for other animals in the forest ecosystem.
What's more, the removal of leaves from plants _____ _____. Consider songbirds, for example. Many songbird species build their nests close to the ground rather than high in the trees. However, _____. These leaves hide the songbirds' eggs from predators. Without the leaves, the eggs are easier to see. As a result, predators eat the eggs, which reduces the number of birds.
Now, we know that these deer can damage the forest ecosystem... The only way the deer can be stopped is _____... One way to achieve this is to introduce more natural predators into the deer's environment. For instance, animals such as mountain lions and wolves can reduce the number of white-tailed deer. However, this alone will not be enough to totally solve the problem. Certainly, the best and fastest method is _____. This is why many states encourage hunting of this species.

Listening Practice 3

Listen to a conversation between a student and an employee at the facilities management office.

C4_P3

Note-taking

---

1 Why does the student visit the facilities management office?

   (A) To ask about the schedule for some exams

   (B) To suggest ways the campus can help students with exams

   (C) To request that a facility extend its opening hours

   (D) To make complaints about the library facilities

2 How does the employee seem to feel about the student café workers?

   (A) He believes that they are happy with their jobs.

   (B) He thinks that they should study harder for exams.

   (C) He is uncomfortable about making them work longer.

   (D) He agrees with their idea to study in the café.

3 What does the student say about the library?

   (A) It fills up with people very quickly.

   (B) It has the cleanest areas to study.

   (C) It is common for people to bring food inside.

   (D) It sometimes gets noisy during the exam period.

4 According to the student, why might the dormitory's common room be a good study area?

   (A) Students can eat and drink in it.

   (B) It has the same furniture as the library.

   (C) Students usually speak quietly there.

   (D) It can be used as long as students want.

Listen again to part of the conversation. Then answer the question.

5 What does the student imply when she says this: 🎧

   (A) She believed that a task would be easy to do.

   (B) She was sure that a payment had already been made.

   (C) She thought it would be hard to convince the employee.

   (D) She was worried about how some workers might respond.

‖ Dictation ‖

Answer Book p. 33

C4_P3_D

Listen again and fill in the blanks.

W: Hello. I'm here to speak with someone about the campus café.

M: OK. Are you looking for a part-time job?

W: No. It's about the café's opening hours. Do you think the school could _____

_____? It's a great place to study, but it closes at 8 p.m.

M: Hmm... Extending the café's hours isn't that simple.

W: You don't think it's possible?

M: Not really. First, we'd have to _____. That would

cost too much. Also, the café usually receives a limited amount of money from the school.

_____ to keep it open for the extra hours.

W: Oh, I didn't think of that. I had no idea it would be so complicated.

M: Yes. In addition, _____. They have to take

exams, too, and need time to study. Besides, _____ during

the exam period. Why don't you study there?

W: The library isn't the best place to study, though. I mean, it's crowded. As you mentioned,

everyone on campus is _____. So it's really difficult to find a

free desk... You have to arrive early to find a spot.

M: What about unused classrooms? You could study in one of those...

W: That's true, but the reason why I prefer the café is because _____

_____.

M: That's a good point, but there's really no way _____.

W: I see... I guess I'll have to think of somewhere else...

M: Um, I have another idea... What about the dormitory's common room?

W: It's a bit noisy with the TVs and people talking...

M: Yes, but you could try talking to the other residents... You know, you could suggest

_____ for the exam period.

W: That could work. The common room has comfortable furniture. And, most importantly, it's

in our dormitory, so _____. I just hope I can convince the

other students.

Answer Book p. 34

Listen to part of a lecture in a business management class.

C4_P4

Note-taking

1 What is the lecture mainly about?

(A) A business strategy that focuses on customers

(B) A way of making employees more effective

(C) An innovative method of producing goods

(D) A way to promote products to new markets

2 According to the professor, what did businesses focus on in the early 20th century?

(A) Reducing production errors

(B) Producing goods efficiently

(C) Training factory workers

(D) Improving the quality of items

3 How does the professor seem to feel about the "Adopt a Customer" program?

(A) It makes the jobs of employees harder.

(B) It could be useful to other businesses.

(C) It is an essential element of market orientation.

(D) It should have been the responsibility of one person.

4 What does the professor say about social media?

(A) It has reduced the importance of market orientation.

(B) It makes it easier to apply market orientation techniques.

(C) It can be too expensive for small companies to use.

(D) It is more popular in some countries than in others.

Listen again to part of the lecture. Then answer the question.

5 What does the professor mean when he says this: 🎧

(A) He thinks a strategy will continue to be widely used.

(B) He hopes more businesses use market orientation.

(C) He believes that market orientation has changed too much.

(D) He feels that a method still has some problems.

‖ Dictation ‖

Listen again and fill in the blanks.

C4_P4_D

P: All right class, let's begin. So, today we're going to study market orientation, which is an important concept in business. Market orientation means that a company is oriented, or directed toward, the market. In other words, the company _____. It sounds like an obvious strategy to us, right? Well, it wasn't always companies' primary focus. In the early 20th century, most companies focused on production. Um, their main goal was to _____ _____. But, by the 1950s, there were plenty of affordable goods. So companies needed a new strategy to earn larger profits... That's when the market orientation strategy was developed. The goal of this strategy is to _____.

Now, how do companies do this? Well, first, the companies need to _____ _____. And the best way to do that is through market research... For instance, many companies use surveys to get information about what customers want. Then, they use this research to create new products or _____ _____.

S: Doesn't every business do that? I mean, all companies have someone that does basic market research, right?

P: That's mostly true. But, with market orientation, _____ _____... It's not just the job of a specific person. You see, there are different ways to satisfy customers, and _____ _____.

Let me give you an example. Several years ago, a chemical manufacturing company started a program called "Adopt a Customer." The idea was that a factory worker visited a customer once a month to discuss the company's products and talk about the customer's needs. And then, the worker returned to the factory and _____. This kind of personal attention made customers feel highly valued and strengthened the relationship between the company's employees and customers. It also _____.

In fact, I think a lot of companies could learn something by studying this program. It really showed that all employees at a company should get involved.

OK. So, over the past few decades, _____ _____ in the business world. It isn't going away anytime soon. But, um, there is one last thing that I'd like to mention. Until recently, there was a problem with market orientation. Small companies could not afford to interact with customers in different areas. It was too expensive for them to travel. But social media has changed all that. Now, companies can _____. Even the smallest businesses can contact their customers and benefit from market orientation.

Answer Book p. 36

TOEFL Listening

C4_T1

Note-taking

1 Why did the professor ask to see the student?

(A) To request his help with planning an event

(B) To invite him to participate in an activity

(C) To encourage him to sign up for a class

(D) To give him feedback on an assignment

2 According to the professor, where did the idea for a project come from?

(A) An article written by a professor in the department

(B) A conversation with a student interested in dance

(C) A discussion among professors during a meeting

(D) A paper submitted by a student in another class

3 What are two reasons that the department is planning to hold dance workshops?

Choose 2 answers.

(A) They will allow students to develop their teaching abilities.

(B) They would be an opportunity for professors and students to interact.

(C) They would be a good way to attract interest in a type of art.

(D) They will inspire young people to study dance in university.

4 What is the student's attitude toward joining a project?

(A) He is concerned that it will take too much time.

(B) He does not think that it will be a useful experience.

(C) He hopes that it involves working with other students.

(D) He thinks that it should be discussed with another professor.

Listen again to part of the conversation. Then answer the question.

5 Why does the student say this: 🎧

(A) To say he does not understand what he has to do

(B) To suggest that he is capable of teaching children

(C) To show that the professor's expectations are reasonable

(D) To indicate he is not confident in doing an activity

Dictation

Listen again and fill in the blanks.

S: Hi, Professor Morris. I got your e-mail. You said you wanted to see me about a project or something?

P: Yes. I wanted to talk to you about a project I'm planning. _____

_____ .

S: That sounds interesting. I've enjoyed your classes a lot, so I'm sure it'll be good.

P: I'm glad to hear that. Uh, the project, well, it's something I've been working on with other professors in the dance department. At one of our meetings, we talked about _____

_____ . And, well, the idea began from there.

S: Um, I'm not sure I understand... What is the project about?

P: Well, we want to _____ .

S: That sounds fun. I mean, I think it's a good idea, but why is the department interested in dance workshops for children?

P: Well, there are a couple of reasons. First, we would like to _____

_____ . Obviously, the department members are passionate about this art form. But we want to get others interested in it as well. _____

_____ seems like a good way to achieve this goal.

S: That makes sense.

P: Another reason is that it would be a great opportunity for students like yourself. Uh, you will get some teaching experience. It would be good for you to learn _____

_____ .

S: I see. So, um, would I be teaching children on my own? I don't know... That would be pretty difficult. Maybe too challenging.

P: No. Actually, the workshops would be _____ .

I'm even going to lead one on ballet. However, we need talented students to

_____ . So you would be like an assistant

teacher.

S: Um, the whole project sounds great. But _____ . I've

been taking extra classes.

P: I understand. Why don't you think about it for a couple of days? And if you have any questions, just contact me.

S: OK. Thanks for considering me.

Answer Book p. 37

TOEFL Listening

C4_T2

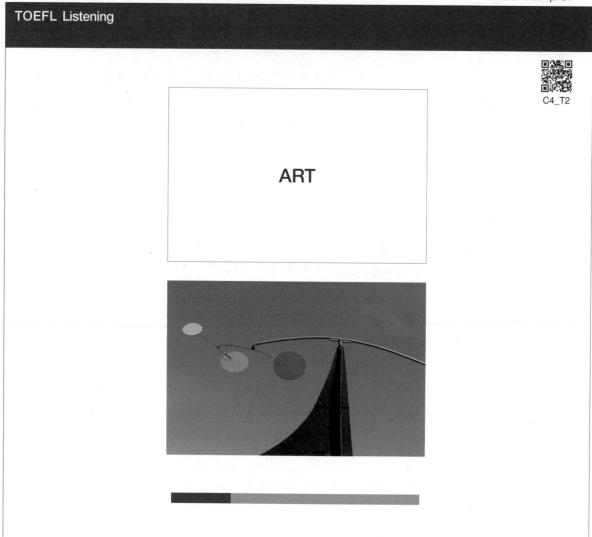

Note-taking

1 What is the lecture mainly about?

   Ⓐ The development of modern art

   Ⓑ A type of art that includes movement

   Ⓒ The impact of mobiles on visual art

   Ⓓ The popularity of kinetic art

2 What does the professor say is an important feature of mobiles?

   Ⓐ They use objects with similar weights.

   Ⓑ They contain items with different materials.

   Ⓒ They rely on the idea of balance.

   Ⓓ They begin with two-dimensional designs.

3 Why does the professor discuss Calder's family background?

   Ⓐ To explain why Calder chose to study art

   Ⓑ To show how Calder's family helped him succeed

   Ⓒ To provide a reason for Calder's interest in art

   Ⓓ To explain why Calder changed his career

4 What is true of the mobiles made by Alexander Calder?

   Ⓐ They used light and dark colors to create contrast.

   Ⓑ Some were standing and others were hanging.

   Ⓒ They were not the first mobiles made by an artist.

   Ⓓ Most required electricity to make them move.

5 What is the professor's opinion of Alexander Calder?

   Ⓐ She believes that Calder greatly influenced the world of art.

   Ⓑ She feels that Calder's artwork is hard to understand.

   Ⓒ She agrees that Calder had limited influence.

   Ⓓ She thinks many people have the wrong idea about Calder.

Listen again to part of the lecture. Then answer the question.

6 Why does the professor say this: ∩

   Ⓐ To show that the materials in kinetic art were cheap

   Ⓑ To specify two objects that are equal in weight

   Ⓒ To provide examples of objects used in mobiles

   Ⓓ To emphasize the importance of making simple art

Dictation

Listen again and fill in the blanks.

C4_T2_D

P: I'm sure you're all familiar with toy mobiles. Parents hang them above a baby's bed. They have colorful shapes and move in the air. But did you know that the earliest mobiles were a type of art called kinetic art? Well, _____.
And this is what we'll be looking at today.
So… In the early 19th century, _____
_____. How did they do this? Well, they typically used one or more sticks made of wood or metal. Then, the artists would attach wires to the sticks and hang objects from the wires. Often, _____… These could be things like small stones or coins… Basically, anything that was possible to hang from wires could be used.
Now, imagine that you hang an object from one end of a stick. What will happen? The stick will be lower on one side, of course. So artists placed objects on both ends of the stick to keep the stick in balance. So, you see, _____
_____. Artists could create a variety of mobiles _____
_____. They could also use multiple sticks with different lengths.
Um, let's look at an example of a famous kinetic artist. His name is Alexander Calder. Now, with Calder's family background, _____.
His parents and grandfather were artists, and they encouraged him to work in art. So, Calder had some interest in art, but _____… The influence of his education is obvious in his work. You see, he used his engineering skills to _____. His early works were sculptures with motors in them. Uh, the motors made the sculptures move. But, later on, he developed other kinds of mobiles that had no motors at all. These included standing mobiles and hanging mobiles.
Standing mobiles had _____. Then, a long metal stick was placed in the center of the stand. From the stick, Calder hung simple objects from wires. _____. They allowed Calder's objects to move with a light touch or even small amounts of wind. Later, Calder designed _____. These mobiles could be hung directly from the ceiling. And, instead of using everyday objects, he cut metal into simple shapes like circles and triangles. He then painted the shapes in different colors.

Anyway, Calder became famous for his mobiles because _____
_____. I mean, they're very creative and fun to look at. They even
inspired professionals that worked in other jobs, such as architects, interior designers, and
jewelry makers. Indeed, Calder _____. Even today,
he is considered one of the most important American artists.

Vocabulary Review

Answer Book p. 39

A. **Choose the correct word for each meaning.**

diversity	habitat	endangered	unlikely

1 having a small chance of happening: _____

2 the place where an animal lives: _____

3 the condition of including many different types of people or things: _____

4 under threat of going extinct or being killed off entirely: _____

B. **Fill in the blanks with the appropriate words from the box.**

features	satisfy	limited	current	adapted

5 Unlike the team's previous coaches, the _____ one makes the players work hard.

6 The best way to _____ guests is to provide them with excellent service.

7 The horseshoe crab has _____ to changes on the planet for over 400 million years.

8 The advertisement should highlight the product's best _____.

9 We have a _____ number of weeks to finish the report.

C. **Choose the closest meaning for each highlighted word.**

10 The rules of the game are too complicated for beginners to understand right away.
(A) complex   (B) comprehensive   (C) compact   (D) competitive

11 There is an urgent need to address the causes of global warming.
(A) attractive   (B) effective   (C) critical   (D) temporary

12 The industrial revolution has had many consequences that no one could have predicted.
(A) decisions   (B) outcomes   (C) elements   (D) reactions

13 The answer to the question is obvious if you think about it.
(A) clear   (B) public   (C) open   (D) bright

14 Building more houses would make them more affordable for everyone.
(A) proper   (B) popular   (C) visible   (D) cheap

CHAPTER 05

Organization

Organization

About the Question Type

Organization questions ask you to identify how a speaker organizes a lecture or presents certain information. Alternatively, you may be asked the reason the speaker mentions a specific piece of information.

Sometimes, you may be asked to determine how specific information relates to the discussion as a whole. Common ways of organizing include: cause and effect, compare and contrast, and problem and solution.

Question Format

- How does the professor introduce/clarify/explain ~?
- How is the lecture organized?
- Why does the man/woman mention ~?
- Why does the man/woman talk about ~?

Key Strategies

- **Step 1** — While listening to the passage, identify the overall organization or structure of the discussion.

- **Step 2** — If the question asks about the organizational structure of the passage, identify how the main idea and its supporting details are organized. If the question asks about the reason why the speaker mentions a specific piece of information, identify how that information connects to the talk as a whole.

- **Step 3** — Select the answer choice that best describes the organizational structure of the passage or the purpose of a specific piece of information.

Example

Answer Book p. 39

A. Listen to a conversation between a student and a dormitory manager.

C5_ExA

Note-taking

Why does the student mention her friend Jamie?

(A) To explain how Jamie fixed the air conditioner
(B) To talk about problems in other dormitory rooms
(C) To emphasize that an air conditioner is broken
(D) To show that Jamie is having a similar problem

Answer Book p. 39

B. Listen to part of a lecture in a nutrition class.

C5_ExB

Note-taking

How does the professor introduce veganism?

(A) By describing its origins and history
(B) By emphasizing its health advantages
(C) By pointing out a moral problem
(D) By comparing it with a similar way of life

Dictation

Listen again and fill in the blanks.

A.

C5_ExA_D

W: Hi, I'm _____.

M: Uh... It's not the air conditioner again, is it? I thought we fixed it last time...

W: That's right. I tried to use it last night and _____. Um, it turns on, but only warm air comes out.

M: Are you using it correctly? As you know, _____

_____.

W: Yes, I am. I even asked my friend Jamie to come over to check. _____.

M: In that case, I'll send someone to your room this afternoon. In the meantime, you might want to stay in the lounge to stay cool.

B.

C5_ExB_D

P: Veganism is a way of life that _____. People who follow this are known as vegans. Um, vegans are kind of like vegetarians, but _____

_____... Although both groups do not eat meat, vegans will not

_____. For example, they don't drink milk or eat cheese because these products come from cows. In addition, _____

_____. Um, vegans do not even use any products made from animals. This means that they do not buy leather shoes, for instance. Now, you may be wondering why people become vegans... Well, some follow veganism for health reasons. But, for others, _____.

Listening Practice 1

Answer Book p. 40

Listen to a conversation between a student and a librarian.

C5_P1

Note-taking

---

1 Why does the student go to see the librarian?

(A) To report problems with the library's computers

(B) To complain about the process for borrowing books

(C) To discuss an issue with the accuracy of a website

(D) To get help finding research materials for an assignment

2 According to the librarian, why is the library's home page updated only once a day?

(A) The library cannot afford a better computer system.

(B) The employee in charge of updates only works part-time.

(C) The university did not approve a request for new computers.

(D) The staff needs time to check every returned book.

3 How does the librarian advise the student?

(A) By mentioning another student's recent experience

(B) By referring the student to a different university library

(C) By presenting the advantages and disadvantages of a plan

(D) By recommending a method for making a request

4 What does the student say she will do?

(A) Attend a meeting to discuss an issue

(B) Contact a staff member to request some help

(C) Ask her friends to help find more students

(D) Call a library employee to confirm a request

Listen again to part of the conversation. Then answer the question.

5 What does the librarian mean when he says this: 🎧

(A) He wants the student to speak more quietly.

(B) He understands how the student is feeling.

(C) He believes the student should come back later.

(D) He knows what the student is looking for.

C5_P1_D

Listen again and fill in the blanks.

M: Hi there. How can I help you?

W: I've got a question about the library's website.

M: Sure. Are you having difficulties using it?

W: Not exactly. It just, uh, seems like _____.

M: What do you mean?

W: I used the website this morning to check if a book was here. It said _____ _____. But when I came this afternoon, I saw the book on a shelf.

M: I understand. I think the previous borrower must have returned the book earlier today. You see, the home page is _____, in the afternoon. Our computer system is quite old. But the library doesn't have enough money for a new one. That's why _____.

W: Doesn't that cause problems? I mean, if the system isn't updated, _____ _____. Students might even come to the library for a book that isn't here. That seems like a waste of time.

M: I hear you. It can be frustrating. _____ at our staff meeting next week. We might be able to improve our computer system this time.

W: That's a good idea. It would really help to _____.

M: I agree. But it might not be enough just to mention it in our meeting. So I would recommend that you also _____.

W: Do you really think that would help?

M: Well, it will get the university's attention. That could _____.

W: You're right. I'll do that.

M: And if I were you, I would get _____. That will also help.

W: Oh, really? Then, I'll tell my friends about this too. I'm sure they know many students who would agree to sign the letter. Thanks!

Listen to part of a lecture in a literature class.

C5_P2

Note-taking

1 What is the main topic of the lecture?
(A) Why an author changed his name
(B) The education system of the 20th century
(C) How children's books became enjoyable
(D) Famous creators of children's literature

2 According to the professor, what was important in Geisel's development as an author?
(A) His personal connections in the publishing industry
(B) His ability to advertise his services
(C) His relationship with an excellent artist
(D) His experience working on advertisements

3 How does the professor introduce Geisel's writing of *The Cat in the Hat*?
(A) By describing a request from a publisher
(B) By mentioning critics' opinions of Geisel
(C) By discussing children's attitudes toward books
(D) By giving a short history of American literature

4 According to the professor, why was *The Cat in the Hat* an important work?
(A) It encouraged more writers to produce schoolbooks.
(B) It changed the way many people thought of children's literature.
(C) It was the first children's book that was taught in schools.
(D) It was published in more languages than any other book.

5 What was the reason Geisel was given a special award?
(A) He sold the most children's books around the world.
(B) He made many contributions to literature and education.
(C) He started a program to teach children how to read.
(D) He developed a new method for illustrating books.

‖ Dictation ‖

Listen again and fill in the blanks.

C5_P2_D

P: OK, so when you think of children's books today, you probably think of interesting stories with colorful pictures. But this wasn't always the case. Traditionally, _____ _____. This changed in the 20th century with the work of Theodor Geisel. Uh, I'm sure you've all read his work, but you probably know him as Dr. Seuss... Anyway, Geisel is the reason _____... Um, let me give you a little background on his career. Geisel started as an illustrator and cartoonist. He drew for magazines, books, and advertisements. _____ _____, he created all sorts of interesting characters. This experience was important in his development as an author. During this time, Geisel learned _____. Then, in 1937, he wrote his first children's book under the name Dr. Seuss. Geisel published several more children's books afterward. However, _____. In fact, he only became really famous much later... In 1957, a publisher of schoolbooks asked Geisel to _____. Geisel was asked to use only a small number of simple words that children could easily understand. And the result was *The Cat in the Hat*. Now, we all know the story... Two children are alone in a house. They are bored because it's raining and they can't go outside. Suddenly, they are visited by a cat wearing a hat. And, um, this cat shows them various tricks and plays games with them. They make a mess in the house. Then, a magical machine cleans up everything just before the children's mother comes home. _____ _____... full of imagination. However, *The Cat in the Hat* was also an important work. In the past, children did not enjoy learning from schoolbooks because the books were boring. *The Cat in the Hat* was the first book in American literature that was both fun and educational. It changed the way many people thought of children's books forever. _____ _____ and encouraged Geisel to publish more books in a similar style. By the time Geisel died in 1991, he had published over 40 children's books as Dr. Seuss. Many of these books became _____. They were even translated into several languages. Geisel was later given a special award in 1984 _____. He really made children's literature entertaining and interesting. And _____.

Listening Practice 3

Listen to a conversation between a student and a professor.

C5_P3

Note-taking

1 What are the speakers mainly discussing?
- (A) A musical performance being held at a university
- (B) A writing seminar the student wants to attend
- (C) An event to raise money for a student organization
- (D) A job opening at the university newspaper

2 What does the professor say about the school newspaper?
- (A) It was started approximately 10 years ago.
- (B) It has had money problems for a long time.
- (C) It does not currently have a head advisor.
- (D) It will be sending members to a conference.

3 Why is the student confident that she will find a band?
- (A) She has many friends who are local musicians.
- (B) She has promised to promote a band at school.
- (C) She has already contacted the leader of a musical group.
- (D) She has decided to pay money to some performers.

4 Why does the professor mention the Central Street Theater?
- (A) To encourage a reservation to be made soon
- (B) To suggest a possible location for an event
- (C) To emphasize the high cost of renting a location
- (D) To express the necessity of a large space

5 What will the student probably do next?
- (A) Find out the cost of using a stage
- (B) Make a list of local musicians
- (C) Contact the owner of a theater
- (D) Ask about using a place on campus

Dictation

Answer Book p. 42

C5_P3_D

Listen again and fill in the blanks.

S: Do you have a moment, Professor Evans?

P: Sure. What's on your mind?

S: I'm the editor for the school newspaper. And, um, there's a writing seminar at the University of Boston in May. We'd like _____.

P: Oh, I've heard about that seminar. It would be a great opportunity to learn about _____.

S: Yes, that's why we'd like to attend. But the problem is... Well, we just don't have enough money for the travel costs. So I was thinking of _____ _____.

P: I see... What kind of event? I've been the head advisor of the paper for 10 years now, and it seems like we never have enough money.

S: Exactly. Well, um, that's why _____.

P: OK, and have you found any bands yet?

S: We're considering a couple... We want one that's _____ _____.

P: That's good. But, um, there are other factors to think about. For example, how much will you pay the band? Will you pay them with money you collect from selling tickets?

S: Oh, I'm confident _____. I have many friends among local musicians. I've even interviewed some of them in the past. They might agree to do the show for free.

P: OK... I see you've thought a lot about this. What about the location? Places on campus are usually _____. You can rent a stage outside campus, but _____. Even a small place like the Center Street Theater costs several hundred dollars per night...

S: I hadn't considered that... I had thought we would be able to use a place on campus.

P: Why don't you check _____, anyway? There might be a place that can still be used.

S: That's true. I should definitely check.

P: If nothing's available, _____...
One of them might let you use the place for free.

S: OK. I'll go to the student activities office first.

Listening Practice 4

Answer Book p. 44

Listen to part of a lecture in a biology class.

Note-taking

C5_P4

1 What is the lecture mainly about?

(A) The deadliest diseases in history

(B) Two kinds of large increases in disease

(C) Why climate influences the spread of disease

(D) Various categories of infectious diseases

2 According to the professor, what is a factor that can cause epidemics?

(A) The quality of health care in a region

(B) A change in weather patterns

(C) A shortage in a country's food supplies

(D) An increase in the population of a local area

3 How does the professor organize the lecture?

(A) She describes several contrasting theories.

(B) She introduces recent scientific research.

(C) She discusses a problem and several solutions.

(D) She compares the differences between terms.

4 According to the professor, what contributed to the extreme danger of the Spanish Flu and Covid?

(A) The limited knowledge about new diseases

(B) The modern travel habits of people

(C) The failure of social distancing

(D) The lack of available masks in many areas

Listen again to part of the lecture. Then answer the question.

5 Why does the professor say this: 🎧

(A) To support a previous statement

(B) To show where an idea came from

(C) To highlight a common misunderstanding

(D) To explain the need for more information

‖ Dictation ‖

Listen again and fill in the blanks.

C5_P4_D

P: Today, we'll discuss the terms *epidemic* and *pandemic*. Both of these terms refer to _____. Most people think these terms apply only to infectious diseases. Uh, these are diseases that get passed from one person to another. However, this is fiction. _____, such as lung cancer. Of course, the disease can also be an infectious one...
OK... First, let's define an epidemic. Epidemics happen when _____
_____. These are quite common, and they can occur anywhere at any time. Epidemics can be _____.
One example is a change in weather patterns. Some epidemics mostly happen at certain times of the year... You know, seasonally. For instance, the flu usually occurs in winter when it is cold. Also, _____, like hurricanes.

S: Um, is that because storms carry diseases?

P: Oh, no. It's because storms can make it harder to find clean drinking water. Dirty water can cause diseases to spread very quickly... Now, in contrast, _____
_____. During pandemics, the spread is very rapid. Many new people are infected every day. And the numbers grow and grow. Within a few weeks or months, _____.
Naturally, this makes pandemics extremely terrifying. The diseases travel too fast and too far... Uh, _____.
So, then, there are two main differences between epidemics and pandemics. These are the scale of the spread of the disease and the rate of the spread. Um, let's explain these differences in more detail... Remember, an epidemic is a disease that spreads in a specific area. It might spread quickly at first, but _____. So, overall, it does not spread as fast or as far... However, a pandemic is a disease that spreads across several countries or continents. In some cases, such as the Spanish Flu and Covid, _____. They were extremely dangerous because both occurred in modern times. Unlike before, people traveled on ships, airplanes, cars, and trains... So, with their modern lifestyles, _____
_____. As a result, millions of people died. But, fortunately, humans have learned a lot about epidemics and pandemics through the years. People have learned to regularly wash their hands. And they have learned to wear masks and practice social distancing... These actions can save many lives.

Answer Book p. 45

TOEFL Listening

C5_T1

Note-taking

1 What are the speakers mainly discussing?

(A) Advice the student needs to hold an activity

(B) The requirements for a temporary job

(C) The best way to learn about a university event

(D) A volunteer position related to the student's major

2 According to the conversation, what might the student be responsible for?

(A) Bringing students to an orientation

(B) Helping students sign up for classes

(C) Showing students around a campus

(D) Introducing students to professors

3 What does the professor say about orientation sessions?

(A) They will take two days for students to complete.

(B) All visiting students have to participate in one.

(C) They will introduce campus life to new students.

(D) Campus guides may choose one of two times to attend.

4 Why does the student mention an exam?

(A) To let the professor know that she is prepared

(B) To show that she is doing well in a class

(C) To give the reason for meeting with a club

(D) To explain why she is not available on Sunday

Listen again to part of the conversation. Then answer the question.

5 What does the student mean when she says this: 🎧

(A) She is happy to be given an opportunity.

(B) She is pleased that her work has been noticed.

(C) She is worried about disappointing her professor.

(D) She is glad that a problem has been solved.

Dictation

Answer Book p. 45

C5_T1_D

Listen again and fill in the blanks.

S: Hi, Professor Wheeler. I'm here to talk about the e-mail that you sent. You mentioned something about _____?

P: Right. I think it's a job you'll be interested in. Please come in and take a seat.

S: Thank you... So _____.

P: Well, as you know, we get applications from new students every year. And some of the students visit the university before deciding if they want to study here. So, in a couple of weeks, we're going to have _____.

S: OK, I see. But what should I expect as a campus tour guide? I mean, what would I be doing?

P: So a guide's responsibilities include _____. That way, they can get an idea of what the university is like. You know, you'll show them where the important buildings are and _____.

S: That's it? It doesn't sound very hard.

P: No, it's not difficult at all. But, um, _____. So that means you won't have much time to do anything else.

S: All right. That won't be a problem.

P: Oh, and _____. Sessions will be held on Thursday night and Sunday afternoon. _____.

S: Well, I'm meeting with my theater club on Thursday night, so that's out. And I can't go on Sunday, either. I have an exam the next day that I was planning to study for.

P: Oh, but _____. You really need to be there on at least one of the days.

S: Hmm... In that case, I'll study for my exam on Saturday, instead. That way, _____.

P: That's a good idea. I'll put your name on the list for Sunday, then. Please _____.

S: I definitely will... And, um, thanks for thinking of me... I'll do my best to help.

P: It's my pleasure! I'm sure you'll do well.

S: Thanks again, Professor. I'll see you around.

Answer Book p. 46

TOEFL Listening

C5_T2

Note-taking

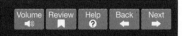

1 What does the professor mainly discuss?

   Ⓐ How humans have survived for so long

   Ⓑ The history of human evolution

   Ⓒ A comparison of human species

   Ⓓ How human beings spread globally

2 What does the professor say about the Out of Africa theory?

   Ⓐ It has been disproven by recent findings.

   Ⓑ It has been updated with new information.

   Ⓒ It is supported by traditional African stories.

   Ⓓ It is based on physical evidence.

3 What is the professor's opinion about why humans originated in Africa?

   Ⓐ He does not think we will ever know the reason.

   Ⓑ He does not believe the explanations of most scientists.

   Ⓒ He believes Africa had the best climate for evolution.

   Ⓓ He thinks food resources were abundant in the region.

4 Why does the professor mention *Homo erectus*?

   Ⓐ To explain how only one species survived

   Ⓑ To discuss the first human species

   Ⓒ To specify the first humans to leave Africa

   Ⓓ To illustrate interactions between human species

5 According to the professor, what is true of the first large movement of *Homo sapiens*?

   Ⓐ It was caused by wars between different groups.

   Ⓑ It probably made it as far as China.

   Ⓒ It occurred mostly within Africa.

   Ⓓ It reached all regions of the world.

Listen again to part of the lecture. Then answer the question.

6 What does the professor mean when he says this: 🎧

   Ⓐ The professor will answer the question later.

   Ⓑ The answer to the student's question is not obvious.

   Ⓒ Climate change had little impact on human movement.

   Ⓓ Population was the biggest factor in human migration.

Dictation

Listen again and fill in the blanks.

C5_T2_D

P: Recently, we were discussing the origins of civilization. I mentioned that all civilizations were started by one species—*Homo sapiens*. *Homo sapiens*, of course, are modern humans like us. But there were other species of humans in the past, and _____ _____. Over time, humans left Africa and spread around the globe. This is what I'd like to talk about today. It is the idea behind the Out of Africa theory.

So _____. This means it tries to explain where humans came from in the past and where they moved around the world. _____, such as old bones and stone tools, scientists believe that all humans started in Africa. Why there? We don't know the exact reason. Personally, I doubt we ever will... However, most of the evidence about early humans is found in Africa. So this strongly suggests that all humans started there _____.

Now, the first humans to leave Africa were not *Homo sapiens*. They were called *Homo erectus*. Uh, _____, but they were humans... Um, *Homo erectus* lived about two million years ago in Eastern Africa. Uh, *Homo erectus* left Africa approximately 1.8 million years ago. But, uh, *Homo sapiens* did not begin moving out of Africa until around 200,000 years ago...

S: Um, why did humans leave Africa, anyway?

P: That's a good question, but it's difficult to say. Remember, this all happened long ago. Scientists believe that _____: climate change and population. Um, climate, as you know, is important for the survival of any species. It's hard to live in a place that is too hot or too cold. And climate also determines _____. As for population, well, if there are many people in one place, then there is less food to share, right? So _____.

Now, going back to the migration itself... According to the theory, _____ _____ and then to Europe and Asia... As I said, *Homo sapiens* started moving around 200,000 years ago. The first large movement probably reached as far as China. This first group did not survive into modern times. However, a second large movement happened, and this group did survive. In fact, it is this group that _____ and eventually created the civilizations that we all know about today. By around 50,000 years ago, _____ _____ . Before long, they had even reached North and South America. And, well… You know the rest of the story… Now, there are few places on Earth where humans have not been to…

Vocabulary Review

A. Choose the correct word for each meaning.

avoid infectious translate civilization

1 an organized and well-developed human society: _____

2 contagious or easily caught as with a sickness: _____

3 to never do something or to do it as little as possible: _____

4 to say or write in a different language: _____

B. Fill in the blanks with the appropriate words from the box.

immediate creative influence moral uninteresting

5 I stopped watching the TV series because I found the characters _____.

6 People often feel an _____ attraction to others who are similar to them.

7 No matter what you think of Warhol's work, it had a huge _____ on the art world.

8 Jony Ive's _____ ideas for product designs contributed to Apple's success.

9 Everyone shares a _____ responsibility to preserve the planet for future generations.

C. Choose the closest meaning for each highlighted word.

10 It can be frustrating to see people make the same mistakes over and over.
   (A) exhausting   (B) tempting   (C) disappointing   (D) confusing

11 Children have an imaginative mind that should be nurtured and developed.
   (A) analytical   (B) logical   (C) inventive   (D) healthy

12 Check your test answers again to make sure they are accurate.
   (A) skillful   (B) correct   (C) punctual   (D) sharp

13 The athlete is being recognized for her accomplishments on the tennis court.
   (A) tasks   (B) acquisitions   (C) achievements   (D) qualifications

14 Our sun will last approximately 5 billion more years before it burns out.
   (A) roughly   (B) closely   (C) slightly   (D) freely

CHAPTER 06

Connecting Contents

Connecting Contents

About the Question Type

Connecting Contents questions ask you to complete a table or chart that shows how the ideas directly mentioned in a conversation or lecture relate to one another.

List questions require you to identify whether the statements listed in a table are true or false. Matching questions ask you to classify the statements or identify which category they belong to, while Ordering questions require you to put the steps of a process or series of events in the correct order.

Question Format

List
- Indicate whether each of the following is mentioned/included/suggested/etc.
  Click in the correct box for each phrase.

	Yes/Included/Suggested	No/Not Included/Not Suggested
Statement A		
Statement B		
Statement C		

Matching
- Indicate for each example what type of ~.

Ordering
- The professor explains the steps ~. Put the steps listed below in the correct order.

Key Strategies

- **Step 1** — Pay attention to the important details and overall flow of the talk.

- **Step 2** — Identify the number of ideas being discussed, and predict which type of question will be asked. Types of questions include List, Matching, and Ordering.

- **Step 3** — Select the answer choices in the table or chart that best represent the information in the passage for each item.

Example

A. Listen to a conversation between a student and a professor.

Note-taking

C6_ExA

The professor explains the steps for a project. Put the steps listed below in the correct order. *Drag each answer choice to the space where it belongs*.

Step 1	
Step 2	
Step 3	
Step 4	

(A) Give a presentation in class

(B) Submit a written report

(C) Choose a business from a list

(D) Do some online research

B. Listen to part of a lecture in a biology class.

Note-taking

C6_ExB

In the lecture, the professor mentions some features of cheetahs and koalas. Indicate whether each sentence below describes a cheetah or a koala. *Click in the correct box for each phrase*.

	Cheetahs	Koalas
(A) They sleep around 12 hours per day.		
(B) They gather food only at night.		
(C) They are active when the temperature is low.		
(D) They sleep a lot because of their diet.		

CHAPTER 06

HACKERS APEX LISTENING for the TOEFL iBT Advanced

‖ Dictation ‖

Listen again and fill in the blanks.

A.

C6_ExA_D

S: Professor, could you tell me about the project for your marketing class? I was absent when you announced it.

P: Sure. So the goal of the project is to create a marketing plan for a business. The first thing you will do is _____.

S: All right. Do I need to contact the business I choose?

P: No. You will do _____.

S: Oh, good. And then what?

P: Next, you will _____. I will give feedback for each presentation.

S: Do I have to give a second presentation after that?

P: That won't be necessary. You will use the feedback to _____

_____.

B.

C6_ExB_D

P: OK... I'd like to continue our discussion of animal sleeping habits. Yesterday, we started talking about cheetahs. Although some animals sleep up to 20 hours a day, _____. They spend much of their time resting to conserve their energy. In fact, they only hunt during the cooler hours of the day.

Now, the animals that sleep the longest are koalas. Uh, they spend up to 22 hours each day sleeping. And _____. The reason koalas sleep so long is their diet. Um, the leaves they consume contain few calories to get energy from. In addition, _____ because they contain a lot of fiber.

Listening Practice 1

Listen to a conversation between a student and a university housing office employee.

C6_P1

Note-taking

---

1 Why does the student visit the housing office?

(A) To report a problem with her dormitory roommate

(B) To make a request to move in to a double room

(C) To complain about the condition of her dormitory

(D) To check on the status of a room change application

2 What is causing delays with the student's request?

(A) The student did not submit an application form in time.

(B) Students rarely leave single rooms before a semester ends.

(C) The student does not have a requirement for a single room.

(D) The housing office has been busy with other requests.

3 According to the employee, what is the reason students leave double rooms during the semester?

(A) They feel the dormitory rooms are not large enough.

(B) They decide to move in with one of their friends.

(C) They have difficulties living with their roommates.

(D) They find cheaper rooms outside the campus.

4 The employee suggests several options to find a room. Indicate whether each of the following is a suggestion. *Click in the correct box for each phrase.*

	Suggested	Not Suggested
(A) Request a double room		
(B) Move in with a friend		
(C) Print out a form		
(D) Place a message on a board		

Listen again to part of the conversation. Then answer the question.

5 What does the student mean when she says this: 🎧

(A) There is some information she needs to gather.

(B) She is not sure what to do about a request.

(C) There is a chance she could get a single room.

(D) She cannot decide between a single and a double room.

Dictation

Answer Book p. 49

C6_P1_D

Listen again and fill in the blanks.

W: Hello, my name is Melissa Sanders. I applied to _____
last month. I just want to see how that's going.

M: Sure. Which dormitory did you want to move in to?

W: Actually, _____ for the Williams dormitory. It's cheaper than
the Nelson dormitory, and most of my friends are there. However, it's been several weeks
and _____ .

M: So are you in the Nelson dormitory now?

W: Yes. It was the only dormitory I could get into because I submitted my application late. But
when I heard I could move rooms, _____ .

M: All right. Let me look up your file... _____ , is that right?

W: That's right.

M: OK, that explains the delay. Single rooms are popular. It's, um, rare for _____
_____ . And according to our records, there are
six people before you on the list.

W: What does that mean?

M: It means that a single room might not be available _____ .

W: I'd really like to move sooner than that. Is there anything I can do?

M: _____ at the Williams dormitory, instead.

W: Actually, I don't want to have a roommate. But if I ask for a double room, will I be able to
move in to the Williams dormitory sooner?

M: Of course. That's because _____
during the semester. You know, many people have trouble with a roommate because of
different sleep schedules and other issues like that. Uh, your only other option is to find
a student who is moving out. _____ about this on the Williams
dormitory notice board.

W: Well, OK. But still, I'd also like to submit a request for a double room and see what
happens.

M: OK, then, _____ ? And do you want me to cancel your single
room request?

W: No, I'd prefer to keep it. You never know about these things, right?

Listening Practice 2

Listen to part of a lecture in a meteorology class.

C6_P2

Note-taking

_____

1 What is the lecture mainly about?
   (A) How weather systems form
   (B) Why storms are difficult to predict
   (C) Why weather is becoming more extreme
   (D) How weather forecasting developed

2 In the lecture, the professor mentions several important events in weather prediction. Put the events listed below in the correct order. *Drag each answer choice to the space where it belongs.*

Event 1	
Event 2	
Event 3	
Event 4	

   (A) Programs can process large amounts of data.
   (B) People are able to get weather data from far away.
   (C) Predictions are made based on clouds and stars.
   (D) Tools are invented for measuring air pressure and wind.

3 According to the professor, how did weather forecasts improve after the 1960s?
   (A) They took less than three days to make.
   (B) They could be made from a longer distance.
   (C) They showed storm locations more accurately.
   (D) They could be reported on the news more quickly.

4 What is the professor's attitude toward the future of weather forecasting?
   (A) She is sure that it will continue improving.
   (B) She thinks it will mostly be done by computers.
   (C) She is worried that it will not help with climate change.
   (D) She believes it needs to be taken more seriously.

Listen again to part of the lecture. Then answer the question.

5 What does the professor imply when she says this: 🎧
   (A) Some scientists forgot to include some data.
   (B) A computer program was not fast enough.
   (C) Some scientists discovered new information.
   (D) A computer program was very advanced.

CHAPTER 06

HACKERS APEX LISTENING for the TOEFL iBT Advanced

Dictation

C6_P2_D

Listen again and fill in the blanks.

P: No one can stop bad weather, but we can prepare for it before it happens. Thanks to improvements in technology, we can learn what the weather will be like in a few hours or days. Of course, _____. Now, today's lesson is about the development of weather forecasting.

Humans have tried to predict the weather for thousands of years. Knowing what the weather will be like is important because it helps _____.

The first people who tried to predict the weather were ancient priests. They used cloud formations and information about the stars. Then, around 350 BC, the Greek philosopher Aristotle wrote about weather patterns in a set of books called *Meteorologica*. Um, this is _____: meteorology. Still, for centuries, people were often wrong when they tried to predict the weather.

Then, from the 1800s, some big developments occurred. First, the invention of the telegraph made it possible to obtain weather data from hundreds of kilometers away. Later, British scientists invented _____.

Air pressure and wind, of course, are important in determining weather.

In the early 20th century, mathematicians suggested that people could _____ _____. However, computers had not yet been invented. So people were not able to collect enough data for accurate predictions. Then, in 1950, some American scientists became the first to _____ _____. However, computers were not very advanced back then. It took 24 hours to produce one weather prediction. Um, this was pointless. Uh, you know, _____. So the predictions were similar to a random guess. With the introduction of supercomputers in the 1960s, _____ _____. Since then, the number of mistakes in predicting the weather has greatly decreased. Predicting the movement of typhoons has also become more accurate. In the 1970s, if scientists tried to predict where a typhoon might occur, they could miss by up to 800 kilometers. Today, _____, so they only miss by less than 200 kilometers.

With new computer models, tools, and data, meteorologists can now predict weather several days in advance. And although weather forecasts are still not perfectly accurate, _____. Today, weather forecasts are much more accurate than they were 25 years ago. Imagine where we will be in another 25 to 50 years. This will be hugely important because _____ _____.

Listening Practice 3

Answer Book p. 52

Listen to a conversation between a student and a career center employee.

C6_P3

Note-taking

_____

1 What is the main topic of the conversation?

(A) Whether a student should accept a job offer or not

(B) The kinds of internships that are suitable for a student

(C) How to use an internship to prepare for graduate school

(D) The process of applying and interviewing for jobs

2 According to the employee, what is an advantage of short internships?

(A) They allow students to try various internships.

(B) They help students choose a career goal.

(C) They accept applicants with no experience.

(D) They motivate students to learn skills quickly.

3 Why does the student decide on a long internship?

(A) She knows someone who can offer her one.

(B) She is disappointed with a previous short internship.

(C) She believes it will let her make many connections.

(D) She has enough past work experience.

4 In the conversation, the employee offers advice about how to use job search sites. Indicate whether each of the following is a piece of advice the employee gives. *Click in the correct box for each phrase.*

	Yes	No
(A) Submit applications early		
(B) Apply to many job positions		
(C) Check job websites frequently		
(D) Consider each offer carefully		

Listen again to part of the conversation. Then answer the question.

5 Why does the student say this: 🎧

(A) To show that she has many skills

(B) To agree with an important point

(C) To indicate that there are other advantages

(D) To express her interest in joining a company

‖ Dictation ‖

Listen again and fill in the blanks.

C6_P3_D

W: Excuse me. My name is Stephanie Davis. I made an appointment to meet with a counselor today.

M: Yes, I'm Mr. Benson. I was expecting you... How can I help?

W: I need your advice. My professor suggested that I _____ after I graduate. But, um, I can't decide _____.

M: Well, that mainly depends on your career goals. First of all, _____ _____?

W: Journalism... I want to work for a travel magazine or a website someday.

M: OK. That's helpful to know. So, let's consider a short internship. What's good is that you can _____. Many students want to experience different internships, but they don't have much time. So, for students like these, _____. But of course, they have less time to, um, learn the job in detail.

W: Right, I see...

M: Next, let's talk about long internships. You'll have more time to _____ _____...

W: Yes, that's definitely true.

M: And, um, another advantage is that you will _____ _____ later on.

W: That's an excellent point. _____, so knowing a lot of people and making connections is important. I guess I should go with a long internship, then. But, um, where's the best place to look?

M: OK, well, _____. They're updated several times a day, so just make sure to check them often. I also suggest _____. Employers often hire someone before the application deadline.

W: I can do that.

M: The other thing I recommend is to _____... Don't worry about finding the perfect one. If you find a post that seems interesting, _____ _____ and see what happens.

W: Thanks for all your advice, Mr. Benson. You've helped me a lot.

Listening Practice 4

Listen to part of a lecture in an astronomy class.

C6_P4

Note-taking
_____

1 What is the lecture mainly about?

(A) How scientists study other planets

(B) Why scientists look for life on other planets

(C) The discovery of new materials on Mars

(D) The pursuit for water on Mars

2 Indicate whether each of the following describes Christiaan Huygens or Percival Lowell. *Click in the correct box for each phrase.*

	Christiaan Huygens	Percival Lowell
(A) Helped an idea about Mars become more popular		
(B) Found dark areas on the surface of Mars		
(C) Believed lines on Mars were caused by water		
(D) Designed a telescope to look at Mars		

3 What is the professor's attitude toward the missions to Mars?

(A) He is disappointed by the results so far.

(B) He still believes they will find water.

(C) He thinks scientists should go to other planets.

(D) He is worried they will be too costly to continue.

4 What is one reason that scientists believe liquid water was once common on Mars?

(A) It has stones that look like ones on Earth.

(B) It has certain land features like mountains.

(C) Its soil has a lot of moisture deep underground.

(D) Its temperatures were much cooler in the past.

Listen again to part of the lecture. Then answer the question.

5 Why does the professor say this:

(A) To show that some evidence is wrong

(B) To introduce an unexpected detail about Mars

(C) To encourage students to answer a question

(D) To identify the purpose of a recent discovery

C6_P4_D

Listen again and fill in the blanks.

P: For centuries, scientists have wondered if there is life on other planets. To find an answer, they look for evidence of water. All living things need water. So, _____

_____, it's possible for life to exist there. So, all right, let's talk about the search for water on the planet Mars.

One of the first scientists who suggested that there was water on Mars was the 17th-century scholar, Christiaan Huygens. Huygens invented a telescope that made it possible to _____. He discovered large, dark shapes on the planet and thought they might be oceans. A couple of centuries later, the astronomer Percival Lowell claimed to see several long, thin lines near the middle of Mars. He believed _____. Lowell also wrote several books about his theory. They helped make the idea of water on Mars more popular. However, research later showed that the dark shapes were completely dry and that the lines were a false image caused by Lowell's telescope. So _____

_____.

Beginning in the 1960s, a number of spacecraft were sent to study Mars. Some of these spacecraft landed on the surface and made measurements. This gave scientists a better idea about conditions on Mars.

S1: Did they find liquid water?

P: Unfortunately, they did not. But, in the 2000s, scientists learned that _____

_____. And, in the past decade, other trips to Mars have found small amounts of frozen water in other parts of the planet. In fact, it has become clear that these amounts of ice are pretty much all over Mars.

S2: So is there still hope that these missions will ever find liquid water?

P: I definitely think so. _____. A couple of years ago, photographs from a spacecraft showed _____. It doesn't sound like much, but guess what? They don't appear in earlier photos. Something on Mars caused the lines and _____. Even if the lines are not caused by liquid water, there is other evidence that _____. For instance, some photographs show an area that looks like a river that dried up. It has many _____. On Earth, stones like these become smooth because of moving water.

Answer Book p. 55

TOEFL Listening

C6_T1

Note-taking

1 Why does the student visit the professor?

(A) To ask for help with a homework assignment

(B) To find out more about a lecture topic

(C) To discuss the professor's teaching experience

(D) To seek advice regarding her choice of major

2 In the conversation, the professor describes some of the benefits of requiring students to do physical work. Indicate whether each of the following is a benefit.

Click in the correct box for each phrase.

	Yes	No
(A) Provided students with job training		
(B) Prepared students to be leaders in society		
(C) Taught respect for other members of society		
(D) Helped students develop useful skills		

3 According to the professor, why did the students of Black Mountain College not have any experience with physical work?

(A) They grew up in small houses.

(B) They had household helpers at home.

(C) They went to college at a young age.

(D) They were too busy with their studies.

Listen again to part of the conversation. Then answer the question.

4 What does the professor imply when he says this: 🎧

(A) The college only accepted wealthy students.

(B) The college stayed open for several years.

(C) The college did not focus on studies alone.

(D) The college did not have many instructors.

Listen again to part of the conversation. Then answer the question.

5 What does the professor mean when he says this: 🎧

(A) The school mainly taught art and science subjects.

(B) Many graduates gave money to the school.

(C) The school's education system produced good results.

(D) Many former students got jobs at the school.

|| Dictation ||

Answer Book p. 55

Listen again and fill in the blanks.

C6_T1_D

S: Hi, Professor Green. Do you have a minute?

P: Sure, come on in. It's Nicole, right? I recognize you from my Introduction to American Education course.

S: Yes, that's me. _____.

P: That's wonderful to hear. Now, how can I help you?

S: Actually, I wanted to learn more about something you talked about in class yesterday. You briefly mentioned an old college. I think _____?

P: Ah, yes. Black Mountain College... It was a private college that was started in 1933 and lasted for 24 years. However, _____.

S: I heard that the students there had to cook and clean. Is that true?

P: Yes. That's _____. Besides studying, students prepared meals, washed their clothes, and did other kinds of physical work.

S: But why did _____? Wouldn't it be better for them to focus on studying?

P: Well, for the college, _____. They didn't want to just develop students' minds. They also wanted to improve students in other ways. Their goal was to _____.

S: How did physical work help them achieve that goal, though?

P: Well, it helped students _____. What I mean is that it taught them to respect the people in society who did physical work as jobs. It also helped them learn skills that could be useful later in life.

S: I see. But hadn't the students done any physical work before they went to Black Mountain College? I mean, didn't they already _____?

P: Actually, no. A lot of these students came from, uh, wealthy backgrounds. So _____ that did the cooking and cleaning for them.

S: OK, I understand. But what about the normal school education that students got? What was it like?

P: The school's record answers that question. Many Black Mountain College graduates _____. They also became leaders in their careers.

S: It all sounds very interesting. I wonder _____.

Answer Book p. 56

C6_T2

ART HISTORY

Note-taking

1 What is the lecture mainly about?

   Ⓐ The skill of artists before the Renaissance

   Ⓑ The reasons Italy produced many artists

   Ⓒ The relationship between art and the economy

   Ⓓ The role of patrons during the Renaissance

2 Why does the professor mention the Black Death?

   Ⓐ To talk about a common art subject

   Ⓑ To give the inspiration for a work of art

   Ⓒ To explain why changes happened in Italy

   Ⓓ To compare art from different periods

3 Indicate whether each of the following is a reason people paid for art during the Renaissance.

Click in the correct box for each phrase.

	Reason	Not a Reason
Ⓐ To celebrate achievements		
Ⓑ To support local artists		
Ⓒ To show their social status		
Ⓓ To display loyalty to the Church		

4 How did artists benefit from their relationship with patrons?

   Ⓐ It gave them more chances to practice art.

   Ⓑ It increased their status in society.

   Ⓒ It allowed them to show art in public galleries.

   Ⓓ It made them famous all over Europe.

5 According to the professor, what changed after the Renaissance?

   Ⓐ Artists had greater control over their work.

   Ⓑ More ordinary citizens became art patrons.

   Ⓒ Artists asked for more money to produce art.

   Ⓓ Patrons started buying more art from other countries.

Listen again to part of the lecture. Then answer the question.

6 What does the professor imply when she says this: 🎧

   Ⓐ Patrons did not always pay artists with money.

   Ⓑ Patrons paid a higher amount for difficult jobs.

   Ⓒ Patrons had a good reason to give artists instructions.

   Ⓓ Patrons stopped supporting artists if they took too long.

Dictation

Listen again and fill in the blanks.

C6_T2_D

P: When people think of the Renaissance, they mostly remember artwork by famous artists like Michelangelo, da Vinci, Botticelli, and others. These artists were certainly very skilled. However, one of the main reasons they became famous is _____ _____. Today, I'd like to discuss the role of patrons during the Renaissance.

So _____. They had an important role in Italy, where the Renaissance began. At the beginning of the Renaissance, Italy was going through many changes. The Black Death, which was a deadly disease, killed millions of people in the 1300s and greatly affected Italy's economy. So _____. Many citizens moved to the city to find work and do business. In the city, merchants, politicians, and religious leaders became wealthy and powerful. They became the largest patrons.

There were many reasons these people paid for art. One is that _____ _____ during the Renaissance. So they wanted to celebrate their achievements. They did this by paying artists to decorate public buildings and churches. The artworks also inspired _____... Another reason patrons supported the arts was to _____. Buying expensive art showed people they were rich and knew about culture. This gave them a high social status... Lastly, patrons paid for religious artwork as a way to honor God and _____. Doing these things was important in Italian society.

Now, what kind of impact did patrons have on artists and art? Generally, patrons influenced the kind of art that was produced. This is because _____ _____. You see, back then, artists were just like ordinary workers... So, um, patrons thought of art _____. They used business contracts, and they gave artists deadlines, and told them how much to spend on materials. And of course, _____. They were paying, after all. Some even had their faces painted in an artwork.

Anyway, this relationship was also good for artists. Normally, producing art took a long time and required expensive materials. Patrons gave artists a way to earn money and practice art. _____

and got more work as a result. This gave them more opportunities to improve their art and try new styles and methods. And, even though patrons mostly told artists what to do, _____. Some patrons developed strong relationships with their favorite artists. Over time, patrons gave these artists _____. In fact, people's attitude to art changed as a result of all this. After the Renaissance, it became more common for artists to create "art for art's sake," which meant that _____.

Vocabulary Review

A. Choose the correct word for each meaning.

| loyalty | merchant | priest | scholar |

1 someone who has studied and is knowledgeable about a topic: _____

2 someone who buys and sells goods: _____

3 someone who conducts ceremonies in some religions: _____

4 the quality of being constantly faithful and supportive: _____

B. Fill in the blanks with the appropriate words or phrases from the box.

| show off | reputation | digest | pointless | physical |

5 An anaconda may take several weeks to _____ an animal it has swallowed.

6 Children like to _____ their favorite toys to impress their friends.

7 It is _____ to ask for a refund because that store will not provide one.

8 Over the years, Paris has developed a _____ as a city of art and culture.

9 At least 30 minutes of _____ activity each day is necessary to stay healthy.

C. Choose the closest meaning for each highlighted word.

10 During the drought, residents of the town were instructed to conserve water.
(A) seek (B) deliver (C) save (D) utilize

11 Polls of voters are conducted in order to predict the winner of an election.
(A) approve (B) debate (C) evaluate (D) anticipate

12 Hundreds of visitors to Loch Ness have claimed that a monster lives in the lake.
(A) noticed (B) pretended (C) asserted (D) advised

13 The professor briefly introduced himself before giving a long lecture about his theory.
(A) decidedly (B) effectively (C) easily (D) quickly

14 The blue-ringed octopus has a deadly venom that can kill a person in minutes.
(A) fatal (B) unique (C) painful (D) rare

CHAPTER 07

Inference

Inference

About the Question Type

Inference questions ask you to infer the correct answer by using information that is implied, or not stated directly, in the conversation or lecture.

These questions require you to draw a conclusion based on a comprehensive understanding of the overall context and by connecting information mentioned in the conversation or lecture. Sometimes, questions may be about a speaker, an idea, or what a speaker will do next.

Question Format

- What can be inferred about ~?
- What does the professor imply about ~?
- What will the man/woman probably do next?

Key Strategies

- **Step 1** — Understand the overall context of the talk, and determine whether the question is about a speaker, an idea, or what a speaker will do next.

- **Step 2** — If the question is about a speaker or an idea, find information that is connected to the speaker or idea. If the question is about what a speaker will do next, listen to the statements that a speaker makes near the end of the conversation or lecture.

- **Step 3** — Select the answer choice that is best supported by information in the conversation or lecture.

Example

Answer Book p. 58

A. Listen to a conversation between a student and a registrar's office employee.

C7_ExA

Note-taking

_____

_____

_____

What will the employee do for the student?

(A) She will make a copy of his student ID.

(B) She will register the student for a class.

(C) She will tell a co-worker to help the student.

(D) She will give the student a description of courses.

Answer Book p. 58

B. Listen to part of a lecture in a sociology class.

C7_ExB

Note-taking

_____

_____

_____

What does the professor imply about people who cross the border illegally?

(A) They often try to enter legally first.

(B) They are looking for a better quality of life.

(C) They have difficulties getting over border walls.

(D) They usually return to their home country.

‖ Dictation ‖

Listen again and fill in the blanks.

A.

C7_ExA_D

M: Hi, I'm interested in _____.

W: Yes, of course.

M: But, uh, I was wondering if you offer financial assistance.

W: Are you a student here?

M: No. I go to a different university, but I'm here visiting my parents for the summer.

W: I see. Well, _____, but I'm not sure you will get it if you're not a student here.

M: That's fine. _____?

W: We'll need a copy of your student ID. And your school will need to confirm that you're a student there. You can just ask them to e-mail this office.

M: OK. And when should I come back?

W: You can come back tomorrow. I won't be here, but I'll _____

_____.

B.

C7_ExB_D

P: The border between the US and Mexico is over 3,000 kilometers long. And, around 350 million people cross it every year... But, um, _____. Another two million or more people also cross it illegally. Many of them are _____. Others are escaping from violence in their home countries. Now, to stop illegal border crossings, the US has _____. However, not everyone agrees with having these walls. One reason is that they are not that effective. Research has shown that people can easily get around them. Also, some people are concerned about a wall's effects on the environment. For them, _____.

Listening Practice 1

Answer Book p. 59

Listen to a conversation between a student and a professor.

C7_P1

Note-taking

---

1 What are the speakers mainly discussing?

(A) The techniques learned in a class

(B) The student's decision to join an exhibit

(C) The requirements for an assignment

(D) The best methods for taking a photograph

2 Why did the professor give the students few guidelines?

(A) To avoid receiving complaints from the students

(B) To make an assignment easier for the students

(C) To encourage the students to work together

(D) To allow the students to be creative

3 What does the professor imply about casual pictures?

(A) They do not require much skill to take.

(B) They will be part of another assignment.

(C) They need to use special camera settings.

(D) They are only good for group photographs.

4 Why does the professor mention a magazine cover?

(A) To remind the student of another requirement

(B) To help explain the main purpose of an assignment

(C) To give an example of a style of photography

(D) To praise the work submitted by another student

5 What should the student remember when submitting more than one picture?

(A) The pictures should all be the same size.

(B) The pictures should have an identical theme.

(C) The student should select unique subjects for the pictures.

(D) There should be some movement in the pictures.

Dictation

C7_P1_D

Listen again and fill in the blanks.

S: Hi, Professor Chapman. I hope you're not busy.

P: Not at all, Kimberly. What can I do for you?

S: Um, it's about the photography assignment you gave us in class yesterday.

P: You mean _____? What would you like to know?

S: Um, well, to be honest, I'm not sure what you want us to do. You didn't give us many guidelines.

P: Oh. I wanted to avoid _____. It's important that you have as much freedom as possible. That way, _____.

S: But, um, I'm still not sure what you're looking for. Can I _____ _____ and submit that? Isn't that like a self-portrait?

P: Well, not exactly. Anyone can take casual pictures. You'll need to use what you've learned. One purpose of this assignment is to _____.

S: Right. So that means we should use a traditional camera as well.

P: Yes, _____. You should choose the right camera settings for your photograph. And _____, lighting, and background, too.

S: Can I pick what to wear?

P: Of course! All of those details are important. _____.

S: I understand now... Still, I don't think I'm an interesting subject. And I don't look good in photos, either.

P: None of those things matter. You're not taking pictures for a magazine cover. The key point of this assignment is to _____. I want you to show your personality.

S: OK. Can I hand in more than one picture?

P: Sure. You can submit several pictures, if you'd like. But _____ _____. They should be about you.

S: All right. I'll try my best, Professor. Thank you for the advice.

Listening Practice 2

Listen to part of a lecture in a history class.

C7_P2

Note-taking

1 What is the main topic of the lecture?

(A) How Britain became a world power

(B) The most important trade products in Britain

(C) How a beverage became popular in Britain

(D) The reasons Britain went to war with China

2 According to the professor, what is one reason that tea was so expensive in Britain?

(A) It was difficult to bring by ship.

(B) It was sold by rich business owners.

(C) It was only available in certain regions.

(D) It was a symbol of social status.

3 In the lecture, the professor provides some reasons why tea became more widely available. Indicate whether each of the following is a reason. *Click in the correct box for each sentence.*

	Reason	Not a Reason
(A) Britain established a company in China.		
(B) The British started growing tea.		
(C) The British discovered tea in India.		
(D) Britain won some wars with China.		

4 What is the professor most likely going to discuss next?

(A) Britain's impact on world economies

(B) The effect of Britain's global trade on tea prices

(C) Why tea became cheaper during the Industrial Revolution

(D) How tea affected Britain during the Industrial Revolution

Listen again to part of the lecture. Then, answer the question.

5 What does the professor imply when he says this: 🎧

(A) Tea was often sold with teapots and cups.

(B) Britain's upper classes did not know how to drink tea.

(C) Drinking tea was considered a special event.

(D) Sugar was expensive because it was used with tea.

Dictation

C7_P2_D

Listen again and fill in the blanks.

P: During the 18th century, Great Britain was a powerful and wealthy country. It had colonies around the world and traded large amounts of goods like sugar, tobacco, and tea. This is when _____ . Today, I'm going to talk about how that happened.

_____ in the 1600s. It was brought there from China by Dutch and Portuguese traders. Um, at the time, most people in Britain drank coffee. However, some people started to drink tea because _____

_____ . Then, in 1662, England's King Charles II married Catherine of Portugal, _____ . Because Catherine enjoyed tea, she convinced others in England to try it, especially in Britain's upper classes.

Unfortunately, _____ . This was mainly because, uh, it had to be brought on long and difficult trips by ship. So _____ .

Moreover, Britain put a heavy tax on all tea that was brought into the country. With the tax, tea became even more expensive than it already was, and _____

_____ .

As tea was so expensive initially, its popularity did not grow beyond Britain's upper classes. It was _____ . The rich held special social events just to drink tea and talk. _____ , which was another expensive product, and drank it from fancy teapots and cups. Eventually, Britain's middle classes copied the habit of drinking tea to, uh, show their status.

Then, two major events happened _____ . First, in the 1820s, Britain started to grow its own tea in India. Seeds were brought from China and planted in places with good soil and weather for growing tea. The second event involves Britain's role in China. Um, in 1839, after many years of trading with China, _____ . Britain won those wars and was able to gain important new trade benefits. For instance, uh, it could obtain certain goods like tea at a lower price. Britain's victory also allowed it to establish a trade center in Hong Kong, which made it easier for Britain to ship goods from China around the world.

Because of these events, Britain was able to provide its people _____

_____ . It became so common and cheap that even the working classes could afford to drink it every day. _____

during the Industrial Revolution. Let's look at this period more closely.

Listening Practice 3

Answer Book p. 62

Listen to a conversation between a student and a university employee at the Department of Student Affairs.

C7_P3

Note-taking

_____

_____

_____

_____

1 Why does the student go to the Department of Student Affairs?

(A) To get money to pay for uniforms

(B) To get permission to join an activity

(C) To check up on an earlier request

(D) To report problems with a uniform company

2 What does the employee imply about the companies that are not on a list?

(A) They usually have higher prices.

(B) They offer a limited number of choices.

(C) They take a longer time to be approved.

(D) They have to submit extra documents.

3 Why does the employee recommend that the student wait?

(A) A company will be offering a discount next week.

(B) It is likely that the school will change its policy.

(C) A new form will be posted on a website.

(D) It is possible that a request will be denied.

4 What does the employee say about the uniforms?

(A) They have to be made of a specific material.

(B) They cannot have more than one image.

(C) They must include the school's symbol.

(D) They should show the name of the school.

Listen again to part of the conversation. Then answer the question.

5 What does the student mean when she says this: 🎧

(A) She has not played a sport before.

(B) She does not know about a process.

(C) She is not sure about a team's skill.

(D) She did not bring some requirements.

|| Dictation **||**

C7_P3_D

Listen again and fill in the blanks.

W: Hi, I'm the captain of the women's football team. We have a competition in three months. But, um, our uniforms are in bad condition. I'd like to know _____ _____.

M: Yes, of course. And good luck to your team... Now, have you done this before?

W: I'm afraid not. This is my first time.

M: That's fine. You can request money up to two times a year. _____ _____. The first step is to visit the Department of Student Affairs website. You'll need to fill out a form with details like the number of uniforms and the names of team members.

W: That shouldn't be a problem.

M: You'll also need to _____.

W: Oh, but we haven't decided on a company yet.

M: In that case, we have a list of companies on our website. You just have to pick one. I, uh, suggest _____. It will save you some time since they've already been approved.

W: OK. What else should I know?

M: Um, the whole process takes about two weeks. _____, you'll get a notice by e-mail to pick up the money. Then, you have to _____ _____.

W: Um, what if we buy the uniforms now and submit a request for the money later?

M: I recommend that you wait. There's always a chance that _____ _____. If you buy the uniforms now, you might have to _____ _____.

W: We don't want that to happen.

M: No. And, um, there's one other thing. The design of the uniforms should _____ _____. You know, the one with the white eagle inside a blue circle. Everything else is up to you.

W: OK. We can _____.

Listening Practice 4

Listen to part of a lecture in an architecture class.

C7_P4

Note-taking

1 What is the professor mainly discussing?

  (A) The benefits of using a variety of building materials

  (B) An alternative material for constructing houses

  (C) The various types of buildings made with straw

  (D) A popular style of home in a region of the US

2 What does the professor imply about many early settlers in Midwest America?

  (A) They had access to machines to process straw.

  (B) They cut down many forests for wood.

  (C) They grew a small number of crops.

  (D) They were the first to use straw.

3 According to the professor, what is an advantage of straw bales as a building material?

  (A) They do not burn as easily as wood.

  (B) They reduce the levels of outside noise.

  (C) They are effective at maintaining a building's temperature.

  (D) They are easy to transport to building sites.

4 In the lecture, the professor explains the steps in building a house with straw bales. Put the steps below in the correct order. *Drag each answer choice to the space where it belongs.*

Stage 1	
Stage 2	
Stage 3	
Stage 4	

  (A) Apply plaster to straw bales.

  (B) Tie straw bales together with wire.

  (C) Construct a hard and flat surface.

  (D) Place straw bales on top of each other.

Listen again to part of the lecture. Then answer the question.

5 Why does the professor say this: 🎧

  (A) To remind the student of an earlier topic

  (B) To suggest that the student read the textbook

  (C) To indicate that the student missed a key idea

  (D) To show that she is confused by the student's question

Dictation

Listen again and fill in the blanks.

C7_P4_D

P: Wood, stone, and cement are probably the most common types of building materials. But there are many other materials you can use. This afternoon, we will look at straw.

For thousands of years, _____. One reason for this is that _____... Um, when farmers grow crops like wheat, they don't use the whole plant. Some parts of the plant are left behind. When farmers dry these parts in the sun, they get straw. Now, imagine the number of farms around the world doing this. That's a lot of straw!

Straw has many uses on a farm. But there is usually _____ _____. Here's how it works. First, you take the straw and _____. This creates large blocks of straw called straw bales. _____ to build the walls of a home. Many early settlers in Midwest America used this method to build their homes... They did this because there weren't many trees where they lived and wood was expensive to buy. But this doesn't mean straw is not a good building material. It actually has a number of advantages.

First, straw bales are excellent at keeping homes cool in the summer and warm in the winter. So _____... Yes?

S: Um, how can straw be good at maintaining the temperature inside a building? It seems like air could pass through it very easily.

P: Yes, but you have to remember something. It's not the straw itself that keeps homes warm or cool... Rather, it's the structure of the straw bales. You see, when you press straw into bales, _____. This makes it hard for cold winds to pass through. Anyway, another benefit of using straw bales is cost. Straw bales are _____. Sometimes, you only have to pay to transport them from a farm. And lastly, _____. First, you just need to make a hard, flat surface to build on, like cement. Once that's done, you can build walls by placing straw bales on top of each other like bricks. Then, you can _____. Finally, you can cover the straw bales with plaster... Um, plaster is a sticky material that hardens after it dries. Straw bales are so easy to use that almost anyone can build houses with them.

Answer Book p. 64

TOEFL Listening

C7_T1

Note-taking

1 Why does the student go to see the professor?

   Ⓐ To pick up a recommendation letter for a program

   Ⓑ To discuss the advantages of attending a school

   Ⓒ To request help in planning for a future career

   Ⓓ To find out how to apply for an overseas program

2 Why does the student want to study at the School of Design?

Choose 2 answers.

   Ⓐ Its professors are good at teaching.

   Ⓑ It will help him become better at French.

   Ⓒ Its students work with famous designers.

   Ⓓ It offers a program that lasts for one year.

3 According to the professor, what should the student include in the personal essay?

   Ⓐ Examples of his previous achievements

   Ⓑ Recommendations from his language teachers

   Ⓒ How the program will support his goals

   Ⓓ Why he is more qualified than other applicants

4 What will the student probably do next?

   Ⓐ Register for an advanced-level French class

   Ⓑ Write about his interest in a program

   Ⓒ Send his application form to a university

   Ⓓ Give the professor a copy of his essay

Listen again to part of the conversation. Then answer the question.

5 What does the student mean when he says this: 🎧

   Ⓐ He feels confident he will be accepted.

   Ⓑ He expected a process to be harder.

   Ⓒ He wants to know more about a school.

   Ⓓ He has completed some requirements.

Dictation

Listen again and fill in the blanks.

C7_T1_D

S: Do you have a moment, Professor Clark? Um, I heard you are the main advisor for the international student exchange program.

P: Yes, Thomas. Come in. How can I help you?

S: Well, uh, I was hoping to _____.

P: Sure. I'm happy to help. We have _____. Is there one in particular that you're interested in?

S: Actually, yes. I'd like to go to the School of Design in Paris. I heard that it has a one-year international exchange program and _____.

P: Excellent. The school has a good reputation, too. And I'm sure a year in France will be a positive experience. But, uh, do you speak French?

S: Actually, I'm in an advanced-level French class right now. That's another reason why I want to go there. I'd like to _____.

P: OK, that's good because all classes at the School of Design will be taught in French. So, uh, _____.

S: I understand. Um, is there an application form I have to fill out?

P: Well, applying for the program is a two-step process. First, you have to submit an application to the university here. This is, uh, to make sure that _____ _____. Once that's approved, we'll send your application to the school in Paris. They'll _____.

S: Is that all? That sounds easy enough.

P: Oh wait... There's one more thing. You need to _____ _____.

S: A personal essay? What do I need to write about?

P: You need to explain _____ and why you've chosen this particular program. In other words, you should explain how this experience is going to _____. And, uh, the sooner you get started, the better. Writing an effective personal essay is not a quick and easy process.

S: Hmm... I'm not good at writing. Could you _____?

P: Absolutely.

S: Thanks for your help, Professor. I'll get started on the essay now.

C7_T2

BIOLOGY

Note-taking

1 What is the main topic of the lecture?

   (A) Why global warming causes many extinctions

   (B) Competition between humans and animals for resources

   (C) The advantages of preserving Earth's biodiversity

   (D) How species are adjusting to rising temperatures

2 According to the professor, what is a common behavior among animals that migrate?

   (A) They use different routes each year.

   (B) They leave before the rainy season starts.

   (C) They only have one mating partner for life.

   (D) They travel during specific times of the year.

3 What do Eurasian blackcaps gain from spending winters in Great Britain?

Choose 2 answers.

   (A) Extra time to find a mate

   (B) More diverse sources of food

   (C) Shorter migration distance

   (D) Larger numbers of offspring

4 How does the professor organize the lecture?

   (A) By mentioning the results of studies from around the world

   (B) By making predictions about changes in animal behavior

   (C) By discussing the animals found in a particular country

   (D) By describing several effects of global warming on animals

5 Why does the professor discuss a disadvantage of early births?

   (A) To emphasize the significance of an early spring

   (B) To show that many animals face similar dangers

   (C) To give a different opinion about an animal

   (D) To bring attention to a recent problem

6 What does the professor imply about the tawny owl?

   (A) Additional colors will develop in the future.

   (B) Cool summers will lead to a population increase.

   (C) Brown feathers will become more common.

   (D) Habitat destruction will affect their numbers.

‖ Dictation ‖

Listen again and fill in the blanks.

C7_T2_D

P: I'm sure you all know what global warming is, right? It refers to the increase in the average temperature of the planet. The planet has always had periods of warming and cooling, but _____. It could cause many extinctions and a loss of biodiversity. Still, some species are _____ _____.

One effect of global warming is a change in migration routes. Normally, animals that migrate move to their feeding grounds in the winter and breeding grounds in the summer. They repeat this process every year. In recent years, though, _____ _____ in response to rising global temperatures. Consider the Eurasian blackcap as an example... Um, this small bird typically lives in Africa during the winter and Northern Europe during the summer. But, recently, a large population has begun spending winters in Great Britain. They are doing this because _____ in recent decades. Um, but this is not a bad thing for the birds. The birds don't have to migrate as far as they did before. Also, they can spend more time finding a mate.

In many parts of the world, other animals are also _____.

For instance, spring is arriving earlier in some places. This lets animals give birth to their offspring earlier in the year. For example, the red squirrel now gives birth 18 days sooner than before. In the past, _____.

Can anyone tell me why?

S: Well, if animals gave birth when the weather was still cold, their offspring would likely die, I guess.

P: Exactly. Lower temperatures, less food... you get the idea. But, _____ _____, that disadvantage is removed. For animals that are born early today, there is more time to eat before winter comes. By the time winter arrives, they are well developed and strong. Of course, _____.

Due to the rising global temperatures, changes to the physical characteristics of some species have occurred as well. The tawny owl is one famous example. _____... Before, most tawny owls were gray. Now, scientists are seeing more brown ones. In fact, these birds now make up 50 percent of the total population. Several decades ago, that number was just 30 percent. So what happened? Well, warmer winters are resulting in less snow on the ground. And since the ground is now mostly brown, more owls have _____ _____. This trend is unlikely to reverse.

Vocabulary Review

A. Choose the correct word for each meaning.

legal	migration	guideline	biodiversity

1 based on or permitted by law: _____

2 a recommended way of doing something: _____

3 the seasonal movement of animals between areas: _____

4 the variety of living organisms in an ecosystem: _____

B. Fill in the blanks with the appropriate words from the box.

specific	obtained	widely	probably	established

5 Stephen King is a _____ known author who has written many popular novels.

6 The seminar will _____ be postponed, but a final decision has not been made.

7 A French explorer _____ a trading post at the site of modern-day Montreal.

8 All students have _____ permission from their parents to participate in the field trip.

9 Choosing _____ words will make your writing less vague.

C. Choose the closest meaning for each highlighted word.

10 Air bags in vehicles have been proven to prevent serious injuries during an accident.
  (A) avert   (B) manage   (C) resolve   (D) treat

11 It is important to choose an appropriate topic for a school report or presentation.
  (A) familiar   (B) suitable   (C) superior   (D) complex

12 The flight attendant refused the passenger's request to change his seat.
  (A) announced   (B) reported   (C) rejected   (D) verified

13 A female black bear produces up to five offspring every two years.
  (A) residences   (B) babies   (C) nests   (D) territories

14 The lawyer tried to convince her client to accept the proposed changes to the contract.
  (A) invite   (B) order   (C) persuade   (D) impress

Actual Test

Actual Test **1**

Actual Test **2**

Answer Book p. 67

TOEFL Listening

PART 1. Passage 1

AT1_P1_1

Note-taking

1   Why does the student visit the housing office?

  Ⓐ To ask why her mailbox is locked
  Ⓑ To find her missing tickets
  Ⓒ To request access to her mail
  Ⓓ To change her mailbox's combination

2   Why is the student unable to get help at the student services office?

  Ⓐ It had to close temporarily.
  Ⓑ She has no time to visit the office.
  Ⓒ It no longer manages student mailboxes.
  Ⓓ She did not fill out a required form correctly.

3   Why does the employee decide to help the student?

  Choose 2 answers.

  Ⓐ He can sympathize with the student's situation.
  Ⓑ He has confirmed that the student owns a mailbox.
  Ⓒ The student received a gift that needs to be used soon.
  Ⓓ The student has promised to do a favor in return.

4   Why does the employee mention another student's dormitory application form?

  Ⓐ To give an example of what the student needs to submit
  Ⓑ To explain why he will be in the office after closing time
  Ⓒ To express that he is busy working on other documents
  Ⓓ To show how easy it is for students to lose their mail

Listen again to part of the conversation. Then answer the question.

5   What does the employee mean when he says this:

  Ⓐ He feels students should be careful with their items.
  Ⓑ He has to follow the rules equally with everyone.
  Ⓒ He wishes the university would change its policy.
  Ⓓ He is not allowed to help students with private matters.

AT1_P1_2

ARCHITECTURE

Note-taking

6 What is the lecture mainly about?

   Ⓐ The differences between old and new architecture styles

   Ⓑ A style of architecture that was popular in America

   Ⓒ The influence of American architecture in Greece

   Ⓓ A group of architects that became very famous

7 Why does the professor mention ancient Greece?

   Ⓐ To show that architecture took many years to develop

   Ⓑ To compare the styles of Britain and Greece

   Ⓒ To explain why old building methods were effective

   Ⓓ To say where British architects got their inspiration

8 Why was Greek Revival architecture called America's National Style?

   Ⓐ It became common throughout America.

   Ⓑ It was originally inspired by American architects.

   Ⓒ It was a standard created by the American government.

   Ⓓ It needed to be different from a similar British style.

9 What led to the development of Greek Revival architecture in America?

   Ⓐ America's close relationship with England

   Ⓑ An increase in the cost of building materials

   Ⓒ America's desire to show its belief in democracy

   Ⓓ A government decision to produce more public buildings

10 Indicate whether each of the following is mentioned as a characteristic of the Greek Revival style.

Click in the correct box for each phrase.

	Yes	No
Ⓐ A roof with decorations		
Ⓑ A building with many large windows		
Ⓒ A portico over the entrance		
Ⓓ A rectangle-shaped building		

Listen again to part of the lecture. Then, answer the question.

11 What does the professor imply when he says this: 🎧

   Ⓐ He thinks more public buildings should look like temples.

   Ⓑ He does not think architects should copy designs.

   Ⓒ He believes white buildings look more significant.

   Ⓓ He wants building colors to be chosen by architects.

Actual Test 1

HACKERS APEX LISTENING for the TOEFL iBT Advanced

PART 2. Passage 1

AT1_P2_1

Note-taking

1 What are the speakers mainly discussing?

  Ⓐ The result of a psychology experiment
  Ⓑ The advantages of doing a survey
  Ⓒ The members of a study group
  Ⓓ The way to accomplish a project

2 Why does the student want to do an experiment about depression?

  Ⓐ He read about the topic in a textbook.
  Ⓑ He got the idea from a recent lecture in class.
  Ⓒ He was inspired by a discussion with students.
  Ⓓ He watched a video on the subject online.

3 What does the professor imply about the student's survey?

  Ⓐ It will be easier to do with a small number of students.
  Ⓑ It may be inaccurate if participants have to give names.
  Ⓒ It might be too detailed to include in a paper.
  Ⓓ It should be about more than one topic.

4 What does the professor recommend for an application?

  Ⓐ Following the guidelines listed on a website
  Ⓑ Mentioning actual stories and cases about students
  Ⓒ Asking an assistant to review it before submitting
  Ⓓ Including plenty of detail about the goals and methods

Listen again to part of the conversation. Then answer the question.

5 What does the student mean when he says this:

  Ⓐ He does not think an experiment will cause harm.
  Ⓑ The experiment will not involve testing students.
  Ⓒ The professor did not understand a goal.
  Ⓓ He will not ask students difficult questions.

Actual Test 1

HACKERS APEX LISTENING for the TOEFL iBT Advanced

AT1_P2_2

ENVIRONMENTAL SCIENCE

Note-taking

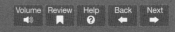

6 What does the professor mainly discuss?

Ⓐ How species survive in the Amazon

Ⓑ Advantages of living in the Amazon region

Ⓒ Different types of Amazon rivers

Ⓓ Various plants and animals in the Amazon

7 Why does the professor mention coffee?

Ⓐ To name an important farm product

Ⓑ To explain the flavor of a type of water

Ⓒ To show how rivers help some plants grow

Ⓓ To describe a river's color more accurately

8 What makes the water in blackwater rivers clean?

Ⓐ The speed of the river

Ⓑ The temperature of the water

Ⓒ The type of soil the water passes

Ⓓ The lack of plants in the river

9 Indicate whether each of the following is a characteristic of whitewater, blackwater, or clearwater rivers.

Click in the correct box for each phrase.

	White-water	Black-water	Clear-water
Ⓐ Difficult to see through			
Ⓑ Contains harmful chemicals			
Ⓒ Supports wide variety of life			
Ⓓ Found in high mountains			

10 What can be inferred about the mountains near the Amazon?

Ⓐ They have existed for millions of years.

Ⓑ Their rivers support many towns near the Amazon.

Ⓒ They are where most of the rivers come from.

Ⓓ Their environment needs to be protected.

Listen again to part of the lecture. Then answer the question.

11 Why does the professor say this: 🎧

Ⓐ To suggest that a natural phenomenon is common

Ⓑ To reassure students that a concept is not difficult

Ⓒ To emphasize the contrast between two river colors

Ⓓ To repeat what she said in a previous lecture

Actual Test 1

HACKERS APEX LISTENING for the TOEFL iBT Advanced

AT1_P2_3

Note-taking

12 What is the main topic of the lecture?

   Ⓐ The differences between government institutions

   Ⓑ The development of modern companies

   Ⓒ The characteristics of a form of organization

   Ⓓ The advantages of having a bureaucracy

13 According to the professor, how are people at the top of an organization different from those at the bottom?

   Ⓐ They usually work longer hours.

   Ⓑ They receive higher pay for their work.

   Ⓒ They have more power to make decisions.

   Ⓓ They have more knowledge about business.

14 Why does the professor mention the Catholic Church?

   Ⓐ To show that bureaucracies can have problems

   Ⓑ To explain why some people leave organizations

   Ⓒ To give an example of a long-lasting institution

   Ⓓ To compare it with other types of bureaucracies

15 According to the professor, what are some drawbacks of bureaucracies?

Choose 2 answers.

   Ⓐ Decisions take a long time to be made.

   Ⓑ Some rules are too difficult to follow.

   Ⓒ People care little about social status.

   Ⓓ People do not respond well to new situations.

Listen again to part of the lecture. Then answer the question.

16 What does the professor mean when he says this: 🎧

   Ⓐ He feels that the student's answer is not complete.

   Ⓑ He thinks that a topic should be discussed later.

   Ⓒ He knows that the textbook has not been updated.

   Ⓓ He believes that the student is confused by the question.

Listen again to part of the lecture. Then answer the question.

17 Why does the professor say this: 🎧

   Ⓐ To suggest that factories should follow a system

   Ⓑ To illustrate the common kinds of jobs in a bureaucracy

   Ⓒ To show that a bureaucracy can be applied to any organization

   Ⓓ To explain a benefit of a bureaucracy's structure

Actual Test 1 | HACKERS APEX LISTENING for the TOEFL iBT Advanced

Answer Book p. 76

TOEFL Listening
PART 1. Passage 1

AT2_P1_1

Note-taking

1 Why does the student go to see the professor?

(A) To check on some graduation requirements

(B) To find out about taking another course

(C) To get help with deciding on a career

(D) To ask for advice about a job interview

2 What does the student say about working for a private company?

(A) She could become very successful.

(B) Her skills will not match the requirements.

(C) She would enjoy the work environment.

(D) Her work might not be exciting enough.

3 What does the professor imply about jobs in advertising?

(A) They do not pay high salaries.

(B) They are usually found in big cities.

(C) They can be difficult to get.

(D) They require lots of experience.

4 Why does the professor mention the student's communication skills?

(A) To explain the reason for her grade

(B) To show how she can be useful

(C) To say that she needs some improvement

(D) To tell her what she should focus on

5 What is the professor's opinion of the student's plans for after graduation?

(A) He feels that a short vacation is necessary.

(B) He thinks she should look for several jobs.

(C) He worries that the student will be too busy.

(D) He recommends that she prepare for a job quickly.

Actual Test 2

HACKERS APEX LISTENING for the TOEFL iBT Advanced

AT2_P1_2

BIOLOGY

Note-taking

6 What is the main topic of the lecture?

(A) The similarities between ants and bees

(B) The benefits of eating a type of fungi

(C) The ways that insects improve agriculture

(D) The useful relationship between two organisms

7 According to the professor, why do leafcutter ants partially chew leaves?

(A) To release nutrients within the leaves

(B) To organize the leaves for the queen ant

(C) To obtain energy from the leaves

(D) To soften the leaves for the fungi

8 In the lecture, the professor mentions several features of Lepiotaceae fungi. Indicate whether each of the following is a feature.

Click in the correct box for each phrase.

	Yes	No
(A) Produce a nutritious substance		
(B) Break down quickly in the soil		
(C) Help to protect the ants' young		
(D) Depend on ants to reproduce		

9 How does the professor explain the job of worker ants?

(A) By describing how it has changed over time

(B) By explaining it from two points of view

(C) By comparing it to a familiar task of humans

(D) By showing its importance to a nest's survival

10 What is the purpose of the white substance on some ants' bodies?

(A) It helps fungi stay healthy.

(B) It lets ants hide from predators.

(C) It allows fungi to reproduce.

(D) It protects ants from diseases.

Listen again to part of the lecture. Then answer the question.

11 What does the student mean when he says this: 🎧

(A) He feels that the ants rely on the fungi too much.

(B) He wants to know how the ants help the fungi.

(C) He wonders if the fungi are harmed by the ants.

(D) He understands the characteristics of ants very well.

Actual Test 2

HACKERS APEX LISTENING for the TOEFL iBT Advanced

AT2_P2_1

Note-taking

1 Why does the professor ask to see the student?

- Ⓐ To find out why her assignment is late
- Ⓑ To give his reactions to her report
- Ⓒ To ask her about her midterms schedule
- Ⓓ To ask her to present a report in class

2 What does the professor say about the novel?

Choose 2 answers.

- Ⓐ The author wanted to be indirect on purpose.
- Ⓑ Many readers think the author is an excellent writer.
- Ⓒ The story is hard for young readers to understand.
- Ⓓ Many students are confused when they first read it.

3 According to the professor, what does the engagement ring in the novel represent?

- Ⓐ The fiancé's unpleasant character
- Ⓑ The feelings Claire has about marriage
- Ⓒ The friendship between two characters
- Ⓓ The importance of making good decisions

4 Why does the professor mention real life?

- Ⓐ To introduce information about the author
- Ⓑ To show that novels are not always complicated
- Ⓒ To show that some characters are realistic
- Ⓓ To remind the student about responsibilities

Listen again to part of the conversation. Then answer the question.

5 What does the student mean when she says this:

- Ⓐ She disagrees with the professor's opinion.
- Ⓑ She believes that she chose the wrong topic.
- Ⓒ She does not understand the professor's comment.
- Ⓓ She thinks her report might have some problems.

Actual Test 2

HACKERS APEX LISTENING for the TOEFL iBT Advanced

AT2_P2_2

GEOLOGY

Note-taking

6 What is the lecture mainly about?

(A) A characteristic of some volcanoes

(B) The main kinds of volcanoes

(C) A newly discovered type of volcano

(D) The danger of volcanic eruptions

7 Why does the professor mention a cooking pot?

(A) To explain the power of eruptions in calderas

(B) To illustrate the shape of a caldera

(C) To introduce a volcano in Spain

(D) To emphasize the strong heat of magma

8 According to the professor, what are the main differences between craters and calderas?

(A) Their depth and location

(B) Their composition and temperature

(C) Their shape and age

(D) Their size and formation

9 What can be inferred about Yellowstone Caldera?

(A) It is unlikely to grow larger in the future.

(B) It was created by multiple volcanoes.

(C) It has not had an eruption for many years.

(D) It is the largest caldera in the world.

10 Indicate whether each of the following describes a crater lake caldera, a shield volcano caldera, or a resurgent caldera.

Click in the correct box for each phrase.

	Crater Lake Caldera	Shield Volcano Caldera	Resurgent Caldera
(A) Forms when the ground collapses and fills with water			
(B) Is the largest volcanic feature on earth			
(C) Has different layers of lava			
(D) Is smaller than other types of calderas			

Listen again to part of the lecture. Then answer the question.

11 Why does the professor say this: 🎧

(A) To compare the lava flow of different volcanoes

(B) To explain the formation of some volcanoes

(C) To show why volcanoes gradually increase in size

(D) To emphasize that an eruption happened a long time ago

Actual Test 2

HACKERS APEX LISTENING for the TOEFL iBT Advanced

AT2_P2_3

BIOLOGY

Note-taking

12 What is the lecture mainly about?

  (A) The characteristics of various insect species

  (B) The reasons that insects have survived for so long

  (C) The advantages that some insects have over others

  (D) The unique features of an insect's wings

13 What does the professor say about dragonflies?

  (A) They need to catch other insects to eat.

  (B) They travel long distances every year.

  (C) They are one of the oldest insects in the world.

  (D) They live in places with strong winds.

14 According to the professor, what do the wing muscles allow dragonflies to do?

Choose 2 answers.

  (A) Keep the wings warm

  (B) Fly without making noise

  (C) Move in different directions

  (D) Use less energy while flying

15 Why does the professor mention colored clothing?

  (A) To identify a weakness of dragonfly wings

  (B) To show why dragonfly wings are transparent

  (C) To illustrate how a feature of dragonfly wings works

  (D) To explain why dragonflies undergo changes

16 What can be inferred about dragonflies that live in cold weather?

  (A) They have thicker bodies.

  (B) They have a shorter lifespan.

  (C) Their wings often have colored spots.

  (D) Their wings move at a faster rate.

Listen again to part of the lecture. Then answer the question.

17 Why does the professor say this: 🎧

  (A) To suggest that a subject requires more research

  (B) To indicate that she will provide an explanation of a concept

  (C) To find out whether the students have understood her point

  (D) To encourage the students to contribute to the discussion

Photo Credits

MEMO

MEMO

| H | A | C | K | E | R | S |

APEX
LISTENING
for the
TOEFL iBT® Advanced

COPYRIGHT © 2023, by Hackers Language Research Institute

January 13, 2023

All rights reserved. No part of this publication may be reproduced, stored in a retrieval system, or transmitted, in any form or by any means, electronic, mechanical, photocopying, recording, or otherwise, without the prior written permission of the author and the publisher.

Hackers Language Research Institute
23, Gangnam-daero 61-gil, Seocho-gu, Seoul, Korea
Inquiries publishing@hackers.com

ISBN 978-89-6542-544-1 (53740)

Printed in South Korea

2 3 4 5 6 7 8 9 10   29 28 27 26 25 24

The Most Preferred Education Brand in Korea,
HACKERS BOOK (www.HackersBook.com)
• Free supplementary study materials

No. 1 in Hankyung Business' Most Preferred Brand Rankings 2019, Education Group category

HACKERS

APEX

LISTENING

for the

TOEFL iBT®

Advanced

HACKERS

APEX
LISTENING
for the
TOEFL iBT® Advanced

Answer Book

CHAPTER 01
Main Purpose/Topic

Example   본문 p. 15

A. (C)   **B.** (B)

A.

Note-taking

S: Sick recently → turn in report late?
P: No, submit tomorrow
S: Exception?
P: X allow extra time for asgmt.
S: Have note ← doctor
P: Assigned @ beg. of semester ∴ enough time
  Finish tonight → give tomorrow

Listen to a conversation between a student and a professor.

S: Hi, Professor Watkins. I've been sick recently, so I was wondering if I could turn in my report a little late.

P: I'm afraid not, Morgan. You have to submit it tomorrow just like everyone else.

S: Couldn't you make an exception for me this time?

P: I explained on the first day that I would not allow extra time for assignments.

S: I know, but I really was sick. I have a note from the doctor...

P: I assigned the paper at the beginning of the semester. So you've had enough time to work on it. I suggest that you finish it tonight and give it to me tomorrow.

학생과 교수 사이의 대화를 들으시오.

S: 안녕하세요, Watkins 교수님. 제가 최근에 아파서, 보고서를 조금 늦게 제출해도 될지 궁금해요.

P: 안 될 것 같구나, Morgan. 너는 다른 사람들과 마찬가지로 내일까지 그것을 제출해야 해.

S: 이번에는 저를 예외로 해주실 수 없을까요?

P: 첫날에 과제물을 위한 추가적인 시간을 허락하지 않을 거라고 설명했단다.

S: 알아요, 하지만 저는 정말 아팠어요. 저는 의사에게 받은 진단서를 가지고 있어요...

P: 그 보고서를 학기 초에 내주었어. 그래서 너는 그것을 할 충분한 시간이 있었지. 네가 오늘 밤에 그것을 끝낸 다음 내일 나에게 제출하는 것을 제안하마.

turn in ~을 제출하다   submit ⑧ 제출하다   exception ⑲ 예외
extra ⑲ 추가적인, 여분의   assignment ⑲ 과제물

학생은 왜 교수를 찾아가는가?

(A) 그의 보고서 초안을 제출하기 위해
(B) 그의 성적에 대한 설명을 요청하기 위해
(C) 과제물을 할 더 많은 시간을 요청하기 위해
(D) 수업에 결석한 이유를 설명하기 위해

B.

Note-taking

Reason Why Antarctica is a Desert

• Largest desert = cold & icy = Antarctic Polar Desert
• Why?
  - Desert = < 25 cm rain/y
  - Temp. & other factors matter X
  - Antarctica = just over 5 cm rain & snow/y = desert

Listen to part of a lecture in a geology class.

P: When you think of a desert, you probably think of a hot, dry, place covered with sand. Well, surprisingly, the largest desert in the world is actually cold and icy. I'm referring to the Antarctic Polar Desert. It's an ecosystem that covers the entire continent of Antarctica.

Now, to understand why Antarctica is considered a desert, we first need to define what a desert is. So, uh, a desert is any area of land that receives less than 25 centimeters of rain each year... Um, temperature and other factors do not matter. And Antarctica receives just over five centimeters of rain and snow per year. As a result, the entire continent is technically one massive desert.

지질학 강의의 일부를 들으시오.

P: 사막을 떠올릴 때, 여러분은 아마 덥고, 건조하고, 모래로 덮인 장소를 떠올릴 거예요. 음, 놀랍게도, 세계에서 가장 큰 사막은 사실 춥고 얼음으로 덮여 있습니다. 저는 남극의 극지 사막을 말하는 거예요. 그것은 남극 대륙 전체를 아우르는 생태계입니다.

자, 남극 대륙이 사막으로 간주되는 이유를 이해하기 위해, 우리는 먼저 사막이 무엇인지 정의해야 합니다. 그러니까, 어, 사막은 연간 25센티미터 미만의 비가 내리는 모든 육지의 지역이에요... 음, 기온과 다른 요소들은 중요하지 않아요. 그리고 남극 대륙에는 연간 5센티미터가 조금 넘는 비와 눈이 내립니다. 결과적으로, 그 대륙 전체는 엄밀히 말하면 하나의 거대한 사막입니다.

Antarctic ⑲ 남극의   ecosystem ⑲ 생태계   continent ⑲ 대륙
consider ⑧ 간주하다   define ⑧ 정의하다
technically ⑭ 엄밀히 말하면

강의는 주로 무엇에 관한 것인가?

(A) 극지 사막이 형성되는 과정
(B) 어떤 지역이 사막으로 분류되는 이유
(C) 남극 대륙의 강우를 제한하는 요소들
(D) 다양한 생태계들 사이의 차이점들

Listening Practice 1

본문 p. 17

1 (C) 2 (B) 3 (B) 4 (D) 5 (A)

Note-taking

W: Dance club member, need place ∵ usual room locked
M: Closed ∵ air con. fixed → finish later afternoon
W: Notified X
M: Univ. update program → issue → back to normal soon
   Check room available
W: Practice w/ loud music
M: Come back in 20 min. ∵ find room & organize
W: Go to lobby, talk w/ group

Listen to a conversation between a student and a university facility manager.

W: Um, do you know where I can find the university facility manager?

M: Actually, that's me. What can I do for you?

W: Oh, great. ¹Um, I'm a member of the dance club, and we need a place to practice today. We went to our usual practice room, but it was locked.

M: I just want to check... When did you reserve the room?

W: Well, we reserved it several months ago for the same time every week. There's never been a problem before, so we were quite surprised when it was locked.

M: OK... What's the room number?

W: ²Um, it's room 302 in the Ryder Building.

M: Just a minute... Oh, that's right. ²It's closed because the air conditioner is being fixed. The repair work will be finished later this afternoon... Nobody told you about this? ³You should have been notified that there was a problem with your schedule.

W: No, and I checked my e-mail just before I came here.

M: I see. ³Actually, the university recently updated one of our computer programs, but there have been some issues with it. That could be why you weren't told. Hopefully, everything will be back to normal soon.

W: OK, but what can we do now? We still don't have a room to use.

M: ⁵Here's what we'll do. Let me check if there are any rooms available. I'll try to reserve one of them for you.

W: Thank you. Um, I should tell you that we practice with loud music... So you probably should not put us next to a place where people are trying to study.

M: That's fine. Could you come back in 20 minutes? I'll need some time to find a room and get everything organized.

W: ⁴OK. I'll just go to the lobby to talk with the rest of the group. I need to tell them about the situation.

M: Oh, in that case, please talk outside the building. There are people working and I don't want you to disturb them.

W: All right. We can meet outside.

학생과 대학교 시설 관리자 사이의 대화를 들으시오.

W: 음, 대학교 시설 관리자를 어디에서 찾을 수 있는지 아시나요?

M: 사실, 그게 저예요. 무엇을 도와 드릴까요?

W: 오, 잘됐네요. 음, 저는 춤 동아리 회원이고, 저희는 오늘 연습할 장소가 필요해요. 저희의 평상시 연습실에 갔는데, 그것은 잠겨 있었어요.

M: 잠깐 확인했으면 하는데... 언제 그 방을 예약하셨나요?

W: 음, 저희는 몇 달 전에 매주 같은 시간에 그것을 예약했어요. 전에는 한 번도 문제가 없어서, 그것이 잠겨 있었을 때 저희는 꽤 놀랐어요.

M: 알겠습니다... 방 번호가 뭐죠?

W: 음, Ryder Building의 302호예요.

M: 잠시만요... 오, 맞아요. 에어컨이 수리되는 중이라 그것은 닫혀있어요. 수리 작업은 오늘 오후 늦게 완료될 거예요... 아무도 이것에 대해 말해주지 않았나요? 일정에 문제가 있다는 것을 통지받으셨어야 하는데.

W: 아뇨, 그리고 여기에 오기 직전에 이메일을 확인했어요.

M: 그렇군요. 사실, 대학은 최근에 컴퓨터 프로그램 중 하나를 업데이트했는데, 그것과 관련한 몇몇 문제가 있었어요. 그게 학생이 전달받지 못한 이유일 수도 있겠네요. 바라건대, 곧 모든 것이 정상으로 돌아갈 거예요.

W: 알겠습니다, 그런데 이제 저희는 어떻게 하죠? 저희는 여전히 이용할 방이 없어요.

M: 이렇게 할게요. 이용 가능한 방이 있는지 확인해 볼게요. 제가 학생을 위해 그것들 중 하나를 예약해 볼게요.

W: 감사합니다. 음, 저희가 음악을 크게 틀고 연습한다는 걸 알려드려야겠네요... 그래서 저희를 사람들이 공부하려고 하는 장소 옆에 들어가게 하시면 아마 안 될 것 같아요.

M: 괜찮습니다. 20분 후에 돌아와 주시겠어요? 방을 찾고 모든 것을 정리하는 데 시간이 좀 필요해요.

W: 알겠습니다. 동아리의 다른 사람들과 얘기하러 로비로 갈게요. 그들에게 상황에 관해 알려줘야 해요.

M: 오, 그러면, 건물 밖에서 얘기해 주세요. 일하는 사람들이 있고 그들을 방해하지 않았으면 해서요.

W: 알겠습니다. 저희는 밖에서 만나도 돼요.

---

usual 형 평상시의   reserve 동 예약하다   repair 명 수리
notify 동 통지하다, 알리다   hopefully 부 바라건대
available 형 이용 가능한   organize 동 정리하다
disturb 동 방해하다

1 학생은 왜 관리자를 찾아가는가?

   (A) 신청서를 제출하기 위해
   (B) 대학 동아리들에 관해 알아보기 위해
   (C) 연습 공간에 관해 문의하기 위해
   (D) 행사를 위한 허가를 얻기 위해

2 관리자는 302호의 수리 작업에 관해 무엇이라고 말하는가?

   (A) 그것은 수개월 전에 예정되었다.

(B) 그것은 오후에 완료될 것이다.

(C) 그것은 교수에 의해 요청되었다.

(D) 그것은 보통 일 년에 두 번 있는 일이다.

3 대화에 따르면, 무엇이 통지에 문제를 일으켰을 수 있는가?

(A) 학생이 이메일에 회답하지 않았다.

(B) 대학이 컴퓨터 프로그램을 업데이트했다.

(C) 동아리가 방 번호를 혼동했다.

(D) 관리자가 중요한 서류를 잃어버렸다.

4 학생은 다음에 무엇을 할 것인가?

(A) 건물의 정책 목록 검토하기

(B) 연습을 위한 다른 날짜 선택하기

(C) 건물에 있는 다른 부서 방문하기

(D) 다른 동아리 회원들과 상황에 관해 논의하기

대화의 일부를 다시 듣고 질문에 답하시오.

M: Here's what we'll do. Let me check if there are any rooms available. I'll try to reserve one of them for you.

W: Thank you. Um, I should tell you that we practice with loud music... So you probably should not put us next to a place where people are trying to study.

5 학생은 이렇게 말함으로써 무엇을 암시하는가:

W: Um, I should tell you that we practice with loud music…

(A) 동아리는 다른 사람들을 방해하고 싶지 않다.

(B) 방에 약간의 음향 장비가 있어야 한다.

(C) 동아리는 큰 소리로 음악을 듣는 것을 즐긴다.

(D) 방은 조용한 곳에 있어야 한다.

Listening Practice 2 본문 p. 19

1 (D)   2 (D)   3 (B)   4 (B)   5 (C)

Note-taking

Role of Extroversion and Introversion in Achievement

- Role of extrov. & introv. in achievement
- Extrov. = gain energy ← time w/ others, approval
  - Act > think, confident, take risk, team work
- Introv. = Think ↑, anxious, serious, like attention X
- Ppl. assume extrov. succeed ↑
- Reality = successful introvert ↑ (e.g. Van Gogh)
- Study = extrov. < introv. in project
- Both have strengths → success

Listen to part of a lecture in a psychology class.

P: OK, so we've spent some time recently talking about the behavior of successful people. ¹Today, we'll move on to the role of extroversion and introversion in personal achievement. But first, let's be sure everyone understands what the terms mean. Um, extroversion and introversion are two opposite personality types that explain how people get and use energy. ²Extroverts are people who gain energy from spending time

with others and who often need other people's approval. They are usually better at acting than thinking. They are confident and more likely to take risks. They are also good at working in teams and making decisions quickly. Introverts, however, are the opposite of extroverts. They, uh, feel exhausted after talking to people and need time alone to regain their energy. In general, introverts are more likely to think long and hard before acting. They pay attention to small details and are generally more anxious than extroverts. They often appear more serious or shy. ³Oh, and they don't like being the center of attention. So introverts feel nervous about talking in front of large groups.

Anyway, that's a basic overview of extroverts and introverts. Um, I want to focus on how we, as a society, perceive these personality types. People often assume that extroverts are more likely to succeed in life. And it's true that many successful people, like politicians and celebrities, are outgoing. In reality, however, there are many successful introverts as well. In fact, many artistic and scientific geniuses, like Van Gogh, Einstein, and Darwin were introverts. ⁵They produced some of history's greatest ideas and creations. This was because they could work well alone and focus on their ideas. Introverts are quite effective leaders, too. This is not my opinion... It's supported by research.

For example, one study showed that extroverts contribute less than introverts in projects. They tend not to listen and lose energy while working on projects. In contrast, introverts listen well and actually gain more energy as projects progress. And another study estimates that over half of the world's CEOs are introverts.

Does that mean employers shouldn't hire extroverts? Not at all. But it does indicate that both extroverts and introverts have strengths that can lead to success. Ideally, extroverts are at their best when they work in large groups. Their personality makes them excellent salespeople and speakers. But that doesn't mean they make the best leaders. My point is that we should think again about success. ⁴We shouldn't force introverts to be more like extroverts. Instead, we should appreciate them for their positive qualities... And there are many!

심리학 강의의 일부를 들으시오.

P: 자, 최근에 우리는 성공한 사람들의 행동에 관해 얘기하면서 시간을 좀 보냈어요. 오늘, 우리는 개인적 성공에 있어 외향성과 내향성의 역할로 넘어갈 거예요. 하지만 먼저, 모두 그 용어들이 의미하는 것을 확실히 이해해 둡시다. 음, 외향성과 내향성은 사람들이 에너지를 얻고 사용하는 방법을 설명하는 두 개의 반대되는 성격 유형들이에요. 외향적인 사람들은 다른 사람들과 시간을 보내는 것에서 에너지를 얻고 종종 다른 사람들의 인정을 필요로 하는 사람들이에요. 그들은 보통 생각하는 것보다는 행동하는 것에 더 능숙해요. 그들은 자신감이 있으며 위험을 감수할 가능성이 더 커요. 그들은 팀에서 일하고 빠르게 결정을 내리는 것에도 능숙합니다. 하지만, 내향적인 사람들은 외향적인 사람들과 반대입니다.

그들은, 어, 사람들과 대화한 후에 지치며 에너지를 되찾기 위해 혼자만의 시간을 필요로 해요. 일반적으로, 내향적인 사람들은 행동하기 전에 오랫동안 열심히 생각할 가능성이 더 커요. 그들은 작은 세부 사항에 주의를 기울이고 보통 외향적인 사람들보다 더 불안해합니다. 그들은 종종 더 진지하거나 수줍은 것처럼 보이죠. 오, 그리고 그들은 관심의 중심이 되는 걸 좋아하지 않아요. 그래서 내향적인 사람들은 큰 무리의 사람들 앞에서 이야기하는 것에 불안해합니다.

어쨌든, 그게 외향적인 사람들과 내향적인 사람들에 대한 기본적인 개요입니다. 음, 저는 우리가 어떻게, 사회로서, 이 성격 유형들을 인식하는지에 초점을 맞추려고 합니다. 사람들은 종종 외향적인 사람들이 인생에서 성공할 가능성이 더 크다고 추정하죠. 그리고 정치인과 유명인 같은 많은 성공한 사람들이 외향적인 것은 사실이에요. 하지만, 실제로는, 성공한 내향적인 사람들도 많이 있습니다. 사실, 반 고흐, 아인슈타인, 다윈 같은 많은 예술과 과학적 천재들은 내향적인 사람들이었습니다. 그들은 역사상 가장 위대한 생각들과 작품들 중 일부를 만들어냈죠. 이는 그들이 혼자서 일을 잘하고 그들의 생각에 집중할 수 있었기 때문이에요. 내향적인 사람들은 상당히 효과적인 지도자들이기도 해요. 이건 제 의견이 아니에요... 그것은 연구에 의해 뒷받침됩니다.

예를 들어, 한 연구는 외향적인 사람들이 내향적인 사람들보다 프로젝트에 덜 기여한다는 것을 보여주었어요. 그들은 경청하지 않고 프로젝트를 하는 동안 에너지를 잃는 경향이 있어요. 반대로, 내향적인 사람들은 잘 경청하며 프로젝트가 진행됨에 따라 사실 더 많은 에너지를 얻어요. 그리고 또 다른 연구는 전 세계 CEO의 절반 이상이 내향적인 사람들이라고 추정해요.

그게 고용주들이 외향적인 사람들을 채용하지 말아야 한다는 뜻일까요? 전혀 아닙니다. 하지만 그것은 외향적인 사람들과 내향적인 사람들 둘 다 성공으로 이어질 수 있는 강점들을 가지고 있다는 걸 시사해요. 이상적으로는, 외향적인 사람들은 큰 집단 안에서 일할 때 가장 뛰어나요. 그들의 성격은 그들을 훌륭한 영업 사원과 연설가로 만듭니다. 하지만 그게 그들이 최고의 지도자가 된다는 뜻은 아니에요. 제 요점은 우리가 성공에 대해 다시 생각해야 한다는 거예요. 우리는 내향적인 사람들에게 더 외향적인 사람들처럼 될 것을 강요하면 안 돼요. 대신, 우리는 그들의 긍정적인 자질들로 그들을 인정해야 해요... 그리고 많은 긍정적인 자질들이 있습니다!

behavior 명 행동 extroversion 명 외향성
introversion 명 내향성 achievement 명 성공, 성취
opposite 형 반대의 approval 명 인정 anxious 형 불안해하는
perceive 동 인식하다 assume 동 추정하다
outgoing 형 외향적인 creation 명 작품, 발명품
contribute 동 기여하다 estimate 동 추정하다
appreciate 동 인정하다

1 강의는 주로 무엇에 관한 것인가?

(A) 성공한 사람들의 공통적인 습관

(B) 함께 일하는 것이 어떻게 직업적 성공으로 이어질 수 있는지

(C) 성공한 사람들의 개인적인 성취

(D) 서로 다른 성격 유형들이 성공을 이루는 방식

2 교수에 따르면, 외향적인 사람들의 자질은 무엇인가?

(A) 큰 소리로 말하는 것

(B) 다른 사람들과 이야기하면서 에너지를 잃는 것

(C) 신중한 결정을 내리는 것

(D) 다른 사람들의 인정을 필요로 하는 것

3 교수에 따르면, 내향적인 사람들은 왜 사람들의 무리 앞에서 이야기하는 것을 싫어하는가?

(A) 그들은 많은 청중에 의해 쉽게 지친다.

(B) 그들은 관심을 받는 것을 피하고 싶어 한다.

(C) 그들은 넓은 공간에서 불편함을 느낀다.

(D) 그들은 실수하는 것을 두려워한다.

4 내향적인 사람들에 대한 교수의 의견은 무엇인가?

(A) 그들은 혼자서 일하도록 장려되어야 한다.

(B) 그들은 많은 좋은 특징들을 가지고 있다.

(C) 그들은 더 외향적이 되도록 노력해야 한다.

(D) 그들은 외향적인 사람들보다 강점들이 더 적다.

강의의 일부를 다시 듣고 질문에 답하시오.

P: They produced some of history's greatest ideas and creations. This was because they could work well alone and focus on their ideas. Introverts are quite effective leaders, too. This is not my opinion... It's supported by research.

5 교수는 왜 이렇게 말하는가:
P: This is not my opinion...

(A) 주장에 이의를 제기하기 위해

(B) 지도자로서의 내향적인 사람들을 비판하기 위해

(C) 견해가 정확하다는 것을 강조하기 위해

(D) 연구의 중요성을 강조하기 위해

Listening Practice 3
본문 p. 21

1 (B)   2 (C)   3 (B)   4 (C)   5 (A)

Note-taking

W: Interested in work as dept. assistant, available?
M: Eng. & math dept, which?
W: Plan = publishing comp. ∴ Eng. dept.
M: Use time well, things = send msg., print, copy, etc.
   Req. = 2nd yr. student ↑, grade > 3.0 or lose job
   Get $11/h, once/month
   Form → write skill, details X ∵ interview later
   Submit end of the week, notified interview later

Listen to a conversation between a student and a university employee.

M: Good afternoon. How can I help you?

W: Hi, my name's Becky Williams. I'm a third-year student here. ¹I'm interested in working as a department assistant. Do you know if there are any positions available?

M: Yes. There are some in the English and math departments. Which one are you interested in?

W: Well, I'm planning to work for a publishing

company after college. So, uh, I'm more interested in the English department.

M: OK. And have you done anything like this before?

W: No, but I think I can do the job. I'm very organized and good at following instructions.

M: Great. You'll be working and studying at the same time. So you'll need to use your time well. Other than that, are you good with computers? [2]You'll be expected to do different things on a computer. You'll, um, need to send and receive messages, print documents, copy files, and so on.

W: I'm sure I can do all of those tasks.

M: All right. You need to have a few requirements to qualify. The first is that you have to be a second-year student at least. So there are no issues there. [3]However, you also need to have a high grade point average of 3.0 or more. This should be maintained while you work. Otherwise, you will lose the job.

W: That shouldn't be a problem. My grades are good.

M: Terrific. Now, do you have any questions before I give you the application form?

W: Yes, uh, could you tell me how much I will be paid for the job?

M: Oh, sure. [5]You'll get $11 an hour. And you'll be paid once a month.

W: Is that right? That's excellent. It's more than I thought. Could I get the form now?

M: Here you go. Make sure you write down all your skills on the form. You don't need to include all the details, though, since there will be an interview later.

W: Thanks! [4]I'll fill it out as soon as I leave here. Um, when should I submit it?

M: I'll need it back by the end of the week. You'll be notified about the interview after that. Good luck!

학생과 교직원 사이의 대화를 들으시오.

M: 안녕하세요. 어떻게 도와드릴까요?

W: 안녕하세요, 제 이름은 Becky Williams입니다. 저는 3학년 학생이에요. 학과 조교로 일하는 데 관심이 있거든요. 구할 수 있는 자리가 있는지 아시나요?

M: 네. 영문과와 수학과에 몇 개가 있어요. 어떤 것에 관심이 있으신가요?

W: 음, 저는 대학교 졸업 후에 출판사에서 일할 계획이에요. 그래서, 어, 영문과에 더 관심이 있습니다.

M: 알겠습니다. 그리고 이전에 이런 일을 해본 적이 있나요?

W: 아뇨, 그렇지만 저는 제가 그 일을 할 수 있을 거라 생각해요. 저는 매우 체계적이고 지시를 따르는 것에 능숙해요.

M: 잘됐네요. 학생은 일과 공부를 동시에 하게 될 거예요. 그러니까 시간을 잘 사용해야 할 겁니다. 그 외에는, 컴퓨터를 잘 다루나요? 컴퓨터로 여러 가지의 것들을 하게 될 거예요. 학생은, 음, 메시지 주고받기, 서류 출력하기, 파일 복사하기 등을 해야 할 거예요.

W: 저는 확실히 그 업무들 모두를 할 수 있어요.

M: 알겠어요. 자격을 얻기 위해 몇 가지 요건을 갖춰야 하는데요. 첫

째로 적어도 2학년 학생이어야 해요. 그러니까 그건 문제가 없네요. 하지만, 3.0이나 그 이상의 높은 학점 평균도 가지고 있어야 해요. 이것은 학생이 일하는 동안 유지되어야 해요. 그렇지 않으면, 일자리를 잃게 될 거예요.

W: 그건 문제가 되지 않겠네요. 제 학점은 좋거든요.

M: 좋아요. 자, 제가 지원서를 드리기 전에 질문이 있나요?

W: 네, 어, 제가 그 일로 얼마를 받게 될지 알려주실 수 있나요?

M: 오, 물론이죠. 시간당 11달러를 받을 거예요. 그리고 한 달에 한 번 지급받을 겁니다.

W: 그런가요? 훌륭하네요. 제가 생각한 것보다 많아요. 지금 지원서를 받을 수 있나요?

M: 여기 있습니다. 지원서에 학생이 가진 기술들을 꼭 모두 적으세요. 하지만, 나중에 면접이 있을 것이기 때문에, 모든 세부 사항들을 포함할 필요는 없어요.

W: 감사합니다! 여기서 나가자마자 그걸 작성할게요. 음, 언제 그것을 제출해야 하나요?

M: 이번 주말까지 가져오셔야 합니다. 그 이후에 면접에 관해 통지받을 거예요. 행운을 빌어요!

department assistant 학과 조교   available 휑 구할 수 있는
organized 휑 체계적인   task 뗑 업무   requirement 뗑 요건
at least 적어도   issue 뗑 문제   maintain 동 유지하다
otherwise 붼 그렇지 않으면   application form 지원서
fill out ~을 작성하다   submit 동 제출하다   notify 동 통지하다

1 학생은 왜 교직원을 찾아가는가?

(A) 직업 훈련 프로그램에 등록하기 위해
(B) 취업 기회에 관해 문의하기 위해
(C) 직장 지원서를 제출하기 위해
(D) 몇몇 일자리 요건에 관해 불평하기 위해

2 직원에 따르면, 학과 조교들은 무엇을 할 것으로 기대되는가?

(A) 학급들을 위한 수업 준비하기
(B) 학생들의 과제물 도와주기
(C) 컴퓨터로 업무 완수하기
(D) 학생들에게 캠퍼스 안내하기

3 학생은 학과 조교가 되기 위해 무엇을 해야 하는가?

(A) 컴퓨터 시험 통과하기
(B) 높은 학점 평균 보유하기
(C) 그녀의 과거 경험 열거하기
(D) 추천서 제출하기

4 학생은 다음에 무엇을 할 것인가?

(A) 학과에 전화하기
(B) 면접에 가기
(C) 지원서 작성하기
(D) 다른 사무실 방문하기

대화의 일부를 다시 듣고 질문에 답하시오.

M: You'll get $11 an hour. And you'll be paid once a month.

W: Is that right? That's excellent. It's more than I thought. Could I get the form now?

5 학생은 이렇게 말함으로써 무엇을 의미하는가:

W: Is that right?

(A) 그녀는 더 낮은 급여를 예상했다.

(B) 그녀는 직원이 실수했다고 생각한다.

(C) 그녀는 파트타임으로 일하는 것을 선호한다.

(D) 그녀는 그녀가 언제 시작할 수 있을지 모른다.

Listening Practice 4

본문 p. 23

1 (C)   2 (D)   3 (B)   4 (C)   5 (D)

Note-taking

Why the UK Army Had Many Young Volunteer Soldiers

- WWI = bet. 2 groups = central & allied
- Why UK had many young volunteers, how?
- Start of WWI = UK had small army ∵ volunteer army
- UK's nat. campaign → successful (5 times more ppl.)
- Many < 18yr. ∵ birth cert. X, easily pretend older
  - In 1918, 250k soldiers < 18yr.
- Reasons = campaign, get away, stories, pressure

Listen to part of a lecture in a history class.

P: World War I was mainly fought between two groups of countries: the Central Powers and Allied Powers. The countries in these groups had agreements with each other. If one country joined a war, the other countries in the group had to join in as well. So when Germany attacked France in 1914, the UK went to war against Germany the next day. Um, Germany, of course, was a Central Power, and the UK and France were Allied Powers. ¹Anyway, what I want to focus on is why the UK army had so many young volunteers during this war. How did this happen?

At the start of World War I, the UK had a small army. It had around 700,000 soldiers. In comparison, Germany had nearly two million soldiers ready to fight. ²One of the reasons for the UK's small army was that, for over a hundred years, it had been a volunteer army. Um, this means no one was forced to join.

So the UK army held a national campaign to find volunteers from the first day of the war... It published requests for help in newspapers and put up posters in public places. And, in towns across the country, leaders gave speeches that encouraged men to join the war. ³Uh, the campaign was very successful. In fact, the UK army found five times more people than it expected in just a few weeks. Now, even though the UK army attracted potential recruits of all ages, a large number were very young. The minimum age to join the army was 18. However, many were much younger than this. You see, back then, few people had birth certificates that showed their real age. So someone could easily pretend to be older. ⁵If a young person just said

he was 18, joining was easy. The UK army was not careful about the requirements. By the time the war ended in 1918, around 250,000 soldiers under the age of 18 had joined the army. Some were as young as 12.

⁴Young men joined the army for many reasons... Uh, some believed the army's campaign and felt a moral duty to fight. Others wanted to get away from their towns because there were no jobs for young people. ⁴Many also grew up reading stories about wars and war heroes. They wrongly thought that going to war would be like an exciting adventure. A lot of young people also felt pressure from society. If they didn't join, people would think they were afraid.

역사학 강의의 일부를 들으시오.

P: 제1차 세계대전은 주로 두 집단의 국가들, 즉 동맹국들과 연합국들 사이에서 싸워졌습니다. 이 집단의 국가들은 서로 협정을 맺었어요. 한 국가가 참전하면, 그 집단에 있는 다른 국가들도 참전해야 했죠. 그래서 1914년에 독일이 프랑스를 공격했을 때, 영국은 다음 날 독일과의 전쟁에 참전했습니다. 음, 독일은 물론, 동맹국이었고, 영국과 프랑스는 연합국이었죠. 하여간, 제가 초점을 맞추고 싶은 것은 이 전쟁 동안 영국에 그렇게나 많은 어린 자원병들이 있었던 이유입니다. 어떻게 이런 일이 일어났을까요?

제1차 세계대전이 시작되었을 때, 영국은 작은 군대를 가지고 있었습니다. 약 70만 명의 군인들이 있었어요. 그에 비해, 독일에는 거의 200만 명의 군인들이 싸울 준비가 되어 있었죠. 영국의 군대가 작았던 이유 중 하나는, 100년이 넘는 동안, 그것이 자원군이어왔기 때문입니다. 음, 이것은 아무도 입대하도록 강요되지 않았다는 것을 의미하죠.

그래서 영국군은 전쟁 첫날부터 자원병을 찾기 위해 국가적인 캠페인을 벌였어요... 그것은 신문에 도움을 요청하는 글을 게재하고 공공장소에 포스터를 붙였습니다. 그리고, 전국의 마을들에서, 지도자들은 남성들에게 참전할 것을 독려하는 연설을 했어요. 어, 그 캠페인은 매우 성공적이었어요. 사실, 영국군은 단 몇 주 안에 예상했던 것보다 5배나 많은 사람들을 얻었죠. 자, 비록 영국군이 모든 연령대의 잠재적 신병들을 끌어모았지만, 많은 사람들이 매우 어렸죠. 입대하기 위한 최소 연령은 18세였어요. 하지만, 많은 사람들이 이것보다 훨씬 더 어렸죠. 그러니까, 당시에는, 그들의 진짜 나이를 보여주는 출생증명서를 가진 사람들이 거의 없었어요. 그래서 손쉽게 더 나이 든 척을 할 수 있었죠. 만약 어린 사람이 그냥 18살이라고 말하면, 입대하는 것은 쉬웠어요. 영국군은 요건에 관해 꼼꼼하지 않았거든요. 1918년에 전쟁이 끝났을 때, 약 25만 명의 18세 미만의 군인들이 입대해 있었습니다. 일부는 12살에 불과했죠.

어린 남성들은 여러 이유로 입대했어요... 어, 몇몇은 군대의 캠페인을 믿었고 싸워야 할 도덕적 의무를 느꼈어요. 다른 이들은 어린 사람들을 위한 일자리가 없었기 때문에 그들의 마을에서 벗어나고 싶어 했어요. 많은 사람들은 전쟁과 전쟁 영웅들에 관한 이야기를 읽으며 자라기도 했죠. 그들은 전쟁에 나가는 것이 신나는 모험과 같을 거라고 잘못 생각했습니다. 많은 어린 사람들이 사회로부터의 압박을 느끼기도 했어요. 그들이 입대하지 않으면, 사람들은 그들이 겁먹었다고 생각했죠.

volunteer 명 자원병; 자원 봉사자   in comparison 그에 비해

nearly 图 거의   attract 图 끌어모으다   minimum 图 최소의
birth certificate 출생증명서   moral 图 도덕적인   duty 图 의무
wrongly 图 잘못되게   adventure 图 모험

1 강의의 주된 목적은 무엇인가?

(A) 영국이 제1차 세계대전에 참전한 이유를 보여주기 위해

(B) 군대가 어떻게 전쟁의 결과를 바꿀 수 있는지 설명하기 위해

(C) 영국군에 많은 어린 자원병들이 있었던 이유를 설명하기 위해

(D) 징병제의 장점들을 논의하기 위해

2 교수에 따르면, 영국군은 왜 작았는가?

(A) 그것은 이전 전쟁에서 많은 군인들을 잃었다.

(B) 그것은 참전한 마지막 국가였다.

(C) 그것은 작은 국가를 방어하기만 하면 됐다.

(D) 그것은 사람들에게 입대하도록 강요하지 않았다.

3 교수는 자원병을 구하기 위한 영국군의 캠페인에 관해 무엇이라고 말하는가?

(A) 그것은 두어 달 동안만 지속되었다.

(B) 그것은 예상보다 좋은 결과를 낳았다.

(C) 그것은 정부에 많은 돈을 들게 했다.

(D) 그것은 해외의 국가들에서 홍보되었다.

4 교수에 따르면, 많은 어린 사람들이 영국군에 입대한 한 가지 이유는 무엇인가?

(A) 그들은 가족 구성원들로부터 전쟁에 대한 이야기를 들었다.

(B) 그들은 그들의 직장에서보다 군대에서 더 많은 임금을 받았다.

(C) 그들은 전쟁에 대한 잘못된 생각을 가지고 있었다.

(D) 그들은 외국에 방문하고 싶어 했다.

강의의 일부를 다시 듣고 질문에 답하시오.

P: If a young person just said he was 18, joining was easy. The UK army was not careful about the requirements. By the time the war ended in 1918, around 250,000 soldiers under the age of 18 had joined the army. Some were as young as 12.

5 교수는 왜 이렇게 말하는가:

P: Some were as young as 12.

(A) 제1차 세계대전 동안의 어린 군인들의 행동을 비판하기 위해

(B) 영국군이 군인들의 나이에 주의를 기울였다는 것을 시사하기 위해

(C) 전쟁 중에 사람의 나이를 아는 것이 얼마나 어려웠는지를 보여주기 위해

(D) 영국군이 요건에 관해 얼마나 부주의했는지를 강조하기 위해

iBT Listening Test 1   본문 p. 25

1 (B)   2 (B)   3 (C)   4 (D)   5 (C)

Note-taking

S: Ask about required book
   Reading asgmt. X ∵ buy required book X
   Campus bookstore = copy X
P: Bookstore only buy small # ∵ univ. policy

Save $ → other uses (e.g. office equip.)
Students cancel class → may sell book
Borrow my book & make copy
Will make copies for all students w/o book yet

Listen to a conversation between a student and a professor.

S: Professor Taylor? Um, I'm George Davis. ¹I'm one of the students in your science class. I wanted to ask you about the required book for class.

P: Sure, George. Are you having difficulties with it? I noticed that you did not participate in the class discussion earlier.

S: Actually, the discussion was interesting. ²However, I didn't participate because I wasn't able to do the reading assignment before class.

P: Why not? Have you been busy with other work?

S: ¹No. Um, the issue is that I wasn't able to buy the required book.

P: I see. Did you check the campus bookstore?

S: Yes, I went right away after I signed up for your class, but the bookstore didn't have any copies.

P: Right. This happens every year. The bookstore only buys a small number of books at the start of the semester. So not everyone is able to buy one.

S: But why doesn't the bookstore just order more copies?

P: ³It's part of a university policy. The university doesn't let the campus bookstore order more than a limited number of books. That way, they can use the money they save for other important uses, like buying office equipment.

S: But then, what are students supposed to do when they can't find a book? ⁴That policy doesn't seem fair. It makes it harder for students to find the books they need.

P: I agree. However, many students cancel their classes after signing up. Um, this happens in the first few weeks of the semester. These students may sell their books to other students.

S: ⁵Oh... So does that mean I can still buy the book from another student?

P: Yes, but you might have to wait one or two weeks... Oh, but hold on. Actually, I have the book right here. You could borrow my book and make copies of the pages you need for the reading assignment.

S: Really? That would be very helpful!

P: Hmm... Now that I think about it... I'll make copies for all of the students who don't have the book yet. I'll ask about that at our next class on Thursday.

S: That's a great idea. I think everyone would appreciate it, Professor Taylor.

학생과 교수 사이의 대화를 들으시오.

S: Taylor 교수님? 음, 저는 George Davis입니다. 저는 교수님의 과학 수업 수강생 중 한 명이에요. 교수님께 수업 필수 도서에 관해 여쭤보고 싶었어요.

P: 물론이지, George. 그것에 관한 어려움이 있니? 예전에 네가 수업 토론에 참여하지 않는다는 걸 알아챘단다.

S: 사실, 토론은 흥미로웠어요. 하지만, 수업 전에 읽기 과제를 할 수 없었기 때문에 참여하지 않았어요.

P: 왜 하지 않았니? 다른 일로 바빴니?

S: 아뇨. 음, 문제는 제가 필수 도서를 구입할 수 없었다는 거예요.

P: 그렇구나. 캠퍼스 서점은 확인했니?

S: 네, 교수님 수업에 등록한 후에 곧바로 갔는데, 서점에는 한 부도 없었어요.

P: 그렇구나. 이런 일은 매년 일어난단다. 그 서점은 학기가 시작할 때 적은 수의 도서만을 구입하지. 그래서 모두가 하나씩 살 수는 없어.

S: 그런데 그 서점은 왜 그냥 더 많은 부수를 주문하지 않나요?

P: 그건 대학 정책의 일부야. 대학은 캠퍼스 서점이 제한된 수의 도서보다 더 많이 주문하도록 허락하지 않아. 그렇게 하면, 그들이 아낀 돈을 사무용 비품 구입 같은 다른 중요한 용도로 사용할 수 있지.

S: 하지만 그러면, 학생들은 도서를 찾을 수 없을 때 어떻게 해야 하나요? 그 정책은 타당해 보이지 않아요. 그것은 학생들이 필요한 도서를 찾는 것을 더 어렵게 만들잖아요.

P: 나도 동의한단다. 하지만, 많은 학생들이 등록한 이후에 수강을 취소해. 음, 이런 일은 학기의 초반 몇 주에 일어나지. 이 학생들이 그들의 도서를 다른 학생들에게 판매할 수도 있어.

S: 오... 그러면 그건 제가 여전히 다른 학생에게 그 도서를 구입할 수 있다는 의미인가요?

P: 맞아, 하지만 너는 한 두 주를 기다려야 할지도 몰라... 오, 기다려보거라. 사실, 내가 그 도서를 바로 여기 가지고 있구나. 네가 내 도서를 빌려서 읽기 과제에 필요한 페이지들의 사본을 만들 수 있겠어.

S: 정말요? 그거 정말 도움이 되겠네요!

P: 흠... 지금 와서 생각해 보니... 아직 그 도서가 없는 학생들 모두를 위해 내가 사본을 만들게. 목요일에 있는 우리의 다음 수업 때 내가 그것에 대해 물어보마.

S: 좋은 생각이네요. 모두가 그것에 감사할 것 같아요, Taylor 교수님.

required 형 필수의   participate in ~에 참여하다
discussion 명 토론   assignment 명 과제   right away 곧바로
limited 형 제한된   office equipment 사무용 비품
fair 형 타당한; 공평한   appreciate 동 감사하다

1 화자들은 주로 무엇을 논의하고 있는가?

(A) 학생의 수업 성적
(B) 수업을 위한 도서의 입수 가능성
(C) 교수의 수업 규칙
(D) 수업 과제물의 주제

2 학생은 왜 토론에 참여할 수 없었는가?

(A) 그는 다른 과제물들로 바빴다.
(B) 그는 자료를 읽지 않았다.
(C) 그는 수업이 어렵다고 생각했다.
(D) 그는 주제에 관심이 없었다.

3 교수는 대학의 도서 주문 정책에 관해 무엇이라고 말하는가?

(A) 그것은 매년 갱신된다.
(B) 그것은 학생들에게 도서를 더 저렴하게 만든다.
(C) 그것은 학교가 비용을 절감하는 데 도움을 준다.
(D) 그것은 서점에 의해 추천되었다.

4 대학 정책에 대한 학생의 의견은 무엇인가?

(A) 그것은 학교의 직원들에게 이로울 것이다.
(B) 그것은 더 많은 대학에서 사용되어야 한다.
(C) 그것은 학생들에게 더 잘 설명될 수 있다.
(D) 그것은 학생들에게 상황을 어렵게 만들지도 모른다.

대화의 일부를 다시 듣고 질문에 답하시오.

S: Oh... So does that mean I can still buy the book from another student?

P: Yes, but you might have to wait one or two weeks... Oh, but hold on. Actually, I have the book right here. You could borrow my book and make copies of the pages you need for the reading assignment.

5 교수는 왜 이렇게 말하는가:

P: Oh, but hold on.

(A) 다른 문제를 지적하기 위해
(B) 요청에 관한 그녀의 혼란을 표현하기 위해
(C) 그녀에게 다른 해결책이 있음을 보여주기 위해
(D) 절차가 얼마나 오래 걸릴 수 있는지를 강조하기 위해

---

iBT Listening Test 2   본문 p. 28

1 (D)   2 (B)   3 (A)   4 (B)   5 (C)   6 (C)

Note-taking
Development of Film Noir

- Film noir = popular in 1940s, dark stories about crime
- Inspired by German artists
  - Violence of WWI → dark subjects (e.g. crime)
  - Small budget ∴ painted walls dark & light
- Hollywood = European ideas mixed w/ American
  - Main characters (e.g. antihero, femme fatale)
  - Began w/ crime, always end well X
  - *The Maltese Falcon* = Sam Spade (antihero)
- 1950s new forms = darker theme & complex character

Listen to part of a lecture in a film class.

P: Imagine a scene from a black-and-white movie... A man in a coat is walking down a city street at night. It is raining and the street is full of shadows... It's the kind of scene you might see in the typical film noir movie. ¹Film noir is a style of film that was popular in the 1940s. Its name came from the French word for *black* because it often involved dark stories about crime. Let's talk about how it developed.

Film noir movies were partly inspired by German artists who painted about the negative aspects of modern life in Germany. [2]But, uh, German filmmakers were also greatly affected by the shocking violence of World War I. This caused them to make films about dark subjects, like crime and horror. Changes in the German film industry also influenced the appearance of film noir. [3]In the early 1900s, many German filmmakers had to work with small budgets because of the country's economic problems. So, instead of lighting scenes with expensive equipment, they painted walls in dark and light colors. Later, other Europeans copied the unusual German films. And, before World War II started, many of these European filmmakers left Europe to work in Hollywood.

In Hollywood, European ideas mixed with American ones. This led to the creation of film noir. [4]The Europeans created the appearance and feel of film noir, but the Americans added new elements like specific types of main characters. Two of the most common character types in film noir were the antihero and the femme fatale. The antihero was a male figure who did the right thing eventually but sometimes did bad things. The femme fatale was a woman who used her beauty to trick other people. Normally, stories began with a serious crime, such as a murder or robbery. This created dramatic tension that continued throughout the movie. And film noir stories did not always end well. Main characters often had unhappy endings.

Now, let's consider an example. One of the most famous film noir movies is called *The Maltese Falcon*. It was filmed in 1941. It includes Humphrey Bogart as a private detective named Sam Spade and Mary Astor as the femme fatale. [6]Before the movie came out, people thought detectives should be like Sherlock Holmes, who had many positive qualities. Sam Spade surprised viewers. He was an antihero who enjoyed being violent toward criminals. During the movie, he even smiles at a character just before punching him in the face.

Film noir's popularity grew throughout the 1940s. Around the world, other filmmakers copied the appearance, characters, and stories about crime. [5]However, by the 1950s, new forms of film noir developed that had darker themes and more complex characters and stories. Since then, generations of filmmakers have continued to make movies that are inspired by film noir.

영화학 강의의 일부를 들으시오.

P: 흑백 영화의 한 장면을 상상해 보세요... 코트를 입은 남자가 밤에 도시의 거리를 따라 걷고 있습니다. 비가 내리고 있고 거리는 그림자로 가득해요... 전형적인 필름 누아르 영화에서 볼 법한 장면이죠. 필름 누아르는 1940년대에 인기 있었던 영화 스타일입니다. 그것의 이름은 '검은색'을 뜻하는 프랑스어 단어에서 유래했는데, 이는 그것이 종종 범죄에 관한 어두운 이야기를 포함했기 때문이에요. 그것이 어떻게 발전했는지에 대해 얘기해 봅시다.

필름 누아르 영화들은 독일의 현대적 삶의 부정적인 측면들에 대

해 그림을 그렸던 독일 예술가들에게 부분적으로 영감을 받았습니다. 하지만, 어, 독일의 영화 제작자들은 제1차 세계대전의 충격적인 폭력으로부터 크게 영향을 받기도 했죠. 이것은 그들로 하여금 범죄와 공포 같은 어두운 주제들에 대한 영화를 만들도록 했어요. 독일 영화 산업의 변화 또한 필름 누아르의 겉모습에 영향을 미쳤어요. 1900년대 초반에, 많은 독일 영화 제작자들은 국가의 경제적 문제들 때문에 적은 예산으로 작업해야 했습니다. 그래서, 비싼 장비로 장면들을 밝히는 대신, 그들은 벽을 어둡고 밝은색들로 칠했어요. 나중에, 다른 유럽인들은 그 독특한 독일 영화들을 모방했어요. 그리고, 제2차 세계대전이 시작되기 전에, 이 유럽 영화 제작자들의 다수가 할리우드에서 일하기 위해 유럽을 떠났어요.

할리우드에서, 유럽의 아이디어들이 미국의 것들과 혼합되었어요. 이는 필름 누아르의 창시로 이어졌죠. 유럽인들이 필름 누아르의 겉모습과 느낌을 만들어냈지만, 미국인들은 독특한 유형의 주인공들 같은 새로운 요소들을 더했어요. 필름 누아르에서 가장 흔한 인물 유형 중 둘은 안티히어로와 팜파탈이었습니다. 안티히어로는 결국 옳은 일을 하지만 가끔 나쁜 짓을 하는 남성 인물이었어요. 팜파탈은 아름다움을 이용해 다른 사람들을 속이는 여성이었어요. 보통, 이야기들은 살인이나 강도 같은 심각한 범죄와 함께 시작되었습니다. 이것은 영화 내내 지속되는 극적인 긴장감을 만들어냈죠. 그리고 필름 누아르의 이야기가 항상 좋게 끝나는 것은 아니었어요. 주인공들은 종종 불행한 결말을 맞았습니다.

이제, 예시를 하나 생각해 봅시다. 가장 유명한 필름 누아르 영화 중 하나는 '말타의 매'입니다. 1941년에 촬영되었죠. 그것은 샘 스페이드라는 사립 탐정 역의 험프리 보가트와 팜파탈 역의 메리 애스터를 포함합니다. 그 영화가 나오기 전에, 사람들은 탐정이 많은 긍정적인 자질을 가진 셜록 홈스 같아야 한다고 생각했어요. 샘 스페이드는 관객들을 놀라게 했어요. 그는 범죄자들에게 폭력적으로 구는 것을 즐기는 안티히어로였죠. 영화 중에, 그는 심지어 한 인물의 얼굴에 주먹을 날리기 직전에 미소를 지어요.

필름 누아르의 인기는 1940년대 내내 증가했습니다. 전 세계에서, 다른 영화 제작자들은 겉모습, 인물, 범죄에 대한 이야기들을 모방했어요. 하지만, 1950년대 무렵에, 더 어두운 주제와 더 복잡한 인물과 이야기를 가진 새로운 형태의 필름 누아르가 발전하기 시작했죠. 그 이후로, 여러 세대의 영화 제작자들은 필름 누아르에서 영감을 받은 영화들을 계속해서 만들어 오고 있습니다.

---

typical 혱 전형적인   involve 통 포함하다   partly 뷔 부분적으로
aspect 몡 측면   filmmaker 몡 영화 제작자
appearance 몡 겉모습, 외관   budget 몡 예산   element 몡 요소
figure 몡 인물   robbery 몡 강도   tension 몡 긴장감
detective 몡 탐정, 형사   violent 혱 폭력적인

1 강의는 주로 무엇에 관한 것인가?
  (A) 몇몇 영화들이 흑백인 이유
  (B) 할리우드 영화에서 예술가들의 역할
  (C) 범죄에 대한 영화들이 만들어지는 방식
  (D) 영화 스타일의 발전

2 교수에 따르면, 제1차 세계대전은 독일의 영화 제작자들에게 어떤 영향을 미쳤는가?
  (A) 그것은 그들이 전쟁에 대한 영화를 만들게 했다.
  (B) 그것은 그들이 어두운 주제에 대한 작품들을 만들게 했다.

(C) 그것은 독일에 대한 그들의 견해를 바꾸었다.

(D) 그것은 그들이 범죄자들과 함께 작업하도록 강요했다.

3 교수에 따르면, 독일의 영화 제작자들은 왜 벽을 어둡고 밝은색들로 칠했는가?

(A) 그들은 비용을 절약해야 했다.

(B) 그들은 미국 예술가들에게 영감을 받았다.

(C) 그들은 유럽의 스타일을 모방하고 싶어 했다.

(D) 그들은 낮은 품질의 카메라를 가지고 있었다.

4 미국의 영화 제작자들은 필름 누아르에 무엇을 기여했는가?

(A) 카메라 기술의 사용

(B) 독특한 주요 인물 유형들

(C) 히어로와 안티히어로

(D) 단순하고 행복한 결말

5 교수에 따르면, 1950년대 무렵에 필름 누아르에 어떤 일이 일어났는가?

(A) 그것은 많은 외국 영화에 영감을 주었다.

(B) 그것은 계속해서 인기가 증가했다.

(C) 그것은 더 어둡고 더 복잡하게 되었다.

(D) 그것은 긍정적인 주제들에 초점을 맞추기 시작했다.

강의의 일부를 다시 듣고 질문에 답하시오.

P: Before the movie came out, people thought detectives should be like Sherlock Holmes, who had many positive qualities. Sam Spade surprised viewers. He was an antihero who enjoyed being violent toward criminals. During the movie, he even smiles at a character just before punching him in the face.

6 교수는 이렇게 말함으로써 무엇을 암시하는가:
P: Sam Spade surprised viewers.

(A) 샘 스페이드의 성격은 셜록 홈스를 기반으로 했다.

(B) 관객들은 보통 영화에서 폭력을 보지 않았다.

(C) 샘 스페이드는 긍정적인 자질들을 많이 가지고 있지 않았다.

(D) 샘 스페이드를 연기한 배우는 유명하지 않았다.

Vocabulary Review 본문 p. 32

1 notify
2 ecosystem
3 continent
4 outgoing
5 exception
6 behavior
7 tension
8 approval
9 budget
10 (A)
11 (C)
12 (C)
13 (A)
14 (D)

Example 본문 p. 35

A. (C)   **B.** (A), (C)

A.

Note-taking
S: Reading textbook, some lessons difficult
P: Join study group
   Understand X → another student can explain

Listen to a conversation between a student and a professor.

S: Excuse me, Professor Gibson. Are we still going to have the biology test next month?

P: Yes, of course. It will happen on October 18. I've already placed this on the schedule. Are you worried about taking it?

S: Um, a little bit. I've been reading the textbook for class, but some of the lessons are difficult.

P: Well, let me give you some advice. I recommend that you join a study group. It will help you understand the lessons in the book.

S: You mean review the lessons with other students from the class?

P: Yes, exactly. That way, if you don't understand a lesson, another student can explain it to you.

학생과 교수 사이의 대화를 들으시오.

S: 실례합니다, Gibson 교수님. 저희가 여전히 다음 달에 생물학 시험을 보나요?

P: 그럼, 물론이지. 그것은 10월 18일에 있을 거야. 이미 일정에 넣었단다. 그것을 보는 게 걱정되니?

S: 음, 약간이요. 수업 교과서를 읽었는데, 몇몇 과가 어려워서요.

P: 음, 내가 약간의 조언을 해주마. 네가 스터디 그룹에 참여하는 것을 추천한단다. 그것은 네가 그 책의 과들을 이해하는 데 도움을 줄 거야.

S: 수업의 다른 학생들과 함께 과를 복습하는 걸 말씀하시는 건가요?

P: 그래, 맞아. 그렇게 하면, 네가 어떤 과를 이해하지 못하면, 다른 학생이 네게 그것을 설명해줄 수 있지.

biology 명 생물학   textbook 명 교과서   lesson 명 (교과서의) 과
advice 명 조언   review 동 복습하다

교수는 학생에게 무엇을 하라고 추천하는가?

(A) 여러 개의 연습 시험 보기

(B) 교과서를 면밀히 읽기

(C) 다른 학생들과 공부하기

(D) 수업 중에 질문하기

B.

Note-taking

Green Roofs

- Green roofs = great for environment
  - Reduce carbon dioxide & provide habitat for birds
  - Lifespan of roof ↑ & keep buildings cool
- Intensive & extensive, difference = soil use
  - Intensive = soil > 1 m ∴ support plants
  - Extensive = soil ↓ ∴ cover wide, other uses X

Listen to part of a lecture in a city planning class.

P: One problem with urban environments is the lack of trees and plants. And one solution is to build green roofs. Green roofs are great for the environment because they reduce carbon dioxide in the atmosphere and provide a habitat for birds. ^AMoreover, they can increase the lifespan of a roof by absorbing rainwater... ^CPlus, green roofs keep buildings cool, which means there is less need for air conditioning.

Now, there are two types of green roofs: intensive and extensive. The main difference between them is how much soil is used. An intensive roof can have soil that's more than a meter deep. So it supports lots of plants. An extensive green roof has less soil. It is good for covering a wide area with grass, but it doesn't have many other uses.

도시 계획학 강의의 일부를 들으시오.

P: 도시 환경의 한 가지 문제는 나무와 식물의 부족입니다. 그리고 한 가지 해결책은 녹화된 옥상을 만드는 것이죠. 녹화된 옥상은 대기 중의 이산화탄소를 줄이고 새들에게 서식지를 제공하기 때문에 환경에 이로워요. 게다가, 그것들은 빗물을 흡수함으로써 옥상의 수명을 늘릴 수 있어요... 이에 더해, 녹화된 옥상은 건물을 시원하게 유지하는데, 이는 냉방의 필요성이 더 작다는 걸 의미해요.

자, 녹화된 옥상에는 집약형과 포괄형 두 종류가 있습니다. 그것들 사이의 주요 차이점은 얼마나 많은 흙이 사용되는가예요. 집약형 옥상에는 1미터가 넘는 깊이의 흙이 있을 수 있어요. 그래서 그것은 많은 식물들을 부양하죠. 포괄형 옥상에는 더 적은 흙이 있어요. 그것은 넓은 구역을 풀로 덮는 데는 좋지만, 다른 용도는 많지 않아요.

urban 형 도시의   lack 명 부족   green roof 녹화된 옥상
carbon dioxide 이산화탄소   atmosphere 명 대기
habitat 명 서식지   lifespan 명 수명   absorb 동 흡수하다
air conditioning 냉(난)방   intensive 형 집약적인
extensive 형 포괄적인

녹화된 옥상의 두 가지 장점은 무엇인가? 2개의 답을 고르시오.

(A) 그것들은 물을 흡수함으로써 옥상이 더 오래 지속되도록 돕는다.

(B) 그것들은 유지 보수를 거의 필요로 하지 않음으로써 비용을 아껴준다.

(C) 그것들은 건물을 시원하게 유지함으로써 에너지를 절감한다.

(D) 그것들은 휴식을 위한 공간을 제공함으로써 도시 생활을 개선한다.

---

1 (B)   **2** (C)   **3** (A)   **4** (C)   **5** (D)

Note-taking

M: Parents coming, need place to stay
   Want room on campus ∵ hotels = expensive
W: Rooms @ conference center, reserved months before
   Rooms = usu. $75, but $45/night for student
M: Places to see?
W: Sugar Falls = close, bus goes twice/day, swimming O
M: Parents prefer art & culture
W: Metro. Art Gallery = special exhibit., transportation O

Listen to a conversation between a student and a university employee.

W: Good morning, and welcome to the student center. How can I help you?

M: ^1Hi, I'd like to ask about rooms. Um, my parents are coming to visit and they need a place to stay. They're watching me play in a music concert.

W: That's wonderful. There are some good hotels nearby.

M: Oh, actually, I'd like them to have a room on campus. Um, most of the hotels in the area are expensive.

W: I see... ^2The university does have rooms at the conference center. But they're usually reserved several months before an event. When are your parents coming?

M: Um, the concert is on Saturday, May 7. They will be here on Friday and stay for two nights.

W: All right, let me check... Oh, we actually have a couple of rooms that can be used on those nights. I can make a reservation now if you'd like...

M: That's great. Um, how much is it for each night?

W: ^5Well, a room usually costs $75 a night. But, because you're a student here, it would just be $45. That's much cheaper than a hotel.

M: I agree! Just one more thing. My parents want to see the city. However, I've only been a student here for a couple of months, so I don't really know where to take them. Could you, uh, recommend some places to see?

W: ^3Oh, Sugar Falls is a good option... It's close and it's really easy to get there. A bus goes from the conference center to the falls twice a day. You can even go swimming if you like. There's more information on the city's website.

M: ^4Actually, is there anything else? My parents don't like doing things outside or being in nature. They prefer art and culture.

W: Then, what about the Metropolitan Art Gallery downtown? They have a special exhibition right now. Plus, transportation is not a problem. You can take a taxi or a bus to get there.

M: That sounds good. Thanks for your help!

학생과 교직원 사이의 대화를 들으시오.

W: 좋은 아침입니다, 그리고 학생지원센터에 오신 것을 환영합니다. 어떻게 도와드릴까요?

M: 안녕하세요, 방에 관해 문의하고 싶은데요. 음, 저희 부모님이 방문하러 오시는데 머물 장소가 필요해요. 부모님께서 제가 음악 콘서트에서 연주하는 걸 보실 거예요.

W: 멋지네요. 근처에 좋은 호텔이 몇 개 있어요.

M: 오, 사실, 저는 부모님이 캠퍼스에 있는 방을 쓰셨으면 해요. 음, 이 지역의 호텔 대부분이 비싸거든요.

W: 그렇군요... 대학은 학회장에 방들을 가지고 있어요. 그런데 그것들은 보통 행사 수개월 전에 예약된답니다. 부모님이 언제 오시나요?

M: 음, 콘서트는 5월 7일 토요일이에요. 부모님은 금요일에 오셔서 이틀 밤 동안 머무실 거예요.

W: 알겠어요, 확인해 볼게요... 오, 사실 그날 밤들에 이용할 수 있는 방이 두어 개 있네요. 원하시면 제가 지금 예약해 드릴게요...

M: 잘됐네요. 음, 하룻밤에 얼마인가요?

W: 음, 방은 보통 하룻밤에 75달러예요. 그런데, 여기 학생이시니까, 45달러가 될 거예요. 호텔보다 훨씬 저렴하죠.

M: 동의해요! 한 가지만 더요. 저희 부모님이 도시를 구경하고 싶어 하세요. 하지만, 저는 겨우 두어 달 동안 이곳의 학생이었어요, 그래서 그들을 어디에 모시고 갈지 잘 모르겠어요. 어, 구경할 만한 몇몇 장소들을 추천해주실 수 있으신가요?

W: 오, Sugar Falls는 좋은 선택지예요... 그것은 가깝고 가기에도 정말 쉬워요. 하루에 두 번 버스가 학회장에서 그 폭포로 가요. 원하시면 심지어 수영하러 갈 수도 있어요. 시 웹사이트에 더 많은 정보가 있어요.

M: 사실은, 다른 게 있나요? 저희 부모님은 밖에서 무언가를 하거나 자연 속에 있는 것을 좋아하지 않으세요. 부모님은 예술과 문화를 선호하시거든요.

W: 그러면, 시내에 있는 Metropolitan Art Gallery는 어떤가요? 그들은 지금 특별 전시회를 열고 있어요. 게다가, 교통은 문제가 아니에요. 거기에 가기 위해 택시나 버스를 탈 수 있죠.

M: 좋네요. 도와주셔서 감사해요!

nearby 툰 근처에   make a reservation 예약하다   falls 명 폭포
prefer 통 선호하다   exhibition 명 전시회   plus 툰 게다가
transportation 명 교통

1 대화는 주로 무엇에 관한 것인가?

(A) 콘서트 티켓을 구매하는 것
(B) 방문객을 위한 방을 찾는 것
(C) 호텔 예약을 변경하는 것
(D) 행사에 참가자들을 초대하는 것

2 직원은 학회장의 방들에 관해 무엇이라고 말하는가?

(A) 그것들은 이틀 밤 동안만 이용될 수 있다.
(B) 그것들은 현재 수리를 위해 닫혀있다.
(C) 그것들은 보통 미리 예약된다.
(D) 그것들은 반드시 온라인으로 지불되어야 한다.

3 Sugar Falls에 가는 것의 장점은 무엇인가?

(A) 그것은 대학에서 가깝다.
(B) 그것은 특별 전시회를 열 것이다.

(C) 그것은 방문하기에 조용한 장소이다.
(D) 그것은 도시 최대의 관광 명소이다.

4 학생은 왜 직원에게 다른 선택지들에 대해 문의하는가?

(A) 그는 교통에 대해 걱정한다.
(B) 그의 아버지는 문화 행사들을 좋아하지 않는다.
(C) 그의 부모님은 야외 활동을 즐기지 않는다.
(D) 그는 활동 비용에 대해 걱정한다.

대화의 일부를 다시 듣고 질문에 답하시오.

W: Well, a room usually costs $75 a night. But, because you're a student here, it would just be $45. That's much cheaper than a hotel.

M: I agree! Just one more thing. My parents want to see the city.

5 학생은 이렇게 말함으로써 무엇을 의미하는가:

M: Just one more thing.

(A) 그는 더 저렴한 선택지를 원한다.
(B) 그는 계획에 관한 그의 생각을 바꾸었다.
(C) 그는 방을 한 개 더 예약하고 싶어 한다.
(D) 그는 더 많은 도움이 필요하다.

Listening Practice 2   본문 p. 39

1 (B)   2 (D)   3 (D)   4 (C)   5 (A)

Note-taking
Sharing Economy

- Sharing econ. = buyers & sellers share resources
- Share underused asset (e.g. car, skill) for $
- Sharing econ. = revolution
  - Econ. efficiency = sellers make $, buyers save $
  - Spread of digital platform = get instant access
- E.g. eBay (buy & sell products) & Uber (share car)
- Sharing econ. = 6% in 2013 → half of all by 2025

Listen to part of a lecture in an economics class.

P: These days, the business environment is changing rapidly. ¹And one of the outcomes of these changes has been the growth of the sharing economy. Um, the sharing economy is an economic system in which individual buyers and sellers share resources. Let's discuss this in more detail...

Um, so, in the sharing economy, people do business by sharing underused assets. An asset is anything that has value to someone else. It can be a physical object like a car or even a skill like designing a website. When these assets are not used all the time, they are called underused assets. The sharing economy lets people share underused assets in exchange for money.

²In recent years, more and more people have been joining the sharing economy. It is truly an economic revolution. There are many reasons for this, but I'll just give a couple... The first is

economic efficiency. People have learned that they can maximize economic efficiency through sharing. This allows sellers to make money and buyers to save money. Uh, the second reason is the spread of digital platforms and devices. [3]With digital technology like apps and smartphones, people can get instant access to sellers and buyers from all over the world… In this way, sharing through digital technology contributes to economic globalization…

Now, let's look at a couple of well-known examples to help us understand the sharing economy better… One good example is eBay. eBay lets people buy and sell products directly… [4]Uh, imagine that you have a hobby, like making jewelry… Where would you sell them? Most likely, you'd use a digital platform like eBay. By using eBay, you don't have to open a physical store or even a personal website. You can simply join the sharing economy… Another example is Uber. Uber allows people to share the use of a car… Anyone with a car can make money by offering ride services through Uber. And riders can use an app to instantly order the service. By sharing the car, the owner can make extra money… And the rider can save money by renting a ride instead of buying their own car.

The success of companies like eBay and Uber has attracted many companies to the sharing economy. It is one of the fastest-growing parts of the global economy. [5]Um, according to a study, the sharing economy was less than 6 percent of all markets in 2013… But, by 2025, researchers expect it to be around half of all markets.

경제학 강의의 일부를 들으시오.

P: 요즘, 사업 환경이 빠르게 변화하고 있습니다. 그리고 이러한 변화들의 결과 중 하나는 공유 경제의 성장이에요. 음, 공유 경제는 그 안에서 개인 구매자와 판매자들이 자원을 공유하는 경제 시스템입니다. 이것에 대해 좀 더 자세히 논의해 봅시다…

음, 그러니까, 공유 경제에서, 사람들은 충분히 활용되지 않는 자산을 공유함으로써 사업을 합니다. 자산이란 다른 사람에게 가치가 있는 모든 것이죠. 그것은 자동차 같은 물체일 수도 있고 심지어는 웹사이트를 디자인하는 것 같은 기술일 수도 있어요. 이러한 자산들이 항상 사용되는 것이 아닌 경우, 그것들은 충분히 활용되지 않는 자산이라고 불려요. 공유 경제는 사람들이 돈을 받는 대가로 충분히 활용되지 않는 자산을 공유하게 해주죠.

최근 몇 년간, 점점 더 많은 사람들이 공유 경제에 참여해 왔어요. 그것은 진정한 경제 혁명이에요. 여기에는 많은 이유가 있지만, 두 가지만 들어볼게요… 첫 번째는 경제적 효율성입니다. 사람들은 공유를 통해 경제적 효율성을 극대화할 수 있다는 걸 알게 됐어요. 이는 판매자들에게는 돈을 벌게 해주고 구매자들에게는 돈을 절약하게 해줍니다. 어, 두 번째 이유는 디지털 플랫폼과 장치의 확산이에요. 애플리케이션과 스마트폰 같은 디지털 기술을 통해, 사람들은 전 세계의 판매자들과 구매자들에게 즉시 접근할 수 있습니다… 이러한 방식으로, 디지털 기술을 통한 공유는 경제의 세계화에 기여해요…

이제, 우리가 공유 경제를 더 잘 이해하는 데 도움이 되는 두 가지의 유명한 예시를 살펴봅시다… 한 가지 좋은 예시는 이베이에요. 이베이는 사람들이 직접 제품을 사고팔게 해줘요… 어, 여러분에게 보석 만들기와 같은 취미가 있다고 상상해 보세요… 그것들을

어디에서 판매할 건가요? 아마도, 여러분은 이베이 같은 디지털 플랫폼을 이용할 거예요. 이베이를 이용함으로써, 여러분은 실제 상점이나 개인 웹사이트조차 개설할 필요가 없어요. 여러분은 간단히 공유 경제에 참여할 수 있죠… 또 다른 예시는 우버예요. 우버는 사람들이 자동차의 사용을 공유할 수 있게 해줘요… 자동차를 가진 사람이라면 누구든지 우버를 통해 승차 서비스를 제공함으로써 돈을 벌 수 있죠. 그리고 승객은 애플리케이션을 이용해서 즉시 서비스를 주문할 수 있어요. 자동차를 공유함으로써, 주인은 여분의 돈을 벌 수 있습니다… 그리고 승객은 자신의 자동차를 구매하는 대신 차편을 대여함으로써 돈을 절약할 수 있어요.

이베이와 우버 같은 회사들의 성공은 많은 회사들을 공유 경제로 끌어들였어요. 그것은 세계 경제에서 가장 빠르게 성장하는 부문 중 하나입니다. 음, 한 연구에 따르면, 공유 경제는 2013년에 전체 시장의 6퍼센트 미만이었어요… 그런데, 2025년까지, 연구자들은 그것이 전체 시장의 절반 정도가 될 것으로 예상하고 있어요.

outcome 명 결과 sharing economy 공유 경제 resource 명 자원
underused 형 충분히 활용되지 않는 asset 명 자산
in exchange for ~을 대가로 revolution 명 혁명
efficiency 명 효율성 spread 명 확산 contribute to ~에 기여하다
globalization 명 세계화 instantly 부 즉시 attract 동 끌어들이다

1 강의는 주로 무엇에 관한 것인가?

(A) 현대 소비자들의 변화하는 태도

(B) 경제 시스템의 성장

(C) 많은 자산을 갖는 것의 장점

(D) 서로 다른 사업 환경의 유사성

2 공유 경제에 대한 교수의 태도는 무엇인가?

(A) 그녀는 그것이 너무 커지고 있음을 걱정한다.

(B) 그녀는 그것이 제품들을 더 비싸게 만들 것이라고 생각한다.

(C) 그녀는 그것이 사회에 부정적인 영향을 미친다고 생각한다.

(D) 그녀는 그것이 경제에 많은 변화를 일으켰다고 생각한다.

3 교수에 따르면, 디지털 기술은 어떻게 경제의 세계화에 기여하는가?

(A) 그것은 회사들이 국제적인 파트너들을 찾을 수 있게 해준다.

(B) 그것은 제품을 해외로 배송하는 것의 비용을 낮춘다.

(C) 그것은 사업체들이 세계적으로 서로 경쟁하게 만든다.

(D) 그것은 전 세계의 개인들에 대한 접근을 제공한다.

4 교수는 왜 보석 만들기를 언급하는가?

(A) 사람들이 창업을 위해 가지고 있는 흔한 아이디어를 명시하기 위해

(B) 공유 경제에 속한 몇몇 사람들이 부유하다는 것을 보여주기 위해

(C) 디지털 플랫폼에서 볼 수 있는 사업의 예시를 제공하기 위해

(D) 종종 충분히 활용되지 않는 자산의 종류를 설명하기 위해

5 연구자들은 공유 경제의 미래에 관해 무엇이라고 말하는가?

(A) 그것은 시장에서 더 큰 비중을 차지할 것이다.

(B) 그것은 많은 근로자들이 그들의 직장을 떠나도록 강요할 것이다.

(C) 그것은 더 많은 사업이 온라인에서 이루어지게 만들 것이다.

(D) 그것은 오늘날보다 느린 속도로 성장할 것이다.

1 (A)   2 (C)   3 (B)   4 (C)   5 (B)

Note-taking

W: Dance competition next month, cost money (e.g. hotel)
M: Univ. pay only for activities on campus
W: Hold event to raise money, how?
M: Need school's permission → fill out form
　 Keep record of $, only for club, for trip O
W: Drama club popular, do sth. similar = dance perform.
　 Exact date X, need to talk to club members
M: Decide quickly ∵ find a place take time

Listen to a conversation between a student and a student activities office employee.

W: Hi. I'm looking for the student activities office. ¹I'm the president of the dance club and I have some questions about holding an event on campus.

M: Yes... What would you like to know?

W: Um, our club will be joining a dance competition in Seattle next month. But it's going to cost a lot of money. We have to pay for hotel rooms, transportation, and meals for all the members...

M: ²I'm sorry, but the university cannot pay for all of those things. The school's policy is to pay only for activities on campus.

W: Oh, I understand. What I mean is, um, we would like to hold an event on campus to raise some money. I just wasn't sure how to organize it.

M: I see. In that case, you will need the school's permission first. Fill out this form and return it to me when you're done.

W: Thank you. But, uh, are there other requirements we should know about?

M: Certainly. Um, the most important one is to keep a record of the money you make from the event. And you need to show how the money was spent. The money can only be used for club-related activities.

W: Got it. But, um, will it be OK to use the money for our trip, then?

M: That will be fine... ³Just make sure to turn in receipts after your trip. ⁵Now, um, what kind of event are you having?

W: Um, the drama club had a play last month... It seemed popular and the tickets were $10 each. We were thinking of doing something similar. Maybe we'll do a dance performance.

M: OK, and when do you want to hold the performance?

W: I'm not sure about the exact date yet... ⁴I'll need to talk about it with the other club members.

M: OK. Discuss it over the next couple of days. You'll need to decide quickly, though. You still need to find a place on campus for your event, and, uh, that also takes time.

학생과 학생활동과 사무실 직원 사이의 대화를 들으시오.

W: 안녕하세요. 학생활동과 사무실을 찾고 있는데요. 저는 춤 동아리 회장이고 캠퍼스에서 행사를 개최하는 것에 관해 질문이 몇 개 있어요.

M: 네... 무엇이 알고 싶으신가요?

W: 음, 저희 동아리는 다음 달에 시애틀에서 춤 대회에 참가할 예정이에요. 그런데 비용이 많이 들 거예요. 저희는 모든 회원을 위해 호텔 방, 교통, 식사를 위한 비용을 지불해야 하거든요...

M: 죄송하지만, 대학은 그것들 전부를 위한 비용을 지불할 수 없어요. 학교의 정책은 캠퍼스 내의 활동에만 비용을 지불하는 거예요.

W: 오, 이해해요. 제 말은, 음, 저희는 돈을 좀 모금하기 위해 캠퍼스에서 행사를 개최하고 싶어요. 저는 단지 그것을 어떻게 준비해야 할지 몰랐어요.

M: 그렇군요. 그런 경우라면, 먼저 학교의 허락이 필요할 거예요. 이 양식을 작성하시고 완료되면 저에게 돌려주세요.

W: 감사합니다. 그런데, 어, 저희가 알아야 하는 다른 요건들이 있나요?

M: 물론이죠. 음, 가장 중요한 것은 행사에서 모은 돈을 기록하는 거예요. 그리고 그 돈이 어떻게 사용되었는지 증명하셔야 해요. 그 돈은 동아리와 관련된 활동에만 사용될 수 있거든요.

W: 알겠습니다. 그런데, 음, 그러면, 그 돈을 저희의 여행을 위해 사용하는 것은 괜찮을까요?

M: 그건 괜찮을 거예요... 여행 후에 영수증을 제출하시는 것만 잊지 마세요. 자, 음, 어떤 종류의 행사를 개최하실 건가요?

W: 음, 연극 동아리가 지난달에 연극을 상연했어요... 인기가 있는 것 같았고 티켓은 각각 10달러였어요. 저희는 무언가 비슷한 것을 하는 걸 생각 중이었어요. 아마 저희는 춤 공연을 할 것 같아요.

M: 알겠어요, 그러면 공연을 언제 개최하시고 싶으세요?

W: 정확한 날짜에 대해서는 아직 잘 모르겠어요... 그것에 대해 다른 동아리 회원들과 얘기해봐야 해요.

M: 알겠어요. 다음 이틀 정도 동안 그것에 관해 논의해 보세요. 하지만, 빠르게 결정하셔야 해요. 학생은 여전히 캠퍼스에서 행사를 위한 장소를 찾아야 하고, 어, 그것에도 시간이 걸려요.

---

student activities office 학생활동과 사무실   president 명 회장
competition 명 대회   transportation 명 교통   policy 명 정책
raise money 돈을 모금하다   organize 통 준비하다, 조직하다
permission 명 허락   requirement 명 요건   receipt 명 영수증
exact 형 정확한

1 학생은 왜 학생활동과 사무실을 찾아가는가?

(A) 학교 행사를 위한 정보를 얻기 위해
(B) 다른 대학의 강의에 등록하기 위해
(C) 학생 동아리에 입회를 신청하기 위해
(D) 학생 공연의 좌석을 예약하기 위해

2 직원은 학교의 정책에 관해 무엇이라고 말하는가?

(A) 그것은 최근에 변경되었다.
(B) 그것은 일부 동아리에만 적용된다.
(C) 그것은 학교가 비용을 지불할 수 있는 것을 제한한다.
(D) 그것은 곧 회의에서 논의될 것이다.

3 여행이 끝날 때 학생은 무엇을 해야 하는가?

(A) 학생들에게 환불 제공하기

(B) 여행 영수증 제출하기

(C) 학교에 편지쓰기

(D) 은행 계좌에 돈 저금하기

4 학생은 다음에 무엇을 할 것인가?

(A) 교직원과 만나기

(B) 연극 동아리 행사에 참석하기

(C) 다른 동아리 회원들과 계획 논의하기

(D) 캠퍼스 내의 행사 장소 검토하기

대화의 일부를 다시 듣고 질문에 답하시오.

M: Now, um, what kind of event are you having?

W: Um, the drama club had a play last month... It seemed popular and the tickets were $10 each. We were thinking of doing something similar. Maybe we'll do a dance performance.

5 학생은 왜 이렇게 말하는가:

W: Um, the drama club had a play last month...

(A) 행사를 개최하는 것이 허용된다는 것을 보여주기 위해

(B) 성공적인 행사의 예를 들기 위해

(C) 행사가 연기된 이유를 설명하기 위해

(D) 행사 장소가 이용된 방법을 묘사하기 위해

Listening Practice 4

본문 p. 43

1 (C)   2 (B)   3 (D)   4 (A), (D)   5 (A)

Note-taking

IUU Fishing

- Illegal, unreported, unregulated fishing = IUU fishing
  - Illegal = violate law (e.g. natl., rgnl., intl.)
  - Unreported = fishers report less fish → more $
  - Unregulated = controlled X, usu. in intl. water
- Common factor = $, rare fish = high price
- Econ. & environ. consequences
  - $23 bil/y, impact on ocean ecosystem
- Regulation needed → recover for future gen.

Listen to part of a lecture in an environmental science class.

P: Fish is an important part of people's diets... I mean, over a billion people eat it every day. The demand is so great that some fishers will do almost anything... Unfortunately, this can lead to overfishing. ¹Although there are laws and agreements that regulate fishing, there are serious problems caused by illegal, unreported, and unregulated fishing, which is also called IUU fishing. Let's review each of these problems in detail.

So, uh, the first problem is illegal fishing. Illegal fishing is any fishing that violates the law. These laws may be national, regional, or international... They may include laws about a country's rivers,

lakes, and coastal waters... Then, the second problem is unreported fishing. Um, many times, fishers must report when, where, and how much fish they've caught. However, dishonest fishers may report less fish than they caught. By doing so, they can have more fish to sell for money. Finally, the third problem is unregulated fishing. This refers to fishing done in areas that aren't controlled by anyone. These areas are usually in international waters.

S: Um, what's wrong with that? ²It's not illegal to catch fish in international waters, right?

P: That's right. And it's because nobody owns international waters. However, it's still a big concern because it worsens the problem of overfishing.

Now, what is a common factor with each of these problems? Well, the reason they happen is because of money. The fishing industry makes a lot of money... Just think of the high demand for fish like tuna and salmon that we eat. ³And, the rarer the fish, the higher its price is on the market. This, of course, greatly contributes to IUU fishing...

Sadly, what these illegal fishers don't realize is the impact that their activities have on the planet. I mean, there are serious economic and environmental consequences. Um, there is an estimate that the global economic losses from IUU fishing are about $23 billion a year. ⁴ᴬThis includes income losses for those who fish legally. ⁴ᴰAnd then there is the impact of IUU fishing on ocean ecosystems... Fish are already suffering from the effects of global warming. But IUU fishing makes this even worse. And, as I said before, the demand for fish is quite high, and it only grows higher as the world's population keeps growing...

So this is why regulations are needed. ⁵Regulations allow fish populations to recover so that there is enough for future generations of people to eat... When IUU fishers violate these regulations, they not only threaten the survival of important fish but also an important food source for humans... Make no mistake... IUU fishing affects everyone.

환경 과학 강의의 일부를 들으시오.

P: 생선은 사람들의 식사에서 중요한 부분입니다... 그러니까, 10억 명 이상의 사람들이 그것을 매일 먹어요. 그 수요가 너무 커서 일부 어부들은 거의 무엇이든 다 할 거예요... 유감스럽게도, 이는 어류 남획으로 이어질 수 있죠. 어업을 규제하는 법률과 협정들이 있긴 하지만, 불법적이고, 보고되지 않으며, 규제되지 않은 어업에 의해 초래되는 심각한 문제들이 있으며, 이는 IUU 어업이라고 불리기도 합니다. 이 문제들 각각에 대해 자세히 검토해 봅시다.

그러니까, 어, 첫 번째 문제는 불법 어업입니다. 불법 어업은 법률을 위반하는 모든 어업이에요. 이 법률들은 국가적이거나, 지역적이거나, 국제적일 수 있어요... 그것들은 국가의 강, 호수, 해안 수역들에 대한 법률들을 포함할 수 있죠... 그다음, 두 번째 문제는 보고되지 않은 어업이에요. 음, 많은 경우에, 어부들은 언제, 어디서, 얼마나 많은 물고기를 잡았는지 반드시 보고해야 합니다. 하

지만, 부정직한 어부들은 그들이 잡은 것보다 더 적은 물고기를 신고할지도 몰라요. 그렇게 함으로써, 그들은 돈을 받고 판매할 수 있는 생선을 더 많이 가질 수 있죠. 마지막으로, 세 번째 문제는 규제되지 않은 어업입니다. 이것은 누구의 통제도 받지 않는 지역에서 행해지는 어업을 가리켜요. 이 지역들은 보통 공해에 있어요.

S: 음, 그게 무슨 문제가 있는 거죠? 공해에서 물고기를 잡는 건 불법이 아니잖아요, 그렇죠?

P: 맞아요. 그리고 그건 아무도 공해를 소유하고 있지 않기 때문이죠. 하지만, 그것이 어류 남획 문제를 악화시키기 때문에 여전히 큰 걱정거리예요.

자, 이 문제들 각각의 공통적인 요소는 무엇일까요? 음, 그것들이 일어나는 이유는 돈 때문이에요. 어업은 큰 수익을 얻거든요... 우리가 먹는 참치와 연어 같은 생선에 대한 높은 수요를 생각해 보세요. 그리고, 생선이 희귀할수록, 시장에서 그것의 가격은 더 높아집니다. 이건, 물론, IUU 어업에 크게 기여하죠...

안타깝게도, 이 불법적인 어부들이 깨닫지 못하는 것은 그들의 활동이 지구에 미치는 영향이에요. 그러니까, 심각한 경제적, 환경적 영향이 있다는 거예요. 음, IUU 어업으로 인한 세계적 경제 손실이 연간 약 230억 달러라는 추정이 있습니다. 이는 합법적으로 낚시를 하는 사람들의 소득 손실을 포함해요. 그리고 IUU 어업이 해양 생태계에 미치는 영향이 있습니다... 물고기들은 이미 지구 온난화의 영향으로 고통받고 있어요. 하지만 IUU 어업은 이것을 훨씬 더 악화시키죠. 그리고, 전에 말했듯이, 생선에 대한 수요는 꽤 높고, 세계의 인구수가 계속해서 증가함에 따라 그것은 더 높아질 수밖에 없어요...

그러니까 이것이 규제가 필요한 이유예요. 규제는 미래 세대의 사람들이 먹을 양이 충분하도록 물고기의 개체 수가 회복하도록 해줘요... IUU 어부들이 이 규제들을 위반하면, 그들은 중요한 어류의 생존을 위협하는 것일 뿐만 아니라 인간에게 중요한 식량 자원을 위협하는 것이기도 해요... 정말이에요... IUU 어업은 모두에게 영향을 미칩니다.

diet 명 식사, 식습관 demand 명 수요 overfishing 명 어류 남획
regulate 동 규제하다 illegal 형 불법적인
unreported 형 보고되지 않은 violate 동 위반하다
regional 형 지역적인 dishonest 형 부정직한
international water 공해 worsen 동 악화시키다
consequence 명 영향, 결과 ecosystem 명 생태계
suffer from ~으로 고통받다 threaten 동 위협하다

1 강의는 주로 무엇에 관한 것인가?

(A) 생태계에서 물고기의 중요성
(B) 어류 남획 문제에 대한 해결책
(C) 다양한 유형의 해로운 어업 관행들
(D) 어부들에 대한 일련의 규제들

2 공해에서의 어업에 대한 교수의 태도는 무엇인가?

(A) 그는 그것이 불법이어야 한다고 생각한다.
(B) 그는 합법적이라고 할지라도 그것이 문제라고 생각한다.
(C) 그는 그것이 몇몇 국가들에만 이롭다고 생각한다.
(D) 그는 그것이 해결하기에 쉽지 않은 문제라고 생각한다.

3 교수에 따르면, IUU 어업에 기여하는 요소는 무엇인가?

(A) 정부에 의해 제공되는 재정 지원
(B) 어선을 유지하는 비용

(C) 낚시하기에 좋은 장소의 부족
(D) 희귀한 생선 종의 높은 가격

4 교수는 IUU 어업의 영향에 대해 무엇이라고 말하는가? 2개의 답을 고르시오.

(A) 그것은 합법적인 어부들의 소득을 감소시킨다.
(B) 그것은 국가들 간의 갈등을 야기한다.
(C) 그것은 물고기들이 더 따뜻한 바다로 이동하도록 강제한다.
(D) 그것은 기존의 환경 문제를 악화시킨다.

강의의 일부를 다시 듣고 질문에 답하시오.

P: Regulations allow fish populations to recover so that there is enough for future generations of people to eat... When IUU fishers violate these regulations, they not only threaten the survival of important fish but also an important food source for humans... Make no mistake... IUU fishing affects everyone.

5 교수는 왜 이렇게 말하는가:

P: Make no mistake...

(A) 문제의 심각성을 강조하기 위해
(B) 문제가 오랜 시간 지속될 것이라고 말하기 위해
(C) 이전에 언급한 내용의 오류를 정정하기 위해
(D) 학생들에게 시험의 주제에 관해 상기시키기 위해

iBT Listening Test 1 본문 p. 45

1 (B) 2 (C) 3 (D) 4 (A) 5 (C)

Note-taking

S: Study-abroad program in England, difficult?
P: Usu. easier < regular courses
About Shakespeare & plays (e.g. *Hamlet*)
Will assign reading = about ancient Greek theater
Shakespeare's plays were inspired by Greek dramas
Other activities = watch *Macbeth*, visit hometown
Help fulfill degree, 4 weeks = shorter < normal

Listen to a conversation between a student and a professor.

S: Hi, Professor Williams. My name is Amelia. Do you have a minute? ¹I want to ask about the study-abroad program in England.

P: Sure, no problem. Are you interested in joining the one we're having this summer?

S: Yes, I think so. I mean, I've always wanted to visit England. But, uh, it's also my first year here. So I'm worried that the course will be difficult.

P: It shouldn't be that hard. Courses in the study-abroad program are usually easier than regular courses. What is your major, by the way?

S: It's English literature, but I especially like drama. I want to write plays for the theater one day.

P: ²Oh, then I'm sure my course will interest you. It will be all about Shakespeare and his plays.

We're going to study famous tragedies, like *Othello* and *Hamlet*.

S: Really? That's perfect. I've read some of his tragedies before.

P: That's good. ³I will also be assigning another reading before the course starts. It'll be about ancient Greek theater.

S: What does that have to do with Shakespeare?

P: Well, some of Shakespeare's plays were inspired by Greek dramas, so I think it's a good idea to understand the topic.

S: ⁵I see... Um, this all sounds great. But are we going to take any field trips while we're abroad? I'm not sure I want to spend the entire summer in a classroom.

P: Oh, don't worry about that. We'll definitely have other activities. For instance, we're going to watch a performance of Shakespeare's *Macbeth* at the Globe Theatre. We'll also visit his hometown, Stratford-upon-Avon...

S: Did you say the Globe Theatre? Isn't that the actual theater where Shakespeare's plays were performed?

P: No, but it looks just like the original one. I've been there several times and my students always love it.

S: That sounds exciting. ⁴Are there any other advantages to joining the program?

P: Yes, actually. Completing the course will help you fulfill your degree requirements. And it's only four weeks long. That's much shorter than a normal college semester.

S: Wow! That is great. Can I sign up today?

학생과 교수 사이의 대화를 들으시오.

S: 안녕하세요, Williams 교수님. 제 이름은 Amelia입니다. 잠깐 시간 있으신가요? 영국에서의 유학 프로그램에 관해 여쭤보고 싶어요.

P: 물론이지, 괜찮단다. 우리가 이번 여름에 하는 것에 참가하는 데 관심이 있니?

S: 네, 그런 것 같아요. 그러니까, 저는 항상 영국을 방문하고 싶었어요. 그런데, 어, 여기에서 저의 첫해이기도 해요. 그래서 그 강의가 어려울까 봐 걱정돼요.

P: 그렇게 어렵지 않을 거야. 유학 프로그램에 있는 강의는 대개 정규 강의보다 쉽단다. 그런데, 네 전공이 무엇이니?

S: 영문학인데, 저는 특히 연극을 좋아해요. 언젠가는 연극을 위한 각본을 쓰고 싶어요.

P: 오, 그럼 내 강의가 분명히 네 관심을 끌겠구나. 그것은 전부 셰익스피어와 그의 연극에 관한 것이 될 거거든. 우리는 '오셀로'와 '햄릿' 같은 유명한 비극들을 공부할 거란다.

S: 정말요? 완벽하네요. 저는 예전에 그의 비극들 중 일부를 읽어봤어요.

P: 잘됐구나. 나는 그 강의가 시작하기 전에 또 다른 읽을거리도 지정할 거야. 그것은 고대 그리스 연극에 관한 것이 될 거야.

S: 그것이 셰익스피어와 어떤 관련이 있나요?

P: 음, 셰익스피어의 연극 중 일부는 그리스의 연극에서 영감을 받았어, 그래서 난 그 주제를 이해하는 게 좋은 생각인 것 같구나.

S: 그렇군요... 음, 전부 아주 좋아요. 그런데 해외에 있는 동안 저희가 현장 학습을 가나요? 제가 여름을 내내 교실 안에서 보내고 싶을지 모르겠어서요.

P: 오, 그건 걱정하지 마라. 우리는 분명히 다른 활동들을 할 거야. 예를 들어, 우리는 Globe Theatre에서 셰익스피어의 '맥베스' 공연을 관람할 거야. 그의 고향인 Stratford-upon-Avon도 방문할 거고...

S: Globe Theatre라고 하셨나요? 그곳은 셰익스피어의 연극이 상연된 실제 극장 아닌가요?

P: 아니야, 그런데 그곳은 꼭 원래의 것처럼 생겼지. 나는 그곳에 여러 번 가보았는데 내 학생들은 항상 그곳을 아주 좋아해.

S: 흥미롭네요. 프로그램에 참가하는 데 다른 장점들이 있나요?

P: 사실, 그렇단다. 강의를 마치는 것은 네가 학위 요건을 충족시키는 데 도움을 줄 거야. 그리고 그건 겨우 4주 길이야. 그것은 보통의 대학교 학기에 비해 훨씬 짧지.

S: 와! 아주 좋네요. 오늘 등록할 수 있나요?

study-abroad program 유학 프로그램 regular [형] 정규의 major [명] 전공 English literature 영문학 tragedy [명] 비극 assign [동] 지정하다, 할당하다 ancient [형] 고대의, 오래된 inspire [동] 영감을 주다 field trip 현장 학습 definitely [부] 분명히 hometown [명] 고향 advantage [명] 장점 degree [명] 학위

1 학생은 왜 교수를 찾아가는가?

(A) 셰익스피어의 몇몇 중요 작품들에 관해 논의하기 위해
(B) 해외 학업 프로그램에 관해 문의하기 위해
(C) 영국에서 온 교수에 관한 정보를 얻기 위해
(D) 공연 관람에 교수를 초대하기 위해

2 교수는 그의 강의에 관해 무엇이라고 말하는가?

(A) 그것은 일 년에 두 번 제공된다.
(B) 그것은 학생들에게 인기가 있다.
(C) 그것은 분명히 학생의 관심을 끌 것이다.
(D) 그것은 몇몇 도전적인 주제를 포함할 것이다.

3 교수는 왜 그의 학생들이 고대 그리스 연극에 대해 읽기를 원하는가?

(A) 그것은 기말시험의 주제가 될 것이다.
(B) 그것은 내년 강의의 일부가 될 것이다.
(C) 그것은 유명한 비극의 많은 예시를 가지고 있다.
(D) 그것은 여러 연극의 집필에 영감을 주었다.

4 프로그램에 참가하는 것의 장점으로 무엇이 언급되는가?

(A) 요건을 더 적은 시간에 완료하는 것
(B) 몇몇 새로운 언어들을 배우는 것
(C) 다른 대학의 학생들을 만나는 것
(D) 유명한 교수와 함께 공부하는 것

대화의 일부를 다시 듣고 질문에 답하시오.

S: I see... Um, this all sounds great. But are we going to take any field trips while we're abroad? I'm not sure I want to spend the entire summer in a classroom.

P: Oh, don't worry about that. We'll definitely have other activities.

5 학생은 이렇게 말함으로써 무엇을 의미하는가:

S: I'm not sure I want to spend the entire summer in a classroom.

(A) 그녀는 여름 동안 어디에 머물지 알지 못한다.

(B) 그녀는 이미 다른 도시를 방문할 계획을 세웠다.

(C) 그녀는 해외에 있는 동안 공부보다 더 많은 것을 하기 원한다.

(D) 그녀는 다른 프로그램에 참가하는 것에 대해 생각하고 있다.

iBT Listening Test 2

1 (C) 2 (D) 3 (A) 4 (B) 5 (B) 6 (D)

Note-taking

Panic Disorder

- Anxiety = normal, natural response to stress
- Anxiety attack → serious = panic attack
  - Shortness of breath = frightening, last long X
- Panic attack → change life ∴ severe problem
- Panic disorder factors = stress, fam. history, environ.
- Not sure why it happens ∴ studying brain
- Now = treat w/ med. or discuss w/ therapist

Listen to part of a lecture in a psychology class.

P: OK, we've been talking about mental disorders. Um, these are conditions of the mind that affect how people normally feel or behave. So, if a person is normally happy, a mental disorder can make them feel unusually sad, angry, or afraid... [1]Now, there are many kinds of mental disorders. Today, we will go over panic disorder.

[6]First, let me be clear. Feeling anxiety is normal. In fact, most of us experience anxiety often. It's a natural response to everyday situations that are stressful. Um, let's say you did something bad and you're afraid to tell your parents about it. This fear can cause your body to react in certain ways. Maybe your heart beats faster, your hands start to sweat, or you feel a little dizzy. These are all signs of anxiety attacks.

Once in a while, however, anxiety attacks can become more serious. When this happens, they are called panic attacks. Panic attacks feel much worse than anxiety attacks. They can also happen suddenly and for no clear reason. You could be walking down the street or just sitting at home when you have a panic attack. [2]Symptoms of panic attacks can include cold skin, sweating, and chest pain. Many times, people also experience shortness of breath, which can be extremely frightening. Some even feel like they are about to die. Thankfully, panic attacks usually don't last very long. Um, maybe five to ten minutes at most. But the anxiety they cause can lead people to develop a panic disorder.

You see, people who have experienced even one panic attack can become very afraid of having another one. So they change how they live in important ways. For instance, if they had a panic attack while driving a car, they may avoid driving ever again. [3]Just imagine what a severe problem this can be. A panic attack can happen almost anywhere without warning. So, instead of living a normal life, people with panic disorders become afraid of doing regular things. As a result, they may have trouble doing things like keeping a job.

Currently, researchers believe that panic disorder may be caused by a number of factors. These may include stress, family history, and the environment. [4]Unfortunately, experts are still not completely sure why it happens. They hope to find answers by studying the human brain. If they can figure out what causes panic disorder, they can develop better ways to treat it. Right now, people who suffer from panic disorders have to see a mental health professional. The mental health professional will usually perform a test to see if a patient has the condition. [5]Then, the condition may be treated with medicine or the patient may be encouraged to discuss his or her concerns with a therapist.

심리학 강의의 일부를 들으시오.

P: 자, 우리는 정신 장애에 대해 얘기해 왔어요. 음, 이것들은 사람들이 일반적으로 생각하거나 행동하는 방식에 영향을 미치는 정신적 질환입니다. 그러니까, 만약 어떤 사람이 일반적으로 행복하다면, 정신 장애는 그들을 대단히 슬프거나, 화가 나거나, 혹은 두려움을 느끼게 만들 수 있어요... 자, 정신 장애에는 여러 종류가 있습니다. 오늘 우리는 공황 장애에 대해 알아볼 거예요.

먼저, 확실히 해둘게요. 불안감을 느끼는 것은 정상입니다. 사실, 우리들 대부분은 종종 불안을 경험해요. 그것은 스트레스를 주는 일상적 상황에 대한 자연스러운 반응이에요. 음, 여러분이 나쁜 일을 저질렀고 부모님께 그것에 대해 말하는 것을 두려워한다고 가정해 보죠. 이 두려움은 여러분의 신체가 특정한 방식으로 반응하게 만들 수 있어요. 아마도 심장이 더 빨리 뛰거나, 손에 땀이 나기 시작하거나, 혹은 약간의 어지러움을 느끼게 되죠. 이것들은 모두 불안 발작의 징후입니다.

하지만, 가끔, 불안 발작은 더 심각해질 수 있습니다. 이런 일이 일어날 때, 그것들은 공황 발작이라고 불려요. 공황 발작은 불안 발작보다 훨씬 더 안 좋습니다. 그것들은 갑작스럽게 분명한 이유 없이 일어날 수도 있어요. 공황 발작이 일어날 때, 여러분은 길을 따라 걷고 있었거나 그냥 집에 앉아 있었을 수도 있어요. 공황 발작의 증상은 차가운 피부, 땀 흘림, 가슴 통증을 포함할 수 있습니다. 많은 경우, 사람들은 호흡 곤란을 겪을 수도 있는데, 이는 극도로 무서울 수 있습니다. 어떤 사람들은 심지어 곧 죽을 것처럼 느껴요. 다행스럽게도, 공황 발작은 보통 아주 오래 지속되지 않습니다. 음, 아마 최대 5분에서 10분 정도 지속됩니다. 하지만 그것들이 야기하는 불안감은 사람들에게 공황 장애가 생기게 할 수 있어요.

그러니까, 한 번이라도 공황 발작을 겪은 사람들은 또 한 번의 공황 발작을 겪는 것을 매우 두려워하게 될 수 있어요. 그래서 그들은 그들이 사는 방식을 크게 바꿉니다. 예를 들어, 그들이 자동차를 운전하는 동안 공황 발작을 겪었다면, 다시는 운전을 하지 않을 수도 있죠. 이것이 얼마나 심각한 문제가 될 수 있을지 상상해 보세요. 공황 발작은 거의 어디에서나 예고 없이 일어날 수 있어요. 그래서, 보통의 삶을 사는 대신, 공황 장애가 있는 사람들은 일상적인 일들을 하는 것을 두려워하게 돼요. 결과적으로, 그들은 직업을 유지하는 것과 같은 것들을 하는 데 어려움을 겪을 수 있습니다.

현재, 연구자들은 공황 장애가 여러 가지 요인들에 의해 발생할 수 있다고 믿습니다. 이것들은 스트레스, 가족력, 그리고 환경을

CHAPTER 02 | Detail **19**

포함할 수 있죠. 안타깝게도, 전문가들은 여전히 그것이 일어나는 이유를 완전히 확신하지 못해요. 그들은 인간의 뇌를 연구함으로써 답을 찾기를 희망하죠. 만약 그들이 무엇이 공황 장애를 일으키는지 알아낼 수 있다면, 그것을 치료할 더 나은 방법을 개발할 수 있어요. 지금은, 공황 장애로 고통받는 사람들은 정신 건강 전문가를 찾아가야 합니다. 일반적으로 정신 건강 전문가는 환자가 그 질환을 앓고 있는지 확인하기 위해 검사를 수행할 거예요. 그런 다음, 그 질환은 약물로 치료되거나 환자가 그 또는 그녀의 걱정거리에 대해 치료사와 상의하도록 권장받을 수도 있습니다.

mental 형 정신의   disorder 명 장애   condition 명 질환
behave 동 행동하다   panic disorder 공황 장애   anxiety 명 불안(감)
react 동 반응하다   attack 명 발작   symptom 명 증상
extremely 부 극도로   professional 명 전문가

1 강의의 주된 주제는 무엇인가?

(A) 정신 건강을 평가하는 방법

(B) 사람들이 여러 감정을 느끼는 이유

(C) 정신 장애의 특징

(D) 정신 건강을 개선하는 행동

2 교수에 따르면, 공황 발작의 증상으로 간주될 수 있는 것은?

(A) 뱃속의 메스꺼움

(B) 제대로 걷지 못하는 문제

(C) 큰 소리로 말해야 할 갑작스러운 필요성

(D) 호흡의 어려움

3 공황 장애에 대한 교수의 태도는 무엇인가?

(A) 그녀는 그것이 심각한 문제를 초래할 수 있다고 생각한다.

(B) 그녀는 그것이 더 흔해지고 있다고 걱정한다.

(C) 그녀는 연구자들이 그것에 대한 해결책을 거의 찾았다고 생각한다.

(D) 그녀는 그것이 관계 문제에 의해 일어난다고 생각한다.

4 전문가들은 공황 장애의 원인에 대해 알아내기 위해 어떻게 노력하고 있는가?

(A) 이전의 실험들을 검토함으로써

(B) 사람들의 뇌를 연구함으로써

(C) 건강 전문가들과 대화함으로써

(D) 서로 다른 장애들을 비교함으로써

5 교수에 따르면, 공황 장애를 가진 환자들을 치료하는 한 가지 방법은 무엇인가?

(A) 그들에게 규칙적인 운동을 하게 하는 것

(B) 그들에게 그들의 생각에 대해 상의하도록 요청하는 것

(C) 그들에게 가족과 시간을 보내도록 권장하는 것

(D) 그들이 그들의 수면 습관을 바꾸도록 돕는 것

강의 일부를 다시 듣고 질문에 답하시오.

P: First, let me be clear. Feeling anxiety is normal. In fact, most of us experience anxiety often. It's a natural response to everyday situations that are stressful.

6 교수는 왜 이렇게 말하는가:

P: First, let me be clear.

(A) 주제가 잘 연구되었음을 보여주기 위해

(B) 잘못된 정보를 제공한 것에 대해 사과하기 위해

(C) 불안감을 가진 사람들이 일반적으로 행동하는 방식을 설명하기 위해

(D) 불안감이 자연스러운 반응이라는 것을 강조하기 위해

Vocabulary Review 본문 p.52

1 urban	2 demand	3 prefer
4 exhibition	5 illegal	6 symptoms
7 worsened	8 disorder	9 lifespan
10 (D)	11 (B)	12 (B)
13 (C)	14 (A)	

CHAPTER 03
Function

Example 본문 p.55

A. (B)   **B.** (C)

A.

Note-taking

S: Not sure what to include in paper
  Many ideas important, some might be unrelated
P: Send copy this evening
S: Evening = football practice → be home late night
P: Send this week

Listen to a conversation between a student and a professor.

S: Hi, Professor Mitchell. I was hoping I could talk to you. Um, it's about the paper I'm writing for your economics class.

P: Oh, hi, Kevin. Are you having difficulties with your research?

S: Yes, I am. Um, I'm not quite sure what to include in the paper. I think a lot of my ideas are important. But I'm worried that some of them might be unrelated.

P: I see. I'd be happy to give you some feedback on your first draft. Send me a copy this evening and I'll take a look.

S: Did you say this evening? I have to go to football practice and I won't be home until late at night.

P: Don't worry. Just send me what you've written this week.

학생과 교수 사이의 대화를 들으시오.

S: 안녕하세요, Mitchell 교수님. 교수님과 이야기하고 싶었어요. 음,

교수님의 경제학 수업을 위해 제가 작성 중인 보고서에 관련한 것인데요.

P: 오, 안녕, Kevin. 연구에 어려움이 있니?

S: 네, 맞아요. 음, 보고서에 어떤 내용을 포함할지 잘 모르겠어요. 제 아이디어 중 많은 것들이 중요한 것 같거든요. 그런데 그것들 중 몇몇이 관련이 없을까 봐 걱정돼요.

P: 그렇구나. 내가 네 초안에 대한 의견을 줄 수 있으면 좋겠구나. 오늘 저녁에 내게 사본을 보내면 내가 살펴보마.

S: 오늘 저녁이라고 하셨나요? 저는 축구 연습에 가야 하고 밤늦게야 집에 올 거예요.

P: 걱정 말거라. 그냥 이번 주에 네가 쓴 것을 내게 보내주렴.

economics 몡 경제학   research 몡 연구, 조사
unrelated 혱 관련이 없는   feedback 몡 의견, 피드백

대화의 일부를 다시 듣고 질문에 답하시오.
P: I'd be happy to give you some feedback on your first draft. Send me a copy this evening and I'll take a look.

S: Did you say this evening? I have to go to football practice and I won't be home until late at night.

학생은 이렇게 말함으로써 무엇을 의미하는가:
S: Did you say this evening?

(A) 그는 보고서를 더 일찍 보내고 싶어 한다.
(B) 그는 그 시간에 끝나지 않을 것이다.
(C) 그는 교수가 말한 것을 이해할 수 없다.
(D) 그는 어떠한 도움 없이도 연구를 완료할 수 있다.

B.

Note-taking
Juneteenth
- Began in 19c. as celebration of end of slavery
- Slaves in Texas = freed in 1865
- 2021 = govt. made Juneteenth nat. holiday
- Past = small family gatherings & church ceremonies
- Recent = larger & more public (e.g. parades & festivals)

Listen to part of a lecture in a history class.

P: Since tomorrow is Juneteenth, I thought we might take some time to talk about this important holiday. So what exactly is Juneteenth? Well, it began in the 19th century as a celebration of the end of slavery. You see, slaves in Texas were freed on June 19, 1865. However, it wasn't until 2021 that the government officially made Juneteenth a national holiday. I would say it's a good thing they did. Today, it's the only holiday that remembers the end of slavery.

Now, in the past, celebrations of Juneteenth usually included small family gatherings and church ceremonies. Recently, however, they have become larger and more public. In fact, many cities across the United States hold parades and festivals on the occasion.

역사학 강의의 일부를 들으시오.
P: 내일이 준틴스이기 때문에, 우리가 이 중요한 휴일에 대해 얘기할 시간을 가져도 좋을 거라 생각했어요. 자, 준틴스가 정확히 무엇

일까요? 음, 그것은 19세기에 노예 제도의 종식을 기념하는 것으로 시작됐어요. 그러니까, 텍사스의 노예들은 1865년 6월 19일에 해방되었어요. 하지만, 정부는 2021년이 되어서야 공식적으로 준틴스를 국경일로 만들었죠. 그들이 한 것은 잘한 일이라고 말하고 싶어요. 오늘날, 그것은 노예 제도의 종식을 상기시키는 유일한 휴일입니다.

자, 과거에, 준틴스를 기념하는 것은 보통 작은 가족 모임과 교회 의식을 포함했습니다. 하지만, 최근에, 그것들은 더 커지고 더 대중적이 됐어요. 사실, 미국 전역의 많은 도시들은 그날 퍼레이드와 축제를 개최합니다.

Juneteenth 몡 준틴스(미국의 노예 해방 기념일)   slavery 몡 노예 제도
officially 뷰 공식적으로   gathering 몡 모임   ceremony 몡 의식

강의의 일부를 듣고 질문에 답하시오.
P: You see, slaves in Texas were freed on June 19, 1865. However, it wasn't until 2021 that the government officially made Juneteenth a national holiday. I would say it's a good thing they did. Today, it's the only holiday that remembers the end of slavery.

교수는 왜 이렇게 말하는가:
P: I would say it's a good thing they did.

(A) 휴일이 인기 있는 이유를 설명하기 위해
(B) 날짜 선택에 동의하기 위해
(C) 기념하는 것이 중요하다는 것을 강조하기 위해
(D) 더 많은 휴일의 필요성을 지적하기 위해

Listening Practice 1
본문 p. 57
1 (C)   2 (C)   3 (D)   4 (D)   5 (C)

Note-taking
M: Bought largest meal plan (225), used around half
W: Get a refund = get half of $ back
M: Sell meal card to another student
W: Good idea X ∵ against rules
M: Final decision when?
W: B.f. winter break, busy final week ∴ try to come early

Listen to a conversation between a student and a student services office employee.

M: Excuse me. Is this the student services office?

W: Yes, it is. What can I help you with?

M: [1]Um, I need to talk to someone about my meal plan. I bought the largest one with 225 meals. But, um, I've only used around half. What can I do about the meals I didn't use?

W: Um, how many do you have left, exactly?

M: I think there are 100 left. And, um, each one is $15. So that's quite a lot of money. I was hoping to get some money back so I can buy a plane ticket to Spain. [2]I'm planning to spend summer break overseas.

W: Well, you have the option to get a refund. But

then, you will only get back half of the money for the remaining meals.

M: I see... ³That doesn't seem like a reasonable policy.

W: Well... Personally, I think you're right. Students should be able to get back all of their money. But I can't do anything about it.

M: Then, I need to think of another solution. Maybe I can sell my meal card to another student. If I sell it at a cheap price, I'm sure someone would buy it.

W: I don't think that's a good idea. ⁵Letting someone else buy your meal card is against university rules. If you are caught doing that, you won't be allowed to get another meal plan next semester. You wouldn't want that to happen, would you?

M: Definitely not. I didn't know that. I'd better think about it some more. When do I have to make a final decision?

W: Well, there are only two weeks left until the end of the semester. And changes have to be made before the winter break. ⁴But it's very busy during the final week. Students sometimes have to wait for hours before they can talk to one of our staff. Try to come earlier, if you can.

M: OK. I'll do that. Thanks for all of your help.

W: My pleasure. Feel free to call us if you need more information.

학생과 학생지원센터 직원 사이의 대화를 들으시오.

M: 실례합니다. 여기가 학생지원센터인가요?

W: 네, 맞아요. 무엇을 도와드릴까요?

M: 음, 제 밀 플랜에 관해 누군가와 이야기해야 해서요. 저는 식사 225끼가 포함된 양이 가장 많은 것을 구입했어요. 그런데, 음, 저는 겨우 반 정도만 사용했어요. 사용하지 않은 식사는 어떻게 할 수 있나요?

W: 음, 정확히 몇 끼나 남아있나요?

M: 100끼가 남아있는 것 같아요. 그리고, 음, 각각은 15달러예요. 그러니까 꽤 많은 돈이죠. 저는 스페인행 비행기표를 살 수 있도록 돈을 돌려받고 싶었어요. 여름 방학을 해외에서 보낼 계획이거든요.

W: 음, 환불받는 선택지가 있어요. 하지만 그러면, 학생은 남아있는 식사에 대한 돈의 절반만 돌려받게 될 거예요.

M: 그렇군요... 합리적인 정책은 아닌 것 같네요.

W: 음... 개인적으로, 저도 학생이 옳다고 생각해요. 학생들은 돈 전부를 돌려받을 수 있어야 해요. 하지만 그것에 대해 제가 할 수 있는 게 없네요.

M: 그러면, 다른 해결책을 생각해 봐야겠어요. 아마 다른 학생에게 제 밀 카드를 판매할 수 있을 거예요. 저렴한 가격에 판매하면, 분명히 누군가가 그걸 구입할 거예요.

W: 그건 좋은 생각이 아닌 것 같아요. 다른 누군가에게 학생의 밀 카드를 구입하게 하는 건 대학 규정에 어긋나요. 그렇게 하다가 발각되면, 다음 학기에 다른 밀 플랜을 얻는 것이 허락되지 않을 거예요. 그런 일이 일어나길 바라지는 않죠, 그렇죠?

M: 절대 아니에요. 그건 몰랐어요. 조금 더 생각해 보는 게 좋겠어요. 제가 언제 최종 결정을 내려야 하나요?

W: 음, 학기 말까지 겨우 2주 남았어요. 그리고 겨울 방학 전까지 변경이 완료되어야 해요. 그런데 마지막 주 동안은 매우 바빠요. 학생들은 때때로 저희 직원 중 한 명과 얘기하기까지 몇 시간을 기다려야 해요. 가능하면, 더 빨리 오세요.

M: 알겠습니다. 그렇게 할게요. 도와주셔서 감사합니다.

W: 천만에요. 더 많은 정보가 필요하시면 언제든지 저희에게 전화하세요.

exactly 閉 정확히   quite 閉 꽤, 상당히   refund 몔 환불
remaining 휑 남아있는   reasonable 휑 합리적인   policy 몔 정책
personally 閉 개인적으로   solution 몔 해결책

1 학생의 문제는 무엇인가?
   (A) 그는 학기 말을 위한 식사가 없다.
   (B) 환불에 대한 그의 요청이 승인되지 않았다.
   (C) 그는 그가 필요한 것보다 많은 식사를 구매했다.
   (D) 그의 밀 플랜은 예상보다 훨씬 더 비쌌다.

2 학생은 무엇을 할 계획이라고 말하는가?
   (A) 다른 밀 플랜 시도해 보기
   (B) 캠퍼스 밖에서 그의 식사 구입하기
   (C) 방학 동안 해외로 출국하기
   (D) 유학 프로그램에 참가하기

3 직원은 대학의 환불 정책에 대해 어떻게 생각하는가?
   (A) 그녀는 학생들이 왜 그것을 싫어하는지 이해하지 못한다.
   (B) 그녀는 그것이 더 명확히 설명되어야 한다고 생각한다.
   (C) 그녀는 그것이 대학에 도움이 된다고 생각한다.
   (D) 그녀는 그것이 학생들에게 공정하다고 생각하지 않는다.

4 직원은 학생에게 무엇을 하라고 제안하는가?
   (A) 그가 결정을 내리면 사무실에 전화하기
   (B) 그의 플랜을 변경하기 위해 다음 학기까지 기다리기
   (C) 직원과 이야기하기 위한 약속 잡기
   (D) 바쁜 시기 이전에 사무실 방문하기

대화의 일부를 다시 듣고 질문에 답하시오.
W: Letting someone else buy your meal card is against university rules. If you are caught doing that, you won't be allowed to get another meal plan next semester. You wouldn't want that to happen, would you?
M: Definitely not. I didn't know that.

5 직원은 왜 이렇게 말하는가:
   W: You wouldn't want that to happen, would you?
   (A) 학생이 나중에 선택하도록 장려하기 위해
   (B) 학생의 결정에 대한 지지를 표현하기 위해
   (C) 문제의 심각성을 강조하기 위해
   (D) 상황을 개선할 방법을 제안하기 위해

Listening Practice 2   본문 p. 59

1 (C)   2 (B)   3 (B)   4 (C)   5 (D)

Note-taking

Fight-or-Flight Response

- When faced danger = face or run away = fight-or-flight
- Fight-or-flight response → physical signs
  - Eyes grow wider = light ↑, see better
  - Heart rate ↑ = send blood to heart & brain & etc.
  - Breathe faster = oxygen ↑
  - Body shaking = muscles become tense
- Quick boost of energy & strength
- Important ∵ help survive danger & perform effectively
- Happen when danger X → attention to physical signs

Listen to part of a lecture in a physiology class.

P: Over the past few weeks, we've been discussing how the body reacts to different situations. For example, we talked about why we feel cold when we're sleepy and why our stomach makes noise when we're hungry. ¹Well, today I want to talk about what happens in our bodies when we feel threatened. It's called the fight-or-flight response.

So, first of all, the fight-or-flight response is a natural reaction to stressful or dangerous situations. It evolved in humans long ago. ²You see, early humans regularly faced danger, such as an attack by a large animal. When this happened, they had only two choices. They could either stay and face the danger or try to run away from it. That is where we get the expression fight-or-flight. Today, of course, we don't have to worry about similar dangers all the time. But we still react the same way whenever we face the possibility of physical or psychological harm. We have an urge to either fight or run away.

Now, it's easy to know when you are having a fight-or-flight response. There are physical signs that you can see and feel. The first thing that happens is that your body's nervous system releases different chemicals, which cause various effects. For instance, they make your eyes grow wider to let in more light. This helps you see better so that you're more aware of what's happening around you. You may also notice your heart rate go up. This sends blood to where it's needed the most, including your heart, brain, and the muscles of your legs and arms. You may also start to breathe much faster. This lets you take in more oxygen. ³Finally, you may feel like your body is shaking and you can't control it. This happens because your muscles become tense in preparation to help you fight or run away. Overall, the fight-or-flight response is your body's way of giving you a quick boost of energy and strength. The effects happen quickly. But you may still feel them for up to an hour even after the threat is gone.

⁵The fight-or-flight response is important because it helps us survive physical dangers. It also helps us perform more effectively in stressful situations. But take note. Sometimes, it can happen when there is no real danger at all. That's why it's important to pay attention to the physical signs. ⁴If you notice these signs when there is no real threat, you can try to reduce its effects. For example, you can close your eyes and breathe slowly to calm your body down.

생리학 강의의 일부를 들으시오.

P: 지난 몇 주 동안, 우리는 신체가 어떻게 다양한 상황에 반응하는지에 대해 논의해 왔어요. 예를 들어, 우리는 졸릴 때 추위를 느끼는 이유와 배고플 때 배가 소리를 내는 이유에 대해 이야기했죠. 음, 오늘은 우리가 위협을 느낄 때 신체에서 어떤 일이 일어나는지에 대해 이야기하려고 합니다. 그것은 투쟁 혹은 도피 반응이라고 불려요.

자, 우선, 투쟁 혹은 도피 반응은 스트레스를 받거나 위험한 상황에 대한 자연스러운 반응이에요. 그것은 오래전에 인간에게 생겨났어요. 그러니까, 초기의 인간은 큰 동물에 의한 공격과 같은 위험에 자주 직면했어요. 이런 일이 일어났을 때, 그들에게는 두 가지 선택밖에 없었죠. 그들은 남아서 위험에 직면하거나 그것으로부터 도망치려 할 수 있었어요. 거기에서 투쟁 혹은 도피라는 표현을 가져온 거예요. 오늘날, 물론, 우리는 항상 이와 비슷한 위험에 대해 걱정할 필요가 없어요. 하지만 신체적이나 심리적 피해의 가능성에 직면할 때마다 여전히 같은 방식으로 반응하죠. 우리는 싸우거나 도망치고 싶은 충동을 느껴요.

자, 여러분이 언제 투쟁 혹은 도피 반응을 보이는지는 알기 쉬워요. 여러분이 보고 느낄 수 있는 신체적인 징후들이 있어요. 가장 먼저 일어나는 것은 신체의 신경계가 다양한 화학물질을 방출한다는 것인데, 그것들은 다양한 효과를 일으켜요. 예를 들어, 그것들은 더 많은 빛이 들어오게 하기 위해 여러분의 눈을 더 커지게 해요. 이는 여러분이 더 잘 볼 수 있도록 도와 주위에서 일어나는 일들을 더 잘 알 수 있게 합니다. 여러분은 또한 심박수가 올라가는 걸 알아챌 수도 있어요. 이는 심장, 뇌, 팔다리의 근육을 포함하여, 가장 필요한 곳에 혈액을 보내죠. 여러분은 훨씬 더 빠르게 호흡하기 시작할 수도 있어요. 이것은 더 많은 산소가 들어올 수 있게 해줘요. 마지막으로, 여러분은 몸이 떨리고 그것을 통제할 수 없는 것처럼 느낄 수도 있어요. 여러분이 싸우거나 도망치는 것을 도울 준비를 하기 위해 근육이 긴장하게 되기 때문에 이런 일이 일어나죠. 전반적으로, 투쟁 혹은 도피 반응은 신체가 에너지와 힘을 빠르게 북돋아 주는 방법입니다. 효과는 빠르게 일어나요. 하지만 심지어 위협이 사라진 후에도 최대 한 시간 동안 그것들을 느낄 수 있어요.

투쟁 혹은 도피 반응은 우리가 물리적 위험에서 살아남도록 도와주기 때문에 중요합니다. 그것은 우리가 스트레스를 받는 상황에서 더 효과적으로 일을 수행하도록 도와주기도 하죠. 하지만 주목하세요. 때때로, 그것은 실제적인 위험이 전혀 없을 때 일어날 수 있습니다. 그게 신체적 징후에 주의를 기울이는 게 중요한 이유예요. 실제적인 위험이 없을 때 이러한 징후들을 알아챈다면, 그것의 효과를 줄이려 노력할 수 있습니다. 예를 들어, 여러분은 신체를 진정시키기 위해 눈을 감고 천천히 호흡할 수 있어요.

---

react 동 반응하다   threaten 동 위협하다
fight-or-flight response 투쟁 혹은 도피 반응
regularly 부 자주, 정기적으로   expression 명 표현
possibility 명 가능성   physical 형 신체적인, 물리적인
psychological 형 심리적인   urge 명 충동   nervous system 신경계
release 동 방출하다   chemical 명 화학물질

1 강의는 주로 무엇에 관한 것인가?

(A) 사람들이 위험한 상황을 피해야 하는 이유

(B) 졸리거나 배고플 때 일어나는 인체의 변화

(C) 인체가 잠재적인 위협들에 반응하는 방식

(D) 신체적 위협과 심리적 위협의 차이

2 초기의 인간들이 직면했던 위험에 대한 교수의 태도는 무엇인가?

(A) 그는 그것이 신체적이기보다는 심리적인 것이었다고 생각한다.

(B) 그는 그것이 그들에게 제한된 선택지를 주었다고 생각한다.

(C) 그는 그것이 그들로 하여금 새로운 지역으로 이주하게 했다고 생각한다.

(D) 그는 그것이 현대의 위협들보다 더 위험했다는 것에 동의하지 않는다.

3 교수에 따르면, 신경계에 의한 화학물질 방출의 효과는 무엇인가?

(A) 심박수가 감소한다.

(B) 걷잡을 수 없이 몸이 떨린다.

(C) 근육의 긴장이 풀린다.

(D) 혈압이 상승한다.

4 교수에 따르면, 사람들은 스트레스를 받는 상황에 대한 신체 반응의 효과를 줄이기 위해 무엇을 할 수 있는가?

(A) 그들이 느끼는 것을 표현하기

(B) 긍정적인 경험을 떠올리기

(C) 천천히 호흡하기

(D) 팔다리를 뻗기

강의의 일부를 다시 듣고 질문에 답하시오.

P: The fight-or-flight response is important because it helps us survive physical dangers. It also helps us perform more effectively in stressful situations. But take note. Sometimes, it can happen when there is no real danger at all.

5 교수는 왜 이렇게 말하는가:

P: But take note.

(A) 투쟁 혹은 도피 반응에 대한 잘못된 믿음을 설명하기 위해

(B) 싸우거나 도망치는 것이 항상 가능하지는 않다는 것을 설명하기 위해

(C) 스트레스와 생존 사이의 관계를 강조하기 위해

(D) 위협 없이도 반응이 일어날 수 있다는 것을 지적하기 위해

Listening Practice 3
본문 p. 61

1 (A)   2 (B)   3 (D)   4 (C)   5 (C)

Note-taking

S: Want to join diff. group ∵ already research @ zoo
P: Midland Zoo = collection of animals & best researchers
   Stay in current group ∵ group can learn from exp.
S: Want to apply for grad. school, know what to study X
   Want to learn about various subjects b.f. graduate
   Topic about marine animals = interesting
P: Share exp. w/ group → join the other group

Listen to a conversation between a student and a professor.

P: Hi, Brad. Is something wrong?

S: No, Professor. I just need to talk about our animal studies course.

P: Sure. What's on your mind?

S: [1]I want to join a different group for the project. Right now, I'm in the group that is studying how animals live in zoos.

P: Oh... Is there a problem with your group?

S: No. But I just started an internship at the Midland Zoo. I'm learning about how animals live in that environment. So I'd like to join another group because I'm already doing research at the zoo.

P: Well, congratulations on the internship. [2]That's a great zoo. I mean, it has a great collection of animals. But also, some of the best researchers work there.

S: [5]Yeah, I was lucky to be selected for the internship. Um, it was really competitive.

P: That's more than just luck, you know. You've always been an excellent student. But I think you should stay in your current group. They can learn from your experience. And the project could also help your work at the zoo.

S: That's true. [3]But I'd like to learn about new things. I want to apply for graduate school, but I don't know what to study yet. That's why I want to learn about various subjects before I graduate.

P: Hmm... I understand what you mean. That sounds like a good idea. Um, do you know which group you want to join?

S: Well, the topic about marine animals sounds interesting. Can I join that group?

P: But then, your current group will have one less member if you leave. That will make the project more difficult for them.

S: Oh... I didn't think about that. Is there anything I can do to help them?

P: [4]How about sharing your experience working at the zoo with your original group? You can join the other group after you do that.

S: Of course. [4]I'll go talk to them right away!

학생과 교수 사이의 대화를 들으시오.

P: 안녕, Brad. 무슨 문제라도 있니?

S: 아뇨, 교수님. 저희의 동물 연구 강의에 대해 좀 말씀드려야 해서요.

P: 물론이지. 무슨 일이니?

S: 프로젝트를 위해 다른 그룹에 참여하고 싶어요. 지금, 저는 동물원에서 동물들이 어떻게 사는지를 연구하는 그룹에 속해 있어요.

P: 오... 네 그룹에 문제가 있니?

S: 아뇨. 그런데 제가 막 Midland Zoo에서 인턴직을 시작해서요. 저는 동물들이 그 환경에서 어떻게 사는지에 대해 배우고 있어요. 그러니까 저는 동물원에서 이미 연구하고 있기 때문에 다른 그룹에 참여하고 싶습니다.

P: 음, 인턴직을 하게 된 걸 축하한단다. 그곳은 멋진 동물원이야. 내 말은, 그곳에는 많은 동물들이 있어. 그런데, 최고의 연구자들 중 몇몇도 그곳에서 일하지.

S: 네, 인턴직에 선발된 건 운이 좋았어요. 음, 경쟁이 정말 심했거든요.

P: 너도 알다시피, 그건 단순한 운 이상이야. 너는 항상 훌륭한 학생이었잖니. 그런데 네가 지금 있는 그룹에 남아있어야 할 것 같구나. 그들은 네 경험으로부터 배울 수 있어. 그리고 프로젝트가 동물원에서의 네 일에 도움을 줄 수도 있지.

S: 맞아요. 그런데 저는 새로운 것들에 대해 배우고 싶어요. 저는 대학원에 지원하고 싶은데, 아직 무엇을 공부할지 모르겠어요. 그게 제가 졸업하기 전에 다양한 과목에 관해 배우고 싶은 이유예요.

P: 흠... 무슨 말인지 이해했다. 좋은 생각 같구나. 음, 네가 어떤 그룹에 참여하고 싶은지 아니?

S: 음, 해양 동물에 관한 주제가 흥미로워 보여요. 그 그룹에 참여해도 될까요?

P: 그런데 그러면, 네가 떠나면 지금 있는 그룹은 그룹원이 한 명 적어질 거야. 그건 그들에게 프로젝트를 더 어렵게 만들 거란다.

S: 오... 그건 생각하지 못했어요. 그들을 돕기 위해 제가 할 수 있는 게 있을까요?

P: 네 원래 그룹과 동물원에서 일한 경험을 공유하는 게 어떠니? 그렇게 한 후에는 다른 그룹에 참여해도 좋아.

S: 물론이죠. 지금 바로 그들에게 얘기할게요!

internship 명 인턴직   research 명 연구
competitive 형 경쟁이 심한   graduate school 대학원
various 형 다양한   original 형 원래의

1 학생은 왜 교수를 찾아가는가?

(A) 프로젝트를 위한 새로운 그룹을 요청하기 위해

(B) 다른 그룹과의 문제를 상의하기 위해

(C) 그의 그룹이 새로운 주제를 선정해도 되는지 문의하기 위해

(D) 그룹 발표에 관해 더 많이 알기 위해

2 Midland Zoo에 대한 교수의 의견은 무엇인가?

(A) 그곳은 인턴직들에 대한 대우가 좋다.

(B) 그곳에는 여러 명의 훌륭한 연구자들이 있다.

(C) 그곳은 더 많은 시 자금을 받아야 한다.

(D) 그곳은 중요한 연구들을 수행한다.

3 학생은 왜 다양한 과목에 관해 배우고 싶어 하는가?

(A) 그는 더 이상 동물 연구에 관심이 없다.

(B) 그는 대학원에 지원하기 위해 그의 성적을 올려야 한다.

(C) 그는 졸업하기 전에 전공을 선택해야 한다.

(D) 그는 대학원에서 무엇을 공부할지 확신하지 못한다.

4 학생은 다음에 무엇을 할 것인가?

(A) 수업 프로젝트를 위한 새로운 주제 선정하기

(B) 몇몇 과제들 완료하기

(C) 그가 동물원에서 배운 것을 그의 그룹에게 얘기하기

(D) 그의 그룹원 중 일부에게 이메일 보내기

대화의 일부를 다시 듣고 질문에 답하시오.

S: Yeah, I was lucky to be selected for the internship. Um, it was really competitive.

P: That's more than just luck, you know. You've always been an excellent student.

5 교수는 이렇게 말함으로써 무엇을 의미하는가:

P: That's more than just luck, you know.

(A) 학생은 인턴직에서 열심히 일해야 한다.

(B) 학생은 인턴직을 위해 추천되었다.

(C) 학생은 인턴직을 할 자격이 있다.

(D) 학생은 인턴직을 해야 한다.

Listening Practice 4

본문 p. 63

1 (C)   2 (B)   3 (C)   4 (C)   5 (D)

Note-taking

How People Have Used Geothermal Energy

- Energy using heat from earth = geothermal energy
- Geo. energy from mantle → released above ground
- First used to heat water (e.g. Chinese & Romans)
- Another use = make electricity
  - Steam → move wheel → energy → generator
  - First generator = town in Italy (5 bulbs → millions)
- Important ∵ renewable for heat & electricity
- Disadvantage = cost → improved w/ new tech.

Listen to part of a lecture in an earth science class.

P: You know we can produce energy from sources like the sun, wind, and water, right? But did you know that we can also produce energy using heat from inside the earth? Well, this is called geothermal energy. [1]Today, we will examine some of the ways humans throughout history have used geothermal energy.

Geothermal energy comes from deep within the earth's mantle. The mantle has temperatures of up to 4,000 degrees Celsius, which is, um, hot enough to melt solid rock. Most of the heat in the mantle has existed for millions of years. Sometimes, the heat goes up and gets released above the ground. [2]Now, when water comes from underground and appears above the surface of the earth, this is called a spring. And, when a spring is heated by geothermal energy, what does it become? Um, can anyone take a guess?

S: It becomes a hot spring?

P: That's right. And this brings us to how geothermal energy was first used. It was used to heat water. Uh, the ancient Chinese and Romans used hot springs for bathing. In fact, there is a hot spring in northeastern China that is among the oldest in the world. People have been using it for about 3,000 years. [3]Meanwhile, in France, a town has been using water from a hot spring since the 1300s. It built pipes to move water from the spring to people's houses. This provided many important benefits. For instance, the springs provided hot water for bathing and kept houses warm in the winter.

OK, another use for geothermal energy is to

make electricity. You see, hot water produces lots of steam. And, uh, this steam can be used to produce energy in a geothermal power facility. First, the steam passes through pipes that go into a building. Inside the building, the steam causes a large wheel to move. As the wheel moves, it creates energy. This energy is then turned into electricity by a machine called a generator. [5]The first generator to produce electricity this way was built in the town of Larderello, Italy, in 1904. At first, the generator made electricity for just five light bulbs. That's not great... But, 10 years later, the town built a larger generator. Today, it provides electricity to millions of people.

Anyway, geothermal energy is important because it is a renewable energy source for both heat and electricity. [4]The only disadvantage is cost. It can be expensive to find the right location and to build a powerful generator. This has improved in recent years, though, with the introduction of new technology.

지구 과학 강의의 일부를 들으시오.

P: 우리가 태양, 바람, 물과 같은 자원으로 에너지를 생산할 수 있다는 것은 알고 있을 거예요, 그렇죠? 그런데 우리가 지구 내부에서 나오는 열을 이용해서 에너지를 생산할 수도 있다는 것을 알고 있었나요? 음, 이것은 지열에너지라고 불립니다. 오늘, 우리는 역사를 통틀어 인간이 지열에너지를 이용해 온 방법들 중 몇 가지를 살펴볼 거예요.

지열에너지는 지구의 맨틀 깊숙한 곳에서 나와요. 맨틀은 섭씨 4,000도에까지 이르는 온도를 가지고 있는데, 그건, 음, 단단한 바위를 녹일 정도로 뜨겁습니다. 맨틀 속에 있는 열의 대부분은 수백만 년 동안 존재해 왔어요. 때때로, 그 열은 위로 올라가 땅 위로 방출됩니다. 자, 물이 지하에서 올라와 지구의 표면 위에 나타날 때, 이것은 샘이라고 불려요. 그리고, 샘이 지열에너지에 의해 가열되면, 그것은 무엇이 될까요? 음, 추측해볼 사람 있나요?

S: 온천이 되나요?

P: 맞아요. 그리고 이것은 지열에너지가 처음에 어떻게 이용되었는지를 알게 해줘요. 그것은 물을 가열하기 위해 이용되었죠. 어, 고대 중국인들과 로마인들은 목욕을 위해 온천을 이용했어요. 사실, 중국 북동부에는 세계에서 가장 오래된 것 중 하나인 온천이 있어요. 사람들은 약 3,000년 동안 그것을 이용해 왔죠. 한편, 프랑스에서, 한 도시는 1300년대부터 온천의 물을 이용해 왔어요. 그것은 물을 온천에서 사람들의 집으로 옮기기 위해 파이프를 건설했죠. 이것은 많은 중요한 이점들을 제공했어요. 예를 들어, 온천은 목욕을 위한 뜨거운 물을 제공했고 겨울에 집을 따뜻하게 유지했죠.

자, 지열에너지의 또 다른 용도는 전기를 만드는 거예요. 그러니까, 뜨거운 물은 많은 증기를 만들어내죠. 그리고, 어, 이 증기는 지열 발전 시설에서 에너지를 생산하는 데 이용될 수 있어요. 먼저, 증기는 건물 안으로 들어가는 파이프를 통과해요. 건물 내부에서, 증기는 큰 바퀴가 움직이게 하죠. 바퀴가 움직이면서, 그것은 에너지를 생산해요. 이 에너지는 그다음 발전기라고 불리는 기계에 의해 전기로 바뀝니다. 이런 방식으로 전기를 생산한 최초의 발전기는 1904년에 이탈리아의 라르데렐로라는 도시에서 만들어졌어요. 처음에, 그 발전기는 겨우 5개의 전구를 위한 전기를 만들어냈어요. 대단하지 않죠... 하지만, 10년 후에, 그 도시는 더 큰 발전기를 만들었어요. 오늘날, 그것은 수백만 명의 사람들에게 전기를 제공합니다.

그래서, 지열에너지는 열과 전기 둘 다를 위한 재생 가능 에너지원이기 때문에 중요합니다. 유일한 단점은 비용이에요. 적절한 장소를 찾는 것과 강력한 발전기를 만드는 것에는 비용이 많이 들 수 있어요. 하지만, 새로운 기술의 도입으로 이것은 최근 몇 년 동안 개선되었습니다.

geothermal energy 지열에너지(지구가 지니고 있는 열에너지)
melt 동 녹이다   solid 형 단단한   release 동 방출하다
underground 형 지하   surface 명 표면   spring 명 샘
hot spring 온천   bathing 명 목욕   benefit 명 이점
electricity 명 전기   generator 명 발전기   bulb 명 전구
renewable 형 재생 가능한   disadvantage 명 단점
introduction 명 도입

1 강의의 주된 주제는 무엇인가?

   (A) 지열에너지가 발명된 방법
   (B) 지열에너지의 주요 장점들
   (C) 사람들이 지열에너지를 이용해 온 방식
   (D) 지열에너지에 활용되는 기술

2 교수는 샘에 관해 무엇이라고 말하는가?

   (A) 그것은 많은 작은 바위들을 포함하고 있다.
   (B) 그것은 땅 밑에서 나오는 물이다.
   (C) 그것은 공기와 만나면 더 차가워진다.
   (D) 그것은 폭풍우 동안 홍수를 일으킬 수 있다.

3 교수는 프랑스의 도시에 관해 무엇이라고 말하는가?

   (A) 그것은 세계에서 가장 오래된 온천을 가지고 있다.
   (B) 그것은 중국으로부터 온천에 관해 배웠다.
   (C) 그것은 다양한 방식으로 온천으로부터 이익을 얻는다.
   (D) 그것은 오직 겨울에만 온천을 이용한다.

4 교수는 새로운 기술에 관해 무엇을 암시하는가?

   (A) 그것은 발전기의 사용을 대체할 수 있다.
   (B) 그것은 열과 전기를 동시에 만들 수 있다.
   (C) 그것은 발전기를 만드는 것을 더 저렴하게 만들었다.
   (D) 그것은 새로운 발전기들을 더 강력하게 만든다.

강의의 일부를 다시 듣고 질문에 답하시오.

P: The first generator to produce electricity this way was built in the town of Larderello, Italy, in 1904. At first, the generator made electricity for just five light bulbs. That's not great... But, 10 years later, the town built a larger generator. Today, it provides electricity to millions of people.

5 교수는 이렇게 말함으로써 무엇을 암시하는가:
   P: That's not great...

   (A) 그 도시는 장비에 너무 많은 돈을 썼다.
   (B) 라르데렐로의 사람들은 잘못된 방법을 이용했다.
   (C) 발전기를 만드는 데 너무 오랜 시간이 걸렸다.
   (D) 그 도시의 첫 번째 발전기는 전기를 거의 생산하지 못했다.

1 (C) 2 (B) 3 (A) 4 (B) 5 (D)

Note-taking

W: 3rd chapter gone, need to write essay
M: Check records → contact student → pay to replace
W: Have another copy?
M: No, book = published X, take a while to replace
　Solution = interlibrary loan system → fill out form
　Take up to 2 weeks, pick up @ library → save time

Listen to a conversation between a student and a librarian.

W: Hi. Uh, could I show you something? It's about this book. I noticed a problem with it last night.

M: A problem? What do you mean? Is it the wrong book?

W: ¹Well, it seems like the entire third chapter is gone. If you look inside, you'll see it's missing. I need that part of the book to write my essay.

M: Really? Let me take a look... Hmm, you're right. It looks like someone actually cut out those pages.

W: Why would someone do that?

M: I'm not quite sure. They could have easily copied the pages that they needed. ²Anyway, I'll check the records and contact the student who borrowed it before you. They will have to pay to replace the book.

W: OK... But that doesn't help me with my problem. Like I said, I need that chapter to complete my assignment. ⁵Does the library have another copy that I can borrow?

M: Um, let me check... Yeah, it's not your day. And the book is no longer published, so you probably won't find it in a bookstore. That means it's going to take us a while to replace it as well.

W: I really need to get another copy of that book. There must be another way to get it. Do you have any suggestions?

M: Well, there is one other option. ³Why don't you see if another library has the book?

W: All right... How exactly can I do that?

M: ³Well, the easiest thing to do would be to use the interlibrary loan system. If the book is available, you can fill out an online form to submit a request. You will be notified by e-mail when the book arrives. Then, you can pick it up...

W: That actually sounds pretty simple. How long does the process usually take?

M: Well, it can take up to two weeks. The book has to be sent here from another location. ⁴However, if I were you, I would pick it up myself at the library. That will save you some time.

W: OK. That would work better for me. If another library has it, I'll go there as soon as possible.

학생과 사서 사이의 대화를 들으시오.

W: 안녕하세요. 어, 뭐 좀 보여드려도 될까요? 이 책에 관한 건데요. 어젯밤에 이것에 문제가 있는 걸 알아챘어요.

M: 문제요? 무슨 말씀이신가요? 잘못된 책인가요?

W: 음, 세 번째 장 전체가 없어진 것 같아요. 안쪽을 보시면, 그것이 없는 게 보이실 거예요. 제 에세이를 쓰려면 책의 그 부분이 필요하거든요.

M: 정말요? 제가 책을 한번 볼게요... 흠, 학생 말이 맞네요. 누군가가 정말로 그 페이지들을 오려낸 것처럼 보이네요.

W: 누군가가 왜 그랬을까요?

M: 잘 모르겠어요. 필요한 페이지를 쉽게 복사할 수 있었을 텐데요. 어쨌든, 제가 기록을 확인하고 이전에 그것을 빌렸던 학생에게 연락할게요. 그분이 책 교체를 위해 비용을 지불해야 할 거예요.

W: 알겠어요... 그런데 그게 제 문제에는 도움이 되지 않아요. 말씀드렸듯이, 저는 과제를 완료하기 위해 그 장이 필요해요. 도서관에 제가 빌릴 수 있는 다른 한 권이 있나요?

M: 음, 확인해 볼게요... 네, 운이 없군요. 그리고 그 책은 더 이상 출간되지 않아요, 그러니까 학생은 아마 서점에서 그것을 찾지 못할 거예요. 저희가 그것을 교체하는 데에도 시간이 좀 걸릴 거라는 의미예요.

W: 저는 정말 그 책을 한 권 구해야 해요. 그것을 구할 다른 방법이 분명히 있을 거예요. 제안해 주실만 한 게 있나요?

M: 음, 한 가지 다른 선택지가 있어요. 다른 도서관에 그 책이 있는지 확인해 보는 게 어때요?

W: 알겠어요... 정확히 어떻게 하면 되죠?

M: 음, 가장 쉬운 건 도서관 상호 대출 제도를 이용하는 것일 거예요. 만약 책을 입수할 수 있으면, 요청을 제출하기 위해 온라인 양식을 작성할 수 있어요. 책이 도착하면 학생은 이메일로 통지받을 거고요. 그런 다음, 그것을 찾아올 수 있어요...

W: 정말 꽤 간단해 보이네요. 그 과정이 보통 얼마나 걸리나요?

M: 음, 2주까지 걸릴 수 있어요. 책은 다른 장소에서 여기로 보내져야 해요. 하지만, 제가 학생이라면, 직접 그 도서관에서 책을 찾아올 거예요. 그렇게 하는 게 시간을 조금 절약해줄 거예요.

W: 네. 그렇게 하는 게 낫겠네요. 만약 다른 도서관이 그것을 보유하고 있으면, 최대한 빨리 그곳으로 갈게요.

---

notice ⑧ 알아채다 chapter ⑲ (책의) 장 replace ⑧ 교체하다 suggestion ⑲ 제안 interlibrary loan system 도서관 상호 대출 제도 notify ⑧ 통지하다 process ⑲ 과정, 절차

1 학생의 문제는 무엇인가?

(A) 그녀는 도서관에서 잘못된 책을 빌렸다.

(B) 그녀는 도서관에 책을 반납하는 것을 잊었다.

(C) 그녀는 분실된 부분이 있는 책을 받았다.

(D) 그녀는 강의를 위해 필요한 책을 잃어버렸다.

2 사서는 왜 다른 학생에게 연락하려 하는가?

(A) 도서관 책의 위치를 알아내기 위해

(B) 파손된 물품에 대한 대금 지불을 요청하기 위해

(C) 일부 계정 정보를 업데이트하기 위해

(D) 책이 언제 반납될지 알아내기 위해

3 다른 도서관에서 책을 구하기 위해 학생은 무엇을 해야 하는가?

(A) 온라인 서류 작성하기

(B) 사무실에서 등록하기

(C) 대학에 이메일 보내기

(D) 다른 사서에게 연락하기

4 사서는 학생에게 시간을 절약하기 위해 무엇을 하라고 제안하는가?

(A) 그와 함께 다른 방문 일정 정하기

(B) 책을 직접 받기

(C) 다른 서점에 연락하기

(D) 책의 자택 배송 요청하기

대화의 일부를 다시 듣고 질문에 답하시오.

W: Does the library have another copy that I can borrow?

M: Um, let me check... Yeah, it's not your day. And the book is no longer published, so you probably won't find it in a bookstore.

5 사서는 이렇게 말함으로써 무엇을 암시하는가:

M: Yeah, it's not your day.

(A) 도서관은 모든 책을 한 권씩만 보유하고 있다.

(B) 학생은 다른 날에 돌아와야 한다.

(C) 책을 나중에 입수할 수 있을지도 모른다.

(D) 학생은 책 한 권을 구할 수 없다.

iBT Listening Test 2
본문 p. 68

1 (C)   2 (C)   3 (D)   4 (A)   5 (A)   6 (B)

Note-taking

Process of Metamorphosis of Caterpillars

• Caterpillar → metamorphosis → monarch butterfly
  - Hatch from egg → eat eggshell → grow quickly
  - Prod. silk → cocoon = protects inside
  - Outer shell → proteins → used as food by pupa
  - Some organs change shape (e.g. brain)
  - Imaginal discs → body part (e.g. eyes & wings & etc.)
  - Pupa break cocoon by breathing in air → grow larger
  - Wait 1~2 hrs. → wings dry → fly away

Listen to part of a lecture in a biology class.

P: [1]In our last class, I mentioned that some insects go through a process called metamorphosis. During this process, insects change their physical form as they grow. A good example is caterpillars, which go through metamorphosis to become monarch butterflies.

OK, so, caterpillars hatch from little eggs. When a caterpillar comes out of its egg, it begins to eat right away. First, it eats its own eggshell, and then it eats the leaves of plants. This allows the caterpillar to grow very quickly. It grows so fast that its skin changes four or five times, and it becomes about a thousand times bigger than its original size.

After about two weeks of eating, chemicals in the caterpillar's brain tell it to go to the next stage of metamorphosis. At this stage, the caterpillar uses all the food it ate to produce silk from its body. The silk is sticky and is used by the caterpillar to attach itself to a leaf or branch. Then, the caterpillar continues to produce silk until its entire body is covered in it. [2]This silk covering is called a cocoon, and it protects the caterpillar inside. The cocoon takes about one day to form.

When the cocoon is complete, the caterpillar's outer shell and other parts of its body are broken down into smaller proteins. At this point, the caterpillar is now a pupa, and it uses the smaller proteins as food. [3]Of course, some parts of the caterpillar are never broken down. These include organs from inside the insect's body, like the stomach or the brain. These organs are not destroyed, but they change shape to fit the insect's growing body. At the same time, the pupa has other groups of cells called imaginal discs. [4]Imaginal discs are groups of cells found on the pupa's skin. They are quite thin and flat, and each one holds a unique set of cells. These cells determine what specific body part an imaginal disc will become. So some imaginal discs will form a butterfly's eyes, others will form the wings, the legs, the antennae, and so on. This stage of development usually lasts from a few weeks to a month, but, for some kinds of butterflies, it can take up to two years.

[6]Once the body parts have fully formed, the pupa is now an adult butterfly. However, it is still inside the cocoon and must break through the cocoon to open its wings. The monarch butterfly, for example, does this by breathing in air. The air fills its body and makes it grow larger. This stretches out the cocoon and causes it to break open.

[5]After the butterfly has left its cocoon, it must wait one to two hours for its wings to dry completely before it can fly away. When that happens, the butterfly has completed its metamorphosis and is now ready to begin its adult life.

생물학 강의의 일부를 들으시오.

P: 지난 수업에서, 일부 곤충들이 변태라고 불리는 과정을 겪는다고 언급했어요. 이 과정 동안, 곤충들은 자라면서 몸의 형태를 바꿔요. 좋은 예시는 애벌레인데, 그것들은 왕나비가 되기 위해 변태를 거쳐요.

자, 그러니까, 애벌레는 작은 알에서 부화합니다. 애벌레가 알에서 나오면, 곧바로 먹기 시작해요. 먼저, 그것은 자신의 알껍데기를 먹은 다음, 식물의 잎을 먹어요. 이것은 애벌레가 매우 빠르게 자라도록 해줍니다. 그것은 너무 빨리 자라서 껍질이 네다섯 번 바뀌고, 원래 크기보다 천 배 정도 더 커져요.

약 2주 동안 먹은 후에, 애벌레의 뇌에 있는 화학물질들은 그것에게 변태의 다음 단계로 가라고 지시합니다. 이 단계에서, 애벌레는 몸에서 실을 생산하기 위해 먹은 음식 전부를 사용해요. 실은 끈적끈적하며 애벌레가 스스로를 잎이나 나뭇가지에 붙이기 위해 사용해요. 그런 다음, 애벌레는 몸 전체가 그 안에 덮일 때까지 계속해서 실을 생산하죠. 이 실로 된 외피를 고치라고 하며, 그것은 안에 있는 애벌레를 보호해요. 고치는 형성되는 데 하루 정도가 걸립니다.

고치가 완성되면, 애벌레의 바깥 껍데기와 몸의 다른 부분들은 더 작은 단백질들로 분해됩니다. 이 시점에, 애벌레는 이제 번데기이며, 그 더 작은 단백질들을 음식으로 이용해요. 물론, 애벌레의 어떤 부분들은 절대 결코 분해되지 않습니다. 이것들은 위나 뇌 같은 그 곤충의 몸 안쪽의 기관들을 포함해요. 이 기관들은 파괴되지 않고, 그 곤충의 성장하는 몸에 맞도록 모양을 바꾸죠. 동시에, 번데기는 성충판이라고 불리는 다른 세포 그룹을 가지고 있어요. 성충판은 번데기의 껍질에서 발견되는 세포 그룹입니다. 그것들은 상당히 얇고 평평하며, 각각은 독특한 일련의 세포들을 가지고 있습니다. 이 세포들은 성충판이 어떤 특정한 몸의 부위가 될지를 결정해요. 그러니까 몇몇 성충판은 나비의 눈을 형성하고, 다른 것들은 날개, 다리, 더듬이 등을 형성하죠. 발달의 이 단계는 보통 몇 주에서 한 달까지 지속되지만, 몇몇 종류의 나비들에게는, 이것이 2년까지 걸릴 수 있습니다.

몸의 부위들이 완전히 형성되면, 번데기는 이제 성충 나비가 돼요. 하지만, 그것은 여전히 고치 안에 있고 그것의 날개를 펴기 위해 고치를 뚫고 나와야 하죠. 예를 들어, 왕나비는 공기를 들이마심으로써 이렇게 해요. 공기가 그것의 몸을 채우고 그것이 더 커지게 하죠. 이것은 고치가 늘어나게 하고 부서지게 해요.

나비가 고치를 떠나면, 날아갈 수 있게 되기 전에 한두 시간 동안 날개가 완전히 마르기를 기다려야 해요. 그런 일이 일어나게 되면, 나비는 변태를 완료하고 그것의 성충으로서의 삶을 시작할 준비가 돼요.

metamorphosis 명 (곤충의) 변태   physical 형 몸의
caterpillar 명 애벌레   hatch 동 부화하다   chemical 명 화학물질
sticky 형 끈적끈적한   attach 동 붙이다   cocoon 명 고치
protein 명 단백질   pupa 명 번데기   organ 명 기관, 장기
imaginal disc 성충판   antenna 명 더듬이

1 강의는 주로 무엇에 관한 것인가?
   (A) 일부 곤충들이 그것들의 모양을 바꾸는 이유
   (B) 과학자들이 곤충들의 삶을 연구하는 방법
   (C) 곤충의 변태 과정
   (D) 곤충들 사이의 몸의 차이점

2 교수는 애벌레의 고치에 관해 무엇이라고 말하는가?
   (A) 그것은 어린 애벌레에게 음식을 제공한다.
   (B) 그것은 매끈하고 빛나는 외관을 가지고 있다.
   (C) 그것은 애벌레에게 보호를 제공한다.
   (D) 그것은 보통 형성되는 데 여러 날이 걸린다.

3 애벌레의 일부 기관들은 발달함에 따라 어떻게 되는가?
   (A) 그것들은 많은 단백질을 생산한다.
   (B) 그것들은 뇌 속에서 화학물질을 방출한다.
   (C) 그것들은 결합하여 새로운 부분들을 형성한다.
   (D) 그것들은 몸에 맞게 모양을 바꾼다.

4 교수에 따르면, 성충판은 무엇인가?
   (A) 몸의 부위를 형성하는 세포
   (B) 나비가 자라는 장소
   (C) 번데기의 껍질에 있는 색깔 패턴
   (D) 번데기 안쪽의 더 작은 곤충들

5 나비는 날아가기 전에 왜 한두 시간을 기다리는가?
   (A) 그것들의 날개가 말라야 한다.
   (B) 그것들은 먼저 무리로 모여야 한다.
   (C) 그것들의 날개가 완전히 펴지는 데 시간이 걸린다.
   (D) 그것들은 하루의 특정 시간에만 날 수 있다.

강의의 일부를 다시 듣고 질문에 답하시오.
P: Once the body parts have fully formed, the pupa is now an adult butterfly. However, it is still inside the cocoon and must break through the cocoon to open its wings. The monarch butterfly, for example, does this by breathing in air.

6 교수는 왜 이렇게 말하는가:
   P: The monarch butterfly, for example, does this by breathing in air.
   (A) 나비가 호흡하는 방법을 설명하기 위해
   (B) 과정 안의 단계를 설명하기 위해
   (C) 전문 용어를 정의하기 위해
   (D) 고치의 견고성을 강조하기 위해

Vocabulary Review
본문 p. 72

1 solution   2 hatch   3 psychological
4 organ   5 competitive   6 replace
7 attach   8 officially   9 possibility
10 (D)   11 (C)   12 (C)
13 (D)   14 (B)

Attitude

Example
본문 p. 75

A. (A)   B. (D)

A.

Note-taking
S: Econ. paper references?
P: Find newer references ∵ econ. changed a lot
   Need to know current ideas
   Look at references used in articles in class

Listen to a conversation between a student and a professor.

S: Hi, Professor. I'm getting ready to start my economics paper. These are the references I'll be using. What do you think?

P: Let's see... Uh, I'm afraid you'll have to find newer references. The ones you've chosen are quite old. Economics has changed a lot since these were published.

S: I thought they would be good because they are well-known.

P: Yes, they are very good books and articles, but you need to know the current ideas about the subject. We read a lot of recent articles in class... Do you still have them?

S: Of course. I kept everything from your class.

P: Well, take a look at the references used in those articles. That would be a good place to start.

학생과 교수 사이의 대화를 들으시오.

S: 안녕하세요, 교수님. 저는 제 경제학 보고서를 시작하려고 준비 중이에요. 이것들은 제가 사용할 참고 문헌들입니다. 어떻게 생각하세요?

P: 어디 보자... 어, 더 최근의 참고 문헌들을 찾아야 할 것 같구나. 네가 고른 것들은 꽤 오래됐어. 이것들이 발표된 이후로 경제학은 많이 변했단다.

S: 그것들이 잘 알려져 있기 때문에 좋을 거라고 생각했어요.

P: 맞아, 그것들은 매우 좋은 책과 논문들이지만, 너는 그 주제에 관한 최신 견해들을 알아야 해. 우리는 수업에서 많은 최근 논문들을 읽었지... 그것들을 여전히 가지고 있니?

S: 물론이죠. 교수님 수업의 모든 것들을 갖고 있었어요.

P: 음, 그 논문들에 사용된 참고 문헌들을 한번 보렴. 시작하기에 좋은 지점이 될 거야.

economics 명 경제학   reference 명 참고 문헌; 참고
publish 동 발표하다; 출판하다   well-known 형 잘 알려진
article 명 논문; 기사   current 형 최신의, 현재의

학생의 상황에 대한 교수의 태도는 무엇인가?

(A) 그는 학생이 좋지 않은 선택을 한 것에 대해 걱정한다.
(B) 그는 학생이 이미 그녀의 보고서를 시작한 것에 놀란다.
(C) 그는 학생이 충분한 조사를 했다고 확신한다.
(D) 그는 학생이 그의 제안을 듣지 않은 것에 마음이 상했다.

B.

Note-taking

Red Tide Phenomenon

- Seawater turns red = red tide
  - Cause = rapid growth of red algae
- Serious consequences for sea life & humans
- Cause health issues for ppl. on the shore
  - Symptom = skin irritation & burning feeling in eyes

Listen to part of a lecture in an environmental science class.

P: Every summer in different parts of the US, the seawater in some places turns red. This phenomenon is called a red tide. Uh, it is caused by a rapid growth of red algae. A red algae bloom has serious consequences for sea life as well as humans. Some species of red algae produce toxins that are released into the air. These can cause health issues for people on the

shore. Some of the common symptoms include skin irritation and, um, a burning feeling in the eyes. And, if anyone with breathing problems is planning a trip to the beach during a red tide... Well, let's just say it'd be better to make other plans.

환경 과학 강의의 일부를 들으시오.

P: 매년 여름 미국의 여러 지역에서는, 일부 장소의 바닷물이 붉게 변합니다. 이 현상은 적조라고 불려요. 어, 그건 홍조류의 빠른 성장 때문에 생깁니다. 홍조류 증식은 인간뿐만 아니라 해양 생물에게도 심각한 결과를 가져와요. 일부 홍조류 종들은 공기 중으로 방출되는 독소를 생산합니다. 이것들은 해안가에 있는 사람들에게 건강 문제를 일으킬 수 있어요. 흔한 증상 중 일부에는 피부 자극과, 음, 눈 따끔거림이 있어요. 그리고, 호흡 문제가 있는 누군가가 적조 중에 해변으로 여행 갈 계획을 세우고 있다면... 음, 그냥 다른 계획을 세우는 게 더 낫다고 해둘게요.

phenomenon 명 현상   red tide 적조   red algae 홍조류
consequence 명 결과   toxin 명 독소   symptom 명 증상

강의의 일부를 다시 듣고 질문에 답하시오.

P: Some of the common symptoms include skin irritation and, um, a burning feeling in the eyes. And if anyone with breathing problems is planning a trip to the beach during a red tide... Well, let's just say it'd be better to make other plans.

교수는 이렇게 말함으로써 무엇을 의미하는가:

P: Well, let's just say it'd be better to make other plans.

(A) 그는 증상이 예상보다 심각하다고 걱정한다.
(B) 그는 적조 문제가 곧 해결되기를 바란다.
(C) 그는 현상이 더 흔해졌다고 생각한다.
(D) 그는 적조가 일부 사람들에게 특히 위험하다고 생각한다.

Listening Practice 1
본문 p. 77

1 (B)   2 (A)   3 (A)   4 (C)   5 (D)

Note-taking

W: Using computer ∵ online exam in 10 min.
   Speakers work X
M: Other ones available X ∵ midterms
   Service engineer = another repair
W: Getting new speakers from supply room?
M: Submit request first → needs to be approved
   Service engineer has to check
W: Own computer O, speakers work X
M: Take my seat ∵ exam now

Listen to a conversation between a student and an assistant in a language lab.

W: Hi. Um... I have a problem. I'm hoping you can help me.

M: Sure. What can I do for you?

W: I'm using the computer in that seat over there...

It's, uh, number 51. I reserved it so I could take an online exam for my Spanish class. [1]The test is in 10 minutes, but the computer's speakers don't seem to be working.

M: Oh, really? Let me see if there are any other ones available... Hmm, it seems that we're full this morning. Midterms are this week, so we have more students than usual.

W: I understand. But I really need to take the exam. Do you think you could fix the speakers?

M: [5]The, uh, service engineer is working on another repair right now. He should be back in about three hours.

W: Hmm... Is there anything you can do in the meantime?

M: I'm sorry. I'd fix them myself if I knew how.

W: The exam is going to start soon. If I miss it, my grade will be affected. [2]How about getting new speakers from the supply room? We could connect them to the computer I'm using.

M: [2]I would do that if I could. But I have to submit a request first. And the request needs to be approved by the head of the maintenance department.

W: But this is kind of urgent... Can't you just get the speakers first and the approval later?

M: No, I can't do that. I have to follow the rules or I could lose my job. Besides, the service engineer has to check the speakers first to make sure they're broken. The problem could be caused by something else.

W: I don't know what to do.

M: Hmm... Don't you have your own computer?

W: [3]Yes, but my laptop is old. The speakers don't work, either. That's why I reserved a spot here at the language lab.

M: [4]I see. Well, I don't need speakers to do my work, so why don't you take my seat, instead? It's usually only for student assistants. However, since you have an exam now, we can switch places.

W: Really? That's so thoughtful of you!

어학실에서 학생과 조교 사이의 대화를 들으시오.

W: 안녕하세요. 음... 문제가 있어요. 절 도와주셨으면 좋겠어요.

M: 물론이죠. 무엇을 도와드릴까요?

W: 저는 저쪽 자리에서 컴퓨터를 사용하는 중인데요... 그것은, 어, 51번이에요. 제 스페인어 수업을 위한 온라인 시험을 볼 수 있도록 그것을 예약했어요. 시험이 10분 후에 있는데, 컴퓨터 스피커가 작동하지 않는 것 같아요.

M: 오, 정말요? 이용 가능한 다른 것들이 있는지 한번 볼게요... 흠, 오늘 아침에는 저희가 만원인 것 같네요. 중간고사가 이번 주라, 평소보다 학생들이 더 많네요.

W: 이해해요. 하지만 저는 정말 그 시험을 봐야 해요. 스피커를 수리해주실 수 있나요?

M: 어, 수리 기사는 지금 다른 수리 작업을 하고 있어요. 그는 대략 3

시간 후에 돌아올 거예요.

W: 흠... 그동안에 해주실 수 있는 게 있나요?

M: 죄송해요. 어떻게 하는지 안다면 제가 직접 수리했을 거예요.

W: 시험이 곧 시작해요. 제가 그걸 보지 못하면 제 성적이 영향을 받을 거예요. 비품실에서 새 스피커를 가져오시는 건 어때요? 우리가 그것들을 제가 사용 중인 컴퓨터에 연결할 수 있을 거예요.

M: 그럴 수 있다면 그렇게 하겠어요. 그런데 저는 먼저 요청을 제출해야 해요. 그리고 그 요청은 관리부장에 의해 승인되어야 해요.

W: 하지만 좀 긴급해요... 그냥 스피커부터 가져오고 승인은 나중에 얻으시면 안 되나요?

M: 아뇨, 그렇게 할 수는 없어요. 저는 규칙에 따라야 하고, 그렇지 않으면 직장을 잃을 수도 있어요. 게다가, 그것들이 고장 난 것임을 확실히 하기 위해 수리 기사가 먼저 스피커를 확인해야 해요. 다른 것에 의해 문제가 발생되었을 수 있어요.

W: 제가 어떻게 해야 할지 모르겠네요.

M: 흠... 본인 컴퓨터를 가지고 있지 않나요?

W: 있는데, 제 노트북 컴퓨터는 낡았어요. 스피커도 작동하지 않아요. 그게 제가 여기 어학실의 자리를 예약한 이유예요.

M: 알겠어요. 음, 저는 업무를 하기 위해서 스피커가 필요하지 않으니까, 대신 제 자리에 앉으시는 게 어때요? 보통은 학생 조교만을 위한 것이에요. 하지만, 학생이 지금 시험을 봐야 하니까, 우리가 자리를 바꿔도 돼요.

W: 정말요? 정말 사려 깊으시네요!

reserve (동) 예약하다 midterms (명) 중간고사
service engineer 수리 기사 in the meantime 그동안에
supply room 비품실 request (명) 요청 approve (동) 승인하다
maintenance department 관리부 urgent (형) 긴급한
approval (명) 승인 switch (동) 바꾸다 thoughtful (형) 사려 깊은

1 여자의 문제는 무엇인가?

   (A) 그녀는 시험을 위한 자리를 예약하고 싶어 한다.

   (B) 그녀는 일부 장비에 문제가 있다.

   (C) 그녀는 기기를 어떻게 사용하는지 모른다.

   (D) 그녀는 컴퓨터에 프로그램을 설치할 수 없다.

2 남자는 왜 비품실에서 새 스피커를 가져올 수 없는가?

   (A) 그는 먼저 승인을 요청해야 한다.

   (B) 그는 부서장에게 연락할 수 없다.

   (C) 그는 비품실에 대한 접근권이 없다.

   (D) 그는 컴퓨터 부품이 이용 가능한지 확인해야 한다.

3 여자는 왜 그녀의 노트북 컴퓨터의 문제를 언급하는가?

   (A) 그녀가 어학실 자리를 예약한 이유를 설명하기 위해

   (B) 컴퓨터의 흔한 문제를 묘사하기 위해

   (C) 그녀가 이미 파일을 다운로드 했음을 확인해주기 위해

   (D) 컴퓨터 관리의 중요성을 강조하기 위해

4 남자는 여자에게 무엇을 해주기로 하는가?

   (A) 부서에 서류 보내기

   (B) 사무실에 메시지 남기기

   (C) 그녀에게 조교를 위한 자리 사용하게 해주기

   (D) 그녀가 필요한 장비 교체하기

대화의 일부를 다시 듣고 질문에 답하시오.

M: The, uh, service engineer is working on another repair right now. He should be back in about three hours.
W: Hmm… Is there anything you can do in the meantime?
M: I'm sorry. I'd fix them myself if I knew how.

5 남자는 이렇게 말함으로써 무엇을 의미하는가:
   M: I'm sorry. I'd fix them myself if I knew how.

   (A) 그는 그가 마감 기한을 맞출 수 없다고 생각한다.
   (B) 그는 물품이 수리하기에 너무 오래 걸릴 거라고 생각한다.
   (C) 그는 그가 몇 개의 더 좋은 도구가 필요할 거라고 생각한다.
   (D) 그는 그가 할 수 있는 것이 있었으면 한다.

Listening Practice 2
본문 p. 79

1 (B) 2 (B) 3 (C) 4 (A), (D) 5 (D)

Note-taking
Effects of White-Tailed Deer Population Increase
- White-tailed deer's ability to adapt = key to success
  - Live in diff. habitats, near humans
- Serious impacts on ecosystem (e.g. forest)
  - Eat young leaves → plants grow X → diversity ↓
  - # of nesting sites ↓ (e.g. songbirds)
- Stop = humans do sth.
  - More natural predators (e.g. lions & wolves)
  - Hunting the deer ↑

Listen to part of a lecture in an ecology class.

P: Recently, we discussed endangered animals. Now, let's talk about a species that is doing well, the white-tailed deer. About 90 years ago, this species was endangered. Due to overhunting, there were only about 300,000 left in the US. But today, there are about 30 million… Obviously, that's a huge increase. ¹So now, let's consider what the effects of this population increase are on the environment.

But first, we need to understand the white-tailed deer's ability to adapt. In fact, this is the key to its success. This species lives in a variety of different habitats. They can survive in grasslands, wetlands, and, of course, forests… Uh, and they also live well near humans, especially, um, in suburban and agricultural areas…

S: ⁵I've heard that they do a lot of damage to crops. Doesn't that cause large economic losses?

P: Yes. The losses are huge. In fact, deer are responsible for more than half of all crop losses caused by wildlife. And that's only the tip of the iceberg… As I was saying, these deer can have serious impacts on whole ecosystems like forests… Um, they significantly influence the plants that grow there. ²Generally, deer prefer to eat young leaves, which can stop plants from growing. And they only eat certain kinds of plants. So, uh, these plants begin to disappear. Why is this a problem? Well, this can lower the diversity of plant species in the forest. And this reduces the food sources for other animals in the forest ecosystem.

What's more, the removal of leaves from plants reduces the number of nesting sites for animals. Consider songbirds, for example. Many songbird species build their nests close to the ground rather than high in the trees. However, deer consume a lot of the low forest leaves. These leaves hide the songbirds' eggs from predators. Without the leaves, the eggs are easier to see. As a result, predators eat the eggs, which reduces the number of birds.

³Now, we know that these deer can damage the forest ecosystem… The only way the deer can be stopped is if humans do something about the problem… ⁴ᴰOne way to achieve this is to introduce more natural predators into the deer's environment. For instance, animals such as mountain lions and wolves can reduce the number of white-tailed deer. However, this alone will not be enough to totally solve the problem. ⁴ᴬCertainly, the best and fastest method is hunting the deer in large numbers. This is why many states encourage hunting of this species.

생태학 강의의 일부를 들으시오.

P: 최근에, 우리는 멸종 위기에 처한 동물들에 대해 논의했어요. 이제, 잘 살고 있는 종인 흰꼬리사슴에 대해 얘기해 봅시다. 약 90년 전에, 이 종은 멸종 위기에 처해 있었어요. 과도한 사냥 때문에, 미국에 겨우 30만 마리 정도만 남아 있었죠. 하지만 오늘날, 약 3천만 마리가 있어요… 분명히, 그건 엄청난 증가예요. 자, 이제, 이 개체 수 증가가 환경에 미치는 영향을 생각해 보죠.

하지만 먼저, 우리는 흰꼬리사슴의 적응하는 능력을 이해해야 해요. 사실, 이건 그것의 성공의 열쇠예요. 이 종은 다양한 서식지에 살아요. 그것들은 초원, 습지, 그리고, 물론, 숲에서 생존할 수 있어요… 어, 그리고 그것들은 인간들 근처, 특히, 음, 교외와 농경지에서도 잘 살아요…

S: 그것들이 농작물에 큰 피해를 준다고 들었어요. 그게 큰 경제적 손실을 초래하지 않나요?

P: 맞아요. 손실이 커요. 사실, 사슴은 야생동물로 인한 모든 농작물 손실의 절반 이상에 책임이 있어요. 그리고 그건 빙산의 일각에 불과해요… 제가 얘기하고 있었듯이, 이 사슴들은 숲 같은 생태계 전체에 큰 영향을 미칠 수 있어요… 음, 그것들은 그곳에서 자라는 식물들에 큰 영향을 미치죠. 일반적으로, 사슴은 어린잎을 먹는 것을 선호하는데, 이는 식물이 자라는 것을 멈추게 할 수 있어요. 그리고 그것들은 특정 종류의 식물만 먹어요. 그래서, 어, 이 식물들은 사라지기 시작하죠. 이게 왜 문제일까요? 음, 이건 숲에 있는 식물 종류의 다양성을 낮출 수 있어요. 그리고 이것은 숲 생태계에 있는 다른 동물들을 위한 먹이 공급원을 줄여요.

게다가, 식물에서 잎을 제거하는 것은 동물들을 위한 둥지 영역의 수를 줄여요. 예를 들어, 명금을 생각해 보세요. 많은 명금 종들은 나무 높은 곳보다 땅 가까이에 둥지를 지어요. 하지만, 사슴은 낮은 곳에 있는 숲 나뭇잎들을 많이 먹어요. 이 잎들은 명금의 알을 포식자들로부터 숨겨주죠. 잎이 없으면, 알은 더 쉽게 발견돼요. 그 결과, 포식자들은 알을 먹는데, 이는 새의 수를 줄입니다.

이제, 우리는 이 사슴들이 숲 생태계에 피해를 줄 수 있다는 걸 알아요… 사슴을 막을 수 있는 유일한 방법은 인간들이 그 문제에 관해 무언가를 하는 거예요… 이것을 해내는 한 가지 방법은 사슴의 환경에 더 많은 자연 포식자들을 들여오는 거예요. 예를 들어, 산사자나 늑대 같은 동물들은 흰꼬리사슴의 수를 줄일 수 있어요. 하지만, 이것만으로는 그 문제를 완전히 해결하기에 충분하지 않을 거예요. 확실히, 가장 좋고 빠른 방법은 사슴을 대량으로 사냥하는 것입니다. 이것이 많은 주들이 이 종의 사냥을 장려하는 이유죠.

endangered 형 멸종 위기에 처한   overhunting 명 과도한 사냥, 남획
adapt 동 적응하다   habitat 명 서식지   suburban 형 교외의
the tip of the iceberg 빙산의 일각   ecosystem 명 생태계
diversity 명 다양성   removal 명 제거
songbird 명 명금(노래하는 새)   predator 명 포식자
achieve 동 해내다

1 강의는 주로 무엇에 관한 것인가?

(A) 멸종 위기에 처한 사슴 종들이 보호가 필요한 이유

(B) 사슴의 증가가 환경에 영향을 미치는 방식

(C) 사슴 종을 과도하게 사냥한 것의 결과

(D) 너무 많은 사슴이 인간의 거주지에 미치는 영향

2 교수에 따르면, 무엇이 몇몇 숲 식물이 사라지는 것에 기여하는가?

(A) 동물들의 활동이 토양의 양을 감소시킨다.

(B) 사슴이 특정한 종류의 잎과 식물을 먹는 것을 선호한다.

(C) 많은 동물들이 둥지를 짓기 위해 잎을 사용한다.

(D) 많은 수의 사슴이 식물을 밟는다.

3 사슴이 숲에 끼치는 피해에 대한 교수의 태도는 무엇인가?

(A) 그것은 사람들의 식량 공급원에 영향을 미칠 것이다.

(B) 그것이 일어나는 것을 막기에는 너무 늦었다.

(C) 그것은 사람들에 의해서만 멈추어질 수 있다.

(D) 그것은 사슴의 수에 부정적인 영향을 끼쳐 왔다.

4 교수에 따르면, 사슴의 수를 줄이는 두 가지 방법은 무엇인가? 2개의 답을 고르시오.

(A) 많은 수의 사슴을 사냥하는 것

(B) 사슴의 먹이 공급원을 제거하는 것

(C) 숲 주변에 울타리와 벽을 만드는 것

(D) 숲에 더 많은 자연 포식자들을 들여오는 것

강의의 일부를 다시 듣고 질문에 답하시오.

S: I've heard that they do a lot of damage to crops. Doesn't that cause large economic losses?

P: Yes. The losses are huge. In fact, deer are responsible for more than half of all crop losses caused by wildlife. And that's only the tip of the iceberg…

5 교수는 왜 이렇게 말하는가:

P: And that's only the tip of the iceberg…

(A) 사슴이 많은 종류의 서식지에서 발견될 수 있다는 것을 시사하기 위해

(B) 농작물에 해로울 수 있는 다른 종을 소개하기 위해

(C) 사슴이 모든 농작물 피해에 책임이 있지는 않다는 것을 보여주기 위해

(D) 사슴이 농업만을 위협하는 것이 아니라는 걸 시사하기 위해

Listening Practice 3

본문 p. 81

1 (C)   2 (C)   3 (A)   4 (D)   5 (A)

Note-taking

W: Café open until midnight during exam? ∵ study
M: Pay employees = cost too much
   Most employees = students ∴ need time to study
W: Library = X ∵ crowded
   Classroom = X ∵ eat & drink X
   Common room = O ∵ can stay late

Listen to a conversation between a student and an employee at the facilities management office.

W: Hello. I'm here to speak with someone about the campus café.

M: OK. Are you looking for a part-time job?

W: No. ¹It's about the café's opening hours. Do you think the school could keep it open until midnight during the exam period? It's a great place to study, but it closes at 8 p.m.

M: Hmm… Extending the café's hours isn't that simple.

W: You don't think it's possible?

M: Not really. First, we'd have to pay our employees to work longer hours. That would cost too much. ⁵Also, the café usually receives a limited amount of money from the school. It's unlikely there is enough money to keep it open for the extra hours.

W: Oh, I didn't think of that. I had no idea it would be so complicated.

M: Yes. ²In addition, most of the café's employees are students. They have to take exams, too, and need time to study. Besides, the library is open until midnight during the exam period. Why don't you study there?

W: ³The library isn't the best place to study, though. I mean, it's crowded. As you mentioned, everyone on campus is preparing for exams right now. So it's really difficult to find a free desk… You have to arrive early to find a spot.

M: What about unused classrooms? You could study in one of those…

W: That's true, but the reason why I prefer the café is because I'm allowed to eat and drink there.

M: That's a good point, but there's really no way the café can stay open later.

W: I see… I guess I'll have to think of somewhere else…

M: Um, I have another idea… What about the dormitory's common room?

W: It's a bit noisy with the TVs and people talking…

M: Yes, but you could try talking to the other residents… You know, you could suggest making the common room a quiet study area for the exam period.

W: That could work. The common room has comfortable furniture. ⁴And, most importantly, it's in our dormitory, so we can stay as late as we want. I just hope I can convince the other students.

시설 관리 사무실에서 학생과 직원 사이의 대화를 들으시오.

W: 안녕하세요. 캠퍼스 카페에 관해 누군가와 얘기하러 왔어요.

M: 네. 아르바이트 자리를 구하고 계신가요?

W: 아뇨. 카페의 영업시간에 관한 거예요. 시험 기간 동안 학교가 그곳을 자정까지 열어둘 수 있을까요? 그곳은 공부하기에 좋은 장소인데, 오후 8시에 닫아서요.

M: 흠... 카페의 영업시간을 연장하는 것은 그렇게 간단하지 않아요.

W: 그게 가능하다고 생각하지 않으시나요?

M: 그럴 것 같지 않아요. 먼저, 저희는 직원들에게 더 긴 시간을 일하도록 급여를 지불해야 할 거예요. 그것은 돈이 너무 많이 들 거고요. 또, 카페는 보통 학교에서 제한된 액수의 돈을 받거든요. 그것을 추가적인 시간 동안 열어둘 충분한 돈이 있을 것 같지 않아요.

W: 오, 그건 생각하지 못했네요. 그렇게 복잡할 줄은 몰랐어요.

M: 네. 게다가, 카페 직원 대부분은 학생이에요. 그들도 시험을 봐야 하고 공부할 시간이 필요해요. 또, 도서관은 시험 기간 동안 자정까지 열어요. 거기서 공부하시는 게 어때요?

W: 하지만, 도서관은 공부하기에 가장 좋은 장소가 아니에요. 그러니까, 그곳은 붐비잖아요. 말씀하신 대로, 캠퍼스 내의 모두가 지금 시험 준비를 하고 있어요. 그래서 사용 중이 아닌 책상을 찾기가 정말 어려워요... 자리를 찾으려면 일찍 도착해야만 해요.

M: 사용하지 않는 교실은 어때요? 그것들 중 하나에서 공부하실 수 있어요...

W: 맞아요, 그런데 제가 그 카페를 선호하는 이유는 거기에서 먹고 마시는 게 허용되기 때문이에요.

M: 좋은 지적이지만, 카페를 더 늦게까지 열 수 있는 방법은 정말 없어요.

W: 알겠습니다... 다른 곳을 생각해 봐야겠네요...

M: 음, 저한테 다른 아이디어가 있어요... 기숙사 공용실은 어때요?

W: 그곳은 TV와 이야기하는 사람들로 약간 시끄러워요...

M: 네, 하지만 학생이 다른 거주자들에게 한 번 얘기해보실 수 있잖아요... 그러니까, 시험 기간 동안 공용실을 조용한 학습 공간으로 만드는 것을 제안하실 수 있어요.

W: 될 수도 있겠네요. 공용실은 편안한 가구를 갖추고 있어요. 그리고, 가장 중요하게도, 그곳은 우리 기숙사 안에 있으니까 원하는 만큼 늦게까지 머물 수 있어요. 제가 다른 학생들을 설득할 수 있으면 좋겠네요.

opening hours 영업시간   midnight 뗑 자정   limited 혱 제한된
unlikely 혱 ~일 것 같지 않은   extra 혱 추가적인
complicated 혱 복잡한   in addition 게다가   besides 뷘 또, 게다가
common room 공용실   convince 뚱 설득하다

1 학생은 왜 시설 관리 사무실을 찾아가는가?

(A) 몇몇 시험의 일정에 대해 문의하기 위해

(B) 캠퍼스가 시험에 관해 학생들을 도울 방법을 제안하기 위해

(C) 시설이 영업시간을 연장할 것을 요청하기 위해

(D) 도서관 시설에 관해 불평하기 위해

2 직원은 카페의 학생 직원들에 대해 어떻게 생각하는가?

(A) 그는 그들이 일자리에 만족한다고 생각한다.

(B) 그는 그들이 시험을 위해 더 열심히 공부해야 한다고 생각한다.

(C) 그는 그들이 더 긴 시간을 일하게 하는 것이 불편하다.

(D) 그는 카페에서 공부한다는 그들의 생각에 동의한다.

3 학생은 도서관에 대해 무엇이라고 말하는가?

(A) 그것은 매우 빠르게 사람들로 가득 찬다.

(B) 그것은 공부하기에 가장 깨끗한 공간들을 보유하고 있다.

(C) 사람들이 실내로 음식을 가져오는 것은 흔한 일이다.

(D) 그것은 시험 기간 동안 때때로 시끄러워진다.

4 학생에 따르면, 기숙사 공용실은 왜 좋은 학습 공간이 될지도 모르는가?

(A) 학생들은 그곳에서 먹고 마실 수 있다.

(B) 그곳은 도서관과 동일한 가구를 보유하고 있다.

(C) 학생들은 보통 그곳에서 조용히 말한다.

(D) 그곳은 학생들이 원하는 만큼 오래 이용될 수 있다.

대화의 일부를 다시 듣고 질문에 답하시오.

M: Also, the café usually receives a limited amount of money from the school. It's unlikely there is enough money to keep it open for the extra hours.

W: Oh, I didn't think of that. I had no idea it would be so complicated.

5 학생은 이렇게 말함으로써 무엇을 암시하는가:

W: Oh, I didn't think of that.

(A) 그녀는 일이 쉬울 것이라고 생각했다.

(B) 그녀는 급여가 이미 지불되었다고 확신했다.

(C) 그녀는 직원을 설득하기 어려울 것이라고 생각했다.

(D) 그녀는 일부 직원들이 어떻게 반응할지에 대해 걱정했다.

Listening Practice 4

1 (A)   2 (B)   3 (B)   4 (B)   5 (A)

Note-taking
Market Orientation

- Market orient. = focus on customer want & need
- Ear. 20c. companies focused on prod.
  - 1950s new strategy = market orient.
- How? market research. (e.g. survey)
- Create value = entire comp. (e.g. Adopt a Customer)
  - Relationship bet. employee & customer ↑, success ↑
- Prob. = small companies afford X ∵ expensive
- Social media changed all → small biz. benefit

Listen to part of a lecture in a business management class.

P: All right class, let's begin. So, today we're going to study market orientation, which is an important concept in business. ¹Market orientation means that a company is oriented, or directed toward, the market. In other words, the company focuses on what customers want and need. It sounds like an obvious strategy to us, right? Well, it wasn't always companies' primary focus. [2]In the early 20th century, most companies focused on production. Um, their main goal was to make large quantities of goods at a low cost. But, by the 1950s, there were plenty of affordable goods. So companies needed a new strategy to earn larger profits... That's when the market orientation strategy was developed. The goal of this strategy is to create more value for customers.

Now, how do companies do this? Well, first, the companies need to understand their customers' preferences. And the best way to do that is through market research... For instance, many companies use surveys to get information about what customers want. Then, they use this research to create new products or add new features to existing products.

S: Doesn't every business do that? I mean, all companies have someone that does basic market research, right?

P: That's mostly true. But, with market orientation, creating value for customers becomes the focus of the entire company... It's not just the job of a specific person. You see, there are different ways to satisfy customers, and every individual in a company can contribute.

Let me give you an example. [3]Several years ago, a chemical manufacturing company started a program called "Adopt a Customer." The idea was that a factory worker visited a customer once a month to discuss the company's products and talk about the customer's needs. And then, the worker returned to the factory and made changes based on the customer's feedback. This kind of personal attention made customers feel highly valued and strengthened the relationship between the company's employees and customers. It also contributed to the company's success. [3]In fact, I think a lot of companies could learn something by studying this program. It really showed that all employees at a company should get involved.

[5]OK. So, over the past few decades, market orientation has become a very popular strategy in the business world. It isn't going away anytime soon. But, um, there is one last thing that I'd like to mention. Until recently, there was a problem with market orientation. Small companies could not afford to interact with customers in different areas. It was too expensive for them to travel. [4]But social media has changed all that. Now, companies can communicate with customers around the world very easily. Even the smallest businesses can contact their customers and benefit from market orientation.

경영학 강의의 일부를 들으시오.

P: 좋아요 여러분, 시작하죠. 자, 오늘 우리는 비즈니스에서 중요한 개념인 시장 지향에 대해 공부할 거예요. 시장 지향이란 회사가 시장을 향해 있다는, 즉 겨냥한다는 것을 의미해요. 다시 말해, 회사는 고객이 원하고 필요로 하는 것에 초점을 맞춰요. 우리에겐 뻔한 전략처럼 들리죠, 그렇죠? 음, 그것이 항상 회사들의 주된 초점이었던 건 아니에요. 20세기 초반에, 대부분의 회사들은 생산

에 초점을 맞췄어요. 음, 그것들의 주된 목표는 적은 비용으로 많은 양의 제품을 만드는 것이었죠. 하지만, 1950년대쯤에는, 적당한 가격의 제품들이 많이 있었어요. 그래서 회사들은 더 큰 이윤을 얻기 위한 새로운 전략이 필요했죠... 그때 시장 지향 전략이 개발되었어요. 이 전략의 목표는 고객을 위해 더 많은 가치를 창출하는 것이죠.

자, 회사는 이것을 어떻게 할까요? 음, 먼저, 회사는 고객들의 선호를 이해할 필요가 있어요. 그리고 그렇게 하는 가장 좋은 방법은 시장 조사를 통해서예요... 예를 들어, 많은 회사들은 고객들이 원하는 것에 대한 정보를 얻기 위해 설문조사를 이용하죠. 그런 다음, 새로운 제품을 만들거나 기존 제품에 새로운 기능을 추가하기 위해 이 조사를 이용합니다.

S: 모든 회사가 그렇게 하지 않나요? 그러니까, 모든 회사에 기본적인 시장 조사를 하는 사람이 있잖아요, 그렇죠?

P: 대부분 사실이에요. 하지만, 시장 지향에서는, 고객을 위해 가치를 창출하는 것이 회사 전체의 초점이 돼요... 그건 단지 특정한 사람의 일이 아니에요. 그러니까, 고객을 만족시키는 데는 다양한 방법이 있고, 회사 내의 모든 개인이 기여할 수 있죠.

예시를 하나 들어 볼게요. 몇 년 전에, 어떤 화학 제조 회사가 "고객을 채용하라"라는 프로그램을 시작했어요. 아이디어는 공장 직원이 한 달에 한 번 고객을 찾아가서 회사의 제품에 대해 논의하고 고객의 니즈에 대해 얘기하는 것이었어요. 그런 다음, 직원은 공장으로 돌아와서 고객의 의견을 기반으로 변화를 주었어요. 이런 종류의 개인적 관심은 고객들이 매우 존중받고 있다고 느끼게 했고 회사 직원과 고객들 사이의 관계를 강화했어요. 그것은 그 회사의 성공에 기여하기도 했습니다. 사실, 많은 회사들이 이 프로그램을 연구함으로써 무언가를 배울 수 있다고 생각해요. 그것은 회사의 모든 직원들이 참여해야 한다는 것을 실제로 보여주었죠.

좋아요. 자, 지난 수십 년 동안, 시장 지향은 비즈니스 세계에서 매우 인기 있는 전략이 되었어요. 그것이 곧 사라지지는 않을 거예요. 하지만, 음, 마지막으로 언급하고 싶은 게 있어요. 최근까지, 시장 지향에는 문제가 있었어요. 작은 회사들은 다양한 지역에 있는 고객들과 교류할 여유가 없었어요. 여행하기에는 너무 비쌌죠. 하지만 소셜 미디어는 그 모든 것을 바꾸었어요. 이제, 회사들은 전 세계의 고객들과 아주 쉽게 소통할 수 있어요. 가장 작은 기업들조차도 그들의 고객에게 연락하고 시장 지향의 혜택을 누릴 수 있습니다.

---

market orientation 시장 지향   concept 몡 개념
obvious 형 뻔한, 명백한   production 몡 생산   quantity 몡 양
affordable 형 (가격이) 적당한   preference 몡 선호
feature 몡 기능   satisfy 동 만족시키다   contribute 동 기여하다
feedback 몡 의견   interact with ~와 교류하다

1 강의는 주로 무엇에 관한 것인가?

   (A) 고객에게 초점을 맞추는 비즈니스 전략

   (B) 직원을 더 효율적으로 만드는 방법

   (C) 제품을 생산하는 혁신적인 방법

   (D) 새로운 시장에 제품을 홍보하는 방법

2 교수에 따르면, 20세기 초반에 회사들은 무엇에 초점을 맞추었는가?

   (A) 생산 오류를 줄이는 것

   (B) 제품을 효율적으로 생산하는 것

   (C) 공장 직원들을 훈련하는 것

   (D) 물품의 품질을 향상하는 것

3 교수는 "고객을 채용하라" 프로그램에 대해 어떻게 생각하는가?

    (A) 그것은 직원들의 일을 더 어렵게 만든다.

    (B) 그것은 다른 회사들에 유용할 수 있다.

    (C) 그것은 시장 지향의 필수 요소이다.

    (D) 그것은 한 사람의 책임이었어야 했다.

4 교수는 소셜 미디어에 대해 무엇이라고 말하는가?

    (A) 그것은 시장 지향의 중요성을 감소시켰다.

    (B) 그것은 시장 지향 기술의 적용을 더 쉽게 만든다.

    (C) 그것은 작은 회사들이 이용하기에 너무 비쌀 수 있다.

    (D) 그것은 다른 곳들보다 일부 국가에서 더 인기가 있다.

강의의 일부를 다시 듣고 질문에 답하시오.

P: OK. So, over the past few decades, market orientation has become a very popular strategy in the business world. It isn't going away anytime soon.

5 교수는 이렇게 말함으로써 무엇을 의미하는가:

P: It isn't going away anytime soon.

    (A) 그는 전략이 계속해서 널리 이용될 것이라고 생각한다.

    (B) 그는 더 많은 회사들이 시장 지향을 이용하기를 바란다.

    (C) 그는 시장 지향이 너무 많이 변했다고 생각한다.

    (D) 그는 방법에 여전히 몇몇 문제점이 있다고 생각한다.

---

iBT Listening Test 1 본문 p. 85

1 (B)   **2** (C)   **3** (A), (C)   **4** (A)   **5** (D)

Note-taking

P: Hope student join project
   How to get ppl. interested in dance @ young age
   Want to hold dance workshops for children
   Promote dance, great opp. for students
S: Teach on my own = challenging
P: Workshop = instructors lead, student = assistant
S: Busy schedule ∵ extra classes
P: Think about it

Listen to a conversation between a student and a professor.

S: Hi, Professor Morris. I got your e-mail. You said you wanted to see me about a project or something?

P: Yes. ¹I wanted to talk to you about a project I'm planning. I was hoping you could join.

S: That sounds interesting. I've enjoyed your classes a lot, so I'm sure it'll be good.

P: I'm glad to hear that. ²Uh, the project, well, it's something I've been working on with other professors in the dance department. At one of our meetings, we talked about how to get people interested in dance at a young age. And, well, the idea began from there.

S: Um, I'm not sure I understand... What is the project about?

P: Well, we want to hold dance workshops at city community centers for children.

S: That sounds fun. I mean, I think it's a good idea, but why is the department interested in dance workshops for children?

P: Well, there are a couple of reasons. ³ᶜFirst, we would like to promote dance in our community. Obviously, the department members are passionate about this art form. But we want to get others interested in it as well. Teaching young people how to dance seems like a good way to achieve this goal.

S: That makes sense.

P: ³ᴬAnother reason is that it would be a great opportunity for students like yourself. Uh, you will get some teaching experience. It would be good for you to learn how to share your skills and knowledge with others.

S: ⁵I see. So, um, would I be teaching children on my own? I don't know... That would be pretty difficult. Maybe too challenging.

P: No. Actually, the workshops would be directed by instructors from the university. I'm even going to lead one on ballet. However, we need talented students to show the dance movements and help the children. So you would be like an assistant teacher.

S: ⁴Um, the whole project sounds great. But I also have a really busy schedule these days. I've been taking extra classes.

P: I understand. Why don't you think about it for a couple of days? And if you have any questions, just contact me.

S: OK. Thanks for considering me.

학생과 교수 사이의 대화를 들으시오.

S: 안녕하세요, Morris 교수님. 이메일 받았습니다. 프로젝트나 그런 것 때문에 저를 보고 싶으셨다고요?

P: 맞아. 내가 계획하고 있는 프로젝트에 관해 너에게 이야기하고 싶었단다. 네가 참여할 수 있었으면 해.

S: 흥미로울 것 같아요. 제가 교수님의 수업들을 매우 즐겁게 들어서, 그건 분명 좋을 거예요.

P: 그 말을 들으니 기쁘구나. 어, 그 프로젝트는, 음, 내가 무용학과의 다른 교수님들과 작업해온 거야. 한 회의에서, 우리는 사람들이 어린 나이에 무용에 관심을 갖게 할 방법에 관해 이야기했어. 그리고, 음, 그 아이디어는 거기에서 시작됐지.

S: 음, 제가 이해하는지 모르겠어요... 프로젝트가 무엇에 관한 것인가요?

P: 음, 우리는 아이들을 위해 시 문화 센터에서 무용 워크숍을 개최하고 싶단다.

S: 재미있을 것 같아요. 그러니까, 좋은 생각인 것 같은데, 학과는 왜 아이들을 위한 무용 워크숍에 관심이 있나요?

P: 음, 두 가지의 이유가 있단다. 첫째로, 우리는 우리 지역 사회에서 무용을 홍보하고 싶어. 분명히, 학과 구성원들은 이 예술 양식에 열정적이야. 그런데 우리는 다른 사람들도 그것에 관심을 갖게 하고 싶어. 젊은 사람들에게 무용하는 법을 가르치는 것은 이 목표

를 달성하는 좋은 방법인 것 같거든.

S: 일리 있는 말씀이네요.

P: 또 다른 이유는 그것이 너와 같은 학생들에게 좋은 기회가 될 거라는 거야. 어, 너는 약간의 가르치는 경력을 얻게 될 거란다. 다른 사람들과 네 기술과 지식을 나누는 방법을 배우는 것은 너에게 좋을 거야.

S: 그렇군요. 그러니까, 음, 제가 혼자 아이들을 가르치게 될까요? 잘 모르겠어요... 꽤 어려울 것 같아요. 아마 너무 어려울 것 같은데요.

P: 아니란다. 사실, 워크숍은 대학에서 온 강사들에 의해 지도될 거야. 심지어 나도 발레 워크숍을 지도할 거란다. 하지만, 우리는 무용 동작을 보여주고 아이들을 도와줄 재능 있는 학생들이 필요해. 그러니까 조교 같을 거야.

S: 음, 프로젝트 전부 좋을 것 같아요. 하지만 저는 요즘 매우 바쁜 일정을 가지고 있어요. 저는 추가적인 수업들을 듣고 있거든요.

P: 이해한다. 그것에 대해 이틀 정도 생각해 보는 게 어떠니? 그리고 질문이 있으면, 나에게 연락하렴.

S: 네. 저를 고려해 주셔서 감사합니다.

hold 图 개최하다   community center 문화 센터
promote 图 홍보하다   obviously 图 분명히
passionate 图 열정적인   achieve 图 달성하다
opportunity 图 기회   knowledge 图 지식
challenging 图 어려운, 도전적인   direct 图 지도하다
instructor 图 강사   talented 图 재능 있는   assistant teacher 조교
extra 图 추가적인   consider 图 고려하다

1 교수는 왜 학생을 보자고 했는가?

(A) 행사를 계획하는 데 그의 도움을 요청하기 위해

(B) 그를 활동에 참여하도록 초대하기 위해

(C) 그를 수업에 등록하도록 독려하기 위해

(D) 그에게 과제에 대한 의견을 주기 위해

2 교수에 따르면, 프로젝트에 대한 아이디어는 어디에서 왔는가?

(A) 학과의 교수가 쓴 기사

(B) 무용에 관심이 있는 학생과의 대화

(C) 회의 중 교수들 간의 논의

(D) 다른 수업의 학생이 제출한 보고서

3 학과가 무용 워크숍 개최를 계획하는 두 가지 이유는 무엇인가? 2개의 답을 고르시오.

(A) 그것들은 학생들이 그들의 가르치는 역량을 개발하도록 해줄 것이다.

(B) 그것들은 교수들과 학생들이 소통할 기회일 것이다.

(C) 그것들은 예술의 종류에 대한 관심을 끌 좋은 방법일 것이다.

(D) 그것들은 젊은 사람들이 대학에서 무용을 공부하도록 영감을 줄 것이다.

4 프로젝트에 참여하는 것에 대한 학생의 태도는 무엇인가?

(A) 그는 그것이 시간이 너무 많이 걸릴까 봐 걱정한다.

(B) 그는 그것이 유용한 경험일 거라고 생각하지 않는다.

(C) 그는 그것이 다른 학생들과 함께 일하는 것을 포함하기를 바란다.

(D) 그는 그것이 다른 교수와 논의되어야 한다고 생각한다.

대화의 일부를 다시 듣고 질문에 답하시오.

S: I see. So, um, would I be teaching children on my own? I don't know... That would be pretty difficult. Maybe too challenging.

P: No. Actually, the workshops would be directed by instructors from the university.

5 학생은 왜 이렇게 말하는가:

S: Maybe too challenging.

(A) 그가 무엇을 해야 하는지 그가 이해하지 못한다는 것을 말하기 위해

(B) 그가 아이들을 가르칠 수 있다는 것을 암시하기 위해

(C) 교수의 기대가 타당하다는 것을 보여주기 위해

(D) 그가 활동을 하는 것에 자신이 없다는 것을 나타내기 위해

iBT Listening Test 2
본문 p. 88

1 (B)   2 (C)   3 (C)   4 (B)   5 (A)   6 (C)

Note-taking

Kinetic Art

- Ear. 19c. artists wanted 3d art that moved
  - How? stick, wire, hang objects (e.g. stones, coins)
- Balance = important feature of mobiles
- Famous artist = Alexander Calder
  - Expected to be artist → study engineering
  - Engin. skills → mobiles (e.g. standing, hanging)
- Standing mobiles = heavy stand, wire important
- Hanging mobiles = stand X, hung ← ceiling, used metal
- Inspired pro. in other jobs, big impact

Listen to part of a lecture in an art class.

P: I'm sure you're all familiar with toy mobiles. Parents hang them above a baby's bed. They have colorful shapes and move in the air. But did you know that the earliest mobiles were a type of art called kinetic art? ¹Well, kinetic art is a type of art that involves movement. And this is what we'll be looking at today.

So... In the early 19th century, kinetic artists wanted to create three-dimensional art that moved. How did they do this? Well, they typically used one or more sticks made of wood or metal. Then, the artists would attach wires to the sticks and hang objects from the wires. ⁶Often, kinetic artists used everyday objects... These could be things like small stones or coins... Basically, anything that was possible to hang from wires could be used.

Now, imagine that you hang an object from one end of a stick. What will happen? The stick will be lower on one side, of course. So artists placed objects on both ends of the stick to keep the stick in balance. ²So, you see, balance is an important feature of mobiles. Artists could create a variety of mobiles using objects with different weights or shapes. They could also use multiple sticks with different lengths.

Um, let's look at an example of a famous kinetic artist. His name is Alexander Calder. ³Now, with Calder's family background, it was expected that he would become an artist. His parents and grandfather were artists, and they encouraged him to work in art. So, Calder had some interest in art, but he chose to study engineering... The influence of his education is obvious in his work. You see, he used his engineering skills to create pieces with movement. His early works were sculptures with motors in them. Uh, the motors made the sculptures move. But, later on, he developed other kinds of mobiles that had no motors at all. ⁴These included standing mobiles and hanging mobiles.

Standing mobiles had a heavy stand on the floor to keep them stable. Then, a long metal stick was placed in the center of the stand. From the stick, Calder hung simple objects from wires. The use of wires was important. They allowed Calder's objects to move with a light touch or even small amounts of wind. Later, Calder designed hanging mobiles that required no stand at all. These mobiles could be hung directly from the ceiling. And, instead of using everyday objects, he cut metal into simple shapes like circles and triangles. He then painted the shapes in different colors.

Anyway, Calder became famous for his mobiles because they let people experience art in a new way. I mean, they're very creative and fun to look at. They even inspired professionals that worked in other jobs, such as architects, interior designers, and jewelry makers. ⁵Indeed, Calder had a big impact on the art world. Even today, he is considered one of the most important American artists.

미술학 강의의 일부를 들으시오.

P: 모두들 장난감 모빌에 익숙할 거예요. 부모들은 그걸 아기 침대 위에 매달아 놓죠. 그것들은 다채로운 모양을 하고 있고 공중에서 움직여요. 그런데 최초의 모빌들이 키네틱 아트라고 불리는 예술의 한 종류였다는 것을 알고 있었나요? 음, 키네틱 아트는 움직임을 포함하는 예술의 종류예요. 그리고 이것이 오늘 우리가 살펴볼 것이에요.

그러니까... 19세기 초반에, 키네틱 아티스트들은 움직이는 3차원 예술품을 만들어내기를 원했어요. 그들이 어떻게 이것을 했을까요? 음, 그들은 일반적으로 나무나 금속으로 만들어진 하나 이상의 막대기를 사용했습니다. 그런 다음, 그 아티스트들은 막대기들에 철사를 붙이고 철사에 물체를 매달았어요. 때때로, 키네틱 아티스트들은 일상적인 물체들을 사용했어요... 이것들은 작은 돌이나 동전 같은 것들이 될 수 있었죠... 기본적으로, 철사에 매달릴 수 있는 것은 무엇이든지 사용될 수 있었습니다.

자, 여러분이 막대기의 한쪽 끝에 물체를 매단다고 상상해 보세요. 어떤 일이 일어날까요? 막대기는 물론, 한 쪽이 더 낮아질 거예요. 그래서 아티스트들은 막대기의 균형을 유지하기 위해 양 끝에 물체를 놓았어요. 자, 그러니까, 균형은 모빌의 중요한 특징이에요. 아티스트들은 다양한 무게나 모양을 가진 물체들을 사용해서 다양한 모빌을 만들 수 있었는데요. 그들은 서로 다른 길이를 가진 여러 개의 막대기를 사용할 수도 있었어요.

음, 유명한 키네틱 아티스트의 예시를 살펴볼게요. 그의 이름은 알렉산더 콜더에요. 자, 콜더의 가족 배경에 따라, 그는 예술가가

될 것으로 기대되었어요. 그의 부모님과 할아버지는 예술가였고, 그들은 그가 예술 분야에서 일하도록 격려했어요. 자, 콜더는 예술에 약간의 관심이 있었지만, 공학을 공부하기로 선택했어요... 그의 작품에서 교육의 영향은 뚜렷해요. 그러니까, 그는 움직임이 있는 작품들을 만들기 위해 그의 공학 기술을 사용했어요. 그의 초기 작품들은 안에 모터가 들어있는 조각품들이었어요. 어, 모터가 그 조각품들을 움직이게 했죠. 하지만, 나중에, 그는 모터가 전혀 없는 다른 종류의 모빌들을 개발했어요. 이것들은 서 있는 모빌과 매달려 있는 모빌을 포함했죠.

서 있는 모빌은 그것들을 안정적으로 유지하기 위해 바닥에 무거운 스탠드를 가지고 있었어요. 그런 다음, 긴 금속 막대기가 스탠드의 중앙에 놓여졌죠. 막대기로부터, 콜더는 철사에 간단한 물체들을 매달았어요. 철사의 사용은 중요했습니다. 그것들은 콜더의 물체들이 가벼운 접촉이나 약간의 바람만으로도 움직이게 했어요. 나중에, 콜더는 스탠드가 전혀 필요 없는 매달려 있는 모빌을 고안했어요. 이 모빌들은 천장에 직접 매달릴 수 있었죠. 그리고, 일상적인 물체들을 사용하는 대신, 그는 금속을 원이나 삼각형 같은 단순한 모양으로 잘라냈어요. 그런 다음 그는 그 모양들을 서로 다른 색으로 칠했죠.

어쨌든, 콜더는 그의 모빌이 사람들에게 새로운 방식으로 예술을 경험하게 해주었기 때문에 유명해졌어요. 그러니까, 그것들은 매우 창의적이었고 보기에 재밌었어요. 그것들은 심지어 건축가, 실내 디자이너, 보석 제작자와 같이 다른 직종에서 일하는 전문가들에게도 영감을 주었죠. 확실히, 콜더는 예술계에 큰 영향을 미쳤습니다. 심지어 오늘날에도, 그는 가장 중요한 미국인 예술가 중 한 명으로 여겨져요.

---

mobile 명 모빌 three-dimensional 형 3차원의
attach 동 붙이다 everyday 형 일상적인 feature 명 특징
variety of ~이 다양한 multiple 형 여러 개의 background 명 배경
engineering 명 공학 influence 명 영향 sculpture 명 조각품
stable 형 안정적인 creative 형 창의적인

1 강의는 주로 무엇에 관한 것인가?

(A) 현대 예술의 발전
(B) 움직임을 포함하는 예술의 종류
(C) 모빌이 시각 예술에 미친 영향
(D) 키네틱 아트의 인기

2 교수는 모빌의 중요한 특징이 무엇이라고 말하는가?

(A) 그것들은 비슷한 무게를 가진 물체들을 사용한다.
(B) 그것들은 서로 다른 재질의 물품들을 포함한다.
(C) 그것들은 균형의 개념에 의존한다.
(D) 그것들은 2차원 디자인으로 시작한다.

3 교수는 왜 콜더의 가족 배경을 이야기하는가?

(A) 콜더가 예술을 공부하기로 선택한 이유를 설명하기 위해
(B) 콜더의 가족이 그가 성공하도록 도운 방법을 보여주기 위해
(C) 예술에 대한 콜더의 관심의 이유를 제공하기 위해
(D) 콜더가 그의 진로를 바꾼 이유를 설명하기 위해

4 알렉산더 콜더에 의해 만들어진 모빌에 관해 사실인 것은?

(A) 그것들은 대조를 만들기 위해 밝고 어두운색들을 사용했다.
(B) 일부는 서 있었고 다른 것들은 매달려 있었다.
(C) 그것들은 예술가에 의해 만들어진 최초의 모빌이 아니었다.
(D) 대부분은 움직이게 하기 위해 전기가 필요했다.

5 알렉산더 콜더에 대한 교수의 의견은 무엇인가?

    (A) 그녀는 콜더가 예술계에 크게 영향을 미쳤다고 생각한다.

    (B) 그녀는 콜더의 작품이 이해하기 어렵다고 생각한다.

    (C) 그녀는 콜더가 제한된 영향력을 가지고 있었다는 데 동의한다.

    (D) 그녀는 많은 사람들이 콜더에 대해 잘못된 생각을 가지고 있다고 생각한다.

강의의 일부를 다시 듣고 질문에 답하시오.

P: Often, kinetic artists used everyday objects… These could be things like small stones or coins… Basically, anything that was possible to hang from wires could be used.

6 교수는 왜 이렇게 말하는가:

    P: These could be things like small stones or coins…

    (A) 키네틱 아트의 재료들이 저렴했다는 것을 보여주기 위해

    (B) 무게가 같은 두 물체를 명시하기 위해

    (C) 모빌에 사용된 물체들의 예시를 제공하기 위해

    (D) 간단한 예술품을 만드는 것의 중요성을 강조하기 위해

Vocabulary Review

본문 p. 92

1 unlikely	2 habitat	3 diversity
4 endangered	5 current	6 satisfy
7 adapted	8 features	9 limited
10 (A)	11 (C)	12 (B)
13 (A)	14 (D)	

CHAPTER 05
Organization

Example

본문 p. 95

A. (C)　　**B.** (D)

A.

Note-taking

W: Issue with dorm. room
    Air con = turns on, only warm air
M: Heater & air con = one system
W: Friend checked → broken
M: Send someone afternoon, stay in lounge

Listen to a conversation between a student and a dormitory manager.

W: Hi, I'm having an issue with my dormitory room.

M: Uh… It's not the air conditioner again, is it? I thought we fixed it last time…

W: That's right. I tried to use it last night and it still isn't working. Um, it turns on, but only warm air comes out.

M: Are you using it correctly? As you know, the heater and air conditioner are all part of one system.

W: Yes, I am. I even asked my friend Jamie to come over to check. It's definitely broken.

M: In that case, I'll send someone to your room this afternoon. In the meantime, you might want to stay in the lounge to stay cool.

학생과 기숙사 관리자 사이의 대화를 들으시오.

W: 안녕하세요, 제 기숙사 방에 문제가 있습니다.

M: 어… 또 에어컨은 아니죠, 그렇죠? 지난번에 저희가 수리했다고 생각했는데요…

W: 맞아요. 어젯밤에 그것을 사용하려고 했는데 여전히 작동하지 않아요. 음, 켜지기는 하는데, 따뜻한 공기만 나와요.

M: 그것을 올바르게 사용하고 계신가요? 아시다시피, 난방기와 에어컨은 모두 하나의 장치의 일부예요.

W: 네, 그렇게 하고 있어요. 저는 심지어 제 친구 Jamie에게 와서 확인해 달라고 했어요. 그것은 분명히 고장 났어요.

M: 그런 경우라면, 오늘 오후에 제가 누군가를 학생의 방에 보낼게요. 그동안에, 시원하게 있기 위해 휴게실에 계시는 게 좋겠네요.

dormitory 몡 기숙사　　turn on 켜다　　correctly 뷔 올바르게
definitely 뷔 분명히　　in the meantime 그동안에　　lounge 몡 휴게실

학생은 왜 그녀의 친구 Jamie를 언급하는가?

    (A) Jamie가 에어컨을 수리한 방법을 설명하기 위해

    (B) 다른 기숙사 방들의 문제에 대해 이야기하기 위해

    (C) 에어컨이 고장 났다는 것을 강조하기 위해

    (D) Jamie가 비슷한 문제를 겪고 있다는 것을 보여주기 위해

B.

Note-taking
Veganism

- Veganism = avoid animal prod., follower = vegan
- Vegan & vegetarian same X
  - Both eat meat X
  - Vegan = consume anything prod. by animal X
- Vegan = use prod. made fr. animal X (e.g. leather shoes)
- Why? health reason, moral decision

Listen to part of a lecture in a nutrition class.

P: Veganism is a way of life that avoids the use of any animal products. People who follow this are known as vegans. Um, vegans are kind of like vegetarians, but they are not exactly the same… Although both groups do not eat meat, vegans will not consume anything produced by an animal. For example, they don't drink milk or eat cheese because these products come from cows. In addition, veganism goes beyond a person's diet. Um, vegans do not even use any products made from animals. This means that they do not buy leather shoes, for instance. Now, you may be wondering why people become vegans... Well, some follow veganism for health reasons. But, for others, it is a moral decision not to kill animals.

영양학 강의의 일부를 들으시오.

P: 비거니즘은 모든 동물성 식품의 사용을 피하는 삶의 방식입니다. 이를 추구하는 사람들은 비건으로 알려져 있어요. 음, 비건은 채식주의자와 비슷하지만, 완전히 같지는 않아요... 두 집단 모두 고기를 먹지 않지만, 비건은 동물에 의해 생산된 어떤 식품도 먹지 않을 거예요. 예를 들어, 그들은 우유를 마시거나 치즈를 먹지 않는데, 이는 이 식품들이 소에서 나오기 때문이죠. 게다가, 비거니즘은 한 사람의 식습관을 넘어서요. 음, 비건은 심지어 동물로 만든 어떤 제품도 사용하지 않아요. 이것은 그들이, 예를 들어, 가죽 신발을 구입하지 않는다는 걸 의미해요. 자, 여러분은 아마 사람들이 비건이 되는 이유가 궁금할 거예요... 음, 어떤 사람들은 건강상의 이유로 비거니즘을 추구해요. 하지만, 다른 사람들에게는, 동물을 죽이지 않는 것이 도덕적인 결정이죠.

---

veganism 명 비거니즘(엄격한 채식주의) avoid 동 피하다
vegetarian 명 채식주의자 go beyond ~을 넘어서다 diet 명 식습관
leather 명 가죽 moral 형 도덕적인

교수는 비거니즘을 어떻게 소개하는가?

(A) 그것의 기원과 역사를 설명함으로써
(B) 그것의 건강상 이점을 강조함으로써
(C) 도덕적인 문제를 지적함으로써
(D) 그것을 비슷한 삶의 방식과 비교함으로써

Listening Practice 1

본문 p. 97

1 (C)   2 (A)   3 (D)   4 (C)   5 (B)

Note-taking

W: Library website = always accurate X
    Website = checked out → library = on shelf
M: Home page = updated once/day
    System = old ∵ not enough $ → late showing update
W: System updated X → waste of time
M: Will mention at staff meeting
    Recommend submit letter requesting change
    Get many students sign letter

Listen to a conversation between a student and a librarian.

M: Hi there. How can I help you?

W: ¹I've got a question about the library's website.

M: Sure. Are you having difficulties using it?

W: Not exactly. ¹It just, uh, seems like the website isn't always accurate.

M: What do you mean?

W: I used the website this morning to check if a book was here. It said the book was checked out. But when I came this afternoon, I saw the book on a shelf.

M: I understand. I think the previous borrower must have returned the book earlier today. ²You see, the home page is only updated once a day, in the afternoon. Our computer system is quite old. But the library doesn't have enough money for a new one. That's why the website can be late in showing updates.

W: Doesn't that cause problems? I mean, if the system isn't updated, a book that's already checked out can be listed as available. ⁵Students might even come to the library for a book that isn't here. That seems like a waste of time.

M: I hear you. It can be frustrating. I'll mention the issue again at our staff meeting next week. We might be able to improve our computer system this time.

W: That's a good idea. It would really help to improve the website's accuracy.

M: I agree. But it might not be enough to just mention it in our meeting. ³So I would recommend that you also submit a letter to the university requesting a change.

W: Do you really think that would help?

M: Well, it will get the university's attention. That could encourage the university to act.

W: You're right. I'll do that.

M: And if I were you, I would get many students to sign the letter. That will also help.

W: Oh, really? ⁴Then, I'll tell my friends about this too. I'm sure they know many students who would agree to sign the letter. Thanks!

학생과 사서 사이의 대화를 들으시오.

M: 안녕하세요. 어떻게 도와드릴까요?

W: 도서관 웹사이트에 관해 질문이 있어요.

M: 물론이죠. 그것을 사용하는 데 어려움이 있으신가요?

W: 꼭 그렇지는 않아요. 그냥, 어, 웹사이트가 항상 정확하지는 않은 것 같아서요.

M: 무슨 말씀이시죠?

W: 저는 어떤 책이 여기에 있는지 확인하기 위해 오늘 아침에 그 웹사이트를 이용했어요. 그건 그 책이 대출되었다고 했어요. 그런데 제가 오늘 오후에 왔을 때, 그 책이 책꽂이에 있는 걸 봤어요.

M: 알겠습니다. 제 생각에는 이전 대출자가 오늘 더 일찍 그 책을 반납했을 것 같네요. 그러니까, 그 홈페이지는 오후에 하루 한 번만 업데이트돼요. 저희의 컴퓨터 시스템은 꽤 낡았어요. 하지만 도서관은 새것을 위한 충분한 돈이 없어요. 그것이 그 웹사이트가 업데이트를 보여주는 데 있어 더딜 수 있는 이유예요.

W: 그게 문제를 일으키지 않나요? 그러니까, 시스템이 업데이트되지 않으면, 이미 대출된 책이 이용 가능한 것으로 기입되어 있을 수도 있잖아요. 학생들은 심지어 여기에 있지 않은 책을 위해 도서관에 올지도 모르고요. 그건 시간 낭비인 것 같아요.

M: 이해해요. 그것이 불만스러울 수 있어요. 제가 다음 주에 직원 회의에서 그 문제를 다시 언급할게요. 이번에는 저희의 컴퓨터 시스템을 개선할 수 있을지도 몰라요.

W: 좋은 생각이에요. 웹사이트의 정확성을 개선하면 정말 도움이 될 거예요.

M: 동의해요. 그런데 회의에서 그것을 언급하는 것만으로는 충분하지 않을지도 몰라요. 그러니까 학생도 대학에 변화를 요청하는 서한을 제출하는 것을 추천할게요.

W: 정말 그게 도움이 될 거라고 생각하세요?

M: 음, 그것이 대학의 주의를 끌 거예요. 그것이 대학이 행동을 취하도록 촉진할 수도 있어요.

W: 맞아요. 그렇게 할게요.

M: 그리고 제가 학생이라면, 많은 학생들이 그 서한에 서명하도록 할 거예요. 그것도 도움이 될 거예요.

W: 오, 정말요? 그럼, 제 친구들에게도 이것에 대해 얘기할게요. 그들은 분명히 그 서한에 서명하는 데 동의할 많은 학생들을 알 거예요. 감사합니다!

accurate 형 정확한   check out (책을) 대출하다   shelf 명 책꽂이   list 동 (명단 등에) 기입하다   frustrating 형 불만스러운   recommend 동 추천하다   attention 명 주의, 관심   encourage 동 촉진하다   act 동 행동을 취하다

1 학생은 왜 사서를 찾아가는가?

(A) 도서관 컴퓨터에 관한 문제를 보고하기 위해

(B) 책 대출을 위한 절차에 관해 불평하기 위해

(C) 웹사이트의 정확성에 관한 문제를 논의하기 위해

(D) 과제를 위한 연구 자료를 찾는 데 도움을 받기 위해

2 사서에 따르면, 도서관 홈페이지는 왜 하루에 한 번만 업데이트되는가?

(A) 도서관은 더 나은 컴퓨터 시스템을 갖출 형편이 안 된다.

(B) 업데이트를 담당하는 직원이 파트타임으로만 일한다.

(C) 대학은 새 컴퓨터를 위한 요청을 승인하지 않았다.

(D) 직원은 반납된 모든 책을 확인하기 위해 시간이 필요하다.

3 사서는 학생에게 어떻게 조언하는가?

(A) 다른 학생의 최근 경험을 언급함으로써

(B) 학생에게 다른 대학 도서관을 알아보게 함으로써

(C) 계획의 장점과 단점을 보여줌으로써

(D) 요청을 하기 위한 방법을 추천함으로써

4 학생은 그녀가 무엇을 할 것이라고 말하는가?

(A) 문제에 관해 논의하기 위해 회의 참석하기

(B) 도움을 요청하기 위해 직원에게 연락하기

(C) 그녀의 친구들에게 더 많은 학생들을 찾는 것을 도와달라고 요청하기

(D) 요청을 확인하기 위해 도서관 직원에게 전화하기

대화의 일부를 다시 듣고 질문에 답하시오.

W: Students might even come to the library for a book that isn't here. That seems like a waste of time.

M: I hear you. It can be frustrating. I'll mention the issue again at our staff meeting next week.

5 사서는 이렇게 말함으로써 무엇을 의미하는가:

M: I hear you.

(A) 그는 학생이 더 조용히 말하기를 원한다.

(B) 그는 학생이 어떻게 느끼는지 이해한다.

(C) 그는 학생이 나중에 돌아와야 한다고 생각한다.

(D) 그는 학생이 무엇을 찾고 있는지 알고 있다.

1 (C)   2 (D)   3 (A)   4 (B)   5 (B)

Note-taking

Theodor Geisel

- Geisel = reason children's book became fun
- Started as illustrator & cartoonist = important exp.
- 1937 = first children's book → success X
- 1957 = publisher asked → wrote The Cat in the Hat
- Important ∵ fun → change ppl. thought → successful
- By 1991 published 40 books as Dr. Seuss
- 1984 = special award ∵ accomplish. & influence
- Changed education forever

Listen to part of a lecture in a literature class.

P: OK, so when you think of children's books today, you probably think of interesting stories with colorful pictures. But this wasn't always the case. Traditionally, most children's books had simple and uninteresting stories. This changed in the 20th century with the work of Theodor Geisel. Uh, I'm sure you've all read his work, but you probably know him as Dr. Seuss... ¹Anyway, Geisel is the reason why children's books became fun and interesting...

Um, let me give you a little background on his career. ²Geisel started as an illustrator and cartoonist. He drew for magazines, books, and advertisements. While working on advertisements for an oil company, he created all sorts of interesting characters. This experience was important in his development as an author. During this time, Geisel learned how to mix entertaining illustrations with words that rhyme and funny expressions. Then, in 1937, he wrote his first children's book under the name Dr. Seuss. Geisel published several more children's books afterward. However, his success was not immediate. In fact, he only became really famous much later... ³In 1957, a publisher of schoolbooks asked Geisel to write an imaginative story with lively illustrations. Geisel was asked to use only a small number of simple words that children could easily understand. And the result was The Cat in the Hat. Now, we all know the story... Two children are alone in a house. They are bored because it's raining and they can't go outside. Suddenly, they are visited by a cat wearing a hat. And, um, this cat shows them various tricks and plays games with them. They make a mess in the house. Then, a magical machine cleans up everything just before the children's mother comes home. It is certainly a creative story... full of imagination.

⁴However, The Cat in the Hat was also an important work. In the past, children did not

enjoy learning from schoolbooks because the books were boring. *The Cat in the Hat* was the first book in American literature that was both fun and educational. It changed the way many people thought of children's books forever. The publication was immediately successful and encouraged Geisel to publish more books in a similar style. By the time Geisel died in 1991, he had published over 40 children's books as Dr. Seuss. Many of these books became the most popular children's books of all time. They were even translated into several languages. [5]Geisel was later given a special award in 1984 for his accomplishments and influence. He really made children's literature entertaining and interesting. And he changed education forever.

문학 강의의 일부를 들으시오.

P: 자, 여러분이 오늘날의 아동 도서를 떠올릴 때, 아마 다채로운 그림이 있는 흥미로운 이야기를 떠올릴 거예요. 하지만 항상 그랬던 것은 아니에요. 전통적으로, 대부분의 아동 도서는 단순하고 재미없는 이야기를 가지고 있었어요. 이것은 20세기에 테오도르 가이젤의 작품으로 인해 바뀌었어요. 어, 여러분 모두 그의 작품을 읽어봤겠지만, 아마 그를 닥터 수스로 알고 있을 거예요... 어쨌든, 아동 도서가 재미있고 흥미로워진 것은 가이젤 덕분이에요...

음, 그의 경력에 대한 약간의 배경을 말해줄게요. 가이젤은 삽화가와 만화가로 시작했어요. 그는 잡지, 도서, 광고를 위해 그림을 그렸어요. 석유 회사를 위한 광고를 작업하는 동안, 그는 온갖 종류의 흥미로운 캐릭터들을 만들어냈어요. 이 경험은 작가로서 그의 발전에 중요했죠. 이 시기 동안, 가이젤은 흥미로운 삽화를 운이 맞는 단어들과 재미있는 표현들과 혼합하는 법을 배웠어요. 그 후, 1937년에, 그는 닥터 수스라는 이름으로 그의 첫 번째 아동 도서를 집필했어요. 가이젤은 그 후에 몇 권의 아동 도서를 더 출간했어요. 하지만, 그의 성공은 즉각적이지 않았죠. 사실, 그는 훨씬 나중이 되어서야 매우 유명해졌어요... 1957년에, 한 교과서 출판사가 가이젤에게 생생한 삽화가 들어있는 창의적인 이야기를 써달라고 요청했어요. 가이젤은 아이들이 쉽게 이해할 수 있는 적은 수의 간단한 단어들만 사용하도록 요청받았죠. 그리고 결과물은 'The Cat in the Hat'이었어요. 자, 우리는 모두 그 이야기를 알죠... 두 아이가 홀로 집에 있어요. 비가 내리고 있고 밖에 나갈 수 없어서 그들은 지루해하죠. 갑자기, 모자를 쓴 고양이가 그들을 방문해요. 그리고, 음, 이 고양이는 다양한 묘기를 보여주고 그들과 함께 게임을 해요. 그들은 집을 엉망으로 만들어요. 그런 다음, 아이들의 엄마가 집에 오기 직전에 마법의 기계가 모든 것을 청소해요. 분명히 창의적인 이야기죠... 상상력으로 가득 차 있어요.

하지만, 'The Cat in the Hat'은 중요한 작품이기도 했어요. 과거에, 아이들은 교과서가 지루했기 때문에 그것들로 학습하는 것을 즐기지 않았어요. 'The Cat in the Hat'은 미국 문학에서 재미있으면서도 교육적인 최초의 도서였어요. 그것은 많은 사람들이 아동 도서에 대해 생각하는 방식을 영원히 바꾸어 놓았어요. 출판은 즉시 성공했고 가이젤이 더 많은 비슷한 스타일의 도서를 출판하도록 독려했죠. 1991년에 가이젤이 사망할 때까지, 그는 닥터 수스라는 이름으로 40권이 넘는 아동 도서를 출판했어요. 이 도서들 중 다수는 역사상 가장 인기 있는 아동 도서가 됐어요. 그것들은 심지어 여러 언어로 번역되기도 했죠. 나중에 가이젤은 그의 업적과 영향에 대한 공로로 1984년에 특별한 상을 받았어요. 그는 진정으로 아동 문학을 재미있고 흥미롭게 만들었어요. 그리고 그는 교육을 영원히 바꾸어 놓았죠.

colorful (형) 다채로운   traditionally (부) 전통적으로

---

uninteresting (형) 재미없는   background (명) 배경
advertisement (명) 광고   rhyme (동) 운이 맞다   expression (명) 표현
immediate (형) 즉각적인   imaginative (형) 창의적인
lively (형) 생생한   creative (형) 창의적인   literature (명) 문학
translate (동) 번역하다   accomplishment (명) 업적
influence (명) 영향

1 강의의 주된 주제는 무엇인가?

(A) 작가가 그의 이름을 바꾼 이유

(B) 20세기의 교육 시스템

(C) 아동 도서가 어떻게 즐길 만하게 되었는지

(D) 아동 문학의 유명한 창작자들

2 교수에 따르면, 작가로서 가이젤의 발전에 있어 중요했던 것은?

(A) 그의 출판업계 내부 인맥

(B) 그의 서비스를 광고하는 능력

(C) 뛰어난 예술가와 그의 관계

(D) 광고를 작업한 그의 경험

3 교수는 가이젤의 'The Cat in the Hat' 집필을 어떻게 소개하는가?

(A) 출판사의 요청을 설명함으로써

(B) 가이젤에 대한 비평가들의 의견을 언급함으로써

(C) 도서에 대한 아이들의 태도를 논함으로써

(D) 미국 문학의 짧은 역사를 말해줌으로써

4 교수에 따르면, 'The Cat in the Hat'은 왜 중요한 작품이었는가?

(A) 그것은 더 많은 작가들이 교과서를 제작하도록 독려했다.

(B) 그것은 많은 사람들이 아동 문학에 대해 생각하는 방식을 바꾸었다.

(C) 그것은 학교에서 가르쳐진 최초의 아동 도서였다.

(D) 그것은 다른 어떤 책보다 더 많은 언어로 출판되었다.

5 가이젤은 왜 특별한 상을 받았는가?

(A) 그는 전 세계에서 가장 많은 아동 도서를 판매했다.

(B) 그는 문학과 교육에 많은 기여를 했다.

(C) 그는 아이들에게 읽는 법을 가르치는 프로그램을 시작했다.

(D) 그는 책에 삽화를 그리는 새로운 방법을 개발했다.

Listening Practice 3   본문 p. 101

1 (C)   2 (B)   3 (A)   4 (C)   5 (D)

Note-taking

S: Writing seminar in Boston → want writers to attend
　Enough $ for travel X → raise money → hold concert
　Confident find band ∵ friend musician → show for free
P: Location on campus = reserved early
　Outside = expensive (e.g. Center Street Theater)
　Check anything available on campus
　Make list → contact owners → might use for free

Listen to a conversation between a student and a professor.

S: Do you have a moment, Professor Evans?

P: Sure. What's on your mind?

S: I'm the editor for the school newspaper. And, um, there's a writing seminar at the University of Boston in May. We'd like some of our writers to attend.

P: Oh, I've heard about that seminar. It would be a great opportunity to learn about how to write better articles.

S: Yes, that's why we'd like to attend. But the problem is... Well, we just don't have enough money for the travel costs. [1]So I was thinking of raising money for the trip by having an event.

P: I see... What kind of event? [2]I've been the head advisor of the paper for 10 years now, and it seems like we never have enough money.

S: Exactly. Well, um, that's why we're thinking of holding a concert.

P: OK, and have you found any bands yet?

S: We're considering a couple... We want one that's popular enough to attract lots of students.

P: That's good. But, um, there are other factors to think about. For example, how much will you pay the band? Will you pay them with money you collect from selling tickets?

S: [3]Oh, I'm confident I can find a band that will play for free. I have many friends among local musicians. I've even interviewed some of them in the past. They might agree to do the show for free.

P: OK... I see you've thought a lot about this. What about the location? Places on campus are usually reserved several months before. [4]You can rent a stage outside campus, but that could be expensive. Even a small place like the Center Street Theater costs several hundred dollars per night...

S: I hadn't considered that... I had thought we would be able to use a place on campus.

P: [5]Why don't you check if anything is available on campus, anyway? There might be a place that can still be used.

S: That's true. I should definitely check.

P: If nothing's available, make a list of places in the city and contact their owners... One of them might let you use the place for free.

S: [5]OK. I'll go to the student activities office first.

학생과 교수 사이의 대화를 들으시오.

S: 잠깐 시간 있으신가요, Evans 교수님?

P: 물론이지. 무슨 일이니?

S: 저는 학교 신문 편집자입니다. 그리고, 음, 5월에 보스턴 대학교에서 글쓰기 세미나가 있어요. 저희는 저희 기자들 중 일부가 참석했으면 합니다.

P: 오, 그 세미나에 관해 들었단다. 더 나은 기사를 쓰는 방법에 관해 배우기에 좋은 기회가 될 거야.

S: 네, 그게 저희가 참석하고 싶은 이유예요. 그런데 문제는... 음, 저희는 여행 경비를 위한 충분한 돈이 없어요. 그래서 행사를 열어 여행을 위한 돈을 모금하는 것을 생각 중이었어요.

P: 그렇구나... 어떤 종류의 행사니? 나는 지금까지 10년 동안 그 신문의 주 지도 교수였는데, 우리는 절대로 충분한 돈을 갖지 못하는 것 같구나.

S: 정확해요. 저, 음, 그게 저희가 콘서트 개최를 생각 중인 이유예요.

P: 알겠다, 그러면 밴드는 찾았니?

S: 두어 개를 고려 중이에요... 많은 학생들을 끌어모을 만큼 충분히 인기 있는 것이었으면 해요.

P: 잘됐구나. 그런데, 음, 생각해봐야 할 다른 요소들이 있어. 예를 들어, 밴드에는 얼마를 지불할 거니? 표를 판매해서 모은 돈으로 그들에게 지불할 거니?

S: 오, 저는 무료로 공연할 밴드를 찾을 자신이 있어요. 저는 지역 음악가들 중에 친구가 많거든요. 저는 심지어 과거에 그들 중 몇 명을 인터뷰했어요. 그들은 아마 무료로 공연하는 것에 동의할 거예요.

P: 그렇구나... 네가 이것에 관해 많이 생각해 봤다는 걸 알겠구나. 장소는 어떠니? 캠퍼스 내의 장소들은 보통 여러 달 전에 예약돼. 네가 캠퍼스 밖의 무대를 대여할 수도 있지만, 그건 비쌀 수도 있어. 심지어 Center Street Theater 같은 작은 장소도 하룻밤에 수백 달러가 들어...

S: 그건 고려하지 못했어요... 저희가 캠퍼스 내의 장소를 사용할 수 있을 거라고 생각했어요.

P: 그래도 캠퍼스 내에 사용 가능한 곳이 있는지 확인하는 건 어떠니? 사용될 수 있는 장소가 아직 있을지도 몰라.

S: 맞아요. 분명히 확인해야겠어요.

P: 사용 가능한 곳이 없으면, 도시에 있는 장소들의 목록을 만들어서 그것들의 주인들에게 연락해 보렴... 그들 중 한 명은 너희에게 무료로 장소를 사용하게 해줄지도 몰라.

S: 네. 학생 활동과 사무실에 먼저 가볼게요.

attend 동 참석하다　article 명 기사　raise money 돈을 모금하다　consider 동 고려하다　attract 동 끌어모으다　factor 명 요소　confident 형 자신이 있는　for free 무료로　reserve 동 예약하다　rent 동 대여하다　definitely 부 분명히

1 화자들은 주로 무엇을 논의하고 있는가?

(A) 대학에서 개최되고 있는 음악 공연

(B) 학생이 참석하기 원하는 글쓰기 세미나

(C) 학생 조직을 위한 돈을 모금할 행사

(D) 대학 신문의 일자리 공석

2 교수는 학교 신문에 관해 무엇이라고 말하는가?

(A) 그것은 약 10년 전에 시작되었다.

(B) 그것은 오랜 시간 동안 돈 문제를 겪어 왔다.

(C) 그것은 현재 주 지도 교수가 없다.

(D) 그것은 학회에 구성원들을 보낼 것이다.

3 학생은 왜 밴드를 찾을 자신이 있는가?

(A) 그녀는 지역 음악가인 친구들이 많다.

(B) 그녀는 학교에서 밴드를 홍보하기로 약속했다.

(C) 그녀는 이미 음악 그룹의 리더에게 연락했다.

(D) 그녀는 일부 공연자들에게 돈을 지불하기로 결정했다.

4 교수는 왜 Central Street Theater를 언급하는가?

(A) 곧 예약할 것을 독려하기 위해

(B) 행사를 위한 가능한 장소를 제안하기 위해

(C) 장소를 대여하는 것의 높은 비용을 강조하기 위해

(D) 넓은 공간의 필요성을 표현하기 위해

5 학생은 다음에 무엇을 할 것인가?

(A) 무대 사용 비용 알아내기

(B) 지역 음악가 목록 만들기

(C) 극장 주인에게 연락하기

(D) 캠퍼스 내의 장소 사용에 관해 문의하기

Listening Practice 4

본문 p. 103

1 (B)　2 (B)　3 (D)　4 (B)　5 (C)

Note-taking

Epidemics and Pandemics

- Epidemic & pandemic = large & unexpected spread
- Only apply to infectious disease = X
- Epidemic = disease increase in specific location
  - Cause = weather pattern (e.g. cold, storm)
- Pandemic = rapid spread to countries & continents
- Difference = scale of spread & rate of spread
  - Epidemic = quick at first → slow down
  - Pandemic = spread across countries & continents
- Spanish flu & Covid = dangerous ∵ modern lifestyle

Listen to part of a lecture in a biology class.

P: [1]Today, we'll discuss the terms epidemic and pandemic. Both of these terms refer to the large and unexpected spread of a disease. [5]Most people think these terms apply only to infectious diseases. Uh, these are diseases that get passed from one person to another. However, this is fiction. They can refer to any disease, such as lung cancer. Of course, the disease can also be an infectious one...

OK... [3]First, let's define an epidemic. Epidemics happen when diseases unexpectedly increase in a specific location. These are quite common, and they can occur anywhere at any time. [2]Epidemics can be caused by a wide range of factors. One example is a change in weather patterns. Some epidemics mostly happen at certain times of the year... You know, seasonally. For instance, the flu usually occurs in winter when it is cold. Also, epidemics can happen after large storms, like hurricanes.

S: Um, is that because storms carry diseases?

P: Oh, no. It's because storms can make it harder to find clean drinking water. Dirty water can cause diseases to spread very quickly... [3]Now, in contrast, pandemics indicate the spread of a disease to many countries or continents. During pandemics, the spread is very rapid. Many new people are infected every day. And the numbers grow and grow. Within a few weeks or months, millions of people can be infected around the world. Naturally, this makes pandemics extremely terrifying. The diseases travel too fast and too far... Uh, there is no easy way to control them.

[3]So, then, there are two main differences between epidemics and pandemics. These are the scale of the spread of the disease and the rate of the spread. Um, let's explain these differences in more detail... Remember, an epidemic is a disease that spreads in a specific area. It might spread quickly at first, but then it slows down. So, overall, it does not spread as fast or as far... However, a pandemic is a disease that spreads across several countries or continents. [4]In some cases, such as the Spanish Flu and Covid, the pandemic reaches almost every place on Earth. They were extremely dangerous because both occurred in modern times. Unlike before, people traveled on ships, airplanes, cars, and trains... So, with their modern lifestyles, people spread these diseases more easily. As a result, millions of people died. But, fortunately, humans have learned a lot about epidemics and pandemics through the years. People have learned to regularly wash their hands. And they have learned to wear masks and practice social distancing... These actions can save many lives.

생물학 강의의 일부를 들으시오.

P: 오늘, 우리는 에피데믹과 팬데믹이라는 용어에 대해 논의할 거예요. 이 용어들은 둘 다 광범위하고 예기치 못한 질병의 확산을 가리킵니다. 대부분의 사람들은 이 용어들이 전염되는 질병에만 적용된다고 생각해요. 어, 이것들은 한 사람에서 다른 사람으로 전해지는 질병이죠. 하지만, 이건 허구입니다. 그것들은 폐암과 같은 어떠한 질병이라도 지칭할 수 있어요. 물론, 그 질병이 전염되는 것일 수도 있겠죠.

자... 먼저, 에피데믹을 정의해 봅시다. 에피데믹은 질병이 특정 지역에서 예기치 않게 증가할 때 발생해요. 이것들은 꽤 흔하며, 언제 어디서나 발생할 수 있어요. 에피데믹은 광범위한 요인들에 의해 야기될 수 있습니다. 한 가지 예시는 날씨 패턴의 변화예요. 몇몇 에피데믹은 대부분 연중 특정 시기에 발생하죠... 그러니까, 계절적으로요. 예를 들어, 독감은 보통 겨울에 추울 때 발생해요. 또한, 에피데믹은 허리케인 같은 큰 폭풍 후에 발생할 수 있어요.

S: 음, 폭풍이 질병을 실어 나르기 때문인가요?

P: 오, 아니요. 폭풍이 깨끗한 식수를 찾는 것을 더 어렵게 만들 수 있기 때문이에요. 더러운 물은 질병이 매우 빠르게 확산되도록 할 수 있거든요... 자, 대조적으로, 팬데믹은 많은 국가나 대륙으로의 질병 확산을 나타내요. 팬데믹 동안, 확산은 매우 빨라요. 많은 새로운 사람들이 매일 감염되죠. 그리고 그 수는 점점 더 늘어나요. 몇 주나 몇 개월 안에, 전 세계에서 수백만 명의 사람들이 감염될 수 있죠. 당연히, 이것은 팬데믹을 매우 무섭게 만들어요. 질병은 너무 빠르게, 그리고 너무 멀리 이동해요... 어, 그것들을 통제할 쉬운 방법은 없습니다.

자, 그럼, 에피데믹과 팬데믹 사이에는 두 가지 주요 차이점이 있어요. 이것들은 질병 확산의 규모와 확산의 속도예요. 음, 이 차이점들을 더 자세히 설명해 보죠... 기억하세요, 에피데믹은 특정 지역에서 확산되는 질병입니다. 그것은 처음에 빠르게 확산될지도

모르지만, 그 후에는 느려집니다. 그래서, 전반적으로, 그렇게 빠르거나 멀리 확산되지 않아요... 하지만, 팬데믹은 여러 국가나 대륙을 가로질러 확산되는 질병입니다. 스페인 독감과 코로나바이러스 같은 몇몇 경우에, 팬데믹은 지구상의 거의 모든 곳에 도달해요. 그것들은 둘 다 현대에 발생했기 때문에 극도로 위험했어요. 이전과 달리, 사람들은 배, 비행기, 자동차, 기차로 이동했죠... 그러니까, 그들의 현대적인 생활방식으로, 사람들은 이 질병들을 더 쉽게 확산시켰어요. 그 결과, 수백만 명의 사람들이 사망했죠. 하지만, 다행히도, 인간은 수년간 에피데믹과 팬데믹에 대해 많은 걸 배웠어요. 사람들은 규칙적으로 손을 씻게 되었죠. 그리고 그들은 마스크를 쓰고 사회적 거리두기를 실천하게 되었어요... 이러한 행동들은 많은 생명을 구할 수 있습니다.

unexpected 형 예기치 못한　apply to ~에 적용되다
infectious 형 전염되는　fiction 명 허구　define 동 정의하다
factor 명 요인, 요소　seasonally 부 계절적으로　continent 명 대륙
naturally 부 당연히　extremely 부 매우, 극도로　scale 명 규모
regularly 부 규칙적으로　social distancing 사회적 거리두기

1 강의는 주로 무엇에 관한 것인가?

(A) 역사상 가장 치명적인 질병들

(B) 질병의 광범위한 증가의 두 가지 종류

(C) 기후가 질병의 확산에 영향을 미치는 이유

(D) 전염되는 질병의 다양한 범주

2 교수에 따르면, 에피데믹을 야기할 수 있는 요인은 무엇인가?

(A) 지역 의료 서비스의 품질

(B) 날씨 패턴의 변화

(C) 국가의 식량 공급 부족

(D) 지역 인구의 증가

3 교수는 강의를 어떻게 구성하는가?

(A) 그녀는 몇 가지 상반되는 이론들을 설명한다.

(B) 그녀는 최근의 과학 연구를 소개한다.

(C) 그녀는 문제와 몇 가지 해결책을 논의한다.

(D) 그녀는 용어들 사이의 차이점을 비교한다.

4 교수에 따르면, 무엇이 스페인 독감과 코로나바이러스의 극도의 위험성에 기여했는가?

(A) 새로운 질병에 대한 제한된 지식

(B) 사람들의 현대적인 이동 습관

(C) 사회적 거리두기의 실패

(D) 많은 지역의 사용 가능한 마스크 부족

강의의 일부를 다시 듣고 질문에 답하시오.

P: Most people think these terms apply only to infectious diseases. Uh, these are diseases that get passed from one person to another. However, this is fiction. They can refer to any disease, such as lung cancer.

5 교수는 왜 이렇게 말하는가:

P: However, this is fiction.

(A) 이전에 말한 것을 뒷받침하기 위해

(B) 견해가 어디에서 비롯되었는지 보여주기 위해

(C) 일반적인 오해를 강조하기 위해

(D) 더 많은 정보의 필요성을 설명하기 위해

iBT Listening Test 1　본문 p. 105

1 (B)　**2** (C)　**3** (D)　**4** (D)　**5** (A)

Note-taking

S: Job for campus tour guide?

P: Guide's responsibility = take students around campus
　Work 3 days straight
　Attend orientation = Thu. & Sun. → pick 1

S: Thu. = X ∵ meet theater club
　Sun. = X ∵ exam next day
　Will study on Sat. → attend orientation on Sun.

Listen to a conversation between a student and a professor.

S: Hi, Professor Wheeler. [1]I'm here to talk about the e-mail that you sent. You mentioned something about a job for a campus tour guide?

P: Right. I think it's a job you'll be interested in. Please come in and take a seat.

S: Thank you... [1]So I'd like to know what the work is about.

P: Well, as you know, we get applications from new students every year. And some of the students visit the university before deciding if they want to study here. So, in a couple of weeks, we're going to have a new group of students visiting the university.

S: OK, I see. [1]But what should I expect as a campus tour guide? I mean, what would I be doing?

P: [2]So a guide's responsibilities include taking students around the campus. That way, they can get an idea of what the university is like. You know, you'll show them where the important buildings are and talk about life on campus.

S: That's it? It doesn't sound very hard.

P: No, it's not difficult at all. But, um, you'll be working for three days straight. So that means you won't have much time to do anything else.

S: All right. That won't be a problem.

P: [3]Oh, and you'll also need to attend an orientation session. Sessions will be held on Thursday night and Sunday afternoon. You can pick which day you want to attend.

S: Well, I'm meeting with my theater club on Thursday night, so that's out. [4]And I can't go on Sunday, either. I have an exam the next day that I was planning to study for.

P: Oh, but the orientation is a requirement. You really need to be there on at least one of the days.

S: Hmm... In that case, I'll study for my exam on Saturday, instead. That way, I can attend the orientation on Sunday.

P: That's a good idea. I'll put your name on the list for Sunday, then. [5]Please make sure you attend.

S: I definitely will... And, um, thanks for thinking of

me... I'll do my best to help.

P: It's my pleasure! I'm sure you'll do well.

S: Thanks again, Professor. I'll see you around.

학생과 교수 사이의 대화를 들으시오.

S: 안녕하세요, Wheeler 교수님. 교수님이 보내신 이메일에 관해 이야기하려고 왔습니다. 캠퍼스 투어 가이드 일자리에 관해 무언가 말씀하셨나요?

P: 맞아. 네가 관심 있어 할 일자리라고 생각한다. 들어와서 앉거라.

S: 감사합니다... 그래서 그 일이 무엇에 관한 것인지 알고 싶어요.

P: 음, 너도 알다시피, 우리는 매년 새로운 학생들에게 지원서를 받는단다. 그리고 학생들 중 일부는 그들이 여기에서 공부하고 싶은지 결정하기 전에 대학을 방문해. 그래서, 2주 후에, 우리는 대학을 방문할 새로운 그룹의 학생들을 맞을 거야.

S: 네, 알겠어요. 그런데 캠퍼스 투어 가이드로서 제가 무엇을 예상해야 하나요? 그러니까, 제가 뭘 하게 되나요?

P: 그러니까 가이드의 책무는 학생들을 캠퍼스 이곳저곳에 데려가는 것을 포함해. 그렇게 해서, 그들은 대학이 어떤지에 대해 알 수 있어. 그러니까, 너는 그들에게 중요한 건물들이 어디에 있는지 보여주고 캠퍼스에서의 생활에 관해 이야기할 거야.

S: 그게 다인가요? 그렇게 어려워 보이지 않네요.

P: 아냐, 전혀 어렵지 않아. 그런데, 음, 너는 3일을 연달아 일하게 될 거야. 그러니까 그건 네가 다른 어떤 것도 할 시간이 많지 않을 거라는 의미야.

S: 괜찮아요. 그건 문제가 되지 않을 거예요.

P: 오, 그리고 너는 오리엔테이션 모임에도 참석해야 할 거야. 모임은 목요일 밤과 일요일 오후에 열릴 거란다. 네가 어떤 날에 참석하고 싶은지 골라도 돼.

S: 음, 저는 목요일 밤에 연극 동아리와 만나니까, 그건 불가능해요. 그리고 저는 일요일에도 갈 수 없어요. 제가 공부하려고 계획했던 시험이 그다음 날에 있어요.

P: 오, 하지만 오리엔테이션은 필요 조건이야. 그날들 중 적어도 하루는 꼭 참석해야 해.

S: 흠... 그런 경우라면, 대신 토요일에 시험을 위해 공부할게요. 그렇게 하면, 일요일에 오리엔테이션에 참석할 수 있어요.

P: 좋은 생각이구나. 그럼, 네 이름을 일요일 명단에 넣어두마. 꼭 참석하렴.

S: 꼭 그럴게요... 그리고, 음, 절 생각해주셔서 감사해요... 돕기 위해 최선을 다할게요.

P: 천만에! 네가 잘할 거라고 확신한다.

S: 다시 한번 감사합니다, 교수님. 나중에 뵐게요.

application 뗑 지원서 expect 동 예상하다
responsibility 뗑 책무, 책임 straight 뷔 연달아서
session 뗑 모임 requirement 뗑 필요 조건 at least 적어도

1 화자들은 주로 무엇을 논의하고 있는가?

(A) 학생이 활동을 개최하기 위해 필요한 조언

(B) 임시 일자리를 위한 필요 조건

(C) 대학 행사에 관해 배우는 가장 좋은 방법

(D) 학생의 전공과 관련이 있는 자원봉사 자리

2 대화에 따르면, 학생은 무엇을 책임질 것인가?

(A) 학생들을 오리엔테이션에 데려오는 것

(B) 학생들이 수업에 등록하는 데 도움을 주는 것

(C) 학생들에게 캠퍼스 이곳저곳을 보여주는 것

(D) 학생들을 교수들에게 소개하는 것

3 교수는 오리엔테이션 모임에 대해 무엇이라고 말하는가?

(A) 학생들이 그것들을 완료하는 데 이틀이 걸릴 것이다.

(B) 모든 방문 학생들은 한 번 참여해야 한다.

(C) 그것들은 새로운 학생들에게 캠퍼스 생활을 소개할 것이다.

(D) 캠퍼스 가이드는 두 번 중 한 번 참석하도록 선택할 수 있다.

4 학생은 왜 시험을 언급하는가?

(A) 교수에게 그녀가 준비되었음을 알리기 위해

(B) 그녀가 수업에서 잘하고 있음을 보여주기 위해

(C) 동아리와 만나는 이유를 대기 위해

(D) 그녀가 일요일에 시간이 안 되는 이유를 설명하기 위해

대화의 일부를 다시 듣고 질문에 답하시오.

P: Please make sure you attend.

S: I definitely will... And, um, thanks for thinking of me... I'll do my best to help.

P: It's my pleasure! I'm sure you'll do well.

5 학생은 이렇게 말함으로써 무엇을 의미하는가:

S: And, um, thanks for thinking of me...

(A) 그녀는 기회를 받게 되어 기쁘다.

(B) 그녀는 그녀의 일을 인정받아 기쁘다.

(C) 그녀는 그녀의 교수를 실망하게 하는 것에 대해 걱정한다.

(D) 그녀는 문제가 해결되어 기쁘다.

iBT Listening Test 2 본문 p. 108

1 (D) 2 (D) 3 (A) 4 (C) 5 (B) 6 (B)

Note-taking

Out of Africa Theory

- Out of Africa theory = where human came & moved
- Evidence → human started in Africa, exact reason X
- *Erectus* = left 1.8 mil yr. ago, *Sapiens* = left 200k yr. ago
  - Reason 1 = climate change = too hot or too cold
  - Reason 2 = population = people ↑, food to share ↓
- Expanded to Middle East → Europe → Asia
- *Sapiens* 1st large mvmt. → China → survive X
- *Sapiens* 2nd large mvmt. → survived → filled world
- 50k yr. ago → reached Australia → America

Listen to part of a lecture in an anthropology class.

P: Recently, we were discussing the origins of civilization. I mentioned that all civilizations were started by one species—*Homo sapiens. Homo sapiens*, of course, are modern humans like us. [1]But there were other species of humans in the past, and all of them are believed to have come from Africa. Over time, humans left Africa and spread around the globe. This is what I'd like to talk about today. It is the idea behind the Out of

Africa theory.

So the Out of Africa theory is a theory of human migration. This means it tries to explain where humans came from in the past and where they moved around the world. 2/3Based on physical evidence, such as old bones and stone tools, scientists believe that all humans started in Africa. [3]Why there? We don't know the exact reason. Personally, I doubt we ever will... However, most of the evidence about early humans is found in Africa. So this strongly suggests that all humans started there before spreading to the rest of the world.

[4]Now, the first humans to leave Africa were not *Homo sapiens*. They were called *Homo erectus*. Uh, they were not modern humans like us, but they were humans... Um, *Homo erectus* lived about two million years ago in Eastern Africa. Uh, *Homo erectus* left Africa approximately 1.8 million years ago. But, uh, *Homo sapiens* did not begin moving out of Africa until around 200,000 years ago...

S: [6]Um, why did humans leave Africa, anyway?

P: That's a good question, but it's difficult to say. Remember, this all happened long ago. Scientists believe that the movements were related to two main factors: climate change and population. Um, climate, as you know, is important for the survival of any species. It's hard to live in a place that is too hot or too cold. And climate also determines how much food and water are available to use. As for population, well, if there are many people in one place, then there is less food to share, right? So people may have moved in order to find more sources of food.

Now, going back to the migration itself... According to the theory, humans first expanded into the Middle East and then to Europe and Asia... As I said, *Homo sapiens* started moving around 200,000 years ago. [5]The first large movement probably reached as far as China. This first group did not survive into modern times. However, a second large movement happened, and this group did survive. In fact, it is this group that filled the world with modern humans and eventually created the civilizations that we all know about today. By around 50,000 years ago, humans had reached the Australian continent. Before long, they had even reached North and South America. And, well... You know the rest of the story... Now, there are few places on Earth where humans have not been to...

인류학 강의의 일부를 들으시오.

P: 최근에, 우리는 문명의 기원에 대해 논의하고 있었어요. 모든 문명은 하나의 종, 즉 '호모사피엔스'에 의해 시작되었다고 말했죠. 물론, '호모사피엔스'는 우리와 같은 현대의 인간이에요. 하지만 과거에는 다른 종의 인간들이 있었고, 그들 모두는 아프리카에서 기원했다고 믿어져요. 시간이 지나면서, 인간들은 아프리카를 떠났고 전 세계로 퍼져나갔어요. 이게 제가 오늘 이야기하고 싶은 거예요. 그것은 아프리카 기원설의 이면에 있는 생각이에요.

자, 아프리카 기원설은 인간의 이주에 대한 이론이에요. 이는 그것이 인간이 과거에 어디에서 기원했으며 세계의 어느 곳으로 이동했는지를 설명하려 한다는 것을 의미해요. 오래된 뼈와 석기 같은 물리적 증거에 근거하여, 과학자들은 모든 인간이 아프리카에서 시작되었다고 믿어요. 왜 그곳일까요? 정확한 이유는 몰라요. 개인적으로, 언젠가 알 수 있게 될지 의심스러워요... 하지만, 초기 인간들에 대한 증거의 대부분은 아프리카에서 발견돼요. 그러니까 이는 모든 인간들이 세계의 나머지 부분으로 퍼져나가기 전에 그곳에서 시작되었다는 걸 암시하죠.

자, 아프리카를 떠난 최초의 인간들은 '호모사피엔스'가 아니었어요. 그들은 '호모에렉투스'라고 불렸어요. 어, 우리와 같은 현대의 인간은 아니지만, 그들은 인간이었어요... 음, '호모에렉투스'는 약 2백만 년 전에 아프리카 동부에 살았어요. 어, '호모에렉투스'는 약 180만 년 전에 아프리카를 떠났어요. 하지만, 어, '호모사피엔스'는 약 20만 년 전이 되어서야 아프리카 밖으로 이주하기 시작했죠...

S: 음, 그런데, 인간들은 왜 아프리카를 떠났나요?

P: 좋은 질문이지만, 답하기에는 어려워요. 기억하세요, 이 모든 것은 오래전에 일어났어요. 과학자들은 그 이동이 기후 변화와 인구라는 두 가지 주된 요인과 관련이 있었다고 생각해요. 음, 알다시피, 기후는 어떤 종의 생존에도 중요하죠. 너무 덥거나 너무 추운 장소에 사는 것은 힘들어요. 그리고 기후는 얼마나 많은 식량과 물을 이용할 수 있는지를 결정하기도 하죠. 인구에 관해서는, 음, 한 장소에 많은 사람이 있으면, 나눌 식량이 더 적어지죠, 그렇죠? 그래서 사람들은 아마 더 많은 식량 공급원을 찾기 위해 이주했을 거예요.

자, 이주 자체로 돌아가서... 그 이론에 따르면, 인간들은 먼저 중동으로, 그 후에 유럽과 아시아로 확장했어요. 제가 말했듯이, '호모사피엔스'는 약 20만 년 전에 이주하기 시작했어요. 최초의 큰 이동은 아마 중국에까지 도달했을 거예요. 이 최초의 집단은 현대까지 생존하지 못했어요. 하지만, 두 번째의 큰 이동이 일어났고, 이 집단은 생존했죠. 사실, 세계를 현대의 인간들로 채우고 결국 오늘날 우리 모두가 알고 있는 문명들을 만든 것이 바로 그 집단이에요. 약 5만 년 전쯤에, 인간들은 호주 대륙에 도달했어요. 머지 않아, 그들은 심지어 북아메리카와 남아메리카에까지 도달했죠. 그리고, 음... 나머지 이야기는 알고 있겠죠... 이제, 지구에는 인간이 가보지 않은 곳이 거의 없어요...

---

origin 몡 기원   civilization 몡 문명   migration 몡 이주
physical 혱 물리적인   exact 혱 정확한   personally 붑 개인적으로
approximately 붑 약   factor 몡 요인   source 몡 공급원
reach 동 도달하다   eventually 붑 결국   continent 몡 대륙

1 교수는 주로 무엇에 관해 논하는가?

   (A) 인간들이 어떻게 그렇게 오래 생존해 왔는지

   (B) 인간 진화의 역사

   (C) 인간종들의 비교

   (D) 인간들이 어떻게 전 세계로 퍼져나갔는지

2 교수는 아프리카 기원설에 관해 무엇이라고 말하는가?

   (A) 그것은 최근의 연구 결과에 의해 반증되었다.

   (B) 그것은 새로운 정보로 갱신되었다.

   (C) 그것은 전통적인 아프리카의 이야기들에 의해 뒷받침된다.

   (D) 그것은 물리적 증거에 근거한다.

3 인간들이 아프리카에서 기원한 이유에 대한 교수의 의견은 무엇인가?

(A) 그는 우리가 언젠가 그 이유를 알게 될 것이라고 생각하지 않는다.

(B) 그는 대부분의 과학자들의 설명을 믿지 않는다.

(C) 그는 아프리카가 진화를 위한 최적의 기후를 가지고 있었다고 믿는다.

(D) 그는 그 지역에 식량 자원이 풍부했다고 생각한다.

4 교수는 왜 '호모에렉투스'를 언급하는가?

(A) 어떻게 한 종만 생존했는지 설명하기 위해

(B) 최초의 인간종에 대해 논의하기 위해

(C) 아프리카를 떠난 최초의 인간들을 명시하기 위해

(D) 인간종들 간의 상호작용을 설명하기 위해

5 교수에 따르면, '호모사피엔스'의 최초의 큰 이동에 대한 설명으로 옳은 것은?

(A) 그것은 서로 다른 집단 사이의 전쟁으로 야기되었다.

(B) 그것은 아마 중국까지 갔을 것이다.

(C) 그것은 대부분 아프리카 내에서 일어났다.

(D) 그것은 세계의 모든 지역들에 도달했다.

강의의 일부를 다시 듣고 질문에 답하시오.

S: Um, why did humans leave Africa, anyway?

P: That's a good question, but it's difficult to say. Remember, this all happened long ago. Scientists believe that the movements were related to two main factors: climate change and population.

6 교수는 이렇게 말함으로써 무엇을 의미하는가:

P: That's a good question, but it's difficult to say.

(A) 교수는 나중에 그 질문에 답할 것이다.

(B) 학생의 질문에 대한 대답은 명확하지 않다.

(C) 기후 변화는 인간의 이동에 거의 영향을 미치지 않았다.

(D) 인구는 인간 이주의 가장 큰 요인이었다.

Vocabulary Review
본문 p. 112

1 civilization   2 infectious   3 avoid
4 translate   5 uninteresting 6 immediate
7 influence   8 creative   9 moral
10 (C)   11 (C)   12 (B)
13 (C)   14 (A)

CHAPTER 06
Connecting Contents

Example
본문 p. 115

A. (C)-(D)-(A)-(B)   B. Cheetahs: (A), (C) Koalas: (B), (D)

A.

Note-taking

S: Project for marketing class?
P: Goal = create marketing plan for biz.
 Choose biz. from list → research online
 Give presentation during class → feedback
 2nd presentation = necessary X
 Improve plan → submit written report

Listen to a conversation between a student and a professor.

S: Professor, could you tell me about the project for your marketing class? I was absent when you announced it.

P: Sure. So the goal of the project is to create a marketing plan for a business. CThe first thing you will do is choose a business from a list I've provided.

S: All right. Do I need to contact the business I choose?

P: No. DYou will do research about it online.

S: Oh, good. And then what?

P: ANext, you will give a presentation during class. I will give feedback for each presentation.

S: Do I have to give a second presentation after that?

P: BThat won't be necessary. You will use the feedback to improve your plan and submit a written report.

학생과 교수 사이의 대화를 들으시오.

S: 교수님, 교수님의 마케팅 수업 프로젝트에 관해 말씀해주실 수 있나요? 그것을 공고하셨을 때 제가 결석해서요.

P: 물론이지. 그러니까 프로젝트의 목표는 기업을 위한 마케팅 계획을 만드는 거야. 네가 할 첫 번째 것은 내가 제공한 목록에서 기업을 선택하는 거야.

S: 그렇군요. 제가 선택한 기업에 연락해야 하나요?

P: 아니. 넌 그것에 관해 온라인으로 조사할 거야.

S: 오, 잘됐네요. 그다음에는요?

P: 그다음에, 너희는 수업 중에 발표를 할 거야. 내가 각 발표에 대해 의견을 줄 거란다.

S: 그 후에 두 번째 발표를 해야 하나요?

P: 그건 필요하지 않을 거야. 너는 그 의견을 이용해서 계획을 개선한 다음 보고서를 제출할 거야.

absent [형] 결석한 announce [동] 공고하다 research [명] 조사
presentation [명] 발표 feedback [명] 의견 necessary [형] 필요한

교수는 프로젝트의 단계를 설명한다. 아래의 단계들을 올바른 순서대로 나열하시오. 각 답변을 해당하는 곳으로 끌어다 놓으시오.

단계 1	(C) 목록에서 기업 선택하기
단계 2	(D) 온라인으로 조사하기
단계 3	(A) 수업에서 발표하기
단계 4	(B) 보고서 제출하기

B.

Note-taking

Sleeping Habits of Cheetahs and Koalas

- Cheetah = sleep 12h/day, hunt during cooler hours
- Koala = 22h/day sleeping
  - Move a few hrs. at night to gather food
  - Sleep so long ∵ diet
  - Leaves = calories ↓, digest req. energy ∵ fiber

Listen to part of a lecture in a biology class.

P: OK... I'd like to continue our discussion of animal sleeping habits. Yesterday, we started talking about cheetahs. AAlthough some animals sleep up to 20 hours a day, cheetahs sleep only 12 hours on average. They spend much of their time resting to conserve their energy. CIn fact, they only hunt during the cooler hours of the day.

Now, the animals that sleep the longest are koalas. BUh, they spend up to 22 hours each day sleeping. And they only move around for a few hours at night to gather food. DThe reason koalas sleep so long is their diet. Um, the leaves they consume contain few calories to get energy from. In addition, digesting them requires much energy because they contain a lot of fiber.

생물학 강의의 일부를 들으시오.

P: 자... 동물의 수면 습관에 대한 논의를 계속하려고 합니다. 어제, 우리는 치타에 대해 이야기하기 시작했죠. 어떤 동물들은 하루에 20시간까지 잠을 자지만, 치타는 평균적으로 겨우 12시간만 잡니다. 그것들은 많은 시간을 에너지를 보존하기 위해 휴식을 취하는 데 써요. 사실, 그것들은 하루 중 더 시원한 시간에만 사냥을 하죠.

자, 가장 오래 자는 동물은 코알라입니다. 어, 그것들은 하루에 22시간까지 자는 데 쓰죠. 그리고 먹이를 모으기 위해 밤에 몇 시간 동안만 돌아다녀요. 코알라가 그렇게 오래 자는 이유는 식습관 때문이에요. 음, 그것들이 먹는 나뭇잎들은 에너지를 얻기 위한 칼로리를 거의 함유하고 있지 않아요. 게다가, 그것들이 많은 섬유질을 함유하고 있기 때문에 그것들을 소화하는 것은 많은 에너지를 필요로 하죠.

on average 평균적으로   conserve 동 보존하다   diet 명 식습관
contain 동 함유하다   digest 동 소화하다   fiber 명 섬유질

강의에서, 교수는 치타와 코알라의 몇몇 특징들을 언급한다. 아래 문장이 치타와 코알라 중 어떤 것을 묘사하는지를 표시하시오. 각 항목에 적절한 칸을 클릭하시오.

	치타	코알라
(A) 그것들은 하루에 12시간 정도 잔다.	V	
(B) 그것들은 밤에만 먹이를 모은다.		V
(C) 그것들은 기온이 낮을 때 활동적이다.	V	
(D) 그것들은 식습관 때문에 많이 잔다.		V

본문 p. 117

Listening Practice 1

1 (D)   2 (B)   3 (C)
4 Suggested: (A), (D) Not Suggested: (B), (C)   5 (C)

Note-taking

W: Name on waiting list for Williams ∵ cheaper & friends
   Been several weeks → nothing
M: Delay ∵ single room = popular → 6 ppl. on list
   Request double room ∵ more students leave
   Many ppl. trouble w/ roommate (e.g. sleep schedule)
   Find student moving out → post msg. on board
   Cancel single room request?
W: Keep

Listen to a conversation between a student and a university housing office employee.

W: Hello, my name is Melissa Sanders. 1I applied to move in to another dormitory room last month. I just want to see how that's going.

M: Sure. Which dormitory did you want to move in to?

W: Actually, I put my name on the waiting list for the Williams dormitory. It's cheaper than the Nelson dormitory, and most of my friends are there. However, it's been several weeks and I still haven't heard anything.

M: So are you in the Nelson dormitory now?

W: Yes. It was the only dormitory I could get into because I submitted my application late. But when I heard I could move rooms, I made a transfer request.

M: All right. Let me look up your file... You asked for a single room, is that right?

W: That's right.

M: 2OK, that explains the delay. Single rooms are popular. It's, um, rare for students to move out in the middle of the semester. And according to our records, there are six people before you on the list.

W: What does that mean?

M: It means that a single room might not be available until next school year.

W: I'd really like to move sooner than that. Is there anything I can do?

M: 4AYou can request a double room at the Williams dormitory, instead.

W: Actually, I don't want to have a roommate. But if I ask for a double room, will I be able to move in to the Williams dormitory sooner?

M: Of course. 3That's because more students leave double rooms than single rooms during the semester. You know, many people have trouble with a roommate because of different sleep schedules and other issues like that. 4DUh, your only other option is to find a student who is moving out. You can post a message about this on the Williams dormitory notice board.

W: Well, OK. But still, I'd also like to submit a request for a double room and see what happens.

M: ⁵OK, then, could you fill out this form? And do you want me to cancel your single room request?

W: No, I'd prefer to keep it. You never know about these things, right?

학생과 대학 기숙사 사무실 직원 사이의 대화를 들으시오.

W: 안녕하세요, 제 이름은 Melissa Sanders입니다. 저는 지난달에 다른 기숙사 방으로 이사 신청을 했어요. 그게 어떻게 되어가는지 알고 싶습니다.

M: 물론이죠. 어떤 기숙사로 이사하고 싶어 하셨죠?

W: 사실은, 제 이름을 Williams 기숙사를 위한 대기 명단에 올려 두었어요. 그곳은 Nelson 기숙사보다 저렴하고, 제 친구들 대부분이 거기에 있거든요. 그런데, 몇 주가 되었는데 아직 아무것도 듣지 못했어요.

M: 그러니까 지금 Nelson 기숙사에 계신가요?

W: 네. 제가 신청서를 늦게 제출해서 그게 제가 들어갈 수 있는 유일한 기숙사였어요. 그런데 제가 방을 옮길 수 있다는 것을 듣고 나서, 이동 신청을 했어요.

M: 좋아요. 학생의 파일을 찾아볼게요... 1인실을 요청하셨죠, 맞나요?

W: 맞아요.

M: 네, 그게 지연의 원인을 설명해 주네요. 1인실은 인기가 많아요. 학생들이, 음, 학기 중간에 이사를 나가는 일은 드물거든요. 그리고 저희 기록에 따르면, 학생 앞에 6명이 명단에 올라와 있어요.

W: 그게 무슨 말이신가요?

M: 다음 학년까지 1인실을 이용할 수 없을지도 모른다는 말이에요.

W: 정말 그것보다는 빨리 이사하고 싶어요. 제가 할 수 있는 일이 있나요?

M: 대신, Williams 기숙사의 2인실을 신청하실 수 있어요.

W: 사실은, 저는 룸메이트를 갖고 싶지 않아요. 그런데 제가 2인실을 요청하면, Williams 기숙사로 더 빨리 이사할 수 있나요?

M: 물론이죠. 그건 학기 중에 1인실보다 2인실을 떠나는 학생들이 더 많기 때문이에요. 아시다시피, 많은 사람들이 서로 다른 수면 시간과 그와 같은 다른 문제들로 룸메이트와 문제를 겪어요. 어, 학생의 유일한 다른 선택지는 이사 나가는 학생을 찾는 거예요. Williams 기숙사 게시판에 이것에 대한 메시지를 게시하실 수 있어요.

W: 음, 알겠어요. 하지만 여전히, 저는 2인실을 위한 신청서를 제출하고 어떻게 되는지 보고 싶어요.

M: 알겠어요, 그럼, 이 양식을 작성해 주시겠어요? 그리고 1인실 신청은 취소해 드릴까요?

W: 아뇨, 그냥 두고 싶어요. 어떻게 될지 모르니까요, 그렇죠?

application 몡 신청서   transfer 몡 이동   delay 몡 지연
rare 혱 드문   post 됭 게시하다   notice board 게시판

1 학생은 왜 기숙사 사무실을 찾아가는가?

(A) 그녀의 기숙사 룸메이트와의 문제를 보고하기 위해

(B) 2인실로의 이사 신청을 하기 위해

(C) 그녀의 기숙사 상태에 관해 불평하기 위해

(D) 방 변경 신청 상황을 확인하기 위해

2 학생의 신청이 지연되는 이유는 무엇인가?

(A) 학생은 제시간에 신청서를 제출하지 않았다.

(B) 학생들은 학기가 끝나기 전에 1인실을 거의 떠나지 않는다.

(C) 학생은 1인실을 위한 필요 조건을 갖추지 못했다.

(D) 기숙사 사무실은 다른 신청들 때문에 바빴다.

3 직원에 따르면, 학생들이 학기 중에 2인실을 떠나는 원인은 무엇인가?

(A) 그들은 기숙사 방이 충분히 넓지 않다고 생각한다.

(B) 그들은 친구 중 한 명과 함께 살러 들어간다.

(C) 그들은 룸메이트와 함께 사는 데 어려움을 겪는다.

(D) 그들은 캠퍼스 밖에서 더 저렴한 방을 구한다.

4 직원은 방을 구하기 위한 몇 가지 선택지를 제안한다. 다음의 항목이 제안인지를 표시하시오. 각 항목에 적절한 칸을 클릭하시오.

	제안됨	제안 안 됨
(A) 2인실 신청하기	V	
(B) 친구와 함께 살러 들어가기		V
(C) 양식 출력하기		V
(D) 게시판에 메시지 게시하기	V	

대화의 일부를 다시 듣고 질문에 답하시오.

M: OK, then, could you fill out this form? And do you want me to cancel your single room request?

W: No, I'd prefer to keep it. You never know about these things, right?

5 학생은 이렇게 말함으로써 무엇을 의미하는가:
W: You never know about these things, right?

(A) 그녀가 수집해야 하는 약간의 정보가 있다.

(B) 그녀는 신청에 관해 무엇을 해야 할지 모른다.

(C) 그녀가 1인실을 얻을 가능성이 있다.

(D) 그녀는 1인실과 2인실 중 하나를 결정할 수 없다.

Listening Practice 2   본문 p.119

1 (D)   2 (C)-(B)-(D)-(A)   3 (C)   4 (A)   5 (B)

Note-taking

Development of Weather Forecasting

- Knowing weather = important ∵ help prepare future
- Ancient priests = use cloud formation & info. abt. stars
- 350 BC, Aristotle's *Meteorologica* → meteorology
- From 1800s, big developments
  - Telegraph = obtain data from far away
  - Tools for measuring air pressure & wind
- 1950, predict w/ computer → not adv. ∵ pointless
- Supercomputers in 1960s → data ↑ & mistakes ↓
- Now = perfect X, success rate ↑

Listen to part of a lecture in a meteorology class.

P: No one can stop bad weather, but we can prepare for it before it happens. Thanks to improvements in technology, we can learn what the weather will be like in a few hours or days. Of course, it wasn't always this easy to predict the weather. [1]Now, today's lesson is about the development of weather forecasting.

Humans have tried to predict the weather for thousands of years. Knowing what the weather will be like is important because it helps people prepare for the future. [2C]The first people who tried to predict the weather were ancient priests. They used cloud formations and information about the stars. Then, around 350 BC, the Greek philosopher Aristotle wrote about weather patterns in a set of books called *Meteorologica*. Um, this is where we get the term for the study of weather: meteorology. Still, for centuries, people were often wrong when they tried to predict the weather.

Then, from the 1800s, some big developments occurred. [2B]First, the invention of the telegraph made it possible to obtain weather data from hundreds of kilometers away. [2D]Later, British scientists invented tools for measuring changes in air pressure and the wind. Air pressure and wind, of course, are important in determining weather.

In the early 20th century, mathematicians suggested that people could predict the weather more accurately by gathering enough data. However, computers had not yet been invented. So people were not able to collect enough data for accurate predictions. [5]Then, in 1950, some American scientists became the first to predict the weather with a computer program. However, computers were not very advanced back then. It took 24 hours to produce one weather prediction. Um, this was pointless. Uh, you know, weather systems change quickly. So the predictions were similar to a random guess. [2A]With the introduction of supercomputers in the 1960s, meteorologists were able to work with larger amounts of data. Since then, the number of mistakes in predicting the weather has greatly decreased. [3]Predicting the movement of typhoons has also become more accurate. In the 1970s, if scientists tried to predict where a typhoon might occur, they could miss by up to 800 kilometers. Today, the accuracy has improved, so they only miss by less than 200 kilometers.

With new computer models, tools, and data, meteorologists can now predict weather several days in advance. [4]And although weather forecasts are still not perfectly accurate, the rate of success has continuously improved. Today, weather forecasts are much more accurate than they were 25 years ago. Imagine where we will be in another 25 to 50 years. This will be hugely important because global warming is already causing many changes in the weather.

기상학 강의의 일부를 들으시오.

P: 아무도 악천후를 막을 수 없지만, 그것이 발생하기 전에 그것에 대비할 수 있습니다. 기술의 발전 덕분에, 우리는 몇 시간이나 며

칠 후에 날씨가 어떨지를 알 수 있죠. 물론, 날씨를 예측하는 게 항상 이렇게 쉽지는 않았어요. 자, 오늘 수업은 기상 예측의 발달에 관한 거예요.

인간은 수천 년 동안 날씨를 예측하려고 노력해 왔어요. 날씨가 어떨지를 아는 건 사람들이 미래에 대비하는 것을 도와주기 때문에 중요해요. 날씨를 예측하기 위해 노력했던 최초의 사람들은 고대의 사제들이었습니다. 그들은 구름의 형태와 별에 대한 정보를 활용했어요. 그 후, 기원전 350년경, 그리스 철학자 아리스토텔레스는 'Meteorologica'라고 불리는 일련의 책들에 기상 패턴에 대해 썼어요. 음, 이것이 날씨를 연구하는 학문을 위한 기상학이라는 용어를 얻는 곳이에요. 그럼에도 불구하고, 수 세기 동안, 날씨를 예측하려 노력할 때 사람들은 종종 틀렸죠.

그 후, 1800년대부터, 몇몇 큰 발전이 일어났어요. 먼저, 전신의 발명이 수백 킬로미터 떨어진 곳으로부터의 기상 데이터를 얻는 것을 가능하게 만들었어요. 후에, 영국 과학자들은 기압과 바람의 변화를 측정하는 도구들을 발명했어요. 물론, 기압과 바람은 날씨를 알아내는 데 있어 중요합니다.

20세기 초에, 수학자들은 충분한 데이터를 수집함으로써 날씨를 더 정확하게 예측할 수 있다고 제안했습니다. 하지만, 컴퓨터는 아직 발명되지 않았었죠. 그래서 사람들은 정확한 예측을 위한 충분한 데이터를 수집할 수 없었어요. 그 후, 1950년에, 몇몇 미국 과학자들은 컴퓨터 프로그램으로 날씨를 예측한 최초의 사람들이 되었어요. 하지만, 당시에는 컴퓨터가 그다지 발달되어 있지 않았어요. 한 번의 날씨 예측을 수행하는 데 24시간이 걸렸죠. 음, 이것은 무의미했어요. 어, 알다시피, 기상 시스템은 빠르게 변해요. 그래서 그 예측들은 무작위적인 추측과 비슷했어요. 1960년대에 슈퍼컴퓨터가 도입되면서, 기상학자들은 더 많은 양의 데이터를 가지고 작업할 수 있었어요. 그 이후로, 날씨 예측에서 실수의 수가 크게 줄어들어 왔어요. 태풍의 움직임을 예측하는 것 또한 더 정확해졌어요. 1970년대에, 과학자들이 태풍이 발생할지도 모르는 장소를 예측하려 하면, 800킬로미터까지 빗나갈 수 있었습니다. 오늘날, 정확도는 200킬로미터 미만의 거리만큼만 빗나갈 정도로 향상되었죠.

새로운 컴퓨터 모델, 도구, 데이터로, 기상학자들은 이제 며칠 앞서 날씨를 예측할 수 있어요. 그리고 기상 예측이 여전히 완벽하게 정확하지는 않지만, 성공률은 계속해서 향상되어 왔어요. 오늘날, 기상 예측은 25년 전에 그랬던 것보다 훨씬 더 정확합니다. 25년에서 50년 후에는 어떨지 상상해 보세요. 지구 온난화가 이미 날씨에 많은 변화를 일으키고 있기 때문에 이것은 매우 중요할 것입니다.

---

predict 동 예측하다   priest 명 사제, 성직자
formation 명 형태; 형성   philosopher 명 철학자
telegraph 명 전신   obtain 동 얻다
determine 동 알아내다; 결정하다   accurately 부 정확하게
pointless 형 무의미한   random 형 무작위적인
meteorologist 명 기상학자   hugely 부 매우

1 강의는 주로 무엇에 관한 것인가?

(A) 기상 시스템이 형성되는 방식

(B) 폭풍을 예측하기 어려운 이유

(C) 날씨가 더 극단적이 되는 이유

(D) 기상 예측이 발달한 방식

2 강의에서, 교수는 기상 예측의 몇 가지 중요한 사건들을 언급한다. 아래의 사건들을 올바른 순서대로 나열하시오. 각 답변을 해당하는 곳으로 끌어다 놓으시오.

사건 1	(C) 구름과 별에 근거하여 예측이 수행된다.
사건 2	(B) 사람들은 멀리 떨어진 곳으로부터 기상 데이터를 얻을 수 있다.
사건 3	(D) 기압과 바람을 측정하기 위한 도구가 발명된다.
사건 4	(A) 프로그램은 많은 양의 데이터를 처리할 수 있다.

3 교수에 따르면, 1960년대 이후에 기상 예측은 어떻게 개선되었는가?

(A) 그것들을 수행하는 데 3일이 채 걸리지 않았다.

(B) 그것들은 더 먼 거리에서 수행될 수 있었다.

(C) 그것들은 폭풍의 위치를 더 정확하게 보여주었다.

(D) 그것들은 더 빨리 뉴스에 보도될 수 있었다.

4 미래의 기상 예측에 대한 교수의 태도는 무엇인가?

(A) 그녀는 그것이 계속해서 개선될 것이라고 확신한다.

(B) 그녀는 그것이 대부분 컴퓨터로 수행될 것이라고 생각한다.

(C) 그녀는 그것이 기후 변화에 도움이 되지 않을까 봐 걱정한다.

(D) 그녀는 그것이 더 진지하게 받아들여져야 한다고 생각한다.

강의의 일부를 다시 듣고 질문에 답하시오.

P: Then, in 1950, some American scientists became the first to predict the weather with a computer program. However, computers were not very advanced back then. It took 24 hours to produce one weather prediction. Um, this was pointless. Uh, you know, weather systems change quickly.

5 교수는 이렇게 말함으로써 무엇을 암시하는가:
P: Um, this was pointless.

(A) 몇몇 과학자들은 일부 데이터를 포함하는 것을 잊었다.

(B) 컴퓨터 프로그램은 충분히 빠르지 않았다.

(C) 몇몇 과학자들은 새로운 정보를 발견했다.

(D) 컴퓨터 프로그램은 매우 발달되어 있었다.

Listening Practice 3
본문 p. 121

1 (B) 2 (A) 3 (C) 4 Yes: (A), (B), (C) No: (D) 5 (B)

Note-taking

W: Internship → can't decide short or long
Interested in journalism (e.g. magazine & website)
M: Short = try many kinds, less time to learn job
Long = knowledge & skill ↑, meet helpful ppl.
W: Journalism = competitive ∴ connection = important
Place to look?
M: Job search sites = good place to start
Apply early ∵ employer hire b.f. deadline
Apply several jobs → apply & see

Listen to a conversation between a student and a career center employee.

W: Excuse me. My name is Stephanie Davis. I made an appointment to meet with a counselor today.

M: Yes, I'm Mr. Benson. I was expecting you... How can I help?

W: I need your advice. ¹My professor suggested that I do an internship to prepare for a job after I graduate. But, um, I can't decide whether to do a short one or a long one.

M: Well, that mainly depends on your career goals. First of all, which field are you interested in?

W: Journalism... I want to work for a travel magazine or a website someday.

M: OK. That's helpful to know. ²So, let's consider a short internship. What's good is that you can try many kinds of internships before you graduate. Many students want to experience different internships, but they don't have much time. So, for students like these, a short internship is the best option. But of course, they have less time to, um, learn the job in detail.

W: Right, I see...

M: Next, let's talk about long internships. ⁵You'll have more time to increase your knowledge and skills in a job...

W: Yes, that's definitely true.

M: And, um, another advantage is that you will meet people who can help you find new jobs later on.

W: That's an excellent point. ³Journalism is extremely competitive, so knowing a lot of people and making connections is important. I guess I should go with a long internship, then. But, um, where's the best place to look?

M: OK, well, job search sites are a good place to start. ⁴ᶜThey're updated several times a day, so just make sure to check them often. ⁴ᴬI also suggest you apply early. Employers often hire someone before the application deadline.

W: I can do that.

M: ⁴ᴮThe other thing I recommend is to apply to several jobs... Don't worry about finding the perfect one. If you find a post that seems interesting, send in your application form and see what happens.

W: Thanks for all your advice, Mr. Benson. You've helped me a lot.

학생과 직업 센터 직원 사이의 대화를 들으시오.

W: 실례합니다. 제 이름은 Stephanie Davis에요. 오늘 상담사와 만나기로 약속했어요.

M: 네, 전 Benson입니다. 기다리고 있었어요... 어떻게 도와드릴까요?

W: 당신의 조언이 필요해요. 제 교수님께서 졸업 후에 취업을 준비하기 위해 인턴직을 하라고 제안하셨어요. 그런데, 음, 단기로 할지 장기로 할지 결정하지 못하겠어요.

M: 음, 그건 주로 학생의 직업 목표에 달려 있어요. 우선, 어떤 분야에 관심이 있으신가요?

W: 저널리즘이요... 저는 언젠가 여행 잡지나 웹사이트를 위해 일하고 싶어요.

M: 알겠습니다. 도움이 되네요. 그러면, 단기 인턴직을 고려해 봅시다. 좋은 점은 학생이 졸업하기 전에 많은 종류의 인턴직을 시도할 수 있다는 거예요. 많은 학생들이 다양한 인턴직을 경험하고 싶어 하지만, 그들은 시간이 많지 않죠. 그래서, 이런 학생들에게는,

단기 인턴직이 가장 좋은 선택이에요. 하지만 물론, 그들은, 음, 업무를 자세히 배울 시간이 더 적죠.

W: 그렇군요, 알겠습니다...

M: 다음으로, 장기 인턴직에 대해 얘기해 봅시다. 학생은 업무에 대한 지식과 기술을 향상할 시간이 더 많을 거예요...

W: 네, 확실히 그래요.

M: 그리고, 음, 또 다른 장점은 학생이 나중에 새로운 일자리를 찾는 걸 도와줄 수 있는 사람들을 만나게 되는 거예요.

W: 훌륭한 요소네요. 저널리즘은 매우 경쟁적이고, 그래서 많은 사람들을 알고 관계를 맺는 것이 중요해요. 그럼, 장기 인턴직을 해야 할 것 같네요. 그런데, 음, 찾아보기에 가장 좋은 곳이 어디인가요?

M: 네, 음, 구직 사이트는 시작하기에 좋은 곳이에요. 그것들은 하루에 여러 번 업데이트되니까, 그것들을 자주 확인하세요. 저는 또 일찍 지원하시는 걸 추천해요. 고용주들은 종종 지원 마감일 전에 누군가를 고용해요.

W: 할 수 있어요.

M: 제가 추천하는 마지막 하나는 여러 일자리에 지원하는 거예요... 완벽한 것을 찾는 것에 대해 걱정하지 마세요. 흥미로워 보이는 공고를 찾으면, 지원서를 보낸 다음 어떻게 되는지 보세요.

W: 조언 감사합니다, Benson씨. 저를 많이 도와주셨어요.

appointment 명 약속 counselor 명 상담사
depend on ~에 달려 있다 knowledge 명 지식
definitely 부 확실히 advantage 명 장점 extremely 부 매우
employer 명 고용주 deadline 명 마감일, 기한

1 대화의 주된 주제는 무엇인가?

(A) 학생이 일자리 제의를 수락해야 할지 여부

(B) 학생에게 알맞은 인턴직의 종류

(C) 대학원을 준비하기 위해 인턴직을 활용하는 방법

(D) 일자리에 지원하고 면접을 준비하는 과정

2 직원에 따르면, 단기 인턴직의 장점은 무엇인가?

(A) 그것들은 학생들이 다양한 인턴직을 시도할 수 있게 해준다.

(B) 그것들은 학생들이 직업 목표를 선택하도록 도와준다.

(C) 그것들은 경험이 없는 지원자들을 받아 준다.

(D) 그것들은 학생들이 기술을 빨리 배우도록 동기를 부여한다.

3 학생은 왜 장기 인턴직을 하기로 결정하는가?

(A) 그녀는 그녀에게 인턴직을 제공할 수 있는 사람을 안다.

(B) 그녀는 이전의 단기 인턴직에 실망했다.

(C) 그녀는 그것이 그녀에게 많은 관계를 맺게 해줄 것이라고 생각한다.

(D) 그녀는 충분한 과거 업무 경험이 있다.

4 대화에서, 직원은 구직 사이트를 이용하는 방법에 대한 조언을 제공한다. 다음의 항목이 직원이 제공하는 조언인지를 표시하시오. 각 항목에 적절한 칸을 클릭하시오.

	예	아니오
(A) 지원서를 일찍 제출하기	V	
(B) 많은 일자리에 지원하기	V	
(C) 구직 웹사이트를 자주 확인하기	V	
(D) 각 제의를 신중히 고려하기		V

대화의 일부를 다시 듣고 질문에 답하시오.

M: You'll have more time to increase your knowledge and skills in a job...

W: Yes, that's definitely true.

M: And, um, another advantage is that you will meet people who can help you find new jobs later on.

5 학생은 왜 이렇게 말하는가:

W: Yes, that's definitely true.

(A) 그녀가 많은 기술을 가지고 있다는 것을 보여주기 위해

(B) 중요한 지적에 동의하기 위해

(C) 다른 장점들이 있다는 것을 나타내기 위해

(D) 회사에 들어가는 것에 대한 그녀의 관심을 표현하기 위해

Listening Practice 4   본문 p. 123

1 (D)   2 Christiaan Huygens: (B), (D)
Percival Lowell: (A), (C)   3 (B)   4 (A)   5 (B)

Note-taking

Search for Water on Mars

- 1st scientist suggested water on Mars = Huygens
  - Invented telescope → large & dark shape → oceans?
- Lowell = saw long & thin lines → caused by water?
  - Wrote books → helped make idea popular
- 1960s, spacecraft study Mars → find water X
- 2000s, ice in north & south pole → ice all over Mars
- Mission will ever find water?
  - Photo show dark line → earlier photo X → water?
  - Area like river dry → smooth stone → moving water?

Listen to part of a lecture in an astronomy class.

P: For centuries, scientists have wondered if there is life on other planets. To find an answer, they look for evidence of water. All living things need water. So, if there is water on a planet, it's possible for life to exist there. ¹So, all right, let's talk about the search for water on the planet Mars.

One of the first scientists who suggested that there was water on Mars was the 17th-century scholar, Christiaan Huygens. ²ᴰHuygens invented a telescope that made it possible to study details on the surface of Mars. ²ᴮHe discovered large, dark shapes on the planet and thought they might be oceans. ²ᶜA couple of centuries later, the astronomer Percival Lowell claimed to see several long, thin lines near the middle of Mars. He believed these were caused by water. ²ᴬLowell also wrote several books about his theory. They helped make the idea of water on Mars more popular. However, research later showed that the dark shapes were completely dry and that the lines were a false image caused by Lowell's telescope. So researchers had to find new ways to see if Mars had water.

Beginning in the 1960s, a number of spacecraft were sent to study Mars. Some of these spacecraft landed on the surface and made measurements. This gave scientists a better idea about conditions on Mars.

S1: Did they find liquid water?

P: Unfortunately, they did not. But, in the 2000s, scientists learned that Mars had ice in its north pole and south pole. And, in the past decade, other trips to Mars have found small amounts of frozen water in other parts of the planet. In fact, it has become clear that these amounts of ice are pretty much all over Mars.

S2: ³So is there still hope that these missions will ever find liquid water?

P: I definitely think so. There are many positive signs. ⁵A couple of years ago, photographs from a spacecraft showed dark lines going down a hill on Mars. It doesn't sound like much, but guess what? They don't appear in earlier photos. Something on Mars caused the lines and it could be water. ⁴Even if the lines are not caused by liquid water, there is other evidence that Mars had lots of water in the past. For instance, some photographs show an area that looks like a river that dried up. It has many smooth stones that are similar to stones on Earth. On Earth, stones like these become smooth because of moving water.

천문학 강의의 일부를 들으시오.

P: 수 세기 동안, 과학자들은 다른 행성에 생명체가 있는지 궁금해 했습니다. 답을 찾기 위해, 그들은 물의 증거를 찾죠. 모든 생명체는 물을 필요로 해요. 그러니까, 어떤 행성에 물이 있다면, 그곳에 생명체가 존재할 가능성이 있습니다. 자, 좋아요, 화성에서의 물 탐색에 대해 얘기해 봅시다.

화성에 물이 있다고 제안한 최초의 과학자 중 한 명은 17세기 학자 크리스티안 하위헌스였어요. 하위헌스는 화성 표면의 세부 사항들을 연구하는 것을 가능하게 만든 망원경을 발명했어요. 그는 그 행성에서 크고 어두운 형상들을 발견했고 그것들이 바다일지도 모른다고 생각했습니다. 두어 세기 후에, 천문학자 퍼시벌 로웰은 화성의 중심부 근처에서 여러 개의 길고 가는 선들을 보았다고 주장했어요. 그는 이것들이 물에 의해 초래되었다고 믿었죠. 로웰은 또한 그의 이론에 대한 몇 권의 책을 썼어요. 그것들은 화성에 물이 있다는 견해를 더 대중적으로 만드는 데 도움을 주었죠. 하지만, 나중에 연구는 그 어두운 형상들이 완전히 메말라 있으며 그 선들은 로웰의 망원경에 의해 만들어진 거짓 이미지라는 것을 보여주었어요. 그래서 연구자들은 화성에 물이 있는지를 확인할 새로운 방법을 찾아야 했죠.

1960년대 초부터, 많은 우주선이 화성을 연구하기 위해 보내졌습니다. 이 우주선들 중 일부는 표면에 착륙했고 측량을 했어요. 이는 과학자들에게 화성의 상태에 대한 더 나은 지식을 제공했어요.

S1: 그것들이 액체 상태의 물을 찾았나요?

P: 안타깝게도, 그러지 못했어요. 하지만, 2000년대에, 과학자들은 화성의 북극과 남극에 얼음이 있다는 것을 알게 됐어요. 그리고, 지난 10년 동안, 화성으로의 다른 항해들이 그 행성의 다른 부분들에서 소량의 언 물을 발견했어요. 사실, 이정도 양의 얼음이 거의 화성 전체에 있다는 것이 분명해졌어요.

S2: 그러니까 이런 우주 비행들이 언젠가 액체 상태의 물을 찾을 희망이 여전히 있는 건가요?

P: 저는 분명히 그렇게 생각해요. 많은 긍정적인 징후들이 있습니다. 두어 해 전에, 한 우주선에서 온 사진들이 화성에서 언덕을 따라 내려가는 어두운 선들을 보여주었어요. 별거 아닌 것 같지만, 짐작할 수 있나요? 그것들은 더 이전의 사진들에는 나타나지 않아요. 화성에 있는 무언가가 그 선들의 원인이 되었고 그건 물일 수도 있어요. 비록 그 선들이 액체 상태의 물에 의해 초래된 것이 아니더라도, 과거에 화성에 많은 물이 있었다는 다른 증거가 있어요. 예를 들어, 몇몇 사진들은 말라버린 강처럼 보이는 지역을 보여줍니다. 그것에는 지구의 돌들과 비슷한 매끄러운 돌들이 많이 있어요. 지구에서, 이와 같은 돌들은 움직이는 물 때문에 매끄러워지죠.

evidence 명 증거 scholar 명 학자 telescope 명 망원경 astronomer 명 천문학자 claim 동 주장하다 false 형 거짓된 spacecraft 명 우주선 measurement 명 측량, 측정 condition 명 상태 mission 명 우주 비행 definitely 부 분명히

1 강의는 주로 무엇에 관한 것인가?

(A) 과학자들이 다른 행성들을 연구하는 방법

(B) 과학자들이 다른 행성들에서 생명체를 찾는 이유

(C) 화성에서의 새로운 물질 발견

(D) 화성에서의 물 추적

2 다음의 항목이 크리스티안 하위헌스와 퍼시벌 로웰 중 누구에 대한 설명인지를 표시하시오. 각 항목에 적절한 칸을 클릭하시오.

	크리스티안 하위헌스	퍼시벌 로웰
(A) 화성에 대한 견해가 더 대중적이 되는 데 도움을 주었다		V
(B) 화성의 표면에서 어두운 지역들을 발견했다	V	
(C) 화성에 있는 선들이 물에 의해 초래되었다고 믿었다		V
(D) 화성을 살펴보기 위한 망원경을 고안했다	V	

3 화성으로의 우주 비행에 대한 교수의 태도는 무엇인가?

(A) 그는 지금까지의 결과에 실망했다.

(B) 그는 여전히 그것들이 물을 찾을 것이라고 믿는다.

(C) 그는 과학자들이 다른 행성들에 가야 한다고 생각한다.

(D) 그는 그것들이 계속하기에 너무 비쌀까 봐 걱정한다.

4 과학자들이 한때 화성에 액체 상태의 물이 흔했다고 믿는 한 가지 이유는 무엇인가?

(A) 그것에 지구의 것들과 비슷해 보이는 돌들이 있다.

(B) 그것에 산과 같은 특정한 지형적 특징이 있다.

(C) 그것의 토양은 깊은 지하에 많은 수분을 가지고 있다.

(D) 그것의 기온은 과거에 훨씬 더 낮았다.

강의의 일부를 다시 듣고 질문에 답하시오.

P: A couple of years ago, photographs from a spacecraft showed dark lines going down a hill on Mars. It doesn't sound like much, but guess what? They don't appear in earlier photos. Something on Mars caused the lines and it could be water.

5 교수는 왜 이렇게 말하는가:

P: It doesn't sound like much, but guess what?

(A) 일부 증거가 틀렸다는 것을 보여주기 위해

(B) 화성에 관한 예상치 못한 세부 사항을 소개하기 위해

(C) 학생들이 질문에 답하도록 독려하기 위해

(D) 최근 발견의 목적을 밝히기 위해

---

iBT Listening Test 1
본문 p. 125

1 (B)　**2** Yes: (C), (D) No: (A), (B)　**3** (B)　**4** (C)　**5** (C)

Note-taking

S: Want to learn more about Black Mountain College
P: Started in 1933 → lasted for 24 yrs.
　Students prepare meal & wash clothes & physical work
　Knowledge = part of edu., goal = produce good citizen
　Appreciate value of physical work, learn useful skills
　Students ← wealthy family w/ workers
　Graduates made contribution in arts & sciences

Listen to a conversation between a student and a professor.

S: Hi, Professor Green. Do you have a minute?

P: Sure, come on in. It's Nicole, right? I recognize you from my Introduction to American Education course.

S: Yes, that's me. I've been enjoying your class.

P: That's wonderful to hear. Now, how can I help you?

S: [1]Actually, I wanted to learn more about something you talked about in class yesterday. You briefly mentioned an old college. I think it was called Black Mountain College?

P: Ah, yes. Black Mountain College... [4]It was a private college that was started in 1933 and lasted for 24 years. However, it wasn't like most colleges.

S: I heard that the students there had to cook and clean. Is that true?

P: Yes. That's what made the college different. Besides studying, students prepared meals, washed their clothes, and did other kinds of physical work.

S: But why did the college require students to do physical work? Wouldn't it be better for them to focus on studying?

P: Well, for the college, knowledge was only one part of education. They didn't want to just develop students' minds. They also wanted to improve students in other ways. Their goal was to produce good citizens for society.

S: How did physical work help them achieve that goal, though?

P: [2C]Well, it helped students appreciate the value of physical work. What I mean is that it taught them to respect the people in society who did physical work as jobs. [2D]It also helped them learn skills that could be useful later in life.

S: I see. [3]But hadn't the students done any physical work before they went to Black Mountain College? I mean, didn't they already do those things at home?

P: Actually, no. A lot of these students came from, uh, wealthy backgrounds. So many of them grew up with workers that did the cooking and cleaning for them.

S: [5]OK, I understand. But what about the normal school education that students got? What was it like?

P: The school's record answers that question. Many Black Mountain College graduates made important contributions in the arts and sciences. They also became leaders in their careers.

S: It all sounds very interesting. I wonder if there are any colleges similar to this today.

학생과 교수 사이의 대화를 들으시오.

S: 안녕하세요, Green 교수님. 잠깐 시간 있으신가요?

P: 물론이지, 들어오렴. Nicole이구나, 그렇지? 내 미국 교육 입문 수업에서 너를 본 기억이 나는구나.

S: 네, 그게 저예요. 교수님의 수업을 즐겁게 듣고 있어요.

P: 그렇게 말해주니 기쁘구나. 자, 어떻게 도와줄까?

S: 사실, 저는 교수님이 어제 수업에서 얘기하신 것에 관해 더 알고 싶었어요. 오래된 대학을 잠깐 언급하셨죠. 블랙마운틴칼리지라고 불린다고요?

P: 아, 그래. 블랙마운틴칼리지... 그건 1933년에 생겨서 24년 동안 존속한 사립 대학이었어. 그런데, 그것은 대부분의 대학들 같지 않았지.

S: 그곳의 학생들은 요리와 청소를 해야 했다고 들었어요. 그게 사실인가요?

P: 맞아. 그게 그 대학을 특이하게 만든 거야. 공부 외에도, 학생들은 식사를 준비하고, 그들의 옷을 빨고, 다른 종류의 육체적인 일을 했어.

S: 그런데 그 대학은 왜 학생들에게 육체적인 일을 하도록 요구했나요? 그들이 공부에 집중하는 게 더 낫지 않았을까요?

P: 음, 그 대학에게, 지식은 교육의 한 부분일 뿐이었어. 그들은 단지 학생들의 정신만 발달시키기를 원하지 않았어. 그들은 다른 방식으로도 학생들을 발달시키기를 원했단다. 그들의 목표는 사회를 위한 좋은 시민을 만들어 내는 것이었거든.

S: 그런데, 육체적인 일이 어떻게 그들이 그 목표를 성취하는 것을 도왔나요?

P: 음, 그것은 학생들이 육체적인 일의 가치를 인정하도록 도움을 주었어. 내 말은 그것이 그들에게 사회에서 육체적인 일을 직업으로 하는 사람들을 존중하도록 가르쳤다는 거야. 그것은 그들이 나중에 인생에서 유용하게 사용할 수 있는 기술을 배우도록 돕기도 했어.

S: 그렇군요. 그런데 학생들이 블랙마운틴칼리지에 가기 전에는 육체적인 일을 하지 않았나요? 그러니까, 그들이 집에서 이미 그런 것들을 하지 않았나요?

P: 사실, 그렇지 않아. 이 학생들 중 다수는, 어, 부유한 환경에서 왔

어. 그래서 그들 중 다수는 그들을 위해 요리하고 청소하는 일꾼들과 함께 자랐지.

S: 네, 이해했어요. 그런데 학생들이 받았던 일반적인 학교 교육은 어떤가요? 그것은 어땠나요?

P: 학교의 기록에 그 질문에 대한 답이 있단다. 많은 블랙마운틴칼리지 졸업생들은 예술과 과학에 중요한 공헌을 했어. 그들은 그들의 직업에서 리더가 되기도 했어.

S: 전부 흥미로워 보이네요. 요즘에도 이것과 비슷한 대학이 있는지 궁금하네요.

briefly 뿐 잠깐   private 형 사립의   last 동 존속하다, 지속하다
physical 형 육체적인   knowledge 명 지식   citizen 명 시민
achieve 동 성취하다   appreciate 동 (가치를) 인정하다
value 명 가치   respect 동 존중하다   wealthy 형 부유한
background 명 환경, 배경   contribution 명 공헌

1 학생은 왜 교수를 찾아가는가?

(A) 과제에 대한 도움을 요청하기 위해

(B) 강의 주제에 관해 더 많은 것을 알아내기 위해

(C) 교수의 강의 경력에 관해 논의하기 위해

(D) 그녀의 전공 선택에 관해 조언을 구하기 위해

2 대화에서, 교수는 학생들에게 육체적인 일을 하도록 요구하는 것의 이점 중 일부를 설명한다. 다음의 항목이 이점인지를 표시하시오. 각 항목에 적절한 칸을 클릭하시오.

	예	아니오
(A) 학생들에게 직업 훈련을 제공했다		V
(B) 학생들이 사회에서 리더가 되도록 준비시켰다		V
(C) 사회의 다른 구성원들에 대한 존중을 가르쳤다	V	
(D) 학생들이 유용한 기술을 발달시키도록 도왔다	V	

3 교수에 따르면, 블랙마운틴칼리지의 학생들은 왜 육체적인 일과 관련된 경험이 없었는가?

(A) 그들은 작은 집에서 자랐다.

(B) 그들은 집에 가사 도우미들이 있었다.

(C) 그들은 어린 나이에 대학에 갔다.

(D) 그들은 공부로 너무 바빴다.

대화의 일부를 다시 듣고 질문에 답하시오.

P: It was a private college that was started in 1933 and lasted for 24 years. However, it wasn't like most colleges.

S: I heard that the students there had to cook and clean. Is that true?

P: Yes. That's what made the college different. Besides studying, students prepared meals, washed their clothes, and did other kinds of physical work.

4 교수는 이렇게 말함으로써 무엇을 암시하는가:

P: However, it wasn't like most colleges.

(A) 그 대학은 부유한 학생들만 받아들였다.

(B) 그 대학은 여러 해 동안 운영되었다.

(C) 그 대학은 공부에만 집중하지 않았다.

(D) 그 대학에는 강사가 많지 않았다.

대화의 일부를 다시 듣고 질문에 답하시오.

S: OK, I understand. But what about the normal school education that students got? What was it like?

P: The school's record answers that question. Many Black Mountain College graduates made important contributions in the arts and sciences. They also became leaders in their careers.

5 교수는 이렇게 말함으로써 무엇을 의미하는가:

P: The school's record answers that question.

(A) 그 학교는 주로 예술과 과학 과목들을 가르쳤다.

(B) 많은 졸업자들은 그 학교에 돈을 주었다.

(C) 그 학교의 교육 제도는 좋은 결과를 낳았다.

(D) 많은 과거의 학생들은 학교에서 일자리를 구했다.

---

iBT Listening Test 2 　　본문 p. 128

1 (D)　　**2** (C)　　**3** Reason: (A), (C), (D) Not a Reason: (B)
4 (A)　　**5** (A)　　**6** (C)

Note-taking

Role of Patrons During the Renaissance

- Patron = pay artists to produce artwork
  - Black Death → rebuild econ. → ppl. moved to city
  - Merchant & religious leader → powerful → patron
- Reasons ppl. paid for art
  - Proud of econ. success ∴ celebrate achievement
  - Show off wealth & status → high social status
  - Honor God & show loyalty to Catholic Church
- Patron influenced ∵ gave deadline & instructions
- Relationship = good for artist
  - Earn $ & practice art → reputation & more work
- After Renaiss. = artist could choose what to create

Listen to part of a lecture in an art history class.

P: When people think of the Renaissance, they mostly remember artwork by famous artists like Michelangelo, da Vinci, Botticelli, and others. These artists were certainly very skilled. However, one of the main reasons they became famous is because of the relationship with patrons. ¹Today, I'd like to discuss the role of patrons during the Renaissance.

So patrons are individuals or groups that pay artists to produce artwork. They had an important role in Italy, where the Renaissance began. ²At the beginning of the Renaissance, Italy was going through many changes. The Black Death, which was a deadly disease, killed millions of people in the 1300s and greatly affected Italy's economy. So there was a huge effort to rebuild the economy. Many citizens moved to the city to find work and do business. In the city, merchants, politicians, and religious leaders became wealthy and powerful. They became the largest patrons.

There were many reasons these people paid for

art. One is that they were proud of their economic success during the Renaissance. ³ᴬSo they wanted to celebrate their achievements. They did this by paying artists to decorate public buildings and churches. The artworks also inspired ordinary citizens to feel pride... ³ᶜAnother reason patrons supported the arts was to show off their wealth and status. Buying expensive art showed people they were rich and knew about culture. This gave them a high social status... ³ᴰLastly, patrons paid for religious artwork as a way to honor God and show loyalty to the Catholic Church. Doing these things was important in Italian society.

Now, what kind of impact did patrons have on artists and art? Generally, patrons influenced the kind of art that was produced. This is because artists only produced what patrons asked for. You see, back then, artists were just like ordinary workers... ⁶So, um, patrons thought of art like a product or service. They used business contracts, and they gave artists deadlines, and told them how much to spend on materials. And of course, patrons gave specific instructions about what to paint. They were paying, after all. Some even had their faces painted in an artwork.

Anyway, this relationship was also good for artists. Normally, producing art took a long time and required expensive materials. ⁴Patrons gave artists a way to earn money and practice art. Artists who were skilled also developed good reputations and got more work as a result. This gave them more opportunities to improve their art and try new styles and methods. And, even though patrons mostly told artists what to do, artists were not always limited. Some patrons developed strong relationships with their favorite artists. Over time, patrons gave these artists more freedom to create art. ⁵In fact, people's attitude to art changed as a result of all this. After the Renaissance, it became more common for artists to create "art for art's sake," which meant that they could choose what type of art to create.

미술사학 강의의 일부를 들으시오.

P: 사람들은 르네상스를 생각할 때, 대부분 미켈란젤로, 다빈치, 보티첼리 등과 같은 유명한 화가들의 작품을 기억합니다. 이 화가들은 분명히 매우 솜씨가 좋았어요. 하지만, 그들이 유명해진 주된 이유 중 하나는 후원자들과의 관계 때문입니다. 오늘은, 르네상스 시대 후원자들의 역할에 대해 논의하려 합니다.

자, 후원자는 작품을 제작하기 위해 예술가에게 돈을 지불하는 개인이나 단체예요. 그들은 르네상스가 시작되었던 이탈리아에서 중요한 역할을 했죠. 르네상스의 초창기에, 이탈리아는 많은 변화를 겪고 있었어요. 치명적인 질병이었던 흑사병은 1300년대에 수백만 명의 사람들을 죽였고 이탈리아의 경제에 크게 영향을 미쳤죠. 그래서 경제를 재건하기 위한 엄청난 노력이 있었어요. 많은 시민들이 일자리를 찾고 사업을 하기 위해 도시로 이사했어요. 도시에서, 상인, 정치인, 종교 지도자들은 부유하고 강력해졌습니다. 그들은 가장 큰 후원자들이 되었죠.

이 사람들이 미술품에 돈을 지불한 데는 많은 이유가 있었어요. 하나는 그들이 르네상스 시대 중에 그들의 경제적 성공을 자랑스러워했다는 거예요. 그래서 그들은 그들의 성공을 기념하고 싶어

했죠. 그들은 공공건물과 교회를 장식하도록 화가들에게 돈을 지불함으로써 이것을 했어요. 그 작품들은 일반 시민들이 자부심을 느끼도록 영감을 주기도 했죠... 후원자들이 미술을 후원했던 또 다른 이유는 그들의 부와 지위를 과시하기 위해서였어요. 값비싼 미술품을 구매하는 것은 사람들에게 그들이 부유하며 교양에 대해 안다는 것을 보여주었죠. 이는 그들에게 높은 사회적 지위를 주었어요... 마지막으로, 후원자들은 신을 숭배하고 가톨릭교회에 대한 충성심을 보여주는 방법으로 종교적인 작품에 돈을 지불했어요. 이런 것들을 하는 것은 이탈리아 사회에서 중요했습니다.

자, 후원자들은 화가들과 미술에 어떤 영향을 미쳤을까요? 일반적으로, 후원자들은 제작되는 미술품의 종류에 영향을 미쳤어요. 이는 화가들이 오직 후원자들이 요청한 것만 제작했기 때문이에요. 그러니까, 당시에, 화가들은 그냥 평범한 근로자 같았어요... 그래서, 음, 후원자들은 미술품을 제품이나 서비스 정도로 생각했죠. 그들은 사업 계약서를 사용했고, 화가들에게 기한을 주고, 재료에 얼마를 쓸지 말해줬어요. 그리고 물론, 후원자들은 무엇을 그릴지에 대한 구체적인 지시를 내렸어요. 어쨌든, 그들이 돈을 지불했으니까요. 어떤 사람들은 심지어 작품에 그들의 얼굴이 그려지게 했죠.

어쨌든, 이 관계는 화가들에게도 좋았어요. 보통, 미술품을 제작하는 데는 오랜 시간이 걸렸고 비싼 재료들이 필요했어요. 후원자들은 화가들에게 돈을 벌고 미술을 실천할 길을 열어주었죠. 솜씨가 좋은 화가들은 좋은 평판을 얻고 결과적으로 더 많은 일감을 얻기도 했어요. 이는 그들에게 그들의 미술을 향상시키고 새로운 양식과 방법을 시도할 수 있는 더 많은 기회를 주었죠. 그리고, 비록 후원자들이 대부분 화가들에게 무엇을 할지 말해주기는 했지만, 화가들이 항상 제한을 받았던 것은 아니에요. 몇몇 후원자들은 그들이 가장 좋아하는 화가들과 끈끈한 관계를 발전시켰어요. 시간이 지남에 따라, 후원자들은 이 화가들에게 미술품을 만들기 위한 더 많은 자유를 주었어요. 사실, 이 모든 것의 결과로 미술품에 대한 사람들의 태도가 바뀌었죠. 르네상스 이후에, 화가가 "미술을 위한 미술품"을 만드는 것이 더 흔해졌는데, 이는 그들이 어떤 종류의 미술품을 만들지 선택할 수 있다는 것을 의미했어요.

skilled (형) 솜씨가 좋은   patron (명) 후원자   role (명) 역할
deadly (형) 치명적인   rebuild (동) 재건하다   merchant (명) 상인
wealthy (형) 부유한   celebrate (동) 기념하다
achievement (명) 성공, 업적   show off ~을 과시하다
culture (명) 교양   honor (동) 숭배하다   loyalty (명) 충성심
deadline (명) 기한   specific (형) 구체적인   reputation (명) 평판

1   강의는 주로 무엇에 관한 것인가?

    (A) 르네상스 이전 화가들의 솜씨

    (B) 이탈리아가 많은 화가들을 배출한 이유

    (C) 미술과 경제 사이의 관계

    (D) 르네상스 시대 후원자들의 역할

2   교수는 왜 흑사병을 언급하는가?

    (A) 흔한 미술 주제에 대해 이야기하기 위해

    (B) 미술 작품을 위한 영감을 주기 위해

    (C) 이탈리아에서 변화가 일어난 이유를 설명하기 위해

    (D) 서로 다른 시대의 미술을 비교하기 위해

3   다음의 항목이 사람들이 르네상스 시대에 미술품에 돈을 지불한 이유인지를 표시하시오.
    각 항목에 적절한 칸을 클릭하시오.

	이유임	이유가 아님
(A) 성공을 기념하기 위해	V	
(B) 지역 화가들을 후원하기 위해		V
(C) 그들의 사회적 지위를 보여주기 위해	V	
(D) 교회에 대한 충성심을 보여주기 위해	V	

4 화가들은 후원자들과의 관계에서 어떻게 이익을 얻었는가?

(A) 그것은 그들에게 미술을 실천할 더 많은 기회를 주었다.

(B) 그것은 사회에서의 그들의 지위를 높였다.

(C) 그것은 그들이 공공 미술관에서 미술품을 전시하게 해주었다.

(D) 그것은 그들을 유럽 전역에서 유명하게 만들었다.

5 교수에 따르면, 르네상스 이후에 무엇이 바뀌었는가?

(A) 화가들은 그들의 작품에 대해 더 큰 통제력을 가졌다.

(B) 더 많은 일반 시민들이 미술 후원자가 되었다.

(C) 화가들은 미술품 제작에 더 많은 돈을 요구했다.

(D) 후원자들은 다른 나라로부터 더 많은 미술품을 구입하기 시작했다.

강의의 일부를 다시 듣고 질문에 답하시오.

P: So, um, patrons thought of art like a product or service. They used business contracts, and they gave artists deadlines, and told them how much to spend on materials. And of course, patrons gave specific instructions about what to paint. They were paying, after all. Some even had their faces painted in an artwork.

6 교수는 이렇게 말함으로써 무엇을 암시하는가:
P: They were paying, after all.

(A) 후원자들이 화가들에게 항상 돈으로 지불한 것은 아니다.

(B) 후원자들은 어려운 작업에 더 많은 금액을 지불했다.

(C) 후원자들은 화가들에게 지시를 내릴 만한 충분한 이유가 있었다.

(D) 후원자들은 화가들이 너무 오래 걸리면 후원하기를 중단했다.

Vocabulary Review

본문 p. 132

1 scholar
2 merchant
3 priest
4 loyalty
5 digest
6 show off
7 pointless
8 reputation
9 physical
10 (C)
11 (D)
12 (C)
13 (D)
14 (A)

CHAPTER 07

Inference

Example

본문 p. 135

A. (C)　　**B.** (B)

A.

Note-taking

M: Interested in summer course, financial assistance?
　Go to diff. university, visiting parents for summer
W: Apply O, sure X ∵ not a student here
　Need student ID & your school will need to confirm
　Come back tomorrow, let another employee know

Listen to a conversation between a student and a registrar's office employee.

M: Hi, I'm interested in taking one of your summer courses.

W: Yes, of course.

M: But, uh, I was wondering if you offer financial assistance.

W: Are you a student here?

M: No. I go to a different university, but I'm here visiting my parents for the summer.

W: I see. Well, you can apply for financial assistance, but I'm not sure you will get it if you're not a student here.

M: That's fine. What documents do I need in order to apply?

W: We'll need a copy of your student ID. And your school will need to confirm that you're a student there. You can just ask them to e-mail this office.

M: OK. And when should I come back?

W: You can come back tomorrow. I won't be here, but I'll let another employee know that you're coming.

학생과 학적과 직원 사이의 대화를 들으시오.

M: 안녕하세요, 여름 계절 학기 수업 수강에 관심이 있습니다.

W: 네, 물론이죠.

M: 그런데, 어, 재정지원을 제공하시는지 궁금해요.

W: 여기 학생이신가요?

M: 아뇨. 저는 다른 대학에 다니는데, 여름 동안 부모님을 뵈러 여기 왔어요.

W: 그렇군요. 음, 재정지원을 신청하실 수는 있는데, 여기 학생이 아니시면 그것을 받게 되실지 잘 모르겠네요.

M: 괜찮아요. 신청하려면 어떤 서류들이 필요한가요?

W: 학생의 학생증 사본이 필요해요. 그리고 학생의 학교가 학생이 그곳의 학생인 것을 확인해줘야 해요. 그냥 그들에게 이 사무실로 이메일을 보내달라고 요청하시면 돼요.

M: 알겠습니다. 그리고 제가 언제 돌아와야 하죠?

W: 내일 돌아오시면 돼요. 저는 여기에 없을 거지만, 다른 직원에게 학생이 올 거라고 알려둘게요.

summer course 여름 계절 학기 수업   financial assistance 재정지원
apply ⑧ 신청하다, 지원하다   confirm ⑧ 확인해주다

직원은 학생을 위해 무엇을 할 것인가?
(A) 그녀는 그의 학생증 사본을 만들 것이다.
(B) 그녀는 학생을 수업에 등록할 것이다.
(C) 그녀는 동료에게 학생을 도와달라고 말할 것이다.
(D) 그녀는 학생에게 수업들을 설명해줄 것이다.

B.

Note-taking

US-Mexico Border Wall

- Border btw. US and Mexico = over 3,000 km
- Around 350 mil ppl. cross = legal crossing
- Another 2 mil ppl. cross = illegal
  - Hope find work in US & escape from violence
- US built walls, everyone agree X
  - Effective X ∵ easily get around
  - Interferes w/ mvmt. of animals

Listen to part of a lecture in a sociology class.

P: The border between the US and Mexico is over 3,000 kilometers long. And, around 350 million people cross it every year… But, um, those are just the legal crossings. Another two million or more people also cross it illegally. Many of them are hoping to find work in the US. Others are escaping from violence in their home countries. Now, to stop illegal border crossings, the US has built walls in some areas. However, not everyone agrees with having these walls. One reason is that they are not that effective. Research has shown that people can easily get around them. Also, some people are concerned about a wall's effects on the environment. For them, it interferes with the movements of animals.

사회학 강의의 일부를 들으시오.

P: 미국과 멕시코의 국경은 3,000킬로미터가 넘습니다. 그리고, 매년 약 3억 5,000만 명의 사람들이 그것을 횡단해요... 하지만, 음, 그것들은 단지 합법적인 횡단일 뿐이에요. 또 다른 200만 명 혹은 그보다 많은 사람들도 그것을 불법적으로 횡단합니다. 그들 중 다수는 미국에서 일자리를 찾기를 희망하고 있어요. 다른 사람들은 고국에서의 폭력으로부터 탈출하고 있죠. 자, 불법적인 국경 횡단을 막기 위해, 미국은 일부 지역에 장벽을 세웠습니다. 하지만, 모두가 이 장벽을 갖는 것에 동의하는 것은 아니에요. 한 가지 이유는 그것들이 그렇게 효과적이지 않기 때문이에요. 연구는 사람들이 그것들을 쉽게 피해 갈 수 있다는 것을 보여주었어요. 또, 몇몇 사람들은 환경에 미치는 장벽의 영향에 대해 걱정합니다. 그들에게, 그것은 동물들의 움직임을 방해하죠.

border ⑲ 국경   cross ⑧ 횡단하다, 건너다   legal ⑱ 합법적인
illegally ⑭ 불법적으로   escape from ~에서 탈출하다
get around ~을 피해 가다   believe in ~이 옳다고 생각하다
prevent ⑧ 막다

교수는 불법적으로 국경을 횡단하는 사람들에 관해 무엇을 암시하는가?
(A) 그들은 종종 먼저 합법적으로 들어가려 한다.
(B) 그들은 더 나은 삶의 질을 찾고 있다.
(C) 그들은 국경 장벽을 넘는 데 어려움이 있다.
(D) 그들은 보통 고국으로 돌아간다.

Listening Practice 1 본문 p. 137

1 (C)   2 (D)   3 (A)   4 (B)   5 (B)

Note-taking

S: Photography asgmt. → what to do? ∵ guidelines ↓
P: Have freedom = important → creative
   Mobile phone = X ∵ anyone can take casual pictures
   Purpose = test photography skill
   Use trad. camera, choose setting & angle & lighting
   Pick what to wear = O, plan carefully
   Key point = show who you are as real person
   Hand in more than one picture = O
   Should have same theme = you

Listen to a conversation between a student and a professor.

S: Hi, Professor Chapman. I hope you're not busy.

P: Not at all, Kimberly. What can I do for you?

S: ¹Um, it's about the photography assignment you gave us in class yesterday.

P: You mean the assignment to do a self-portrait? What would you like to know?

S: Um, well, to be honest, I'm not sure what you want us to do. ²You didn't give us many guidelines.

P: Oh. I wanted to avoid giving instructions that were too specific. It's important that you have as much freedom as possible. That way, you can be creative with your pictures.

S: But, um, I'm still not sure what you're looking for. Can I take a picture of myself on my mobile phone and submit that? Isn't that like a self-portrait?

P: ³Well, not exactly. Anyone can take casual pictures. You'll need to use what you've learned. One purpose of this assignment is to test your photography skills.

S: Right. So that means we should use a traditional camera as well.

P: Yes, I'd like you to use a traditional camera. You should choose the right camera settings for your photograph. And make sure to choose the appropriate angles, lighting, and background, too.

S: Can I pick what to wear?

P: Of course! All of those details are important. They have to be planned carefully.

S: I understand now... Still, I don't think I'm an interesting subject. And I don't look good in photos, either.

P: ⁴None of those things matter. You're not taking pictures for a magazine cover. The key point of this assignment is to show who you are as a real person. I want you to show your personality.

S: OK. Can I hand in more than one picture?

P: Sure. ⁵You can submit several pictures, if you'd like. But they should all have the same theme. They should be about you.

S: All right. I'll try my best, Professor. Thank you for the advice.

학생과 교수 사이의 대화를 들으시오.

S: 안녕하세요, Chapman 교수님. 바쁘지 않으시면 좋겠네요.

P: 전혀 아니야, Kimberly. 무엇을 도와줄까?

S: 음, 어제 수업에서 저희에게 내주신 사진 촬영 과제에 관한 거예요.

P: 자화상을 촬영하는 과제를 말하는 거니? 무엇을 알고 싶니?

S: 음, 저, 솔직히 말씀드리면, 교수님이 저희가 무엇을 하기를 원하시는지 잘 모르겠어요. 저희에게 많은 지침을 주지 않으셔서요.

P: 오. 나는 너무 구체적인 설명을 주는 것을 피하고 싶었단다. 네가 최대한의 자유를 갖는 것이 중요해. 그렇게 하면, 너는 네 사진을 창의적으로 할 수 있어.

S: 그런데, 음, 여전히 교수님이 무엇을 기대하시는지 잘 모르겠어요. 제가 스스로를 휴대폰으로 촬영해서 그걸 제출해도 되나요? 그게 자화상 같은 거 아닌가요?

P: 음, 꼭 그런 건 아니야. 누구나 캐주얼한 사진을 촬영할 수 있단다. 넌 네가 배운 것을 이용해야 해. 이 과제의 한 가지 목적은 네 사진 촬영 기술을 테스트하는 거란다.

S: 그렇군요. 그러니까 그건 저희가 또한 전통적인 카메라를 사용해야 한다는 말씀이시죠.

P: 맞아, 나는 네가 전통적인 카메라를 사용했으면 해. 너는 네 사진을 위한 올바른 카메라 설정을 선택해야 해. 그리고 적절한 각도, 조명, 배경을 꼭 선택하렴.

S: 제가 무엇을 입을지 골라도 되나요?

P: 물론이지! 그런 모든 세부 사항들은 중요해. 그것들은 신중하게 계획되어야 해.

S: 이제 이해했어요... 그래도, 제가 흥미로운 피사체가 아닌 것 같아요. 그리고 저는 사진이 잘 받지도 않아요.

P: 그런 것들은 하나도 중요하지 않아. 너는 잡지 표지를 위한 사진을 촬영하는 게 아니야. 이 과제의 요점은 진짜 사람으로서 네가 누구인지를 보여주는 거란다. 나는 네가 네 개성을 보여주었으면 좋겠어.

S: 알겠습니다. 한 장 보다 많은 사진을 제출해도 되나요?

P: 물론이지. 원한다면, 여러 장의 사진을 제출해도 돼. 그런데 그것들은 모두 동일한 주제를 가지고 있어야 해. 그것들은 너에 관한 것이어야 해.

S: 알겠습니다. 최선을 다해 볼게요, 교수님. 조언 감사합니다.

---

photography 몡 사진 촬영, 사진   self-portrait 몡 자화상
guideline 몡 지침   instruction 몡 설명   specific 혱 구체적인
creative 혱 창의적인   purpose 몡 목적   appropriate 혱 적절한
angle 몡 각도   lighting 몡 조명   background 몡 배경
subject 몡 피사체; 주제   personality 몡 개성, 성격   theme 몡 주제

---

1 화자들은 주로 무엇을 논의하고 있는가?
  (A) 수업에서 배운 기술
  (B) 전시회에 참여하기로 한 학생의 결정
  (C) 과제를 위한 필요 조건
  (D) 사진을 촬영하는 가장 좋은 방법

2 교수는 왜 학생들에게 지침을 거의 주지 않았는가?
  (A) 학생들의 불평을 받는 것을 피하기 위해
  (B) 학생들을 위해 과제를 더 쉽게 만들기 위해
  (C) 학생들에게 함께 작업할 것을 권장하기 위해
  (D) 학생들이 창의적이 되도록 하기 위해

3 교수는 캐주얼한 사진에 관해 무엇을 암시하는가?
  (A) 그것들은 촬영하는 데 많은 기술을 필요로 하지 않는다.
  (B) 그것들은 다른 과제의 일부가 될 것이다.
  (C) 그것들은 특수한 카메라 설정 사용을 필요로 한다.
  (D) 그것들은 단체 사진에만 적절하다.

4 교수는 왜 잡지 표지를 언급하는가?
  (A) 학생에게 다른 필요 조건을 상기시키기 위해
  (B) 과제의 주요 목적 설명을 돕기 위해
  (C) 사진 촬영 스타일의 예시를 들기 위해
  (D) 다른 학생에 의해 제출된 작품을 칭찬하기 위해

5 학생은 한 장 보다 많은 사진을 제출할 때 무엇을 기억하여야 하는가?
  (A) 사진들은 모두 같은 크기여야 한다.
  (B) 사진들은 동일한 주제를 가지고 있어야 한다.
  (C) 학생은 사진들을 위해 독특한 피사체들을 선택해야 한다.
  (D) 사진들에 약간의 움직임이 있어야 한다.

Listening Practice 2   본문 p. 139

1 (C)   2 (A)   3 Reason: (B), (D) Not a Reason: (A), (C)
4 (D)   5 (C)

Note-taking

How Tea Became Popular in Britain

- 18c. Britain = powerful & wealthy, tea → favorite
- 1st introduced in 1600s from China, sold in coffee house
- 1662 = Catherine convinced others, esp. upper classes
- Tea = expensive ∵ long & difficult trip by ship
- Tea = luxury item & status symbol → mid. class copied
- 2 events made tea widely available
  - 1820s = grow tea in India
  - War w/ China → won → trade benefit (e.g. tea)
- Became common & cheap → working class afford

Listen to part of a lecture in a history class.

P: During the 18th century, Great Britain was a powerful and wealthy country. It had colonies around the world and traded large amounts of goods like sugar, tobacco, and tea. ¹This is when tea became Britain's favorite drink. Today, I'm going to talk about how that happened.

Tea was first introduced to Britain in the 1600s. It was brought there from China by Dutch and Portuguese traders. Um, at the time, most people in Britain drank coffee. However, some people started to drink tea because it was sold in coffee houses as a health drink. Then, in 1662, England's King Charles II married Catherine of Portugal, a country where tea was already popular. Because Catherine enjoyed tea, she convinced others in England to try it, especially in Britain's upper classes.

²Unfortunately, tea in Britain was expensive. This was mainly because, uh, it had to be brought on long and difficult trips by ship. So traders often sold it at high prices. Moreover, Britain put a heavy tax on all tea that was brought into the country. With the tax, tea became even more expensive than it already was, and only wealthy people could afford it.

⁵As tea was so expensive initially, its popularity did not grow beyond Britain's upper classes. It was considered a luxury item and a status symbol. The rich held special social events just to drink tea and talk. They made the tea sweeter with sugar, which was another expensive product, and drank it from fancy teapots and cups. Eventually, Britain's middle classes copied the habit of drinking tea to, uh, show their status.

Then, two major events happened that made tea more widely available. ³ᴮFirst, in the 1820s, Britain started to grow its own tea in India. Seeds were brought from China and planted in places with good soil and weather for growing tea. The second event involves Britain's role in China. ³ᴰUm, in 1839, after many years of trading with China, Britain started wars with China over some trade policies. Britain won those wars and was able to gain important new trade benefits. For instance, uh, it could obtain certain goods like tea at a lower price. Britain's victory also allowed it to establish a trade center in Hong Kong, which made it easier for Britain to ship goods from China around the world.

Because of these events, Britain was able to provide its people with large amounts of tea at low prices. It became so common and cheap that even the working classes could afford to drink it every day. ⁴It even had an impact on Britain's economy during the Industrial Revolution. Let's look at this period more closely.

역사학 강의의 일부를 들으시오.

P: 18세기 동안, 영국은 강력하고 부유한 국가였습니다. 그것은 전 세계에 식민지들을 갖고 있었고 설탕, 담배, 차와 같은 상품들을 대량으로 무역했어요. 이것이 차가 영국이 가장 좋아하는 음료가 된 때입니다. 오늘은, 그런 일이 어떻게 일어났는지에 대해 말해 보려 합니다.

차는 1600년대에 영국에 처음 소개되었습니다. 그것은 네덜란드와 포르투갈 상인들에 의해 중국으로부터 들여와졌어요. 음, 당시에, 대부분의 영국 사람들은 커피를 마셨어요. 하지만, 차가 커피 하우스에서 건강 음료로 판매되었기 때문에 몇몇 사람들이 차를 마시기 시작했어요. 그 후, 1662년에, 영국의 왕 찰스 2세가 포르투갈의 캐서린과 결혼했는데, 그 나라에서는 이미 차의 인기가 높았어요. 캐서린이 차를 즐겼기 때문에, 그녀는 영국에 있는 다른 사람들, 특히 상류층 사람들에게 그것을 마셔 보라고 설득했어요.

안타깝게도, 영국의 차는 비쌌어요. 이것은 주로, 어, 그것이 길고 힘든 항해를 통해 선편으로 들여와져야 했기 때문이에요. 그래서 상인들은 종종 그것을 높은 가격에 판매했어요. 게다가, 영국은 그 국가로 들여와지는 모든 차에 무거운 세금을 부과했죠. 세금으로 인해, 차는 원래 그랬던 것보다 심지어 더 비싸졌고, 오직 부유한 사람들만 그것을 살 여유가 있었죠.

처음에는 차가 너무 비쌌기 때문에, 그것의 인기는 영국의 상류층을 넘어서까지 증가하지 않았어요. 그것은 사치품이자 지위의 상징으로 여겨졌어요. 부유한 사람들은 단지 차를 마시고 이야기를 하기 위해 특별한 사교 행사를 열었어요. 그들은 또 다른 비싼 제품이었던 설탕으로 차를 더 달게 만들었고, 화려한 찻주전자와 잔으로 그것을 마셨어요. 결국, 영국의 중산층은, 어, 그들의 지위를 보여주기 위해 차를 마시는 습관을 모방했어요.

그 후, 차를 더 널리 구할 수 있게 만든 두 가지 주요 사건이 일어났습니다. 먼저, 1820년대에, 영국은 인도에서 차를 직접 재배하기 시작했습니다. 씨앗이 중국에서 가져와진 다음 차를 재배하기 좋은 토양과 날씨를 가진 곳에 심어졌어요. 두 번째 사건은 중국에서의 영국의 역할과 관련이 있어요. 음, 1839년에, 중국과 수년간의 무역 후에, 영국은 몇몇 무역 정책을 놓고 중국과 전쟁을 시작했습니다. 영국은 그 전쟁들에서 승리했고 중요한 새로운 무역 혜택들을 얻을 수 있었어요. 예를 들어, 어, 그것은 차와 같은 특정 상품들을 더 낮은 가격에 얻을 수 있었죠. 영국의 승리는 또한 그것이 홍콩에 무역 센터를 설립할 수 있게 해주었는데, 이는 영국이 중국에서 전 세계로 상품을 운송하는 것을 더 쉽게 만들어 주었습니다.

이러한 사건들 때문에, 영국은 국민들에게 많은 양의 차를 낮은 가격에 제공할 수 있었어요. 그것은 노동자 계층 사람들조차 매일 마실 수 있을 정도로 흔하고 저렴해졌어요. 그것은 심지어 산업혁명 시기 동안 영국의 경제에 영향을 미쳤습니다. 이 시기를 더 자세히 살펴보죠.

wealthy 형 부유한   colony 명 식민지   Dutch 형 네덜란드의
convince 동 설득하다   popularity 명 인기   luxury 형 사치의
widely 부 널리   policy 명 정책   obtain 동 얻다
establish 동 설립하다   working class 노동자 계층
Industrial Revolution 산업혁명   closely 부 자세히

1 강의의 주된 주제는 무엇인가?

(A) 영국이 세계적인 강국이 된 방법

(B) 영국에서 가장 중요한 무역 상품들

(C) 음료가 어떻게 영국에서 인기를 얻게 되었는지

(D) 영국이 중국과 전쟁을 한 이유

2 교수에 따르면, 영국에서 차가 매우 비쌌던 한가지 이유는 무엇인가?

(A) 그것을 선편으로 들여오는 것은 힘들었다.

(B) 그것은 부유한 사업주들에 의해 판매되었다.

(C) 그것은 특정한 지역들에서만 구할 수 있었다.

(D) 그것은 사회적 지위의 상징이었다.

3 강의에서, 교수는 차를 더 널리 구할 수 있게 된 몇 가지 이유를 제시한다. 다음의 각 항목이 이유인지를 표시하시오. 각 항목에 적절한 칸을 클릭하시오.

	이유임	이유가 아님
(A) 영국이 중국에 회사를 설립했다.		V
(B) 영국이 차를 재배하기 시작했다.	V	
(C) 영국이 인도에서 차를 발견했다.		V
(D) 영국이 중국과의 몇몇 전쟁에서 승리했다.	V	

4 교수는 다음에 무엇에 대해 논의할 것인가?

(A) 세계 경제에 대한 영국의 영향

(B) 영국의 국제 무역이 차 가격에 미치는 영향

(C) 산업혁명 시기에 차가 더 저렴해진 이유

(D) 산업혁명 시기에 차가 영국에 영향을 미친 방식

강의의 일부를 다시 듣고 질문에 답하시오.

P: As tea was so expensive initially, its popularity did not grow beyond Britain's upper classes. It was considered a luxury item and a status symbol. The rich held special social events just to drink tea and talk. They made the tea sweeter with sugar, which was another expensive product, and drank it from fancy teapots and cups.

5 교수는 이렇게 말함으로써 무엇을 암시하는가:

P: They made the tea sweeter with sugar, which was another expensive product, and drank it from fancy teapots and cups.

(A) 차는 종종 찻주전자 및 잔과 함께 판매되었다.

(B) 영국의 상류층은 어떻게 차를 마시는지 몰랐다.

(C) 차를 마시는 것은 특별한 행사로 여겨졌다.

(D) 설탕은 차와 함께 사용되었기 때문에 비쌌다.

Listening Practice 3

본문 p.141

1 (A)   2 (C)   3 (D)   4 (C)   5 (B)

Note-taking

W: Captain of football team, competition in 3 months
   Uniform = bad condition ∴ request money for new?
M: Can request money 2 times/yr
   Visit website → fill out form w/ detail (e.g. # of uniform)
   Provide name of company & price
   Comp. on website → suggest use one → save time
   Approved → notice → pick up $ → submit receipt
W: Buy now & submit request later?
M: Recommend wait ∵ school refuse request
   Design should have school logo

Listen to a conversation between a student and a university employee at the Department of Student Affairs.

W: Hi, I'm the captain of the women's football team. We have a competition in three months. But, um, our uniforms are in bad condition. ¹I'd like to know if we can request money to buy new ones.

M: ⁵Yes, of course. And good luck to your team... Now, have you done this before?

W: I'm afraid not. This is my first time.

M: That's fine. You can request money up to two times a year. It's a simple process to follow. The first step is to visit the Department of Student Affairs website. You'll need to fill out a form with details like the number of uniforms and the names of team members.

W: That shouldn't be a problem.

M: You'll also need to provide the name of the uniform company and their prices.

W: Oh, but we haven't decided on a company yet.

M: In that case, we have a list of companies on our website. You just have to pick one. ²I, uh, suggest you use one of the companies on the list. It will save you some time since they've already been approved.

W: OK. What else should I know?

M: Um, the whole process takes about two weeks. If your request is approved, you'll get a notice by e-mail to pick up the money. Then, you have to submit a receipt when you're done.

W: Um, what if we buy the uniforms now and submit a request for the money later?

M: ³I recommend that you wait. There's always a chance that the school will refuse your request. If you buy the uniforms now, you might have to pay for them yourselves.

W: We don't want that to happen.

M: No. And, um, there's one other thing. ⁴The design of the uniforms should have the official school logo on it. You know, the one with the white eagle inside a blue circle. Everything else is up to you.

W: OK. We can follow that guideline.

대학 학생처에서 학생과 교직원 사이의 대화를 들으시오.

W: 안녕하세요, 저는 여자 축구팀의 주장입니다. 저희는 3개월 후에 대회가 있어요. 그런데, 음, 저희 유니폼의 상태가 좋지 않아요. 저희가 새것을 구입할 자금을 요청할 수 있는지 알고 싶어요.

M: 네, 물론이죠. 그리고 학생의 팀에 행운을 빌어요... 자, 전에 이걸 해보신 적이 있나요?

W: 유감스럽게도 아니에요. 이게 처음이에요.

M: 괜찮아요. 1년에 두 번까지 자금을 요청할 수 있어요. 그것은 따르기에 간단한 절차예요. 첫 번째 단계는 대학 학생처 웹사이트에 방문하는 거예요. 유니폼의 수와 팀원의 이름 같은 세부 사항들로 양식을 작성해야 할 거예요.

W: 그건 문제가 되지 않겠네요.

M: 유니폼 회사의 이름과 그것들의 가격도 제공해야 할 거예요.

W: 오, 그런데 저희는 아직 회사를 결정하지 못했어요.

M: 그렇다면, 저희 웹사이트에 회사들의 명단이 있어요. 그냥 하나를 고르시면 돼요. 저는, 어, 그 명단에 있는 회사 중 하나를 이용하시는 것을 추천해요. 그것들은 이미 승인되었기 때문에 시간을 좀 아껴줄 거예요.

W: 알겠어요. 제가 또 무엇을 알아야 하죠?

M: 음, 전체 절차는 약 2주가 걸려요. 요청이 승인되면, 돈을 찾으러 오라는 안내문을 이메일로 받으실 거예요. 그다음, 끝나면 영수증을 제출하셔야 해요.

W: 음, 저희가 지금 유니폼을 구입하고 자금 요청서를 나중에 제출하면요?

M: 저는 기다리시는 것을 추천해요. 언제나 학교가 요청을 거절할 가능성이 있어요. 지금 유니폼을 구입하시면, 그것들을 위해 직접 지불하셔야 할지도 몰라요.

W: 저희는 그런 일이 일어나기를 원하지 않아요.

M: 그렇지 않죠. 그리고, 음, 또 하나 있어요. 유니폼의 디자인은 그 위에 학교의 공식 로고를 포함해야 해요. 파란색 원 안에 흰색 독수리가 있는 거 있잖아요. 다른 모든 건 학생에게 달려 있어요.

W: 알겠어요. 그 지침은 따를 수 있겠네요.

competition 몡 대회   process 몡 절차   approve 통 승인하다
refuse 통 거절하다   official 혱 공식적인   guideline 몡 지침

1 학생은 왜 대학 학생처를 찾아가는가?

(A) 유니폼을 위해 지불할 자금을 얻기 위해
(B) 활동에 참여하기 위한 허락을 얻기 위해
(C) 이전에 요청한 것을 확인하기 위해
(D) 유니폼 회사와 관련한 문제를 보고하기 위해

2 직원은 명단에 없는 회사들에 관해 무엇을 암시하는가?

(A) 그것들은 보통 더 높은 가격을 가지고 있다.
(B) 그것들은 제한된 수의 선택권을 제공한다.
(C) 그것들은 승인되는 데 더 오랜 시간이 걸린다.
(D) 그것들은 추가적인 서류를 제출해야 한다.

3 직원은 왜 학생이 기다릴 것을 추천하는가?

(A) 한 회사가 다음 주에 할인을 제공할 것이다.
(B) 학교가 정책을 바꿀 것으로 예상된다.
(C) 새로운 양식이 웹사이트에 게시될 것이다.
(D) 요청이 거부될 가능성이 있다.

4 직원은 유니폼에 관해 무엇이라고 말하는가?

(A) 그것들은 특정한 재료로 만들어져야 한다.
(B) 그것들은 한 개보다 많은 그림을 포함할 수 없다.
(C) 그것들은 반드시 학교의 상징을 포함해야 한다.
(D) 그것들은 학교의 이름을 보여주어야 한다.

대화의 일부를 다시 듣고 질문에 답하시오.

M: Yes, of course. And good luck to your team... Now, have you done this before?

W: I'm afraid not. This is my first time.

M: That's fine. You can request money up to two times a year. It's a simple process to follow.

5 학생은 이렇게 말함으로써 무엇을 의미하는가:

W: I'm afraid not.

(A) 그녀는 전에 스포츠를 해본 적이 없다.
(B) 그녀는 절차에 관해 알지 못한다.
(C) 그녀는 팀의 기량에 관해 확신하지 못한다.
(D) 그녀는 몇몇 필요한 것들을 가져오지 않았다.

Listening Practice 4 본문 p. 143

1 (B)   2 (A)   3 (C)   4 (C)-(D)-(B)-(A)   5 (C)

Note-taking

Using Straw as Building Material

• Ppl. have used straw ∵ easy to get
• Straw → compress → straw bales → used like bricks
• Early settler in Am. used ∵ trees X & wood expensive
• Straw has advantages
  - Keep home cool & warm ∵ less energy required
  - Cost < other materials
  - Easy = flat surface → place → tie → cover w/ plaster

Listen to part of a lecture in an architecture class.

P: ¹Wood, stone, and cement are probably the most common types of building materials. But there are many other materials you can use. This afternoon, we will look at straw.

For thousands of years, people have used straw to build houses. One reason for this is that straw is easy to get... Um, when farmers grow crops like wheat, they don't use the whole plant. Some parts of the plant are left behind. When farmers dry these parts in the sun, they get straw. Now, imagine the number of farms around the world doing this. That's a lot of straw!

Straw has many uses on a farm. But there is usually plenty left over to use as a building material. Here's how it works. ²First, you take the straw and compress it in a machine for processing. This creates large blocks of straw called straw bales. The straw bales are then used like bricks to build the walls of a home. Many early settlers in Midwest America used this method to build their homes... They did this because there weren't many trees where they lived and wood was expensive to buy. But this doesn't mean straw is not a good building material. It actually has a number of advantages.

³First, straw bales are excellent at keeping homes cool in the summer and warm in the winter. So less energy is required to heat or cool a building... Yes?

S: ⁵Um, how can straw be good at maintaining the temperature inside a building? It seems like air could pass through it very easily.

P: Yes, but you have to remember something. It's not the straw itself that keeps homes warm or cool... Rather, it's the structure of the straw bales. You see, when you press straw into bales, it becomes tightly packed. This makes it hard for cold winds to pass through. Anyway, another benefit of using straw bales is cost. Straw bales are much cheaper than other materials. Sometimes, you only have to pay to transport them from a farm. And lastly, straw bales are easy to use in building homes. ⁴ᶜFirst, you just need to make a hard, flat surface to build on, like cement. ⁴ᴰOnce that's done, you can build walls by placing straw bales on top of each other like bricks. [4B]Then, you can tie the bales together with wire to keep them stable. [4A]Finally, you can cover the straw bales with plaster... Um, plaster is a sticky material that hardens after it dries. Straw bales are so easy to use that almost anyone can build houses with them.

건축학 강의의 일부를 들으시오.

P: 목재, 돌, 시멘트는 아마도 가장 흔한 건축 자재 종류일 거예요. 하지만 사용할 수 있는 많은 다른 자재들이 있습니다. 오늘 오후에, 우리는 짚을 살펴볼 거예요.

수천 년 동안, 사람들은 집을 짓기 위해 짚을 사용해 왔어요. 이것의 한 가지 이유는 짚을 구하기 쉽다는 것이죠... 음, 농부들이 밀 같은 작물을 기를 때, 그들은 작물 전체를 사용하지 않아요. 작물의 일부는 남겨져요. 농부들이 이 부분들을 햇볕에 말리면, 그들은 짚을 얻게 되죠. 이제, 이렇게 하는 전 세계의 농장 수를 상상해 보세요. 정말 많은 짚이죠!

짚은 농장에서 많은 용도를 가지고 있습니다. 하지만 보통 건축 자재로 사용하기에 충분한 양이 남아 있어요. 그것이 가공되는 과정은 이렇습니다. 먼저, 짚을 가져와서 가공을 위해 기계에 넣고 압축해요. 이것은 짚 더미라고 불리는 짚의 큰 사각형 덩어리를 만들어내요. 짚 더미는 그 후에 집의 벽을 짓기 위해 벽돌처럼 사용돼요. 미국 중서부의 많은 초기 정착민들은 그들의 집을 짓기 위해 이 방법을 사용했어요... 그들이 살았던 곳에 나무가 많지 않았고 목재는 구입하기에 비쌌기 때문에 이렇게 했어요. 하지만 이게 짚이 좋은 건축 자재가 아니라는 의미는 아니에요. 그것은 사실 많은 장점을 가지고 있어요.

먼저, 짚 더미는 여름에는 집을 시원하게 유지하고 겨울에는 집을 따뜻하게 유지하는 데 탁월합니다. 그래서 건물을 따뜻하거나 시원하게 만드는 데 더 적은 에너지가 요구되죠... 네?

S: 음, 어떻게 짚이 건물의 내부 온도를 잘 유지할 수 있나요? 공기가 그것을 매우 쉽게 통과할 수 있을 것처럼 보이는데요.

P: 네, 하지만 기억해야 할 게 있어요. 집을 따뜻하거나 시원하게 유지하는 건 짚 자체가 아니에요... 대신, 그건 짚 더미의 구조예요. 그러니까, 짚을 눌러 더미로 만들면, 그것은 빽빽이 다져져요. 이것은 찬바람이 통과하는 것을 어렵게 만들죠. 그건 그렇고, 짚 더미를 사용하는 것의 또 다른 이점은 비용이에요. 짚 더미는 다른 자재들보다 훨씬 저렴합니다. 때때로, 그것들을 농장으로부터 운송하는 비용만 지불하면 돼요. 그리고 마지막으로, 짚 더미는 집을 지을 때 사용하기 쉬워요. 먼저, 시멘트같이 단단하고 평평한 표면을 만들기만 하면 돼요. 그게 끝나면, 짚 더미를 벽돌처럼 서로의 위에 놓음으로써 벽을 만들 수 있어요. 그런 다음, 더미들을 철사로 묶어 안정적으로 유지할 수 있죠. 마지막으로, 짚 더미를 석고 반죽으로 덮을 수 있어요... 음, 석고 반죽은 마른 후에 단단해지는 끈적끈적한 물질이에요. 짚 더미는 사용하기 매우 쉬워서 거의 누구나 그것들로 집을 지을 수 있죠.

---

probably [부] 아마도 building material 건축 자재 straw [명] 짚
wheat [명] 밀 compress [동] 압축하다 bale [명] 더미
settler [명] 정착민 maintain [동] 유지하다 tightly [부] 빽빽이
pack [동] 다지다 transport [동] 운송하다 flat [형] 평평한
plaster [명] 석고 반죽

1 교수는 주로 무엇을 논의하고 있는가?

(A) 다양한 건축 자재를 사용하는 것의 이점

(B) 집 건설을 위한 대안적 자재

(C) 짚으로 만들어진 다양한 종류의 건물

(D) 미국의 한 지역에서 인기 있는 주택 양식

2 교수는 미국 중서부의 많은 초기 정착민들에 관해 무엇을 암시하는가?

(A) 그들은 짚을 가공하는 기계들을 이용할 수 있었다.

(B) 그들은 목재를 위해 많은 숲을 베어냈다.

(C) 그들은 적은 수의 작물을 재배했다.

(D) 그들은 짚을 사용한 최초의 사람들이었다.

3 교수에 따르면, 건축 자재로서 짚 더미의 장점은 무엇인가?

(A) 그것들은 목재만큼 쉽게 불타지 않는다.

(B) 그것들은 외부 소음의 수준을 낮춘다.

(C) 그것들은 건물의 온도를 유지하는 데 효과적이다.

(D) 그것들은 건설 현장으로 운송하기 쉽다.

4 강의에서, 교수는 짚 더미로 집을 짓는 단계들을 설명한다. 아래의 단계들을 올바른 순서대로 나열하시오. 각 답변을 해당하는 곳으로 끌어다 놓으시오.

단계 1	(C) 단단하고 평평한 표면 건설하기.
단계 2	(D) 짚 더미를 서로의 위에 놓기.
단계 3	(B) 철사로 짚 더미 묶기.
단계 4	(A) 짚 더미에 석고 반죽 바르기.

강의의 일부를 다시 듣고 질문에 답하시오.

S: Um, how can straw be good at maintaining the temperature inside a building? It seems like air could pass through it very easily.

P: Yes, but you have to remember something. It's not the straw itself that keeps homes warm or cool... Rather, it's the structure of the straw bales.

5 교수는 왜 이렇게 말하는가:

P: Yes, but you have to remember something.

(A) 학생에게 이전의 주제를 상기시키기 위해

(B) 학생이 교과서를 읽을 것을 제안하기 위해

(C) 학생이 핵심 아이디어를 놓쳤다는 것을 나타내기 위해

(D) 그녀가 학생의 질문에 혼란스럽다는 것을 보여주기 위해

---

iBT Listening Test 1   본문 p. 145

1 (D)   2 (B), (D)   3 (C)   4 (B)   5 (B)

Note-taking

S: Intl. student exchange program, hope to get info.
Want School of Design ∵ 1-yr. program, prefer long
In adv. French class, want to improve language abilities

P: Apply for program = 2-step process
Submit appl. to univ. here → make sure qualified
Approved → send appl. to Paris → Final decision
Essay = how exp. help academic & career goal

S: Not good at writing, look over essay?

P: Yes

Listen to a conversation between a student and a professor.

S: Do you have a moment, Professor Clark? [1]Um, I heard you are the main advisor for the international student exchange program.

P: Yes, Thomas. Come in. How can I help you?

S: [1]Well, uh, I was hoping to get some information about the application process.

P: Sure. I'm happy to help. We have programs with several universities overseas. Is there one in particular that you're interested in?

S: Actually, yes. I'd like to go to the School of Design in Paris. [2D]I heard that it has a one-year international exchange program and I would prefer a long program to a short one.

P: Excellent. The school has a good reputation, too. And I'm sure a year in France will be a positive experience. But, uh, do you speak French?

S: Actually, I'm in an advanced-level French class right now. [2B]That's another reason why I want to go there. I'd like to improve my language abilities.

P: OK, that's good because all classes at the School of Design will be taught in French. So, uh, you need to be familiar with the language.

S: I understand. Um, is there an application form I have to fill out?

P: Well, applying for the program is a two-step process. First, you have to submit an application to the university here. This is, uh, to make sure that you're qualified to join the program. [5]Once that's approved, we'll send your application to the school in Paris. They'll make the final decision about your acceptance.

S: Is that all? That sounds easy enough.

P: Oh wait... There's one more thing. You need to submit a personal essay as part of your application.

S: [3]A personal essay? What do I need to write about?

P: You need to explain why you want to study abroad and why you've chosen this particular program. In other words, you should explain how this experience is going to help you with your academic and career goals. And, uh, the sooner you get started, the better. Writing an effective personal essay is not a quick and easy process.

S: Hmm... I'm not good at writing. Could you look over my essay once it's finished?

P: Absolutely.

S: Thanks for your help, Professor. [4]I'll get started on the essay now.

학생과 교수 사이의 대화를 들으시오.

S: 잠시 시간 있으신가요, Clark 교수님? 음, 교수님이 국제 교환 학생 프로그램의 주 지도 교수님이라고 들었어요.

P: 그래, Thomas. 들어오렴. 어떻게 도와줄까?

S: 음, 어, 지원 절차에 관한 정보를 좀 얻고 싶어요.

P: 물론이지. 돕게 되어 기쁘구나. 우리는 해외의 여러 대학과의 프로그램이 있단다. 관심 있는 특정한 것이 있니?

S: 사실, 있어요. 저는 파리에 있는 School of Design에 가고 싶어요. 그곳에 1년짜리 국제 교환 학생 프로그램이 있다고 들었고 저는 단기보다는 장기 프로그램을 선호해요.

P: 잘됐구나. 그 학교는 좋은 평판을 가지고 있기도 해. 그리고 프랑스에서의 1년이 긍정적인 경험이 될 거라고 확신해. 그런데, 어, 프랑스어를 할 줄 아니?

S: 사실, 저는 지금 고급 프랑스어 수업을 듣고 있어요. 그게 제가 그곳에 가고 싶은 또 다른 이유예요. 제 언어 구사력을 향상하고 싶거든요.

P: 알았다, School of Design의 모든 수업이 프랑스어로 가르쳐질 것이기 때문에 그건 잘됐구나. 그러니까, 어, 너는 그 언어에 익숙해야 해.

S: 이해했어요. 음, 제가 작성해야 하는 지원서가 있나요?

P: 음, 프로그램에 지원하는 것은 두 단계로 된 절차야. 먼저, 너는 여기 대학에 지원서를 제출해야 해. 이건, 어, 네가 프로그램에 참여할 자격이 있는지 확인하기 위해서야. 그게 승인되면, 우리는 네 지원서를 파리에 있는 학교에 보낼 거야. 그들이 합격에 관한 최종 결정을 내릴 거란다.

S: 그게 전부인가요? 쉬워 보이네요.

P: 오 기다려보거라... 하나 더 있구나. 너는 네 지원서의 일부로 개인 에세이를 제출해야 해.

S: 개인 에세이요? 무엇에 관해 써야 하나요?

P: 네가 해외에서 공부하고 싶은 이유와 이 특정 프로그램을 선택한 이유를 설명해야 해. 다시 말해, 너는 이 경험이 네 학업 및 직업적 목표에 어떻게 도움이 될 것인지 설명해야 해. 그리고, 어, 네가 빨리 시작할수록 더 좋아. 효과적인 개인 에세이를 쓰는 것은 빠르고 쉬운 과정이 아니야.

S: 흠... 저는 글쓰기를 잘하지 못해요. 제 에세이가 마무리되면 살펴봐 주실 수 있나요?

P: 물론이지.

S: 도와주셔서 감사합니다, 교수님. 이제 에세이를 시작할게요.

---

international 형 국제적인   application 명 지원(서)
overseas 형 해외의   particular 형 특정한   prefer 동 선호하다
reputation 명 평판   positive 형 긍정적인   fill out ~을 작성하다
acceptance 명 합격   academic 형 학업의
look over ~을 살펴보다

1 학생은 왜 교수를 찾아가는가?

   (A) 프로그램을 위한 추천서를 찾아가기 위해

   (B) 학교에 다니는 것의 장점을 논의하기 위해

   (C) 미래의 직업에 대한 계획을 세우는 데 도움을 요청하기 위해

   (D) 해외로 가는 프로그램에 지원하는 방법을 알아내기 위해

2 학생은 왜 School of Design에서 공부하고 싶어 하는가?
   2개의 답을 고르시오.

   (A) 그것의 교수들은 가르치는 데 능숙하다.

   (B) 그것은 그가 프랑스어를 더 잘하도록 도울 것이다.

   (C) 그것의 학생들은 유명한 디자이너들과 함께 일한다.

   (D) 그것은 1년 동안 지속되는 프로그램을 제공한다.

3 교수에 따르면, 학생은 개인 에세이에 무엇을 포함해야 하는가?

(A) 그가 이전에 성취한 것들의 예시

(B) 그의 어학 선생님들의 추천서

(C) 프로그램이 어떻게 그의 목표를 지원할 것인지

(D) 그가 다른 지원자들에 비해 더 자격이 있는 이유

4 학생은 다음에 무엇을 할 것인가?

(A) 고급 프랑스어 수업에 등록하기

(B) 프로그램에 대한 그의 관심에 관해 쓰기

(C) 그의 지원서를 대학에 보내기

(D) 교수에게 그의 에세이 한 부를 건네기

대화의 일부를 다시 듣고 질문에 답하시오.

P: Once that's approved, we'll send your application to the school in Paris. They'll make the final decision about your acceptance.

S: Is that all? That sounds easy enough.

P: Oh wait... There's one more thing.

5 학생은 이렇게 말함으로써 무엇을 의미하는가:

S: Is that all?

(A) 그는 합격할 자신이 있다.

(B) 그는 절차가 더 어려울 것이라고 예상했다.

(C) 그는 학교에 관해 더 알고 싶어 한다.

(D) 그는 몇 가지 요구사항을 완료했다.

iBT Listening Test 2

본문 p. 148

1 (D)   2 (D)   3 (A), (C)   4 (D)   5 (A)   6 (C)

Note-taking

How Species are Adapting to Warming Climate

• Some species finding way to adapt to warm climate
• 1 effect of global warming = change in migration route
 - Eurasian blackcap = winters in GB ∵ warmer & wetter
 - Migrate far X & more time find mate
• Benefit from change in season
 - Spring earlier → offspring earlier (e.g. red squirrel)
 - Past = disadv. ∵ lower temp. → less food
 - Today = born early → more time to eat ∴ survival ↑
• Changes in physical characteristics
 - Tawny owl = more brown ∵ less snow on ground

Listen to part of a lecture in a biology class.

P: I'm sure you all know what global warming is, right? It refers to the increase in the average temperature of the planet. The planet has always had periods of warming and cooling, but the current rise in temperatures is happening very quickly. It could cause many extinctions and a loss of biodiversity. ¹Still, some species are finding ways to adapt to the warming climate.

⁴One effect of global warming is a change in migration routes. ²Normally, animals that migrate move to their feeding grounds in the winter and breeding grounds in the summer. They repeat this process every year. In recent years, though,

some migrating animals have chosen new seasonal destinations in response to rising global temperatures. Consider the Eurasian blackcap as an example... Um, this small bird typically lives in Africa during the winter and Northern Europe during the summer. But, recently, a large population has begun spending winters in Great Britain. They are doing this because the climate in Great Britain has become warmer and wetter in recent decades. Um, but this is not a bad thing for the birds. ³ᶜThe birds don't have to migrate as far as they did before. ³ᴬAlso, they can spend more time finding a mate.

⁴In many parts of the world, other animals are also benefiting from changes in the seasons. ⁵For instance, spring is arriving earlier in some places. This lets animals give birth to their offspring earlier in the year. For example, the red squirrel now gives birth 18 days sooner than before. In the past, an early birth would have been a big disadvantage for animals. Can anyone tell me why?

S: Well, if animals gave birth when the weather was still cold, their offspring would likely die, I guess.

P: Exactly. Lower temperatures, less food... you get the idea. But, with warmer temperatures today, that disadvantage is removed. For animals that are born early today, there is more time to eat before winter comes. By the time winter arrives, they are well developed and strong. Of course, this greatly improves their chances of survival.

⁴Due to the rising global temperatures, changes to the physical characteristics of some species have occurred as well. The tawny owl is one famous example. It now has two distinct colors... ⁶Before, most tawny owls were gray. Now, scientists are seeing more brown ones. In fact, these birds now make up 50 percent of the total population. Several decades ago, that number was just 30 percent. So what happened? Well, warmer winters are resulting in less snow on the ground. And since the ground is now mostly brown, more owls have developed brown feathers to match their surroundings. This trend is unlikely to reverse.

생물학 강의의 일부를 들으시오.

P: 모두 지구 온난화가 무엇인지 알고 있을 거라 생각해요, 그렇죠? 그건 지구 평균 기온의 상승을 가리켜요. 지구는 항상 온난화와 냉각화 기간을 가져왔지만, 현재의 기온 상승은 매우 빠르게 일어나고 있어요. 그건 많은 멸종과 생물 다양성의 상실을 초래할 수 있어요. 그럼에도 불구하고, 몇몇 종들은 온난화되는 기후에 적응하는 방법을 찾고 있습니다.

지구 온난화의 한 가지 결과는 이주 경로의 변화입니다. 보통, 이주를 하는 동물들은 겨울에는 먹이를 먹는 곳으로 이동하고 여름에는 번식지로 이동해요. 그것들은 이 과정을 매년 반복하죠. 하지만, 최근 몇 년 동안, 몇몇 이주를 하는 동물들은 지구의 기온 상승에 대응하여 새로운 계절적 목적지를 선택했습니다. 유라시아 검은머리꾀꼬리를 예로 들어 보죠... 음, 이 작은 새는 일반적으로 겨울 동안에는 아프리카에 살고 여름 동안에는 북유럽에 살아요. 하지만, 최근에, 큰 개체군이 영국에서 겨울을 보내기 시작했어

요. 영국의 기후가 최근 수십 년 동안 더 따뜻하고 습해졌기 때문에 그것들을 이렇게 하고 있어요. 음, 하지만 이게 새들에게 나쁜 것은 아니에요. 그 새들은 이전에 그랬던 것만큼 멀리 이주할 필요가 없죠. 또, 그것들은 짝을 찾는 데 더 많은 시간을 쓸 수 있어요.

세계의 많은 곳에서, 다른 동물들도 계절의 변화로부터 이익을 얻고 있어요. 예를 들어, 어떤 곳들에서는 봄이 더 일찍 오고 있어요. 이것은 동물들이 연중에 더 일찍 새끼를 낳게 해주죠. 예를 들어, 붉은날다람쥐는 이제 예전보다 18일 더 빨리 새끼를 낳아요. 과거에는, 조산이 동물들에게 큰 불이익이 되었을 거예요. 왜 그런지 말해볼 사람 있나요?

S: 음, 동물들이 날씨가 아직 추울 때 새끼를 낳으면, 아마 새끼가 죽을 가능성이 클 것 같아요.

P: 정확해요. 더 낮은 기온, 더 적은 먹이... 무슨 말인지 알겠죠. 하지만, 오늘날의 더 따뜻한 기온으로 인해, 그 불이익은 제거돼요. 오늘날 더 일찍 태어나는 동물들에게는, 겨울이 오기 전에 먹을 시간이 더 많아요. 겨울이 올 때쯤이면, 그것들은 잘 발달되어 있고 튼튼합니다. 물론, 이건 그들의 생존 확률을 크게 높이죠.

상승하는 지구 기온 때문에, 몇몇 종들의 신체적 특징에도 변화가 일어났어요. 올빼미는 한 가지 유명한 예시예요. 그것은 이제 두 가지의 뚜렷한 색을 가지고 있죠... 이전에는, 대부분의 올빼미가 회색이었어요. 이제, 과학자들은 갈색 올빼미들을 더 많이 보고 있어요. 사실, 이 새들은 이제 전체 개체수의 50퍼센트를 차지합니다. 수십 년 전에, 그 수는 겨우 30퍼센트였어요. 그래서 무슨 일이 일어났을까요? 음, 더 따뜻한 겨울은 땅에 더 적은 눈이 쌓이게 되는 결과를 낳고 있어요. 그리고 이제 땅이 대부분 갈색이기 때문에, 더 많은 올빼미들이 주변 환경에 맞게 갈색 깃털을 발달시켜 왔죠. 이 추세는 역전될 것 같지 않습니다.

extinction 명 멸종 biodiversity 명 생물 다양성
migration 명 이주 breed 동 번식하다 mate 명 짝
offspring 명 새끼, 자손 disadvantage 명 불이익
physical 형 신체적인; 물리적인 distinct 형 뚜렷한
feather 명 깃털

1 강의의 주된 주제는 무엇인가?

(A) 지구 온난화가 많은 멸종을 초래하는 이유
(B) 자원을 위한 인간과 동물의 경쟁
(C) 지구의 생물 다양성을 보존하는 것의 이점
(D) 종들이 상승하는 기온에 적응하고 있는 방식

2 교수에 따르면, 이주하는 동물들의 공통된 행동은 무엇인가?

(A) 그것들은 매년 다른 경로를 이용한다.
(B) 그것들은 우기가 시작되기 전에 떠난다.
(C) 그것들은 평생 한 마리의 짝을 갖는다.
(D) 그것들은 연중 특정 시간 동안 이동한다.

3 유라시아 검은머리꾀꼬리는 영국에서 겨울을 보냄으로써 무엇을 얻는가?
2개의 답을 고르시오.

(A) 짝을 찾기 위한 추가적인 시간
(B) 더 다양한 먹이 공급원
(C) 더 짧은 이주 거리
(D) 많은 수의 새끼

4 교수는 강의를 어떻게 구성하는가?

(A) 전 세계의 연구 결과를 언급함으로써
(B) 동물 행동의 변화에 대해 예측함으로써
(C) 특정 국가에서 발견되는 동물들에 대해 논의함으로써
(D) 지구 온난화가 동물들에게 미치는 여러 영향들을 설명함으로써

5 교수는 왜 조산의 불이익을 이야기하는가?

(A) 이른 봄의 중대성을 강조하기 위해
(B) 많은 동물들이 비슷한 위험에 직면한다는 것을 보여주기 위해
(C) 동물에 대한 다른 의견을 제공하기 위해
(D) 최근의 문제로 주의를 돌리기 위해

6 교수는 올빼미에 관해 무엇을 암시하는가?

(A) 미래에 추가적인 색이 발달될 것이다.
(B) 시원한 여름이 개체수 증가로 이어질 것이다.
(C) 갈색 깃털이 더 흔해질 것이다.
(D) 서식지 파괴가 그것들의 수에 영향을 미칠 것이다.

Vocabulary Review

본문 p. 152

1 legal	2 guideline	3 migration
4 biodiversity	5 widely	6 probably
7 established	8 obtained	9 specific
10 (A)	11 (B)	12 (C)
13 (B)	14 (C)	

Actual Test 1

PART 1. Passage 1

본문 p. 154

1 (C) 2 (A) 3 (A), (C) 4 (B) 5 (B)

Note-taking

W: Sth. delivered, forgot combination, look it up?
M: Can't give info. even w/ student ID
Issues w/ stealing ∴ school changed rules
Fill out a form ← student services office
W: Office = closed for repairs until Monday
Basketball ticket = expensive, game = tomorrow
M: Tell combination or give new one X → open for you
Need extra ID w/ name (e.g. passport) → compare
Stay for another 15 min. ∵ wait for another student

Listen to a conversation between a student and a university housing office employee.

M: Hi there, what can I do for you?

W: Um, hi... [1]I've got a problem. Something was

delivered to my mailbox today and I need to pick it up... But, um, I forgot the combination... Could you look it up for me? I brought my student ID.

M: I see... I'm sorry, but I can't give you that information, even with your student ID.

W: Oh, how come? I've done it before. Last semester, I was able to get my combination here.

M: Yes, well... [5]We've had a lot of issues with stealing lately... A few people have had important documents and personal packages disappear. So the school has changed the rules. I know that's inconvenient, but... It's nothing personal... The school is only trying to protect students.

W: OK, I understand. But what can I do?

M: Well, you'll need to fill out a form that shows the mailbox belongs to you. You can get it at the student services office...

W: [2]Actually, I passed by the student services office on my way over here... A sign on the door said that it's closed for repairs until Monday. Please... My brother sent me basketball tickets as a birthday present, and they were really expensive!

M: I'd like to help, but I need to follow the rules... You'll have to wait until Monday.

W: But the game is tomorrow evening, so I really need those tickets. Is there anything you can do?

M: Well, there is one way I can help you. I'm not really supposed to do this, but I guess your case is special. [3C]Your tickets will be useless if you don't open the mailbox today. [3A]And, I've been in a similar situation before, so I know how it feels. I was grateful when somebody helped me. I can't tell you your combination, or give you a new one. But I will open your mailbox for you so that you can get your tickets.

W: Wow! Thank you so much!

M: And one more thing. I'll need to see an extra form of ID with your name on it... Something like a passport would be fine... That way, I can compare it with the name on the envelope from your brother. Would that be OK?

W: Yes, that'd be great. I really appreciate it... But, um, I don't have any extra ID right now. I'll have to go back to my dormitory room. What time does this office close?

M: In 20 minutes.

W: My dormitory is on the other side of campus... I'm not sure if I can come back in 20 minutes...

M: Well, how about this... [4]I'll stay for another 15 minutes... I'm waiting for another student to bring his dormitory application form, anyway.

W: That's so kind of you. I'll go as fast as I can.

학생과 대학 기숙사 사무실 직원 사이의 대화를 들으시오.

M: 안녕하세요, 무엇을 도와드릴까요?

W: 음, 안녕하세요... 문제가 있어요. 오늘 제 우편함으로 무언가가 배달되었고 저는 그것을 찾아와야 해요... 그런데, 음, 자물쇠의 숫자

조합을 잊어버렸어요... 그것을 찾아봐 주실 수 있나요? 제 학생증을 가져왔어요.

M: 그렇군요... 죄송하지만, 학생증을 갖고 계시더라도 그 정보를 드릴 수 없어요.

W: 오, 왜 그런가요? 이전에도 해봤어요. 지난 학기에, 여기서 제 자물쇠의 숫자 조합을 받을 수 있었어요.

M: 네, 음... 저희는 최근에 절도와 관련된 문제가 아주 많았어요... 몇몇 사람들은 중요한 서류와 개인 소포가 사라졌어요. 그래서 학교는 규칙을 바꿨어요. 그게 불편하다는 건 알아요, 하지만... 기분 나쁘게 하려는 건 아니에요... 학교는 단지 학생들을 보호하려고 하는 거예요.

W: 네, 이해합니다. 그런데 제가 무엇을 할 수 있죠?

M: 음, 그 우편함이 학생의 소유라는 것을 보여주는 양식을 작성해야 해요. 그것은 학생지원 센터에서 구할 수 있어요...

W: 사실은, 여기에 오는 길에 학생지원 센터 옆을 지나쳤어요... 문에 있는 표지판에 그곳이 수리를 위해 월요일까지 문을 닫는다고 쓰여 있었어요. 저... 제 오빠가 생일 선물로 농구 경기 티켓을 보냈고, 그것들은 정말 비쌌어요!

M: 도와드리고 싶지만, 저는 규칙을 따라야 해요... 월요일까지 기다리셔야 할 거예요.

W: 하지만 경기는 내일 저녁이에요, 그래서 저는 정말로 그 티켓들이 필요해요. 해 주실 수 있는 게 있나요?

M: 음, 제가 도와드릴 수 있는 한 가지 방법이 있어요. 사실 제가 이렇게 하면 안 되지만, 학생의 경우는 특수한 것 같네요. 학생이 오늘 우편함을 열지 않으면 티켓들은 쓸모없어질 거예요. 그리고, 저도 이전에 비슷한 상황에 처한 적이 있어서, 그게 어떤 느낌인지 알아요. 누군가가 저를 도와주었을 때 감사했죠. 자물쇠의 숫자 조합을 말씀드리거나 새로운 것을 드릴 수는 없어요. 하지만 티켓을 받으실 수 있도록 우편함을 열어드릴게요.

W: 와! 정말 감사합니다!

M: 한 가지 더요. 학생의 이름이 적힌 다른 종류의 신분증을 확인해야 해요... 여권 같은 거면 괜찮을 거예요... 그렇게 하면, 제가 그것을 학생의 오빠가 보낸 봉투 위의 이름과 비교할 수 있어요. 괜찮으시겠어요?

W: 네, 그거 좋겠네요. 정말 감사해요... 그런데, 음, 지금은 다른 신분증이 없어요. 제 기숙사 방으로 돌아가야겠네요. 이 사무실은 몇 시에 문을 닫나요?

M: 20분 후에요.

W: 제 기숙사는 캠퍼스 반대편에 있어요... 20분 안에 돌아올 수 있을지 모르겠네요...

M: 음, 이건 어때요... 제가 15분 더 머물러 있을게요... 어차피, 저는 다른 학생이 그의 기숙사 신청서를 가져오기를 기다리고 있거든요.

W: 정말 친절하시네요. 최대한 빨리 갈게요.

---

combination 명 자물쇠의 숫자 조합   look up ~을 찾아보다
stealing 명 절도   disappear 동 사라지다
inconvenient 형 불편한   protect 동 보호하다
belong to ~의 소유이다   pass by ~의 옆을 지나치다
useless 형 쓸모없는   grateful 형 감사한   compare 동 비교하다
envelope 명 봉투   application form 신청서

1 학생은 왜 기숙사 사무실을 찾아가는가?

(A) 그녀의 우편함이 잠겨 있는 이유를 묻기 위해

(B) 그녀의 잃어버린 티켓을 찾기 위해

(C) 그녀의 우편물에 대한 접근을 요청하기 위해

(D) 그녀의 우편함 자물쇠의 숫자 조합을 바꾸기 위해

2 학생은 왜 학생지원 센터에서 도움을 받을 수 없는가?

(A) 그곳은 일시적으로 문을 닫아야 했다.

(B) 그녀는 그 사무실에 방문할 시간이 없다.

(C) 그곳은 더 이상 학생 우편함을 관리하지 않는다.

(D) 그녀는 필요한 양식을 올바르게 작성하지 않았다.

3 직원은 왜 학생을 돕기로 했는가?
2개의 답을 고르시오.

(A) 그는 학생의 상황에 공감할 수 있다.

(B) 그는 학생이 우편함을 소유한다는 것을 확인했다.

(C) 학생은 곧 사용되어야 하는 선물을 받았다.

(D) 학생은 보답으로 부탁을 들어주겠다고 약속했다.

4 직원은 왜 다른 학생의 기숙사 신청서를 언급하는가?

(A) 학생이 제출해야 하는 것의 예시를 들기 위해

(B) 그가 문 닫는 시간 이후에 사무실에 있는 이유를 설명하기 위해

(C) 그가 다른 서류를 작업하느라 바쁘다는 것을 표현하기 위해

(D) 학생들이 그들의 우편물을 잃어버리는 것이 얼마나 쉬운지 보여주기 위해

대화의 일부를 다시 듣고 질문에 답하시오.

M: We've had a lot of issues with stealing lately... A few people have had important documents and personal packages disappear. So the school has changed the rules. I know that's inconvenient, but... It's nothing personal... The school is only trying to protect students.

5 직원은 이렇게 말함으로써 무엇을 의미하는가:

M: It's nothing personal...

(A) 그는 학생들이 그들의 물품에 주의해야 한다고 생각한다.

(B) 그는 모두와 똑같이 규칙을 따라야 한다.

(C) 그는 대학이 정책을 바꾸기를 바란다.

(D) 그는 개인적인 문제에 관해 학생들을 도울 수 없다.

PART 1. Passage 2 　　　　　　本文 p. 156

6 (B)　　7 (D)　　8 (A)　　9 (C)
10 Yes: (C), (D) No: (A), (B)　　11 (C)

Note-taking
Greek Revival Architecture
- 1750 = Brit. architect travel to Greece to see temple
- Style spread to Europe → America → widely used
- Why was it popular?
  - Interest in bldg. of Greece & Rome
  - America = young democracy → come from Greece
- Mostly used for govt. bldg. → later for bank, etc.
- Large & shaped like rect., front = portico
- Top of portico = triangle roof held by pillars & columns
- Am. architect follow Greek style → some differences
  - Am. = marble expensive → used wood & brick
  - Am. = paint bldg. white, Greek = paint various colors

Listen to part of a lecture in an architecture class.

P: Let's continue with our discussion of American architecture. Um, we've already talked about common American buildings and homes in the 17th century. Um, they were mostly built in the Georgian and Federal styles. ⁶Now, let's move on to a popular style from the late 18th and early 19th centuries. It's called Greek Revival architecture.

⁷So, as the name suggests, this style of architecture was inspired by Greece. But, to be specific, it was inspired by the architecture of ancient Greece. Um, that's why it's called Greek Revival. It revived or brought back an old style of architecture. You see, in 1750, British architects traveled to Greece to see its ancient temples. When they returned to Britain, they wrote about the experience and this led to the style's revival. Eventually, the style spread to Europe and then to America. In America, it was especially popular from about 1825 to 1860. ⁸It was used so widely that it became known as America's National Style.

Why was it so popular? Well, there are a couple of reasons. First, during the 17th and 18th centuries, there was a lot of interest in studying the buildings of ancient Greece and Rome. This started a revival of classical architecture throughout England and the rest of Europe. ⁹Second, America was a young democracy at the time. And of course, the idea of democracy actually comes from ancient Greece. So America used Greek Revival architecture to show that it strongly believed in democracy. This is also why the style was mostly used for important government buildings. Of course, it was later used for banks, libraries, public monuments, and even people's homes. There are several famous examples that you can still see today. These include the Second Bank of the United States and the Philadelphia Museum of Art.

OK. So, as you might expect, buildings in the Greek Revival style looked very much like ancient Greek temples. You may have seen pictures before. ¹⁰ᴰIn general, Greek Revival buildings were large and shaped like rectangles. ¹⁰ᶜAt the front, they had a smaller structure that covered the entrance to the building. This was called a portico. At the top of the portico was a triangle-shaped roof. It was held by six to eight pillars or columns. These columns were very tall and usually had a simple design. However, some of them also had decorations. On the inside of the buildings, American architects sometimes added smaller columns next to fireplaces and windows.

Now, most of the time, American architects tried to follow the Greek style closely. However, there were also some differences. For instance, Greek temples were mostly built with marble. However, marble was expensive in America, so architects sometimes used wood and brick instead. When they used wood or brick, they painted the buildings white so that it looked more like the marble of Greek temples. But, interestingly, Greek temples were actually often painted in various colors. However, nobody knew this during the 1700s and 1800s. [11]After thousands of years, most of the original paint on the temples had disappeared. So architects saw the white color of the temples and copied that in their designs. Personally, I think that was a good development. The buildings look more important in white. They would look less serious if they were painted in many different colors.

건축학 강의의 일부를 들으시오.

P: 미국의 건축 양식에 대한 논의를 계속해 봅시다. 음, 17세기에 흔했던 미국의 건물과 집들에 대해서는 이미 얘기했죠. 음, 그것들은 대부분 조지언 양식과 연방 양식으로 지어졌어요. 이제, 18세기 후반과 19세기 초반에 인기 있었던 양식으로 넘어가 봅시다. 그것은 그리스 부흥 건축 양식이라고 불립니다.

자, 이름이 암시하듯이, 이 건축 양식은 그리스에서 영감을 받았습니다. 하지만, 구체적으로 말하자면, 그것은 고대 그리스의 건축 양식에서 영감을 받았어요. 음, 그게 그것이 그리스 부흥이라고 불리는 이유죠. 그것은 오래된 건축 양식을 부활시키거나 다시 도입했어요. 그러니까, 1750년에, 영국 건축가들은 고대의 신전들을 보기 위해 그리스에 갔어요. 영국으로 돌아왔을 때, 그들은 그 경험에 대해 글을 썼고 이것이 그 양식의 부흥으로 이어졌어요. 결국, 그 양식은 유럽으로 그 후에는 미국으로 퍼졌습니다. 미국에서, 그것은 약 1825년부터 1860년까지 특히 인기가 있었어요. 그것은 너무나 널리 사용되어서 미국의 국가적 양식이라고 알려지게 되었죠.

그것이 왜 그렇게 인기가 많았을까요? 음, 두 가지의 이유가 있습니다. 첫째로, 17세기와 18세기 동안, 고대 그리스와 로마의 건물들을 연구하는 것에 많은 관심이 있었어요. 이것은 영국과 나머지 유럽 전역에서 고전 건축의 부흥이 시작되게 했어요. 둘째로, 당시에 미국은 젊은 민주주의 국가였어요. 그리고 물론, 민주주의 개념은 실제로 그리스에서 비롯되었죠. 그래서 미국은 민주주의를 강하게 믿고 있다는 것을 보여주기 위해 그리스 부흥 건축 양식을 사용했습니다. 이것은 그 양식이 주로 중요한 정부 건물들을 위해 사용된 이유이기도 해요. 물론, 그것은 나중에 은행, 도서관, 공공 기념물, 그리고 심지어는 사람들의 집을 위해 사용되었어요. 오늘날에도 여전히 볼 수 있는 여러 유명한 예시들이 있어요. 이것들은 제2합중국은행과 필라델피아 미술관을 포함해요.

좋아요. 자, 여러분이 예상할 수 있듯이, 그리스 부흥 건축 양식의 건물들은 고대 그리스의 신전들과 매우 비슷해 보였어요. 여러분은 전에 사진을 본 적이 있을 거예요. 일반적으로, 그리스 부흥 양식 건물들은 컸고 직사각형 같은 모양으로 만들어졌어요. 정면에, 그것들은 건물의 입구를 덮는 더 작은 구조물을 가지고 있었어요. 이것은 포르티코라고 불렸어요. 포르티코의 꼭대기에는 삼각형 모양의 지붕이 있었습니다. 그것은 6개에서 8개의 받침이나 기둥으로 지탱되었어요. 이 기둥들은 매우 높았고 보통 단순한 디자인을 가지고 있었어요. 하지만, 그것들 중 일부에는 장식이 있기도 했어요. 건물의 안쪽에, 미국 건축가들은 때때로 벽난로와 창문 옆에 더 작은 기둥들을 추가했어요.

자, 대부분의 경우, 미국 건축가들은 그리스 양식을 면밀히 모방하려고 노력했습니다. 하지만, 몇몇 차이점들도 있었어요. 예를 들어, 그리스 신전들은 대부분 대리석으로 지어졌어요. 하지만, 미국에서 대리석은 비쌌기 때문에 건축가들은 때때로 목재나 벽돌을 대신 사용했어요. 목재나 벽돌을 사용할 때, 그들은 건물을 하얗게 칠해서 그것이 좀 더 그리스 신전의 대리석처럼 보이게 했

어요. 그런데, 흥미롭게도, 그리스 신전들은 종종 다양한 색으로 칠해졌어요. 하지만, 1700년대와 1800년대에는 이를 아무도 몰랐죠. 수천 년이 지난 후에, 신전의 원래 칠의 대부분이 사라졌어요. 그래서 건축가들은 신전의 하얀색을 보고 그들의 디자인에 그것을 모방했죠. 개인적으로, 저는 그게 좋은 발전이었다고 생각합니다. 건물들은 하얀색일 때 더 중요해 보이죠. 그것들이 많은 서로 다른 색으로 칠해지면 덜 진지해 보일 거예요.

architecture [명] 건축 양식   revive [동] 부활시키다   temple [명] 신전
spread [동] 퍼지다   widely [부] 널리   classical [형] 고전적인
democracy [명] 민주주의 국가, 민주주의   rectangle [명] 직사각형
pillar [명] 받침, 기둥   column [명] 기둥   fireplace [명] 벽난로
closely [부] 면밀히   marble [명] 대리석

6 강의는 주로 무엇에 관한 것인가?

(A) 오래된 건축 양식과 새로운 건축 양식의 차이점

(B) 미국에서 인기 있었던 건축 양식

(C) 미국 건축 양식이 그리스에 미친 영향

(D) 매우 유명해진 건축가 집단

7 교수는 왜 고대 그리스를 언급하는가?

(A) 건축 양식이 발전하는 데 오랜 시간이 걸렸다는 것을 보여주기 위해

(B) 영국과 그리스의 양식을 비교하기 위해

(C) 오래된 건축 방법이 효과적이었던 이유를 설명하기 위해

(D) 영국 건축가들이 어디에서 영감을 얻었는지 말하기 위해

8 그리스 부흥 건축 양식은 왜 미국의 국가적 양식이라고 불렸는가?

(A) 그것이 미국 전역에서 보편화되었다.

(B) 그것이 원래 미국 건축가들에게서 영감을 받았다.

(C) 그것이 미국 정부에 의해 만들어진 표준이었다.

(D) 그것이 비슷한 영국의 양식과 달라야 했다.

9 무엇이 미국에서 그리스 부흥 건축 양식의 발전을 이끌었는가?

(A) 미국의 영국과의 긴밀한 관계

(B) 건축 자재 비용의 상승

(C) 민주주의에 대한 믿음을 보여주려는 미국의 열망

(D) 더 많은 공공건물을 만들기 위한 정부의 결정

10 다음의 항목이 그리스 부흥 건축 양식의 특징으로 언급된 것인지를 표시하시오.
각 항목에 적절한 칸을 클릭하시오.

	예	아니오
(A) 장식이 있는 지붕		V
(B) 많은 큰 창문이 있는 건물		V
(C) 입구 위에 있는 포르티코	V	
(D) 직사각형 모양의 건물	V	

강의의 일부를 다시 듣고 질문에 답하시오.

P: After thousands of years, most of the original paint on the temples had disappeared. So architects saw the white color of the temples and copied that in their designs. Personally, I think that was a good development. The buildings look more important in white. They would look less serious if they were painted in many different colors.

11 교수는 이렇게 말함으로써 무엇을 암시하는가:

P: Personally, I think that was a good development.

(A) 그는 더 많은 공공건물이 신전처럼 보여야 한다고 생각한다.

(B) 그는 건축가들이 디자인을 모방해야 한다고 생각하지 않는다.

(C) 그는 하얀 건물들이 더 중요해 보인다고 생각한다.

(D) 그는 건물의 색이 건축가에 의해 선택되기를 원한다.

PART 2. Passage 1
본문 p. 158

1 (D)　2 (C)　3 (B)　4 (D)　5 (A)

Note-taking

S: Not sure what to do w/ final project
　Talked about depression → want to do experiment
　Want to do survey = ask about feelings
P: Get approval from school → make sure harm X
　Could cause mental stress ∴ be careful
　Reveal names X = better ∵ may not be honest
　Work on application ASAP
　Specific in application, mention why & how

Listen to a conversation between a student and a professor.

P: Good morning, Alex. Is there something you need?

S: Hi, Professor Daniels. ¹Um, I need your advice. I'm not sure what to do with my final project.

P: Oh? What is it about?

S: ²Well, I was with my study group yesterday and we were talking about depression... It seems to be very common among university students.

P: You're probably right.

S: ²Yes, so our discussion made me want to do an experiment about it for the final project. Um, I know it's not directly related to what we've talked about in class.

P: Well, that's fine. Your final project doesn't have to be about the exact topics we've covered in class. And I'm happy you're interested in the subject. What exactly are you planning to do?

S: I want to do a survey... You know, collect information from students on campus. I want to ask about their feelings and how campus life affects them.

P: I see... ⁵That could be a problem, actually. You would be using people in an experiment. That means you'll have to get approval from the school. This is necessary to make sure that your experiment doesn't harm students.

S: Really? But it's just a survey. It's not like I'm testing a new medicine...

P: Well, I know a survey seems harmless. But you'll be asking students about personal feelings...

If they're feeling depressed or nervous, they probably don't want others to know that. This could cause mental stress, so it's important to be careful. That's why research like this requires the school's approval.

S: Oh, that's something I hadn't considered.

P: Many universities require it. ³You can probably do the survey, but you won't be able to reveal any names... It's better that way, anyway. Otherwise, participants may not be honest about their feelings.

S: You're right. That could affect the results... Is there anything else I should know?

P: Yes. It could take a while to get the school's approval. So you should work on the application as soon as possible. That way, if you can't do this project, you'll have time to think of a new one.

S: I really hope this one is approved. I mean, depression is a big problem for students. The experiment could show it's a problem on our campus, too. If it is, then the school can help the students by offering programs or counseling...

P: That's a good point. Still, you should apply soon. ⁴And make sure you are specific in your application... You should mention why you are doing the experiment and how you plan to do the survey. Very often, applications are rejected because they are unclear about their purpose and plans.

S: Thanks for the advice. And can I come to you if I have any other questions?

P: Of course. I'll help if I can. I look forward to seeing your results.

학생과 교수 사이의 대화를 들으시오

P: 좋은 아침이구나, Alex. 필요한 게 있니?

S: 안녕하세요, Daniels 교수님. 음, 교수님의 조언이 필요해요. 제 기말 과제와 관련해서 어떻게 해야 할지 모르겠어요.

P: 오? 무엇에 관한 거니?

S: 음, 어제 제 스터디 그룹과 함께했고 저희는 우울증에 관해 얘기했어요... 그것은 대학생들 사이에서 매우 흔해 보여요.

P: 아마 네가 맞을 거야.

S: 네, 그러니까 저희의 논의는 제가 기말 과제를 위해 그것에 대한 실험을 하고 싶게 만들었어요. 음, 그것이 수업에서 저희가 얘기한 것과 직접적인 관련이 없다는 건 알아요.

P: 음, 그건 괜찮아. 네 기말 과제가 우리가 수업에서 다룬 정확한 주제에 관한 것일 필요는 없어. 그리고 네가 그 주제에 관심이 있다니 기쁘구나. 정확히 무엇을 하려고 계획 중이니?

S: 저는 설문조사를 하고 싶어요... 그러니까, 캠퍼스의 학생들에게 정보를 수집하는 거요. 그들의 감정과 캠퍼스 생활이 그것들에 어떻게 영향을 미치는지에 관해 묻고 싶어요.

P: 그렇구나... 사실, 그건 문제가 될 수도 있어. 너는 실험에 사람들을 이용할 거야. 그건 네가 학교의 승인을 받아야 한다는 걸 의미해. 이것은 네 실험이 학생들에게 해를 끼치지 않는다는 걸 확실히 하기 위해 필요해.

S: 정말요? 하지만 그건 그냥 설문조사예요. 새로운 약을 시험하는 것 같은 게 아니에요...

P: 음, 설문조사에 악의가 없어 보이는 건 안단다. 하지만 너는 학생들에게 개인적인 감정에 관해 물어볼 거야... 만약 그들이 우울하거나 초조함을 느낀다면, 그들은 아마 다른 사람들이 그걸 알기를 원치 않을 거야. 이것은 정신적 스트레스를 초래할 수 있어, 그래서 조심하는 것은 중요해. 그것이 이런 조사가 학교의 승인을 필요로 하는 이유야.

S: 오, 그건 제가 고려하지 못했던 것이네요.

P: 많은 대학들이 그걸 요구해. 너는 아마 설문조사를 할 수 있겠지만, 어떠한 이름도 밝힐 수 없을 거야... 어차피, 그 방식이 더 나아. 그렇지 않으면, 참여자들은 그들의 감정에 관해 솔직하지 않을 수도 있어.

S: 맞아요. 그게 결과에 영향을 미칠 수도 있겠네요... 제가 또 알아야 하는 게 있나요?

P: 있어. 학교의 승인을 받으려면 시간이 좀 걸릴 수도 있어. 그러니까 너는 가능한 한 빨리 그 신청서를 써야 해. 그렇게 하면, 네가 이 과제를 할 수 없게 되더라도, 새로운 것을 생각해낼 시간이 있을 거야.

S: 정말로 이게 승인되었으면 좋겠어요. 제 말은, 우울증은 학생들에게 큰 문제잖아요. 실험은 우리 캠퍼스에서도 그것이 문제임을 보여줄 수도 있어요. 만약 그렇다면, 학교는 프로그램이나 상담을 제공함으로써 학생들을 도울 수 있어요...

P: 좋은 지적이구나. 그래도, 너는 곧 신청해야 해. 그리고 네 신청서를 꼭 구체적으로 쓰렴... 네가 실험을 하는 이유와 어떻게 설문조사를 할 계획인지 언급해야 해. 종종, 신청서는 목적과 계획에 관해 불분명하기 때문에 거절돼.

S: 조언 감사합니다. 그리고 다른 질문이 있으면 교수님께 와도 되나요?

P: 물론이지. 내가 도울 수 있다면 도와줄게. 결과를 보기를 기대하마.

depression 명 우울증   experiment 명 실험   exact 형 정확한
affect 동 영향을 미치다   approval 명 승인   harm 동 해를 끼치다
mental 형 정신적인   reveal 동 밝히다, 드러내다
participant 명 참여자   counseling 명 상담   specific 형 구체적인
reject 동 거절하다   unclear 형 불분명한
look forward to ~을 기대하다

1 화자들은 주로 무엇을 논의하고 있는가?

(A) 심리학 실험의 결과

(B) 설문조사를 하는 것의 장점

(C) 스터디 그룹의 구성원

(D) 과제를 완료할 방법

2 학생은 왜 우울증에 관한 실험을 하고 싶어 하는가?

(A) 그는 교과서에서 그 주제에 관해 읽었다.

(B) 그는 수업의 최근 강의에서 아이디어를 얻었다.

(C) 그는 학생들과의 논의에서 영감을 받았다.

(D) 그는 온라인으로 그 주제에 대한 영상을 보았다.

3 교수는 학생의 설문조사에 관해 무엇을 암시하는가?

(A) 그것은 적은 수의 학생들과 함께 하는 것이 더 쉬울 것이다.

(B) 만약 참여자들이 이름을 제공해야 한다면 그것은 정확하지 않을 수 있다.

(C) 그것은 보고서에 포함하기에 너무 상세할지도 모른다.

(D) 그것은 한 가지 이상의 주제에 관한 것이어야 한다.

4 교수는 신청서를 위해 무엇을 추천하는가?

(A) 웹사이트에 열거된 지침을 따르는 것

(B) 학생들에 관한 실제 이야기와 사례들을 언급하는 것

(C) 제출 전에 조교에게 그것을 검토해 달라고 요청하는 것

(D) 목표와 방법에 관한 많은 세부 사항을 포함하는 것

대화의 일부를 다시 듣고 질문에 답하시오.

P: That could be a problem, actually. You would be using people in an experiment. That means you'll have to get approval from the school. This is necessary to make sure that your experiment doesn't harm students.

S: Really? But it's just a survey. It's not like I'm testing a new medicine...

5 학생은 이렇게 말함으로써 무엇을 의미하는가:

S: It's not like I'm testing a new medicine...

(A) 그는 실험이 해를 끼칠 것이라고 생각하지 않는다.

(B) 실험은 학생들을 시험하는 것을 포함하지 않을 것이다.

(C) 교수는 목표를 이해하지 못했다.

(D) 그는 학생들에게 어려운 질문을 하지 않을 것이다.

PART 2. Passage 2   본문 p. 160

6 (C)   **7** (D)   **8** (C)
9 Whitewater: (A), (C) Blackwater: (B) Clearwater: (D)
10 (A)   **11** (C)

Note-taking
Three Different Kinds of Amazon Rivers

- Most common type = whitewater river
  - Light brown ∵ pick up sediments ↑
  - Muddy & difficult to see through
  - Many nutrients = provide food for animals & plants
- Blackwater river
  - Dark brown, smaller, slow, pass forest & sandy soil
  - Cleaner & clearer > whitewater
  - Dark color ∵ dead leaves & plants, produce chemicals
- Clearwater = mostly clear, can be blue or light green
  - Found in high mountains, little sediment
  - Nutrients ↓, support more fish > blackwater

Listen to part of a lecture in an environmental science class.

P: Most people have heard of the Amazon River. Um, it's famous for being one of the longest rivers in the world. It, uh, starts somewhere in Peru and ends in the Atlantic Ocean. ⁶But the Amazon River isn't just one long river. Throughout the region, there are actually many smaller rivers that connect to it. And, in general, there are three kinds of rivers with distinct features. This is what I want to discuss today.

So the three main kinds of rivers in the Amazon are whitewater, blackwater, and clearwater rivers. Um, Alfred Russel Wallace, an English scientist, created the terms in 1853. However, the rivers also have other key differences. For instance, they have different amounts of nutrients and sediments, or loose rocks and soil, depending on the lands they pass through. Now, let's look at each type...

The most common type is the whitewater river. [7]Um, these rivers are light brown, like coffee with cream. They have this color because they pick up lots of sediments from low, flat areas of land. [9A]The sediments make the water muddy and difficult to see through. The sediments also give whitewater rivers many nutrients. [9C]These provide food for a wide variety of animals and help plants in nearby areas grow. In fact, that's why there are many farms near whitewater rivers.

Next, um, we have blackwater rivers. These rivers are dark brown, like the color of black tea. They are usually smaller, slow-moving rivers. They pass through thick forests and places with sandy soil. [8]The sandy soil removes large sediments from the water, which makes it cleaner and clearer than the water in whitewater rivers. However, blackwater rivers get their dark color from dead leaves and plants that fall into them. And, um, this produces some interesting results. You see, dead plants produce chemicals that make the water acidic.

S: Sorry. Could you explain that some more?

P: Sure... Um, river water has different characteristics depending on what is in it. So when river water has large amounts of materials like dead plants, it becomes more acidic. This is because of the chemicals in those materials... In addition, many plants in the Amazon produce harmful chemicals to protect themselves from being eaten. [9B]And when these plants die, their harmful chemicals also enter the water. So the combination of acidic water and harmful chemicals can make blackwater rivers unsafe for many plants and animals.

Finally, um, let's talk about clearwater rivers. These kinds of rivers have the most accurate name. They really are mostly clear, but they can also be blue or light green. [9D]Clearwater rivers are mostly found in the high mountains near the Amazon. [10]For millions of years, water has passed over the rocks in these mountains. So very little sediment is produced. The rivers also tend to have fast-moving sections, so loose materials are carried away quickly. Also, clearwater rivers do not have many nutrients. However, they are not as acidic as blackwater rivers and can support more types of fish.

[11]If you get a chance, visit the city of Manaus, Brazil. It has a popular tourist attraction called The Meeting of Waters. There, you will see a blackwater river meet a whitewater river. The difference is easy to see. Where the rivers meet, it looks like one large river with two distinct colors!

환경 과학 강의의 일부를 들으시오.

P: 대부분의 사람들은 아마존강에 대해 들어봤어요. 음, 그것은 세계에서 가장 긴 강 중 하나로 유명하죠. 그것은, 어, 페루의 어딘가에서 시작해서 대서양에서 끝나요. 하지만 아마존강은 단지 하나의 긴 강이 아니에요. 그 지역 도처에, 사실 그것에 연결된 더 작은 하천들이 많이 있어요. 그리고, 일반적으로, 뚜렷한 특징을 가진 세 종류의 하천이 있어요. 이게 오늘 논의하고자 하는 거예요.

자, 아마존의 세 가지 주요 하천의 종류는 백수, 흑수, 청수 하천입니다. 음, 영국 과학자 Alfred Russel Wallace는 1853년에 그 용어들을 만들었어요. 하지만, 그 하천들에는 다른 중요한 차이점들도 있어요. 예를 들어, 그것들은 통과해 지나가는 땅에 따라 서로 다른 양의 영양물과 침전물, 즉 느슨한 바위들과 흙을 가지고 있어요. 이제, 각 종류를 살펴봅시다...

가장 흔한 종류는 백수 하천이에요. 음, 이 하천들은 크림이 들어간 커피처럼 연한 갈색이에요. 그것들은 땅의 낮고 평평한 부분에서 많은 침전물을 들어올리기 때문에 이런 색을 가지고 있죠. 침전물은 물을 탁하고 투시하기 어렵게 만들어요. 침전물은 또한 백수 하천에 많은 영양물을 제공합니다. 이것들은 매우 다양한 동물들에게 먹이를 제공하고 근처 지역의 식물들이 성장하는 것을 도와요. 사실, 그것이 백수 하천 근처에 농장이 많은 이유예요.

다음으로, 음, 흑수 하천이 있습니다. 이 하천들은 홍차의 색처럼 어두운 갈색이에요. 그것들은 보통 더 작고, 천천히 움직이는 하천이에요. 그것들은 무성한 숲과 모래흙이 있는 장소들을 통과해 지나가요. 모래흙은 물에서 큰 침전물을 제거하는데, 이는 그것을 백수 하천의 물보다 더 깨끗하고 투명하게 만들어요. 하지만, 흑수 하천은 그것들로 떨어지는 죽은 나뭇잎과 식물들로 인해 그것의 어두운색을 갖게 돼요. 그리고, 음, 이는 몇 가지 흥미로운 결과를 낳아요. 그러니까, 죽은 식물은 물을 산성으로 만드는 화학물질을 만들어내요.

S: 죄송합니다. 조금 더 설명해 주실 수 있나요?

P: 물론이죠... 음, 하천수는 그 안에 무엇이 있느냐에 따라 서로 다른 특징을 가지고 있어요. 그러니까 하천수에 죽은 식물 같은 물질들이 많으면, 그것은 더 산성이 돼요. 이것은 그 물질들에 있는 화학물질들 때문이죠... 게다가, 아마존의 많은 식물들은 먹히는 것으로부터 자신을 보호하기 위해 해로운 화학물질들을 만들어내요. 그리고 이 식물들이 죽을 때, 그것들의 해로운 화학물질들이 물로 들어가기도 하죠. 그래서 산성인 물과 해로운 화학물질의 결합은 흑수 하천을 많은 식물들과 동물들에게 안전하지 않게 만들 수 있어요.

마지막으로, 음, 청수 하천에 대해 얘기해 봅시다. 이 종류의 하천들은 가장 정확한 이름을 가지고 있어요. 그것들은 실제로 대부분 투명하지만, 파란색이거나 연한 녹색일 수도 있어요. 청수 하천들은 대부분 아마존 근처의 높은 산에서 발견돼요. 수백만 년 동안, 물은 이 산들의 바위 위로 흘러갔어요. 그래서 침전물이 거의 만들어지지 않았죠. 그 하천들에는 또한 빠르게 움직이는 구간들이 있는 경향이 있어서, 느슨한 물질들이 빠르게 휩쓸려가요. 또, 청수 하천들에는 영양물이 많지 않아요. 하지만, 그것들은 흑수 하천만큼 산성이지 않고 더 많은 종류의 물고기를 부양할 수 있어요.

기회가 된다면, 브라질의 도시 마나우스를 방문해 보세요. 그곳은 The Meeting of Waters라고 불리는 인기 있는 관광 명소를 가지고 있어요. 그곳에서, 여러분은 흑수 하천이 백수 하천과 만나는 것을 볼 거예요. 차이는 쉽게 알 수 있어요. 하천들이 만나는 곳에서, 그것은 두 가지 뚜렷한 색을 가진 하나의 큰 하천처럼 보여요!

---

distinct 휑 뚜렷한　feature 몡 특징　term 몡 용어
nutrient 몡 영양물　sediment 몡 침전물　loose 휑 느슨한
flat 휑 평평한　muddy 휑 탁한　chemical 몡 화학물질
acidic 휑 산성의　harmful 휑 해로운　combination 몡 결합, 조합
unsafe 휑 안전하지 않은　accurate 휑 정확한
tourist attraction 관광 명소

6 교수는 주로 무엇에 관해 논하는가?

    (A) 종들이 아마존에서 생존하는 방법

    (B) 아마존 지역에 사는 것의 장점

    (C) 서로 다른 종류의 아마존 하천

    (D) 아마존의 다양한 식물과 동물

7 교수는 왜 커피를 언급하는가?

    (A) 중요한 농산물의 이름을 대기 위해

    (B) 물 종류의 맛을 설명하기 위해

    (C) 하천이 일부 식물의 성장을 돕는 방법을 보여주기 위해

    (D) 하천의 색을 더 정확하게 묘사하기 위해

8 흑수 하천의 물을 깨끗하게 만드는 것은 무엇인가?

    (A) 하천의 속도

    (B) 물의 온도

    (C) 물이 통과하는 흙의 종류

    (D) 하천의 식물 부족

9 다음의 항목이 백수, 흑수, 청수 하천 중 어떤 것의 특징인지를 표시하시오.

각 항목에 적절한 칸을 클릭하시오.

	백수	흑수	청수
(A) 투시하기 어렵다	V		
(B) 해로운 화학물질을 포함하고 있다		V	
(C) 매우 다양한 생물을 부양한다	V		
(D) 높은 산에서 발견된다			V

10 아마존 근처의 산에 관해 추론할 수 있는 것은 무엇인가?

    (A) 그것들은 수백만 년 동안 존재해 왔다.

    (B) 그것들의 하천은 아마존 근처의 많은 마을을 부양한다.

    (C) 그것들은 대부분의 하천이 비롯되는 곳이다.

    (D) 그것들의 환경은 보호되어야 한다.

강의의 일부를 다시 듣고 질문에 답하시오.

P: If you get a chance, visit the city of Manaus, Brazil. It has a popular tourist attraction called The Meeting of Waters. There, you will see a blackwater river meet a whitewater river. The difference is easy to see. Where the rivers meet, it looks like one large river with two distinct colors!

11 교수는 왜 이렇게 말하는가:

P: The difference is easy to see.

    (A) 자연 현상이 흔하다는 것을 시사하기 위해

    (B) 학생들에게 개념이 어렵지 않다는 것을 재확인해주기 위해

    (C) 두 하천의 색 대비를 강조하기 위해

    (D) 그녀가 이전 강의에서 말했던 것을 반복하기 위해

PART 2. Passage 3
본문 p. 162

12 (C)   13 (C)   14 (C)   15 (A), (D)   16 (A)
17 (D)

Note-taking

Bureaucracy

- Bureaucracy = found in large institution (e.g. company)
- Have distinct roles, focus on particular job ∴ efficient
  - Factory = specific task → pass it to next person
- Follow hierarchy = top-down structure
  - Low-level employee < manager < CEO
  - Ppl. at the top = responsibility & authority ↑
  - Easier to control ppl. & activities
- Formal rules & procedures (e.g. manual)
  - Accomplish task efficiently → ensure continuity
- Make things fairer ∵ clear guideline
- Downside = respond new situation & long time decision

Listen to part of a lecture in a sociology class.

P: Let's get started. [12]Hopefully, you all did the assigned reading, which covers today's topic. It's the organizational structure known as a bureaucracy. OK, who can give me a quick definition of a bureaucracy?

S: [16]A bureaucracy is like a government office, right? I mean, the textbook gave the example of a post office as a well-known type of bureaucracy.

P: Well, that's part of it. But the concept is broader than that... Bureaucracies are found in many large institutions, including schools, churches, armies, and companies. They are simply a type of organization or a way of organizing people. Every organization needs to have a certain structure so that it can achieve its goals in the best way possible.

Now that we know what a bureaucracy is, what are some of its characteristics? Well, first of all, people in a bureaucracy usually have distinct roles. Each person focuses on a particular job and has clear responsibilities. [17]This is what makes a bureaucracy efficient. Think of it like a factory... Each worker performs a specific task on a product and then passes it on to the next person. The result is that goods are produced faster and at a lower cost.

Another characteristic is that bureaucracies follow a hierarchy. In other words, they have a top-down structure, like a pyramid. Take a company as an example... You've got low-level employees at the bottom. They follow the orders of managers above them. Then, above the managers, you have people like the CEO. [13]In a hierarchy, people at the top of the organization control the people below them. They have the widest responsibilities and the most authority to make decisions. Meanwhile, those at the bottom have fewer responsibilities and almost no authority to make decisions. Having a hierarchy like this makes it easier for the organization to control the many people and activities within it... I mean, just imagine if everyone did whatever they wanted.

This leads to my next point. Bureaucracies also have many formal rules and procedures. These are usually written down in manuals and other documents. These rules are important because they tell workers how to handle different types of tasks and situations. That way, they can accomplish tasks efficiently. Rules also help to ensure an organization's continuity, or its ability to last a long time. For example, if people leave an organization, it is very easy for others to come in and continue what they started. [14]This is how large bureaucracies like national governments or the Catholic Church are able to last for hundreds of years even though the people inside them come and go.

Aside from providing efficiency, control, and continuity, bureaucracies also help to make things fairer... For instance, in a bureaucracy, decisions are based on clear guidelines that everyone knows. So, uh, for example, employees know what to do to get a raise or a promotion. Managers can't decide these things simply based on their personal feelings either. Of course, bureaucracies also have downsides, though... [15D]Sometimes, people are not able to respond to a new situation because they don't have a specific rule that tells them how to handle it. [15A]Another drawback comes from having a hierarchy. Because many decisions have to come from the top of an organization, it can take a long time for decisions to be made.

다른 문서들에 기재돼요. 이 규칙들은 근로자들에게 여러 종류의 업무와 상황을 처리하는 방법을 알려주기 때문에 중요해요. 그렇게 하면, 그들은 업무를 효율적으로 완수할 수 있죠. 규칙들은 조직의 연속성, 즉 오랫동안 존속할 능력을 보장하는 데 도움을 주기도 해요. 예를 들어, 사람들이 조직을 떠나면, 다른 사람들이 들어와서 그들이 시작한 것을 계속하는 것은 매우 쉬워요. 이것이 국가 정부나 가톨릭교회 같은 큰 관료 체제가 그 안의 사람들이 드나듦에도 불구하고 수백 년 동안 존속할 수 있는 방법이에요.

효율성, 통제력, 연속성을 제공하는 것 외에도, 관료 체제는 일을 더 공평하게 만드는 데 도움이 됩니다... 예를 들어, 관료 체제에서, 결정은 모두가 알고 있는 명확한 지침들에 기초해요. 그러니까, 어, 예를 들어, 직원들은 임금 인상이나 승진을 위해 무엇을 해야 하는지 알고 있죠. 관리자들은 이러한 것들을 단순히 개인적인 감정에 기초하여 결정할 수 없어요. 그럼에도 불구하고, 물론, 관료 체제에는 단점들도 있습니다... 때때로, 사람들은 새로운 상황에 대응하지 못하는데, 이는 그것을 어떻게 처리할지 알려주는 구체적인 규칙이 없기 때문이에요. 또 다른 단점은 계급제를 갖는 것에서 비롯돼요. 많은 결정들이 조직의 최고위층에서 나와야 하기 때문에, 결정이 내려지는 데 오랜 시간이 걸릴 수 있어요.

사회학 강의의 일부를 들으시오.

P: 시작합시다. 바라건대, 여러분 모두 오늘의 주제를 다루는 읽기 과제를 했겠죠. 주제는 관료 체제라고 알려진 조직의 구조입니다. 자, 관료 체제에 대해 간단한 정의를 해줄 수 있는 사람 있나요?

S: 관료 체제는 관공서 같은 거죠, 그렇죠? 그러니까, 교과서는 관료 체제의 잘 알려진 유형으로 우체국의 예시를 들었어요.

P: 음, 그것은 일부예요. 그런데 개념은 그것보다 더 광범위해요... 관료 체제는 학교, 교회, 군대, 회사와 같은 많은 큰 기관들에서 볼 수 있어요. 그것은 그저 조직의 한 유형이나 사람들을 조직하는 방식이에요. 모든 조직은 가능한 최선의 방법으로 목표를 달성할 수 있도록 특정한 구조를 가질 필요가 있어요.

이제 관료 체제가 무엇인지 알았으니, 그것의 특징에는 어떤 것들이 있을까요? 음, 가장 먼저, 관료 체제에서 사람들은 보통 뚜렷한 역할을 가지고 있어요. 각자는 특정한 일에 집중하고 분명한 책무를 가지고 있죠. 이것이 관료 체제를 효율적으로 만드는 거예요. 그것을 공장 같은 거라고 생각해 보세요... 각 작업자는 제품에 대해 특정한 작업을 수행한 다음 그걸 다음 사람에게 전달해요. 그 결과 상품은 더 빠르게 더 낮은 비용으로 생산되죠.

또 다른 특징은 관료 체제가 계급제를 따른다는 거예요. 다시 말해서, 그것은 피라미드 같은 상의하달식 구조를 가지고 있습니다. 회사를 예로 들어 보죠... 최하위층에는 하급 직원들이 있죠. 그들은 그들 위에 있는 관리자들의 명령에 따라요. 그리고, 관리자들 위에는, CEO 같은 사람들이 있어요. 계급제에서, 조직의 최고위층에 있는 사람들은 그들 아래에 있는 사람들을 통제해요. 그들은 가장 광범위한 책무와 결정을 내릴 가장 큰 권한을 가지고 있어요. 한편, 최하위층에 있는 사람들은 더 적은 책무를 가지고 있고 결정을 내릴 권한이 거의 없어요. 이와 같은 계급제를 갖는 것은 조직이 그 안에서 많은 사람들과 활동을 통제하는 것을 더 쉽게 만들죠... 그러니까, 모든 사람이 원하는 대로 한다면 어떨지 상상해 보세요.

이는 저의 다음 요점으로 이어져요. 관료 체제는 또한 많은 공식적인 규칙들과 절차들을 가지고 있어요. 이것들은 보통 매뉴얼과

hopefully 男 바라건대   organizational 형 조직의
bureaucracy 명 관료 체제   definition 명 정의
government office 관공서   concept 명 개념   broad 형 광범위한
institution 명 기관   distinct 형 뚜렷한   particular 형 특정한
specific 형 특정한, 구체적인   hierarchy 명 계급제
top-down 형 상의하달식의   authority 명 권한
formal 형 공식적인   procedure 명 절차   accomplish 통 완수하다
continuity 명 연속성   promotion 명 승진   downside 명 단점
drawback 명 단점

12 강의의 주된 주제는 무엇인가?

(A) 정부 기관들 사이의 차이점

(B) 현대 회사들의 발전

(C) 조직 형태의 특징

(D) 관료 체제를 갖추는 것의 장점

13 교수에 따르면, 조직의 최고위층에 있는 사람들은 최하위층에 있는 사람들과 어떻게 다른가?

(A) 그들은 보통 더 긴 시간을 일한다.

(B) 그들은 그들의 일에 대해 더 높은 임금을 받는다.

(C) 그들은 결정을 내릴 더 많은 권한을 가지고 있다.

(D) 그들은 사업에 대한 더 많은 지식을 가지고 있다.

14 교수는 왜 가톨릭교회를 언급하는가?

(A) 관료 체제에 문제점이 있을 수 있다는 것을 보여주기 위해

(B) 일부 사람들이 조직을 떠나는 이유를 설명하기 위해

(C) 오래 존속하는 기관의 예시를 들기 위해

(D) 그것을 다른 종류의 관료 체제들과 비교하기 위해

15 교수에 따르면, 관료 체제의 단점은 무엇인가?
2개의 답을 고르시오.

(A) 결정이 내려지는 데 오랜 시간이 걸린다.

(B) 일부 규칙들은 따르기에 너무 어렵다.

(C) 사람들은 사회적 지위에 대해 거의 신경 쓰지 않는다.

(D) 사람들은 새로운 상황에 잘 대응하지 못한다.

강의의 일부를 다시 듣고 질문에 답하시오.

S: A bureaucracy is like a government office, right? I mean, the textbook gave the example of a post office as a well-known type of bureaucracy.

P: Well, that's part of it. But the concept is broader than that... Bureaucracies are found in many large institutions, including schools, churches, armies, and companies.

16 교수는 이렇게 말함으로써 무엇을 의미하는가:

P: Well, that's part of it.

(A) 그는 학생의 대답이 완전하지 않다고 생각한다.

(B) 그는 주제가 나중에 논의되어야 한다고 생각한다.

(C) 그는 교과서가 개정되지 않았다는 것을 알고 있다.

(D) 그는 학생이 질문에 혼란스러워한다고 생각한다.

강의의 일부를 다시 듣고 질문에 답하시오.

P: This is what makes a bureaucracy efficient. Think of it like a factory... Each worker performs a specific task on a product and then passes it on to the next person. The result is that goods are produced faster and at a lower cost.

17 교수는 왜 이렇게 말하는가:

P: Think of it like a factory...

(A) 공장이 체제를 따라야 한다고 제안하기 위해

(B) 관료 체제에서 흔히 볼 수 있는 직업의 종류를 설명하기 위해

(C) 관료 체제가 어느 조직에나 적용될 수 있다는 것을 보여주기 위해

(D) 관료 체제 구조의 이점을 설명하기 위해

Actual Test 2

PART 1. Passage 1

1 (C)   2 (D)   3 (C)   4 (B)   5 (D)

Note-taking

S: Not sure what to do after graduation, advice?
P: Most obvious job = marketing manager
S: Lose interest working for 1 comp., want more exciting
P: Job in advertising = creative & work w/ many comp.
  Very competitive, become good → long & successful
S: Charity org.? ∵ like helping ppl.
P: Always need help, you could be very helpful
  Try different jobs → find the right one
  Internship = great way to learn if job is right
  Apply ASAP, if need break → too long X

Listen to a conversation between a student and a professor.

P: Hi, Rose. Come on in. How can I help you?

S: Hi, Professor Collins. I'll be graduating in a couple of months... ¹But, uh, I'm still not sure what to do for work after graduation. Um, could I ask for your advice?

P: Oh, sure! What did you want to know?

S: Well, as a marketing major, there are so many jobs I could do. ¹I'm having a hard time choosing a specific career.

P: Well, let's see... There are so many options. ²For instance, the most obvious job would be to work as a marketing manager for a private company. You would, um, do things like promote the company's brand, develop marketing plans, and so on...

S: ²That sounds all right. But I might lose interest working for just one company. I'd like to do something more exciting.

P: Hmm... In that case, you may want to look at a job in advertising. You would get to be creative and work with many companies.

S: I enjoy being creative, so that's definitely a possibility. I've heard the work environment isn't so great, though.

P: ³Well, jobs in advertising are usually very competitive. They have lots of applicants wanting those positions. Also, the hours are long and clients can be difficult. But if you become good at your job, you can have a long and successful career.

S: I see. I guess I could consider that job... What about doing events for charity organizations? I like the idea of helping people.

P: Why not? They always need help raising money and letting people know about important issues. ⁴You could be very helpful in both those areas. You're organized and have excellent communication skills.

S: Thank you, Professor.

P: The truth is, you will probably do well in any career you choose. You just have to find out what you enjoy doing and what you're good at. And sometimes, the only way to do that is to try different jobs. Eventually, you will find the right one for you.

S: That's true. I wasn't thinking of it that way. Maybe I should apply for an internship first.

P: Actually, I highly recommend that you do that. It's a great way to learn if a job is right for you. And the experience will also help you find other jobs later.

S: That's what I'll do, then. But, um, do you think I should apply for an internship now or wait until after graduation? I was hoping to take a short vacation after graduation.

P: If I were you, I would apply for an internship as soon as possible. That's probably what most students will do. However, if you feel like you need a break, then make sure it isn't too long. ⁵And you should start preparing for a job right away when you get back.

76   영어 실력을 높여주는 다양한 학습 자료 제공 HackersBook.com

S: Thanks for the advice, Professor. I'll think carefully about everything you've said.

학생과 교수 사이의 대화를 들으시오.

P: 안녕, Rose. 들어오렴. 어떻게 도와줄까?

S: 안녕하세요, Collins 교수님. 저는 두 달 후에 졸업해요... 그런데, 어, 저는 여전히 졸업 후에 어떤 일을 할지 잘 모르겠어요. 음, 교수님의 조언을 여쭤봐도 될까요?

P: 오, 물론이지! 무엇을 알고 싶었니?

S: 음, 마케팅을 전공하는 학생으로서, 제가 할 수 있는 일이 아주 많아요. 저는 구체적인 진로를 선택하는 데 어려움을 겪고 있어요.

P: 음, 어디 보자... 아주 많은 선택지가 있지. 예를 들어, 가장 확실한 일은 민간 회사의 마케팅 관리자로 일하는 것이겠구나. 너는, 음, 회사의 브랜드를 홍보하고, 마케팅 계획을 수립하는 등의 일을 하게 될 거야...

S: 괜찮은 것 같아요. 그런데 저는 한 회사만을 위해 일하는 것에 흥미를 잃을지도 몰라요. 저는 더 재미있는 일을 하고 싶어요.

P: 흠... 그런 경우라면, 광고 분야의 일을 고려해보고 싶어 할 수도 있겠구나. 너는 창의적이 될 수 있고 많은 회사들과 일하게 될 거야.

S: 저는 창의적이 되는 걸 즐거워해서, 그건 분명히 하나의 가능성이에요. 그런데, 근무 환경이 그렇게 좋지 않다고 들었어요.

P: 음, 광고 분야의 일자리들은 보통 매우 경쟁적이야. 그 자리를 원하는 지원자들이 많이 있어. 또, 근무 시간은 길고 고객은 까다로울 수 있어. 하지만 네가 일을 잘하게 되면, 길고 성공적인 경력을 가질 수 있단다.

S: 그렇군요. 그 일도 고려할 수 있겠네요... 자선 단체를 위한 행사를 하는 건 어떤가요? 저는 사람들을 돕는다는 발상이 좋아요.

P: 왜 안 되겠어? 그들은 돈을 모금하고 중요한 문제에 관해 사람들에게 알리는 데 항상 도움이 필요해. 너는 그 두 분야 모두에서 큰 도움이 될 수 있어. 너는 체계적이고 훌륭한 의사소통 기술을 갖고 있잖니.

S: 감사합니다, 교수님.

P: 사실은, 너는 아마 네가 선택하는 어떤 직업에서도 잘할 거야. 너는 단지 네가 하기를 좋아하는 것과 잘하는 것을 알아내면 돼. 그리고 가끔은, 그렇게 하는 유일한 방법은 여러 가지 일을 해보는 거야. 결국, 너는 너에게 맞는 것을 찾을 거야.

S: 맞아요. 그런 방식으로는 생각하지 못했어요. 어쩌면 저는 인턴직에 먼저 지원해 봐야겠어요.

P: 사실, 나는 네가 그렇게 하는 걸 적극적으로 추천해. 그것은 어떤 일이 네게 맞는지를 배울 좋은 기회야. 그리고 그 경험은 나중에 네가 다른 일을 찾는 데도 도움이 될 거야.

S: 그럼, 그렇게 해야겠어요. 그런데, 음, 교수님은 제가 지금 인턴직에 지원해야 한다고 생각하시나요 아니면 졸업 후까지 기다려야 한다고 생각하시나요? 저는 졸업 후에 짧은 휴가를 보냈으면 했어요.

P: 내가 너라면, 가능한 한 빨리 인턴직에 지원할 거야. 그게 아마 대부분의 학생들이 할 것이 거야. 하지만, 네가 휴식이 필요하다고 생각하면, 그것이 너무 길어지지 않도록 하렴. 그리고 네가 돌아오면 곧바로 일을 위한 준비를 시작해야 해.

S: 조언 감사합니다, 교수님. 말씀하신 모든 것에 대해 신중하게 생각해 볼게요.

advice 명 조언 specific 형 구체적인 career 명 진로; 경력; 직업
obvious 형 확실한, 분명한 promote 동 홍보하다
develop 동 수립하다, 개발하다 advertising 명 광고 분야, 광고

creative 형 창의적인 definitely 부 분명히
competitive 형 경쟁적인 applicant 명 지원자
charity organization 자선 단체 organized 형 체계적인
probably 부 아마 right away 곧바로

1 학생은 왜 교수를 찾아가는가?

(A) 몇몇 졸업 요건들을 확인하기 위해

(B) 다른 수업을 수강하는 것에 관해 알아보기 위해

(C) 진로 결정에 관해 도움을 받기 위해

(D) 일자리 면접에 관한 조언을 구하기 위해

2 학생은 민간 회사에서 일하는 것에 대해 무엇이라고 말하는가?

(A) 그녀는 매우 성공적일 수 있다.

(B) 그녀의 기술은 필요 조건에 부합하지 않을 것이다.

(C) 그녀는 그 근무 환경을 좋아할 것이다.

(D) 그녀의 일은 충분히 재미있지 않을 수도 있다.

3 교수는 광고 분야의 일자리들에 관해 무엇을 암시하는가?

(A) 그것들은 높은 급여를 주지 않는다.

(B) 그것들은 보통 큰 도시에 있다.

(C) 그것들은 구하기 어려울 수 있다.

(D) 그것들은 많은 경험을 요구한다.

4 교수는 왜 학생의 의사소통 기술을 언급하는가?

(A) 그녀의 성적에 대한 이유를 설명하기 위해

(B) 그녀가 어떻게 도움이 될 수 있는지 보여주기 위해

(C) 그녀에게 약간의 개선이 필요하다는 것을 말하기 위해

(D) 그녀가 집중해야 하는 것을 말해주기 위해

5 학생의 졸업 이후 계획에 대한 교수의 의견은 무엇인가?

(A) 그는 짧은 휴가가 필요하다고 생각한다.

(B) 그는 그녀가 여러 개의 일을 찾아봐야 한다고 생각한다.

(C) 그는 학생이 너무 바빠질까 봐 걱정한다.

(D) 그는 그녀가 빠르게 일을 위해 준비할 것을 추천한다.

PART 1. Passage 2　　　　본문 p. 166

6 (D)　　7 (D)　　8 Yes: (A), (D) No: (B), (C)　　9 (C)
10 (A)　　11 (B)

Note-taking
Leafcutter Ants and Lepiotaceae Fungi
- How does relationship work?
  - Ants cut leaves into small pieces → carry to nest
  - Chew leaf to soften → spit leaves onto fungi
  - Fungi digest leaves → prod. gongylida → ants eat
  - Ants digest other food X → need fungi to survive
- Fungi depend on ants to survive
  - Queen ant take fungi to new nest ∴ survive & spread
  - Fungi use energy for reproduction X ∴ grow food
  - Ants maintain health of fungi ∵ cut harmful parts
  - Ants develop white substance = work like antibiotic
  - Ants prod. acid = stop growth of harmful organism

Listen to part of a lecture in a biology class.

P: There are many examples of species with mutually beneficial relationships. You know, that's where two different species provide each other with benefits. You can see this type of relationship between, um, flowers and bees, sharks and small fish, and some birds and large animals. [6]Well, today, I'm going to talk about leafcutter ants and a type of fungi called Lepiotaceae fungi. While many ants use fungi as a food source, leafcutter ants have developed a special relationship with Lepiotaceae fungi.

So how does this relationship work? Well, first, leafcutter ants cut leaves into many small pieces. Then, they carry these pieces to their nest, where they grow the Lepiotaceae fungi. [7]The ants partially chew the leaf pieces to soften them. Next, they spit the softened leaves onto the fungi. This allows the fungi to digest the leaves. [8A]After digesting the leaves, the fungi produce gongylidia, which is a highly nutritious substance. The leafcutter ants eat the gongylidia and feed it to their young. It grows nowhere else. And it is the only thing that the leafcutter ants can eat. [11]Over time, you see, leafcutter ants have lost the ability to digest other kinds of food. So the ants truly need the fungi to survive.

S: But what do the fungi get out of it? So far, it's all about the ants.

P: Of course, the fungi also depend on the ants to survive. Normally, fungi reproduce by releasing spores. Spores are like, uh, the seeds of a plant. They get released into the air and grow into new fungi if they land in a place with the right conditions. Among Lepiotaceae fungi, however, this no longer happens. [8D]The Lepiotaceae fungi completely depend on the ants for reproduction. This happens when a new colony is built. The queen ant takes a piece of the original fungi and carries it to the new nest. In this way, the fungi can survive and spread. And, because the fungi do not need to use all their energy for reproduction, they have lots of energy to grow food for the ants.

And there are other benefits besides the ones I've mentioned. You see, lots of things can grow on fungi, including some harmful organisms. Well, the ants have several ways to stop this. [9]First, worker ants have the job of maintaining the health of the fungi. So they constantly cut away parts of the fungi that might be harmful. Um, this is similar to the way that gardeners cut dead leaves from a plant. [10]Second, worker ants develop a white substance on their bodies. It's, um, a kind of bacteria that looks similar to powdered sugar. Anyway, what's important is that it works like an antibiotic. Um, for humans, antibiotics are a type of medicine that are used to stop infections, right? Well, this type of bacteria works in a similar way on the fungi. As the worker ants move around the Lepiotaceae fungi, the bacteria get transferred from the ant's body to the fungi. This stops the growth of harmful organisms and helps to keep the Lepiotaceae healthy. Lastly, leafcutter ants also produce a type of acid that stops the growth of harmful organisms… However, recent studies have shown that some organisms are becoming resistant to this acid, so the ants may need to develop a new defense method in the future.

생물학 강의의 일부를 들으시오.

P: 서로 이익이 되는 관계를 맺는 종들에는 많은 예시가 있습니다. 그러니까, 그건 두 개의 서로 다른 종이 서로에게 이익을 제공하는 경우예요. 이러한 종류의 관계는, 음, 꽃과 벌, 상어와 작은 물고기, 몇몇 새와 큰 동물들 사이에서 볼 수 있습니다. 음, 오늘, 저는 잎꾼개미와 Lepiotaceae 균류라고 불리는 균류의 유형에 대해 얘기할 거예요. 많은 개미들이 균류를 먹이 공급원으로 사용하는 반면, 잎꾼개미는 Lepiotaceae 균류와 특수한 관계를 발달시켜 왔어요.

그래서 이 관계는 어떻게 작동하는 걸까요? 음, 먼저, 잎꾼개미는 잎을 많은 작은 조각들로 자릅니다. 그러고 나서, 이 조각들을 둥지로 옮기는데, 그곳에서 그것들은 Lepiotaceae 균류를 길러요. 개미들은 그 잎 조각들을 부드럽게 만들기 위해 부분적으로 그것들을 씹어요. 다음으로, 그것들은 부드러워진 잎들을 그 균류 위에 뱉어내요. 이것은 그 균류가 잎을 소화할 수 있게 해줍니다. 잎을 소화한 후에, 그 균류는 매우 영양가가 높은 물질인 공길리디아를 만들어내요. 잎꾼개미는 공길리디아를 먹고 그것을 새끼들에게 먹여요. 그것은 다른 어디에서도 자라지 않아요. 그리고 그것은 잎꾼개미가 먹을 수 있는 유일한 것이에요. 시간이 지나면서, 그러니까, 잎꾼개미는 다른 종류의 먹이를 소화하는 능력을 잃어버렸어요. 그래서 개미들은 생존하기 위해 정말로 그 균류가 필요하죠.

S: 그런데 그 균류는 거기에서 무엇을 얻나요? 지금까지는, 모두 개미에 관한 것인데요.

P: 물론, 그 균류 또한 생존하기 위해 개미에게 의존해요. 보통, 균류는 포자를 방출함으로써 번식해요. 포자는, 어, 식물의 씨앗 같은 거예요. 그것들은 공기 중으로 방출되고 적절한 조건을 갖춘 장소에 착륙하면 새로운 균류로 자라요. 하지만, Lepiotaceae 균류에서는 더 이상 이런 일이 일어나지 않아요. Lepioaceae 균류는 번식을 위해 완전히 개미에게 의존하죠. 이런 일은 새로운 군락이 건설될 때 일어나요. 여왕개미는 원래 균류의 조각을 가지고 그것을 새로운 둥지로 옮겨요. 이렇게 하면, 그 균류는 생존하고 퍼질 수 있죠. 그리고, 그 균류가 번식을 위해 모든 에너지를 사용할 필요가 없기 때문에, 개미를 위한 먹이를 기를 많은 에너지를 가지게 돼요.

그리고 제가 언급한 것들 외에도 다른 이점들이 있어요. 그러니까, 몇몇 해로운 유기체들을 포함하여 많은 것들이 균류에서 자랄 수 있어요. 음, 개미들은 이를 막기 위한 여러 가지 방법들을 가지고 있어요. 첫 번째로, 일개미들은 그 균류의 건강을 유지하는 임무를 가지고 있어요. 그래서 그것들은 해로울지도 모르는 균류의 일부를 계속해서 잘라내요. 음, 이것은 정원사들이 식물에서 죽은 잎을 잘라내는 방식과 비슷해요. 두 번째로, 일개미들은 그것들의 몸에 하얀 물질을 발달시켜요. 그것은, 음, 가루 설탕과 비슷하게 생긴 일종의 박테리아죠. 어쨌든, 중요한 것은 그것이 항생제처럼 작용한다는 거예요. 음, 인간들에게, 항생제는 감염을 막기 위해 사용되는 약의 일종이죠, 그렇죠? 음, 이 종류의 박테리아는 그 균류에 비슷한 방식으로 작용합니다. 일개미가 Lepiotaceae 균류 주위를 돌아다니면, 그 박테리아가 개미의 몸에서 균류로 옮겨져요. 이는 해로운 유기체의 성장을 막고 Lepiotaceae가 건강을 유지하는 데 도움을 줘요. 마지막으로, 잎꾼개미는 또한 해로운 유기체의 성장을 막는 일종의 산을 만들어내요… 하지만, 최근의 연구들은 일부 유기체들이 이 산에 저항력이 있게 되어서 개미들이 미래에 새로운 방어 방법을 개발해야 할지도 모른다는 것을 보여주었어요.

mutually 퉈 서로 beneficial 휑 이익이 되는 fungi 뎽 균류
partially 퉈 부분적으로 chew 뙁 씹다 soften 뙁 부드럽게 만들다
spit 뙁 뱉다 digest 뙁 소화하다 nutritious 휑 영양가가 높은
substance 뎽 물질 reproduce 뙁 번식하다 spore 뎽 포자
colony 뎽 군락 harmful 휑 해로운 organism 뎽 유기체, 생물
constantly 퉈 계속해서 antibiotic 뎽 항생제 infection 뎽 감염
transfer 뙁 옮기다 resistant 휑 저항력이 있는

6 강의의 주된 주제는 무엇인가?

(A) 개미와 벌의 유사점

(B) 일종의 균류를 먹는 것의 이점

(C) 곤충들이 농업을 개선하는 방식

(D) 두 유기체 간의 유용한 관계

7 교수에 따르면, 잎꾼개미는 왜 부분적으로 잎을 씹는가?

(A) 잎 안에 있는 영양물을 방출하기 위해

(B) 여왕개미를 위해 잎을 정리하기 위해

(C) 잎에서 에너지를 얻기 위해

(D) 균류를 위한 잎을 부드럽게 만들기 위해

8 강의에서, 교수는 Lepiotaceae 균류의 여러 가지 특징을 언급한다. 다음의 항목이 특징인지를 표시하시오.
각 항목에 적절한 칸을 클릭하시오.

	예	아니오
(A) 영양가가 높은 물질을 만들어내기	V	
(B) 토양에서 빠르게 분해되기		V
(C) 개미의 새끼를 보호하는 것을 돕기		V
(D) 번식을 위해 개미에 의존하기	V	

9 교수는 일개미의 임무를 어떻게 설명하는가?

(A) 그것이 시간이 지남에 따라 어떻게 변했는지 묘사함으로써

(B) 그것을 두 가지 관점에서 설명함으로써

(C) 그것을 인간에게 익숙한 작업과 비교함으로써

(D) 둥지의 생존에 있어 그것의 중요성을 보여줌으로써

10 일부 개미의 몸에 있는 하얀 물질의 목적은 무엇인가?

(A) 그것은 균류가 건강을 유지하도록 도와준다.

(B) 그것은 개미가 포식자들로부터 숨게 해준다.

(C) 그것은 균류가 번식하게 해준다.

(D) 그것은 개미를 질병으로부터 보호한다.

강의의 일부를 다시 듣고 질문에 답하시오.

P: Over time, you see, leafcutter ants have lost the ability to digest other kinds of food. So the ants truly need the fungi to survive.

S: But what do the fungi get out of it? So far, it's all about the ants.

P: Of course, the fungi also depend on the ants to survive.

11 학생은 이렇게 말함으로써 무엇을 의미하는가:
S: But what do the fungi get out of it?

(A) 그는 개미가 균류에 너무 많이 의존한다고 생각한다.

(B) 그는 개미가 어떻게 균류를 돕는지 알고 싶어 한다.

(C) 그는 균류가 개미에 의해 해를 입는지 궁금해한다.

(D) 그는 개미의 특징을 아주 잘 이해하고 있다.

PART 2. Passage 1
본문 p. 168

1 (B)　　2 (A), (D)　　3 (A)　　4 (C)　　5 (D)

Note-taking

P: Looked at work, wanted to give feedback
Format = great & info. = well organized
What was confusing?
S: Couldn't understand main character
Very much in love w/ fiancé → canceling wedding
P: Author wrote that way intentionally
Show about people in indirect way
Claire's fiancé = good partner X, ring = indirect clue
Characters = believable = real life = choice w/o reason
Read closely = important as English major

Listen to a conversation between a student and a professor.

S: Hi, Professor Brown. Did you want to see me?

P: Yes, I did. Thanks for coming... I, uh, know you must be busy since midterms are coming up.

S: It's not a problem, Professor. ¹Um, is this about the writing assignment?

P: Yes, I looked at your work, and I wanted to give you some feedback...

S: Now I'm nervous. I hope it wasn't that bad.

P: No, it's nothing serious. ⁵The format of your report is great and your information is well organized...

S: Thank you, Professor. I tried to organize it well... I created different sections to discuss the theme, the characters, and the story. Reviewing literature this way helps me understand it better. But, um, I guess you have other feedback?

P: Yes. I was about to talk about that. Um... I'm a little worried about the content of your report.

S: OK... I thought you might say something about that. Actually, I was quite confused about some parts of the novel.

P: Uh-huh, I could see that in your writing. So I thought it would help if we discussed the novel together... Can you tell me what was confusing?

S: Well, I couldn't understand the main character, Claire. At first, she seems very much in love with her fiancé and happy about her upcoming wedding. I mean, she makes wedding plans and talks with friends about her marriage.

P: Go on... You're doing well...

S: OK, but then, suddenly, she thinks about canceling the wedding. It doesn't make sense to me... Why did she change her mind? The author doesn't seem to give a reason for this. [2D]So it's a bit confusing...

P: Yes, many students have that reaction when they read the novel for the first time... They can't understand why Claire changes her mind. [2A]But the author wrote it that way intentionally. He wanted to show us something about people in an indirect way. [3]I mean, in the novel, you'll notice that Claire's fiancé wasn't a good partner... There were clues that he was a bad person... Um, can you think of any examples?

S: Hmm... Oh, I know. [3]There's a part where Claire notices that the engagement ring he gives her has a scratch.

P: Good. [3]The author uses the ring to give you an indirect clue. The ring tells us that, uh, something about the fiancé is not quite right. [4]You know, if you think about it, the characters are quite believable. Think of real life. Sometimes, people make choices without a clear reason. Many times, they do things without exactly knowing why.

S: OK, that makes more sense to me now. I guess I should, um, read more carefully to notice clues like that...

P: Absolutely. The ability to read closely is important to succeed as an English major.

S: Well, thank you, Professor. I really appreciate the advice.

학생과 교수 사이의 대화를 들으시오

S: 안녕하세요, Brown 교수님. 저를 보고 싶어 하셨다고요?

P: 맞아, 그랬단다. 와줘서 고맙구나... 나는, 어, 중간고사가 다가오고 있어서 네가 바쁠 거란 건 안다.

S: 괜찮아요, 교수님. 음, 글쓰기 과제에 관한 것인가요?

P: 그래, 네 작업물을 살펴봤고, 네게 의견을 좀 주고 싶었어...

S: 이제 긴장이 되네요. 그게 그렇게 나쁘지는 않았으면 좋겠어요.

P: 아냐, 전혀 심각한 게 아니야. 네 보고서의 형식은 아주 좋고 정보도 잘 정리되어 있어...

S: 감사합니다, 교수님. 그것을 잘 정리하려고 노력했어요... 주제, 인물, 줄거리를 논하기 위해 서로 다른 부분들을 만들었어요. 이런 방식으로 문학을 비평하는 건 제가 그것을 더 잘 이해하도록 도와주거든요. 그런데, 음, 다른 의견이 있으시겠죠?

P: 맞아. 그것에 관해 얘기하려던 참이다. 음... 네 보고서의 내용에 관해 약간 걱정이 되는구나.

S: 네... 그것에 관한 걸 말씀하실지도 모른다고 생각했어요. 사실, 저는 소설의 몇몇 부분들이 꽤 혼란스러웠어요.

P: 그래, 네 글에서 그걸 알 수 있었단다. 그래서 우리가 소설에 대해 같이 논의하면 도움이 될 거라 생각했어... 무엇이 혼란스러웠는지 말해주겠니?

S: 음, 저는 주인공인 Claire를 이해할 수 없었어요. 처음에, 그녀는 그녀의 약혼자를 매우 사랑하고 다가오는 결혼식으로 행복해하는 것처럼 보여요. 그러니까, 그녀는 결혼식 계획을 세우고 그녀의 결혼에 관해 친구들과 이야기해요.

P: 계속하거라... 잘하고 있어...

S: 네, 그런데 그때, 갑자기, 그녀는 결혼식을 취소하는 것에 대해 생각해요. 저는 그게 이해가 안 돼요... 그녀가 왜 그녀의 마음을 바

꿨나요? 작가는 이것에 대한 이유를 밝히지 않는 것 같아요. 그래서 그게 좀 혼란스러워요...

P: 그래, 많은 학생들이 그 소설을 처음 읽을 때 그런 반응을 보인단다... 그들은 Claire가 왜 그녀의 마음을 바꾸는지 이해하지 못하지. 그런데 작가는 의도적으로 그걸 그런 방식으로 썼어. 그는 간접적인 방식으로 우리에게 사람들에 대한 무언가를 보여주고 싶어 했어. 그러니까, 그 소설에서, 너는 Claire의 약혼자가 좋은 애인이 아니었다는 것을 알아챌 거야... 그가 나쁜 사람이라는 단서들이 있었지... 음, 예시를 떠올려볼 수 있겠니?

S: 흠... 오, 맞아요. 그가 그녀에게 주는 약혼반지에 긁힌 자국이 있다는 걸 Claire가 알아채는 부분이 있어요.

P: 좋아. 작가는 간접적인 단서를 제공하기 위해 그 반지를 사용한단다. 그 반지는 우리에게, 어, 약혼자에 관한 무언가가 옳지 않다는 걸 말해줘. 그러니까, 생각해 보면, 그 인물들은 꽤 그럴듯해. 현실의 삶을 생각해 보렴. 가끔, 사람들은 분명한 이유 없이 선택을 해. 많은 경우, 그들은 정확히 이유를 알지 못한 채 일을 하지.

S: 네, 이제 더 잘 이해가 되네요. 저는, 음, 그런 단서를 알아채기 위해 더 신중하게 읽어야 할 것 같아요...

P: 물론이지. 면밀히 읽는 능력은 영문학 전공자로서 성공하는 데 중요해.

S: 음, 감사합니다, 교수님. 조언 정말 감사해요.

---

midterms 명 중간고사   feedback 명 의견
organize 동 정리하다, 조직하다   section 명 부분
review 동 비평하다; 검토하다   literature 명 문학   content 명 내용
confused 형 혼란스러운   upcoming 형 다가오는   author 명 작가
intentionally 부 의도적으로   indirect 형 간접적인
engagement ring 약혼반지   scratch 명 긁힌 자국
believable 형 그럴듯한   closely 부 면밀히, 자세히

1 교수는 왜 학생을 보자고 했는가?

(A) 그녀의 과제가 늦은 이유를 알아내기 위해

(B) 그녀의 보고서에 대한 그의 의견을 주기 위해

(C) 그녀의 중간고사 일정에 관해 묻기 위해

(D) 그녀에게 수업에서 보고서를 발표할 것을 요청하기 위해

2 교수는 소설에 관해 무엇이라고 말하는가?
2개의 답을 고르시오.

(A) 작가는 의도적으로 간접적이 되기를 원했다.

(B) 많은 독자들은 작가가 훌륭한 저술가라고 생각한다.

(C) 줄거리는 어린 독자들이 이해하기에 어렵다.

(D) 많은 학생들은 그것을 처음 읽을 때 혼란스러워한다.

3 교수에 따르면, 소설 속의 약혼반지는 무엇을 나타내는가?

(A) 약혼자의 불쾌한 성격

(B) Claire가 결혼에 대해 갖는 생각

(C) 두 인물 사이의 우정

(D) 좋은 결정을 내리는 것이 중요성

4 교수는 왜 현실의 삶을 언급하는가?

(A) 작가에 관한 정보를 소개하기 위해

(B) 소설들이 항상 복잡하지는 않다는 것을 보여주기 위해

(C) 몇몇 인물들이 사실적이라는 것을 보여주기 위해

(D) 학생에게 맡은 일을 상기시키기 위해

대화의 일부를 다시 듣고 질문에 답하시오.

P: The format of your report is great and your information is well organized...

S: Thank you, Professor. I tried to organize it well... I created different sections to discuss the theme, the characters, and the story. Reviewing literature this way helps me understand it better. But, um, I guess you have other feedback?

5 학생은 이렇게 말함으로써 무엇을 의미하는가:

S: But, um, I guess you have other feedback?

(A) 그녀는 교수의 의견에 동의하지 않는다.

(B) 그녀는 그녀가 잘못된 주제를 선택했다고 생각한다.

(C) 그녀는 교수의 지적을 이해하지 못한다.

(D) 그녀는 그녀의 보고서에 몇몇 문제점이 있을지도 모른다고 생각한다.

PART 2. Passage 2 본문 p. 170

6 (A) 7 (B) 8 (D) 9 (B)
10 Crater Lake Caldera: (A) Shield Volcano Caldera: (C), (D)
Resurgent Caldera: (B) 11 (B)

Note-taking

Caldera

- Caldera = large depression inside volcano
- Craters & calderas = similar, diff. = size & how formed
  - Crater = small & form when magma break ground
  - Caldera = big & form when crater collapse
- Crater lake caldera
  - Eruption → chamber empty → ground collapse
  - Fills w/ water → lake (e.g. Crater Lake in Oregon)
- Shield volcano caldera
  - Smaller than others (e.g. Kilauea Caldera in Hawaii)
- Resurgent caldera
  - Biggest on the planet, caused by more than one

Listen to part of a lecture in a geology class.

P: Last time, we went over the main types of volcanoes. For instance, some volcanoes are tall and shaped like a cone. They usually have powerful eruptions and lava that is thick. Other volcanoes are shorter and flatter. They erupt more often and tend to have lava that is less thick. ⁶Well, today, we will look at a specific feature of some volcanoes. This feature is called a caldera. It can be seen in different types of volcanoes.

⁷So, um, calderas are large depressions, or holes, that form inside a volcano. Um, their name comes from the Spanish word for a cooking pot. This is because they have the same shape as a cooking pot or bowl... Yes? Did you have a question?

S1: Yes, sorry, I'm confused... You said a caldera is a hole. But isn't a crater also a hole? How are they different?

P: ⁸Actually, craters and calderas are similar. They are both depressions. The main differences between them are their size and how they're formed. Craters are usually less than a few hundred meters in size. They form when magma breaks through the ground in an eruption. However, calderas can be thousands of meters wide. And they usually form when a crater collapses or breaks down. Um, now let's look at the three types of calderas.

¹⁰The first type of caldera is known as a crater lake caldera. These usually form in tall volcanoes during powerful eruptions. Um, but first, does anyone remember what I said about a volcano's magma chamber?

S2: Yes, isn't that the space under a volcano that holds most of its magma?

P: Yes, exactly. It's an area deep beneath a volcano that contains lots of magma. In powerful eruptions, all of the magma in the magma chamber gets released. And, uh, this leaves the chamber empty. Because the chamber is empty, it cannot hold the weight of the ground above it. ¹⁰ᴬSo the ground collapses into the chamber and forms a caldera. Over time, this caldera fills with water and becomes a lake. Um, Crater Lake in Oregon is one example. The volcano had several extremely powerful eruptions over 7,000 years ago. Eventually, all of the magma was used up, and the caldera was filled with rain and melted snow. Today, Crater Lake is the deepest lake in the United States.

Now let's look at the second type of caldera. It's called a shield volcano caldera. ¹¹Shield volcanoes are a short type of volcano. They erupt more often, but the eruptions are less powerful. So, um, the lava comes out slowly and regularly in thin layers. This is why shield volcanoes appear low and flat. ¹⁰ᴰSo the calderas of shield volcanoes are also smaller than the other types of calderas. ¹⁰ᶜAnd you can see where the different layers of lava have formed over time. A good example of this is Kilauea Caldera in Hawaii.

Lastly, we have what is called a resurgent caldera. ¹⁰ᴮResurgent calderas are usually big in size. In fact, they are the biggest volcanic features on the planet. They form when powerful eruptions happen over a wide area. ⁹Um, these eruptions are caused by more than one volcano. And, because the eruptions are so strong, some magma goes back into the ground beneath the volcano. Then, during later eruptions, this magma resurges, or rises again. ⁹That's why they're called resurgent calderas. You can see one in Yellowstone Park in Wyoming. The Yellowstone Caldera is about 80,000 meters across.

지질학 강의의 일부를 들으시오.

P: 지난 시간에, 우리는 화산의 주요 유형들을 살펴보았어요. 예를 들어, 일부 화산들은 높고 원뿔처럼 생겼죠. 그것들은 보통 강력한 폭발과 걸쭉한 용암을 가지고 있어요. 다른 화산들은 더 낮고

평평해요. 그것들은 더 자주 폭발하고 덜 걸쭉한 용암을 가지고 있는 경향이 있죠. 음, 오늘, 우리는 몇몇 화산들의 독특한 특징에 대해 알아볼 거예요. 이 특징은 칼데라라고 불려요. 여러 유형의 화산들에서 볼 수 있죠.

그러니까, 음, 칼데라는 화산 내부에 형성되는 크게 움푹 파인 곳, 즉 구멍이에요. 음, 그것들의 이름은 요리용 냄비를 의미하는 스페인어 단어에서 유래되었어요. 그것들이 요리용 냄비나 그릇 같은 모양을 가지고 있기 때문이죠.. 네? 질문 있나요?

S1: 네, 죄송한데, 헷갈려서요... 칼데라가 구멍이라고 하셨죠. 그런데 분화구도 구멍 아닌가요? 그것들이 어떻게 다른가요?

P: 사실, 분화구와 칼데라는 비슷합니다. 그것들은 둘 다 움푹 파인 곳들이에요. 그것들 사이의 주요 차이점은 크기와 형성되는 방식이에요. 분화구는 보통 크기가 수백 미터 미만이에요. 그것들은 폭발할 때 마그마가 땅을 뚫고 들어가면서 형성돼요. 하지만, 칼데라의 너비는 수천 미터가 될 수 있어요. 그리고 그것들은 보통 분화구가 무너지거나 붕괴될 때 형성돼요. 음, 이제 칼데라의 세 가지 유형을 살펴봅시다.

첫 번째 유형은 화구호 칼데라로 알려진 칼데라입니다. 이것들은 보통 강력한 폭발 동안 높은 화산에서 형성돼요. 음, 하지만 먼저, 제가 화산의 마그마 체임버에 대해 얘기했던 걸 기억하는 사람 있나요?

S2: 네, 마그마의 대부분을 담고 있는 화산 아래의 공간 아닌가요?

P: 네, 정확해요. 그건 많은 마그마를 담고 있는 화산 아래 깊은 곳에 있는 부분이죠. 강력한 폭발이 일어나면, 마그마 체임버에 있는 모든 마그마가 방출돼요. 그리고, 어, 이것은 체임버가 비어있는 상태가 되게 해요. 체임버가 비어있기 때문에, 그것은 위에 있는 땅의 무게를 지탱할 수 없죠. 그래서 땅은 체임버 속으로 무너지고 칼데라를 형성해요. 시간이 지나면서, 이 칼데라는 물로 채워지고 호수가 돼요. 음, 오리건의 화구호가 한 가지 예시입니다. 그 화산은 7,000년도 더 전에 몇 차례 매우 강력한 폭발이 있었어요. 결국, 마그마가 모두 소진되었고, 칼데라는 빗물과 녹은 눈으로 채워졌어요. 오늘날, 그 화구호는 미국에서 가장 깊은 호수예요.

이제 두 번째 칼데라 유형을 살펴봅시다. 그것은 순상화산 칼데라라고 불려요. 순상화산은 낮은 형태의 화산이에요. 그것들은 더 자주 폭발하지만, 폭발은 덜 강력해요. 그래서, 음, 용암은 얇은 층으로 천천히 그리고 규칙적으로 흘러나와요. 이것이 순상화산이 낮고 평평해 보이는 이유예요. 그래서 순상화산의 칼데라는 또한 다른 유형의 칼데라보다 더 작아요. 그리고 시간이 지남에 따라 서로 다른 용암의 층이 어디에 형성되었는지를 볼 수 있어요. 이것의 좋은 예시는 하와이의 킬라웨아 칼데라예요.

마지막으로, 소생 칼데라라고 불리는 것이 있어요. 소생 칼데라는 보통 크기가 커요. 사실, 그것들은 지구상에서 가장 큰 화산 지형입니다. 그것들은 강력한 폭발이 광범위한 지역에 걸쳐 발생할 때 형성돼요. 음, 이 폭발들은 하나보다 많은 화산에 의해 초래됩니다. 그리고, 폭발이 매우 강하기 때문에, 일부 마그마는 화산 아래의 땅으로 되돌아가죠. 그리고, 더 나중의 폭발 동안, 이 마그마는 소생, 즉 다시 상승해요. 그게 그것들이 소생 칼데라라고 불리는 이유입니다. 와이오밍의 옐로스톤 공원에서 하나를 볼 수 있죠. 옐로스톤 칼데라는 지름이 약 8만 미터입니다.

cone 명 원뿔   eruption 명 폭발, 분출   lava 명 용암
thick 형 걸쭉한; 두꺼운   flat 형 평평한   depression 명 움푹 파인 곳
crater 명 분화구   collapse 동 무너지다   contain 동 담고 있다
extremely 부 매우, 극도로   layer 명 층   feature 명 지형, 지세
resurge 동 소생하다, 다시 나타나다   across 부 지름으로

6 강의는 주로 무엇에 관한 것인가?

(A) 일부 화산들의 특징

(B) 화산의 주요 종류

(C) 새롭게 발견된 화산 유형

(D) 화산 폭발의 위험성

7 교수는 왜 요리용 냄비를 언급하는가?

(A) 칼데라에서 일어나는 폭발의 힘을 설명하기 위해

(B) 칼데라의 모양을 설명하기 위해

(C) 스페인에 있는 화산을 소개하기 위해

(D) 마그마의 강한 열을 강조하기 위해

8 교수에 따르면, 분화구와 칼데라의 주요 차이점은 무엇인가?

(A) 그것들의 깊이와 위치

(B) 그것들의 구성과 온도

(C) 그것들의 모양과 나이

(D) 그것들의 크기와 형성 과정

9 옐로스톤 칼데라에 관해 추론할 수 있는 것은 무엇인가?

(A) 그것은 미래에 더 커질 가능성이 작다.

(B) 그것은 여러 화산에 의해 만들어졌다.

(C) 그것은 수년 동안 폭발하지 않았다.

(D) 그것은 세계에서 가장 큰 칼데라이다.

10 다음의 항목이 화구호 칼데라, 순상화산 칼데라, 혹은 소생 칼데라 중 어떤 것에 대한 설명인지를 표시하시오.
각 항목에 적절한 칸을 클릭하시오.

	화구호 칼데라	순상화산 칼데라	소생 칼데라
(A) 땅이 무너지고 물로 채워질 때 형성된다	V		
(B) 지구상에서 가장 큰 화산 지형이다			V
(C) 서로 다른 용암의 층을 가지고 있다		V	
(D) 다른 유형의 칼데라보다 작다		V	

강의의 일부를 다시 듣고 질문에 답하시오.

P: Shield volcanoes are a short type of volcano. They erupt more often, but the eruptions are less powerful. So, um, the lava comes out slowly and regularly in thin layers. This is why shield volcanoes appear low and flat.

11 교수는 왜 이렇게 말하는가:

P: So, um, the lava comes out slowly and regularly in thin layers.

(A) 서로 다른 화산들의 용암 흐름을 비교하기 위해

(B) 일부 화산의 형성 과정을 설명하기 위해

(C) 화산의 크기가 점점 커지는 이유를 보여주기 위해

(D) 폭발이 오래전에 일어났다는 것을 강조하기 위해

12 (D)　　13 (A)　　14 (C), (D)　　15 (C)　　16 (C)
17 (B)

Note-taking

Wings of Dragonflies

- Dragonflies = type of flying insect > 3k species
- Need powerful wings ∵ they're predators
- Go 35 to 50 km/h ∴ help catch insect & fly long dist.
- Wing muscles control how fast ea. wing moves
  - Can move body in diff. directions
  - Change style of flight depending on situation
- Wings = quite tough ∴ break X at high speed, why?
  - Wings made of chitin = make body hard & light
- Veins = send blood to wings → warm up wings
- Dark-colored spots = similar purpose
  - Usu. found on dragonflies live in cold weather

Listen to part of a lecture in a biology class.

P: Let's continue our discussion of insects. As I said before, about one million different species exist today. And many of those insects have been around for a long time. Through evolution, some of these insects have developed special characteristics that help them survive. [12]Today, we are going to discuss a specific characteristic of dragonflies. We will talk about their wings.

First, dragonflies are a type of flying insect. There are over 3,000 different species. They can range in size from a few centimeters to around 10 centimeters. Most live in tropical places near fresh water. Their bodies usually have bright colors like green, yellow, red, and blue. They also have large eyes that can see almost all the way around. But what's most interesting about dragonflies are the wings. Dragonflies have two sets of powerful wings. When the wings are open, they can be up to 16 centimeters from one wing to the other.

S1: Wow. That's even longer than their bodies.

P: Right. [13]Dragonflies need powerful wings because they're predators. This means that they eat other insects. Sometimes, those insects are even larger than the dragonfly. So it helps that the dragonfly has powerful wings. And, um, the wings are powerful because they are connected directly to muscles on the dragonfly's body. Most dragonflies fly at around 16 kilometers an hour. But they can also go as fast as 35 to 50 kilometers an hour. This helps dragonflies catch other insects and lets them fly long distances.

[14C]The wing muscles also let dragonflies move each wing independently. This means they can control how fast each wing moves. Because of this, dragonflies can move their bodies in many different directions. They can even stay still in the air. All of this is useful because it lets dragonflies change their style of flight depending on the situation. So, when dragonflies need to fly away quickly or attack prey, they use their wing muscles to move all of their wings together. [14D]At other times, they move some wings slower than the others to save energy while flying in the air.

[17]The wings are quite tough, too. Uh, they don't break even when the dragonfly is moving at high speed. The question is, why not? Well, there are a few reasons. One reason is that the wings are made of chitin. Chitin is a material that is common in many insects. It's what makes the bodies of insects hard and light... Um, what else do you notice about the wings?

S2: Um, they look transparent? I mean, you can see right through them.

P: Yes, but if you look closely, you will see veins. These veins send blood to the wings. You see, dragonflies have to warm up their wings before they fly. So many dragonflies sit in the sun before flying or move their wings at high speed to warm up the blood. Um, you'll also notice that some dragonflies have dark-colored spots on their wings. These have a similar purpose. [15]You probably know that dark colors absorb more sunlight than light colors. That's why you feel warmer in dark-colored clothes than in light-colored clothes. [16]Well, that's also how the dark-colored spots on a dragonfly's wings work. They help to keep the wings warm. That's why they're usually found on dragonflies that live in places with cold weather.

생물학 강의의 일부를 들으시오.

P: 곤충에 대한 논의를 계속해 봅시다. 전에 말했듯이, 오늘날에는 약 백만 개의 서로 다른 종이 존재합니다. 그리고 그 곤충들 중 다수는 오랫동안 존재해 왔어요. 진화를 통해, 이 곤충들 중 일부는 생존에 도움이 되는 특별한 특징들을 발달시켜왔죠. 오늘, 우리는 잠자리의 구체적인 특징에 대해 논의해볼 거예요. 그것들의 날개에 대해 얘기해 보죠.

먼저, 잠자리는 날아다니는 곤충의 한 종류입니다. 약 3천 개의 서로 다른 종들이 있죠. 그것들은 크기가 몇 센티미터에서 약 10 센티미터까지 다양할 수 있습니다. 대부분은 민물 근처의 열대 지역에서 살아요. 그것들의 몸은 보통 초록, 노랑, 빨강, 그리고 파랑 같은 밝은색을 가지고 있어요. 그것들은 또한 주위의 거의 모든 방향을 볼 수 있는 큰 눈들을 가지고 있죠. 하지만 잠자리에 관한 가장 흥미로운 점은 날개입니다. 잠자리는 두 짝의 강력한 날개를 가지고 있어요. 날개가 펴졌을 때, 그것들은 한 날개에서 다른 날개까지의 길이가 16센티미터까지 될 수 있습니다.

S1: 와. 심지어 몸보다 더 기네요.

P: 맞아요. 잠자리는 포식자이기 때문에 강력한 날개가 필요합니다. 이는 그것들이 다른 곤충들을 먹는다는 걸 의미해요. 때때로, 그 곤충들은 잠자리보다 훨씬 더 커요. 그래서 잠자리에게 강력한 날개가 있다는 것은 도움이 됩니다. 그리고, 음, 날개들은 잠자리 몸의 근육과 직접적으로 연결되어 있기 때문에 강력해요. 대부분의 잠자리는 약 시속 16킬로미터로 날아요. 하지만 그것들은 시속 35에서 50킬로미터만큼 빠르게 갈 수도 있죠. 이는 잠자리가 다른 곤충을 잡도록 도와주고 먼 거리를 날 수 있게 해줘요.

날개 근육 또한 잠자리가 각 날개를 독립적으로 움직이게 해줍니다. 이는 그것들이 각 날개가 얼마나 빨리 움직일지 조절할 수 있다는 걸 의미해요. 이것 때문에, 잠자리는 많은 서로 다른 방향로 몸을 움직일 수 있어요. 심지어 공중에 가만히 있을 수도 있죠. 이 모든 것은 잠자리가 상황에 따라 비행 방식을 바꾸게 해주기 때문에 유용해요. 그러니까, 잠자리가 빠르게 날아가거나 먹이를 공격해야 할 때, 그것들은 날개 근육을 이용해서 모든 날개를 함께 움직여요. 다른 때에는, 그것들은 일부 날개를 다른 것들보다 느리게 움직여서 공중을 나는 동안 에너지를 절약하죠.

그 날개들은 꽤 튼튼하기도 해요. 어, 그것들은 심지어 잠자리가 빠른 속도로 움직일 때도 찢어지지 않아요. 궁금한 건, 왜 그런 걸까요? 음, 몇 가지 이유가 있습니다. 한 가지 이유는 그 날개들이 키틴으로 만들어졌다는 거예요. 키틴은 많은 곤충들에게서 흔한 물질이에요. 곤충의 몸을 단단하고 가볍게 만들어주는 게 그거예요... 음, 그 외에 날개에 대해 무엇을 알 수 있죠?

S2: 음, 그것들이 투명해 보인다는 거요? 그러니까, 그것들을 바로 꿰뚫어 볼 수 있잖아요.

P: 맞아요, 하지만 자세히 들여다보면, 시맥이 보일 거예요. 이 시맥들은 날개로 혈액을 보내죠. 그러니까, 잠자리는 날기 전에 그것들의 날개를 따뜻하게 해야 해요. 그래서 많은 잠자리들이 혈액을 따뜻하게 하기 위해 날기 전에 햇볕에 앉아 있거나 날개를 빠른 속도로 움직여요. 음, 일부 잠자리의 날개에 어두운색의 반점이 있다는 것도 눈치챌 거예요. 이것들은 비슷한 목적을 가지고 있어요. 여러분은 아마 어두운색이 밝은색보다 더 많은 햇빛을 흡수한다는 걸 알 거예요. 그게 밝은색 옷을 입었을 때보다 어두운색 옷을 입었을 때 더 따뜻하게 느껴지는 이유죠. 음, 그것은 잠자리 날개의 어두운색 반점이 작용하는 방식이기도 해요. 그것들은 날개가 따뜻하게 유지되도록 도와요. 그게 그것들이 보통 추운 날씨를 가진 지역에 사는 잠자리에서 발견되는 이유예요.

evolution 몡 진화 dragonfly 몡 잠자리 tropical 혱 열대의
fresh water 민물, 담수 predator 몡 포식자
independently 뷔 독립적으로 chitin 몡 키틴
transparent 혱 투명한
vein 몡 시맥(곤충의 날개에 무늬처럼 갈라져 있는 맥), 정맥
absorb 통 흡수하다

12 강의는 주로 무엇에 관한 것인가?

(A) 다양한 곤충 종의 특징

(B) 곤충이 매우 오랫동안 생존해온 이유

(C) 다른 곤충들에 비해 일부 곤충들이 가지고 있는 이점

(D) 곤충 날개의 독특한 특징

13 교수는 잠자리에 관해 무엇이라고 말하는가?

(A) 그것들은 먹기 위해 다른 곤충들을 잡아야 한다.

(B) 그것들은 매년 먼 거리를 이동한다.

(C) 그것들은 세상에서 가장 오래된 곤충 중 하나이다.

(D) 그것들은 강한 바람이 부는 지역에 산다.

14 교수에 따르면, 날개 근육은 잠자리들이 무엇을 할 수 있게 하는가?
2개의 답을 고르시오.

(A) 날개를 따뜻하게 유지하기

(B) 소리를 내지 않고 날기

(C) 서로 다른 방향으로 움직이기

(D) 나는 동안 더 적은 에너지 사용하기

15 교수는 왜 색이 있는 옷을 언급하는가?

(A) 잠자리 날개의 약점을 확인하기 위해

(B) 잠자리의 날개가 투명한 이유를 보여주기 위해

(C) 잠자리 날개의 기능이 작동하는 방식을 설명하기 위해

(D) 잠자리가 변화를 겪는 이유를 설명하기 위해

16 추운 날씨에 사는 잠자리에 관해 추론할 수 있는 것은 무엇인가?

(A) 그것들은 더 두꺼운 몸을 가지고 있다.

(B) 그것들은 더 짧은 수명을 가지고 있다.

(C) 그것들의 날개는 종종 색이 있는 반점을 가지고 있다.

(D) 그것들의 날개는 더 빠른 속도로 움직인다.

강의의 일부를 다시 듣고 질문에 답하시오.

P: The wings are quite tough, too. Uh, they don't break even when the dragonfly is moving at high speed. The question is, why not? Well, there are a few reasons.

17 교수는 왜 이렇게 말하는가:

P: The question is, why not?

(A) 주제에 대한 더 많은 연구가 필요하다는 것을 시사하기 위해

(B) 그녀가 개념에 대한 설명을 제공할 것임을 나타내기 위해

(C) 학생들이 그녀의 요점을 이해했는지 알아내기 위해

(D) 학생들에게 토론에 참여할 것을 독려하기 위해

HACKERS

APEX
LISTENING
for the
TOEFL iBT® Advanced

Answer Book